CONTEMPORARY COMMUNITY HEALTH SERIES

A Mad People's History of Madness

A Mad People's History of Madness

Dale Peterson, Editor

UNIVERSITY OF PITTSBURGH PRESS

Published by the University of Pittsburgh Press, Pittsburgh, Pa. 15260

Copyright © 1982, University of Pittsburgh Press
All rights reserved
Feffer and Simons, Inc., London
Manufactured in the United States of America

Library of Congress Cataloging in Publication Data

Main entry under title:

A Mad people's history of madness.

  (Contemporary community health series)
  Bibliography: p. 353
  1. Mental illness—History—Biography. 2. Psychiatric hospital care—History—
Biography. I. Peterson, Dale. II. Series. [DNLM: 1. Mental disorders—Biog-
raphy. WM 40 P485m]
RC464.A1M32   362.2'09   81–50430
ISBN 0–8229–3444–2   AACR2
ISBN 0–8229–5331–5 (pbk.)

Publication of this book was assisted by a grant from the Maurice Falk Medical Fund.

To "Tom" and "Andy"

Contents

Acknowledgments

SEVERAL PEOPLE supported and guided my work on this project. Professor Thomas Moser of the Stanford English Department, in particular, watched over, criticized, and nurtured it. Professor Irvin Yalom of the Stanford Department of Psychiatry, and Professor Robert Polhemus and Wyn Kelley of the Stanford English Department generously gave time and energy as readers and critics; I appreciate their intelligence and standards. I thank William Allen and Florence Chu of the Stanford libraries for the many hours they spent, with good humor, helping me gather and examine many far-flung books. I wish to thank Patricia Allderidge, archivist of the Bethlem Royal Hospital in London, for calling my attention to Urbane Metcalf's work of 1818 and for allowing me to look at some early "Bedlam" case notes; and I wish to thank Charles Steir for his extensive help on my bibliography. The many quotations from ancient, classical, and medieval authors on madness, which comprise Appendix I, were collected by Professor Bert Kaplan of the University of California at Santa Cruz and Jasper Rose; I wish to thank Professor Kaplan for passing them on to me and for allowing me to make use of them. I also want to thank two patient and supportive people from the University of Pittsburgh Press: Frederick Hetzel, for his continuing interest in this project, and Cathy Miller, for her pleasant manner and eagle eye.

In large part, I have been supported by a Stanford Department of English Fellowship and a Teaching Assistantship, also by some shorter-term grants from the Stanford English Department, the Office of the Graduate Dean at Stanford, and the Maurice Falk Medical Fund. I am grateful for that support.

My parents and siblings have given moral, emotional, and financial support for this project; to them I am uniquely indebted.

Finally, I should acknowledge my particular reliance on the following sources: Albert Deutsch, *The Mentally Ill in America*; Henri Ellenberger, *The Discovery of the Unconscious*; William Parry-Jones, *The Trade in Lunacy*; and Gregory Zilboorg, *A History of Medical Psychology*.

Grateful acknowledgement is made to the following publishers for permission to reprint excerpts that appear in this book. From *The Book of Margery Kempe*, translated into modern English by W. Butler-Bowden, copyright ©

Introduction

IN MARCH 1969, after two weeks' training, I entered a psychiatric ward to begin two years of full-time work as an attendant.

The head nurse described the patients on her ward as "chronic burnt-out schizophrenics" and proceeded to introduce me to them. I met a patient we might call Andy. He shook my hand, smiled, and said in a childish voice, "I'm glad you've come! You better take good care of me, I'm crazy. I'm loony as they come." He smiled and stared directly into my eyes. "Take good care of me. Look: I can't move my eyes to the right or to the left. I speak three languages." I was introduced to another patient—let's call him Tom—who certainly looked mad, his face ravaged with deep arroyo wrinkles, his hair yellow, short, and chaotic, shreds of tobacco around his lips, his eyes pale blue and blank. He whined. "Well, go to school. Well, Tom, Tom, go to school." I reached out to shake his hand. He took my hand, and bent down and kissed it with a loud, wet smack, leaving a half-dollar sized spot of saliva and tobacco fragments. Then he frowned, turned away, and shuffled off, his pants falling down his narrow hips, again and again thumping his rib cage with a strange, awkward, stereotyped gesture.

Certainly Andy said such things with some degree of mockery, including, perhaps, self-mockery. But it was a desire to take Andy seriously, at his word, as well as a curiosity perhaps first stimulated by Tom, and an affection for them both and for others in their position, that originally motivated my work on this history.

This history is simply a collection of pieces from the published autobiographical works of mad people and mental patients, written about the experience of being mad or being a mental patient, from a period of more than five centuries. I have seen fit to include historical background and commentary of my own; but I have tried, mostly, to have mad people and mental patients themselves address the most serious, difficult, and complex issues.

Is there meaning in madness? Can we know it? What is madness? What *was* madness? What is the history of madness? What is the history of how people have seen madness? Is it a disease, or is it simply a private religion, a little harmless deviance of thought and action? Which is better, institution or no institution? Which is better, psychiatry or no psychiatry? Are we all, in our own obscure ways, mad, and is madness really so close to sanity?

Experts and authorities have addressed these questions for centuries, with confused results. It is time to hear from those who, by experience, are more closely connected to the issues— mad people, mental patients, themselves. Perhaps they are less confused.

A Mad People's History of Madness

1436 ᛰ

The Book of Margery Kempe

The earliest theories on madness were spiritual, assuming a possession of the mind by an alien deity. By the time of Hippocrates (460–
377 B.C.), most bodily illnesses were thought to be the result of material events, of various fluidic or humoral imbalances in the body. Still,
madness, abnormalities of behavior, and epilepsy, were generally regarded as the workings of the gods.

In his treatise *The Sacred Disease*, however, Hippocrates argued for
the natural rather than the supernatural origin of epilepsy. "It . . .
appears to me to be in no way more divine, nor more sacred than
other diseases, but has a natural cause from which it originates like
other afflictions," he wrote. "If you cut open the head, you will find
the brain humid, full of sweat and smelling badly. And in this way
you may see that it is not a god which injures the body, but disease."[1]
Hippocrates also described other similar ailments in natural terms,
identifying not only epilepsy, but also mania, melancholy, and a form
of mental deterioration he called "paranoia."

The Greeks had developed a quadripartite theory of the universe.
The universe was composed of four elements: earth, air, fire, and
water. All four elements, and therefore all matter, partook of four
basic qualities: hot, cold, moist, and dry. Earth was cold and dry. Air
was hot and moist. Fire was hot and dry. And water was cold and
moist.

As a tradition of secular medicine developed, the Greeks applied
the quadripartite system to their concept of the body. Hippocrates
taught that the healthy body had a balance of four basic humors:
black bile from the liver, yellow bile from the spleen, blood, and
phlegm. Black bile, like earth, was considered to be cold and dry; its
predominance was supposed to cause solitary behavior and a
melancholic temperament. Yellow bile, like fire, was hot and dry; its
predominance supposedly caused an angry, violent, and splenetic
personality. Blood, like air, was considered hot and moist; its predominance supposedly resulted in a ruddy countenance and a cheerful, sanguine temperament. And finally, phlegm, like water, was cold

---

[1] Zilboorg, *A History of Medical Psychology*, pp. 43, 44.

and moist; its predominance caused a pale appearance and a sluggish, phlegmatic temperament.

Hippocrates believed that both physical illnesses and madness were caused by some imbalance of the four humors, and therefore his treatment was to restore the natural balance of the body. For instance, in the case of severe depression, presumably caused by excesses of black bile, he would attempt to rid the body of bile by administering the herbal purgative hellebore. At the same time, he would counteract bile's cold and dry qualities by giving the patient plenty of food and drink, thus building up his supply of hot, moist blood.

Classical medicine and psychiatry reached a peak of innovation and progress in the second century A.D., with the school of the Roman court physician, Galen (130–200 A.D.). Galen taught an eclectic system of medicine which combined the humoral theories of Hippocrates and the so-called pneumatic theories with a strong interest in anatomy.[2] But the importance of Galen and Hippocrates has less to do with the rightness or wrongness of their theories than with their insistence on careful observation and their recognition of the inadequacies of traditional and popular lore. "Do not go to the gods," wrote Galen, "to make inquiries and thus attempt by soothsaying to discover the nature of the directing soul . . . or the principle of action of nerves; but go and take instruction on the subject from an anatomist."[3]

After Galen died, the classical tradition of medicine lapsed into a stagnation that lasted for more than a thousand years. Medicine during the medieval period became a discipline based not upon firsthand observation, but rather upon the simple rote memorization of the teachings of Hippocrates and Galen. Dissection of bodies was forbidden until the thirteenth century, and the teachings of classical medicine became as rigid as the pronouncements of the Church.

Alongside the somewhat enlightened view of those educated in the classical lore of Hippocrates and Galen, which taught that the origins of madness could be understood in comprehensible, natural systems, there continued the ancient view of madness as the possession of an

---

[2]Neaman, *Suggestion of the Devil*, p. 10. The *pneuma* was an invisible vital principle in the body and mind, similar to our concept of spirit. Galen believed that pneuma began as air, was inhaled into the lungs, and was then somehow transformed into a vital life force animating both body and brain.

[3]Zilboorg, *A History of Medical Psychology*, p. 87.

individual by alien, spiritual forces. In pre-Christian Rome, it had been popularly believed that the spirits of the forest, the *sylvani* and the *fauni*, caused madness. Mad people were sometimes called *larvarum plenus* or *larvatus*, meaning "full of *larvae*, or phantoms."[4] After the death of Galen, such popular superstitions came to have greater significance. Early Christianity, instead of countering such beliefs, often appears to have absorbed them. The Christian Gnostics in particular believed that they had an essential *gnosis*, or wisdom, which, among other things, involved an awareness of large numbers of spiritual mediators between God and man. The early Christian Father, Origen (who castrated himself soon after his conversion), theorized that the body was made up of thirty-six basic parts, each one under the control of a different deity, and that sterility in women and famine were the work of evil spirits. Demonologists catalogued signs of demonic possession that became known after the second century as *stigmata diaboli*, the stigmata of the Devil. And finally, in 429 A.D., in the *Codex Theodesianus*, the Church officially denounced the practice of magic as criminal, and authorities prepared to prosecute anyone who conspired with demonic powers. Shortly thereafter a magician in Spain was executed for heresy.[5]

In short, the single most powerful institution of medieval times, the Church, gradually accepted the validity of popular superstitions about the existence of spiritual powers, and the reality of possession by them, at last recognizing those superstitions as part of its own sacred canon. Spiritual psychiatry had arrived.

Of course, not all cases of madness in medieval times were thought to be caused by possession. Theologians, lawyers, and physicians generally were careful to distinguish between madness of natural origin and demonic possession. Yet the Church and its followers had come to accept St. Augustine's vision of the world as a battleground between the forces of good and evil, the legions of God and the Devil. It is therefore not surprising that some mad people in medieval times were seen as victims of the Devil or his minions.

For the classically trained physician, then, at least some of the pathologies of the mind were thought to be of natural origin. The theologian may have agreed that some mental pathologies were of natural origin, but for him the mind was essentially equal to the soul.

---

[4] Ibid., p. 106.
[5] Ibid., pp. 99, 100, 110.

Regardless of theory, in practice it was the theologian—not the physician—who put forth a language and metaphor for the inner drama of the mind. And so it was that the earliest autobiographies of the inner life, the life of the mind, always described that life in spiritual or religious terms. I use the term *spiritual autobiography* to describe that kind of autobiography. Although seventeenth-century English Puritans and Quakers applied this term to a traditional narrative of the inner life, I use it more broadly to include all autobiographies of the inner life which describe that life in spiritual or religious terms.

Margery Kempe's *Book* is one such spiritual autobiography.

Margery Kempe was the daughter of the mayor of Lynn, a town in Norfolk, England. She was born around 1373, grew up illiterate, and married young. Soon after the birth of her first child, perhaps in 1393 or 1394, Kempe went "out of her mind" (her words) for about eight months, during which time she thought she saw and heard flame-tongued devils. For much of her life after that Margery Kempe experienced unusual visions or hallucinations, both visual and auditory, usually about religious or spiritual matters. In 1413 she went on a pilgrimage to Rome and the Holy Land, dressed in white according to what she felt to be a divine injunction. Upon arriving in Jerusalem, she began "crying and roaring though she should have died for it." That was her first attack of crying out, but the attacks quickly became chronic, often occurring several times a day, especially during times of devotion and contemplation, and often in church.

In England, her persistent eccentric behavior aroused a lot of public attention. Occasionally people assumed she was ill. We are told that at one time people thought she had "the falling evil," presumably epilepsy: "Some said she had the falling evil, for she, with the crying, wrested her body, turning from one side to the other, and waxed all blue and livid, like the colour of lead." But mostly, perhaps because so much of her behavior was focused on religious matters, people assumed that she was either possessed by the Devil or was a heretic. In 1417 she was brought to trial for heresy in the Church of All Hallows at Leicester, but on examination she appeared orthodox and was acquitted, saved from a possible death by fire.

Apparently a few people thought of Kempe as a holy woman, a prophet, or visionary. According to her account, certain "worthy and worshipful" clergy urged her to make "a book of her feelings and revelations," perhaps patterned on the book of revelations written by a contemporary, Juliana of Norwich. Since she herself was illiterate, she dictated the original version of the long first part of her autobiography to an unknown amanuensis, possibly her son. Finished in 1432, that copy was poorly written, "nor were the letters shaped or formed as other letters." In 1436 her second amanuensis, a priest, began rewriting the original version of the first part of the *Book*, putting it into recognizable English. By 1438 the priest had begun transcribing a shorter second part as Kempe dictated it. The manuscript later disappeared—for a few centuries—at last discovered in 1934, in the home of Colonel William Erdeswick Ignatius Butler-Bowden, who soon after published it in modern English.

As a picture of medieval life, Margery Kempe's book is unparalleled. In at least two places, for instance, we are given rare descriptions of seemingly ordinary fifteenth-century treatment of persons who were recognized as mad. When Kempe was "out of her mind," we learn that she "was bound and kept with strength, day and night," to prevent her from biting and scratching herself. Later, she visited a woman who had become "alienated from her wits," after childbirth. The woman "roared and cried" and would "both smite and bite": "Then was she taken to the furthest end of town, into a chamber, so that the people should not hear her crying, and there was she bound, hand and foot, with chains of iron, so that she should smite nobody."

Margery Kempe's *Book* is of greatest interest as the first fully developed example in English of autobiographical description of inner experience—normal or abnormal. And it is from that perspective that we might best examine the work.

Perhaps the most notable quality of Kempe's inner experience is her sense of her own separation from the origins of that experience. She sees herself as a passive recipient, rather than an active originator. Thus she first loses her mind partly because the Devil placed in her mind a fear of damnation. In describing her preparations for the pilgrimage to Rome and the Holy Land, Kempe does mention that she "had a desire" to see those places, but almost immediately after, in the text, we learn that before the desire was followed, it was ratified by a spiritual command: "as she was in these desires, Our Lord bade her, in her mind . . . that she should go." Such a separation of the self from the origins of thought and action is consistent with the theocratic view of the psyche, and in the spiritual autobiographies to follow, we shall see this theoretical system repeated. But Kempe seems to take it to extremes. All her unusual mental experiences are described in passive form, denoting the intrusion of spiritual forces onto the self. Even ordinary, minor mental events are likely to be described in passive form: "she was led to think" is as likely a construction as "she thought."

The following excerpts have been selected for their interest and clarity. In the first, the narrator describes Kempe's experience of being "out of her mind" (although she dictated her story, it is presented as third-person narrative). In the second excerpt, we read of her persecution in Canterbury, where she is accused of heresy and threatened with death by fire. The third excerpt presents a description of many of Kempe's visions and spiritual experiences; we might compare them with some twentieth-century accounts of madness such as Daniel Paul Schreber's *Memoirs* (1903) and the anonymous, *I Question* (1945). In the last excerpt, the Devil tempts her with foul thoughts for twelve days. We may note how passive Kempe's mind seems here. She becomes almost entirely the pawn and victim of external spiritual forces.

WHEN THIS CREATURE was twenty years of age, or some deal more, she was married to a worshipful burgess (of Lynne) and was with child within a short time, as nature would. And after she had conceived, she was belaboured with great accesses till the child was born and then, what with the labour she had in childing, and the sickness going before, she despaired of her life, weening she might not live. And then she sent for her ghostly father, for she had a thing on her conscience which she had never shewn before that time in all her life. For she was ever hindered by her enemy, the devil, evermore saying to her that whilst she was in good health she needed no confession, but to do penance by herself alone and all should be forgiven, for God is merciful enough. And therefore this creature often-times did great penance in fasting on bread and water, and other deeds of alms with devout prayers, save she would not shew that in confession.

And when she was at any time sick or dis-eased, the devil said in her mind that she should be damned because she was not shriven of that default. Wherefore after her child was born, she, not trusting to live, sent for her ghostly father, as is said before, in full will to be shriven of all her lifetime, as near as she could. And when she came to the point for to say that thing which she had so long concealed, her confessor was a little too hasty and began sharply to reprove her, before she had fully said her intent, and so she would no more say for aught he might do. Anon, for the dread she had of damnation on the one side, and his sharp reproving of her on the other side, this creature went out of her mind and was wondrously vexed and laboured with spirits for half a year, eight weeks and odd days.

And in this time she saw, as she thought, devils opening their mouths all inflamed with burning waves of fire, as if they would have swallowed her in, sometimes ramping at her, sometimes threatening her, pulling her and hauling her, night and day during the aforesaid time. Also the devils cried upon her with great threatenings, and bade her that she should forsake Christendom, her faith, and deny her God, His Mother and all the Saints in Heaven, her good works and all good virtues, her father, her mother and all her friends. And so she did. She slandered her husband, her friends and her own self. She said many a wicked word, and many a cruel word; she knew no virtue nor goodness; she desired all wickedness; like as the spirits tempted her to say and do, so she said and did. She would have destroyed herself many a time at their stirrings and have been damned with them in Hell, and in witness thereof, she bit her own hand so violently, that the mark was seen all her life after.

And also she rived the skin on her body against her heart with her nails spitefully, for she had no other instruments, and worse she would have done, but that she was bound and kept with strength day and night so that she might not have her will. And when she had long been laboured in these and many other temptations, so that men weened she should never have escaped or lived, then on a time as she lay alone and her keepers were from her, Our Merciful Lord Jesus Christ, ever to be trusted, worshipped be His Name, never forsaking His servant in time of need, appeared to His creature who had forsaken Him, in the likeness of a man, most seemly, most beauteous and most amiable that ever might be seen with man's eye, clad in a mantle of purple silk, sitting upon her bedside, looking upon her with so blessed a face that she was strengthened in all her spirit, and said to her these words:—

"Daughter, why hast thou forsaken Me, and I forsook never thee?"

And anon, as He said these words, she saw verily how the air opened as bright as any lightning. And He rose up into the air, not right hastily and quickly, but fair and easily, so that she might well behold Him in the air till it was closed again.

And anon this creature became calmed in her wits and reason, as well as ever she was before, and prayed her husband as soon as he came to her, that she might have the keys of the buttery to take her meat and drink as she had done before. Her maidens and her keepers counselled him that he should deliver her no keys, as they said she would but give away such goods as there were, for she knew not what she said, as they weened.

Nevertheless, her husband ever having tenderness and compassion for her, commanded that they should deliver to her the keys; and she took her meat and drink as her bodily strength would serve her, and knew her friends and her household and all others that came to see how Our Lord Jesus Christ had wrought His grace in her, so blessed may He be, Who ever is near in tribulation. When men think He is far from them, He is full near by His grace. Afterwards, this creature did all other occupations as fell to her to do, wisely and soberly enough, save she knew not verily the call of Our Lord.

*   *   *

On a time, as this creature was at Canterbury in the church amongst the monks, she was greatly despised and reproved because she wept so fast, both by the monks and priests, and by secular men, nearly all day both forenoon and afternoon also, so much indeed that her husband went away from her as if he had not known her, and left her alone amongst them, choose how she might. Further comfort had she none of him that day.

So an old monk, who had been Treasurer with the Queen whilst he was in secular clothing, a rich man, and greatly dreaded by many people, took her by the hand, saying unto her:—

"What canst thou say of God?"

"Sir," she said, "I will both speak of Him, and hear of Him," repeating to the monk a story of Scripture.

The monk said:—"I would thou wert enclosed in a house of stone, so that, there, no man should speak with thee."

"Ah! Sir," she said, "ye should maintain God's servants. Ye are the first that hold against them. Our Lord amend you."

Then a young monk said to her:—"Either thou hast the Holy Ghost, or else thou hast the devil within thee, for what thou speakest to us here is Holy Writ, and that hast thou not of thyself."

Then said this creature:—"I pray you, sir, give me leave to tell you a tale."

Then the people said to the monk:—"Let her say what she will."

Then she said:—"There was once a man who had sinned greatly against God, and when he was shriven, his confessor enjoined him as part of his penance, that he should for one year hire men to chide him and reprove him for his sins, and he should give them silver for their labour. And one day he came amongst many great men, such as are now here, God save you all, and stood among them as I do now amongst you, despising him as ye do me, the man laughing and smiling and having good game at their words. The greatest master of them said to the man:—

"'Why laughest thou, wretch? Thou art greatly despised!'

"'Ah! Sir, I have great cause to laugh, for I have many days put silver out of my purse and hired men to chide me for remission of my sin, and this day I may keep my silver in my purse. I thank you all.'

"Right so I say to you, worshipful sirs. Whilst I was at home in my own country, day by day with great weeping and mourning, I sorrowed because I had no shame, scorn or contempt, as I was worthy. I thank you all, sirs, highly for what, forenoon and afternoon, I have had in good measure this day, blessed be God for it."

Then she went out of the monastery, they following and crying upon her:—

"Thou shalt be burnt, false Lollard. Here is a cartful of thorns ready for thee, and a tun to burn thee with."

And the creature stood outside the gates of Canterbury, for it was in the evening, many people wondering at her.

Then said the people:—"Take and burn her!"

She stood still, trembling and quaking full sore in her flesh, without earthly comfort, and knew not where her husband had gone.

Then prayed she in her heart to Our Lord in this manner:—

"Here came I, Lord, for Thy love. Blessed Lord, help me and have mercy on me."

And anon, after she had made her prayer in her heart to Our Lord, there came two fair young men, who said to her:—

"Damsel, art thou neither heretic nor Lollard?"

And she said:—"No, sirs, I am neither heretic nor Lollard."

They asked her, where was her inn. She said she knew not what street; nevertheless it would be at a Dewchman's house. Then these two young men brought her home to her hostel, and made her great cheer, asking her to pray for them, and there she found her husband.

And many people in N . . . had said evil of her whilst she was out, and slandered her over many things she was said to have done whilst she was in the country.

Then, after this, she was in great rest of soul a long while, and had high contemplation day by day, and much holy speech and dalliance with Our Lord Jesus Christ, both forenoon and after-noon with many sweet tears of high devotion, so plenteously and continually, that it was a marvel that her eyes endured, or that her heart should last, without being consumed with the ardour of love, which was kindled with the holy dalliance of Our Lord, when He said to her many times:—

"Dear daughter, love thou Me with all thy heart, for I love thee with all My heart and the might of My Godhead, for thou wert a chosen soul without beginning in My sight and a pillar of Holy Church. My merciful eyes are even upon thee. It would be impossible for thee to suffer the scorn and contempt that thou shalt have, were not My grace supporting thee."

*   *   *

As this creature was in the Apostles' Church in Rome on Saint Lateran's Day, the Father of Heaven said to her:—

"Daughter, I am well pleased with thee, inasmuch as thou believest in all the Sacraments of Holy Church and in all faith that belongeth thereto, and especially because thou believest in the manhood of My Son, and for the great compassion thou hast for His bitter Passion."

Also the Father said to this creature:—"Daughter, I will have thee wedded to My Godhead because I shall shew thee My secrets and My counsels, for thou shalt live with Me without end."

Then the creature kept silence in her soul and answered not thereto, for she was full sore afraid of the Godhead; and she had no knowledge of the dalliance of the Godhead, for all her love and all her affection were set in the manhood of Christ, and there-of she had knowledge, and she would not for anything be parted therefrom.

She had so much affection for the manhood of Christ, that when she saw women in Rome bearing children in their arms, if she could ascertain that any were men-children, she would then cry, roar, and weep as if she had seen Christ in His childhood.

And if she might have had her will, oftentimes she would have taken the children out of their mothers' arms and have kissed them in the stead of Christ.

If she saw a seemly man, she had great pain in looking at him, lest she might have seen Him Who was both God and man.

And therefore she cried many times and often when she saw a seemly man, and wept and sobbed full sore on the manhood of Christ, as she went in the streets of Rome, so that they that saw her wondered full much at her, for they knew not the cause.

Therefore it was no wonder if she was still and answered not the Father of Heaven when He told her that she should be wedded to His Godhead.

Then said the Second Person, Christ Jesus, Whose manhood she loved so much, to her:—

"What sayest thou, Margery, daughter, to My Father of these words He spake to thee? Art thou well pleased that it be so?"

And then she would not answer the Second Person, but wept wondrous more, desiring to have still Himself and in no wise to be parted from Him. Then the Second Person in the Trinity answered to His Father for her, and said:—

"Father, hold her excused, for she is yet but young, and not fully learned how she should answer."

And then the Father took her by the hand, (ghostly) in her soul, before the Son and the Holy Ghost; and the Mother of Jesus and all the twelve Apostles and Saint Katherine and Saint Margaret and many other saints and holy virgins with a great multitude of angels, saying to her soul:—

"I take thee, Margery, for My wedded wife, for fairer, for fouler, for richer, for poorer, so that thou be kindly and gentle to do as I bid thee. For, daughter, there was never a child so gracious to its mother as I shall be to thee, both in weel and in woe, to help thee and comfort thee. And thereto I make thee surety."

Then the Mother of God, and all the saints that were present in her soul, prayed that they might have much joy together. And then the creature with high devotion with great plenty of tears, thanked God for His ghostly comfort, holding herself, in her own feeling, right unworthy to any such grace as she felt, for she felt many great comforts, both ghostly comforts and bodily ones. Sometimes she felt sweet smells with her nose. They were sweeter, she thought, than ever was any sweet earthly thing that she smelt before, for could she ever tell how sweet they were, for she thought she might have lived thereby, if they had lasted.

Sometimes she heard with her bodily ears such sounds and melodies that she could not well hear what a man said to her at that time, unless he spoke the louder. These sounds and melodies had she heard nearly every day for the term of twenty-five years, when this book was written, and especially when she was in devout prayer, and also many times while she was at Rome and in England both.

She saw with her bodily eyes many white things flying all about her on every side, as thick, in a manner, as specks in a sunbeam. They were right subtle and comfortable, and the brighter the sun shone, the better might she see them. She saw them many divers times and in many divers places, both in church and in her chamber, at her meat, and at her prayers, in the fields, and in town, both going and sitting. And many times she was afraid what they might be, for she saw them as well at night in darkness, as in daylight. Then, when she was afraid of them, Our Lord said to her:—

"By this token, daughter, believe that it is God Who speaketh in thee, for, wheresoever God is, Heaven is, and where God is, there be many angels, and God is in thee and thou art in Him. And therefore be not afraid, daughter, for these be tokens that there are many angels about thee, to keep both day and night so that no devil shall have power over thee, nor evil men to harm thee."

Then from that time forward, she used to say, when she saw them coming:—"Benedictus qui venit in nomine Domini."

Also Our Lord gave her another token which endured about sixteen years, and it increased ever more and more, and that was a flame of fire, wondrous and hot and delectable, and right comfortable, not wasting but ever increasing, of love; for though the weather were never so cold, she felt the heat burning in her breast and at her heart, as verily as a man could feel the material fire if he put his hand or his finger therein.

When she first felt the fire of love burning in her breast, she was afraid thereof, and then Our Lord answered to her mind and said:—

"Daughter, be not afraid, for this heat is the heat of the Holy Ghost, which shall burn away all thy sins; for the fire of love quencheth all sins. And thou shalt understand by this token that the Holy Ghost is in thee, and thou knowest well that wherever the Holy Ghost is, there is the Father, and where the Father is, there is the Son, and so thou hast fully in thy soul all the Holy Trinity. Therefore thou hast great cause to love Me right well; and yet thou shalt have greater cause than ever thou hadst to love Me, for thou shalt hear what thou hast never heard, and see what thou hast never seen, and thou shalt feel what thou hast never felt.

"For daughter, thou art as secure in the love of God, as God is God. Thy soul is more certain of the love of God, than of thine own body, for thy soul shall part from thy body, but God shall never part from thy soul, for they are united together without end. Therefore, daughter, thou hast as great cause to be merry as any lady in this world; and if thou knew, daughter, how much thou pleasest Me when thou sufferest Me wilfully to speak in thee, thou wouldst never do otherwise, for this is a holy life, and the time is right well spent. For daughter, this life pleaseth Me more than the wearing of the haburion or the hair-cloth, or fasting on bread and water; for, if thou saidst every day a thousand Pater Nosters, thou wouldst not please Me so well as thou dost when thou art in silence and sufferest Me to speak in thy soul."

*   *   *

Thus, through hearing holy books and holy sermons, she ever increased in contemplation and holy meditation. It is in a manner impossible to write all the holy thoughts, holy speeches and high revelations which Our Lord shewed unto her, both of herself and other men and women, and also of many souls, some to be saved and some to be damned, and it was to her a great punishment and a sharp chastisement. To know of those that should be saved, she was full glad and joyful, for she desired, as much as she durst, all men to be saved, and when Our Lord shewed to her any that should be damned, she had great pain. She would not hear or believe that it was God who shewed her such things, and put it out of her mind as much as she might. Our Lord blamed her therefor, and bade her believe that it was His high mercy and His goodness to shew her His privy counsels, saying to her mind:—

"Daughter, thou must as well hear of the damned as of the saved."

She would give no credence to the counsel of God, but rather believed it was some evil spirit deceiving her.

Then for her frowardness and her unbelief, Our Lord withdrew from her all good thoughts and all good remembrance of holy speeches and dalliance, and the high contemplation which she had been used to before, and suffered her to have as many evil thoughts as she before had good ones.

And this vexation endured for twelve days; and just as, before, she had four hours of the forenoon in holy speeches and dalliance with Our Lord, so now she had as many hours of foul thoughts and foul memories of lechery and all uncleanness, as though she had been common to all manner of people.

And so the devil deluded her, dallying unto her with cursed thoughts, as Our Lord dallied to her before with holy thoughts.

And, as she before had many glorious visions and high contemplation in the Manhood of Our Lord, in Our Lady and in many other holy saints, even right so had she now horrible sights and abominable, for aught she could do, of beholding men's members, and such other abominations.

She saw, as she thought verily, divers men of religion, priests and many others, both heathen and Christian, coming before her sight, so that she might not eschew them or put them out of her sight, shewing their bare members unto her.

And therewith the devil bade her, in her mind, choose whom she would have first of them all, and she must be common to them all.

And he said she liked better some one of them than all the others.

She thought that he said truth; she could not say nay; and she must needs do his bidding, and yet she would not have done it for all this world.

Yet she thought it should be done, and she thought these horrible sights and cursed memories were delectable to her, against her will.

Wherever she went, or whatever she did, these cursed memories remained with her. When she should see the Sacrament, make her prayers, or do any other good deed, ever such cursedness was put into her mind.

She was shriven, and did all that she might, but she found no release, until she was near at despair. It cannot be written what pain she felt, and what sorrow she was in.

Then she said:—"Alas! Lord, Thou hast said before that Thou shouldst never forsake me. Where now is the truth of Thy word?"

And anon, came her good angel unto her, saying:—

"Daughter, God hath not forsaken thee, and never shall forsake thee, as He hath promised thee; but, because thou believest not that it is the spirit of God that speaketh in thy soul, and sheweth thee His privy counsels, of some that shall be saved and some that shall be damned, therefore God chastiseth thee in this wise and manner. And this chastising shall endure twelve days, until thou wilt believe that it is God Who speaketh to thee, and no devil."

Then she said to her angel:—"Ah! I pray thee, pray for me to My Lord Jesus Christ that He will vouchsafe to take from me these cursed thoughts, and speak to me as He did before time, and I shall make a promise to God that I shall believe it is God Who hath spoken to me beforetime, for I may no longer endure this great pain."

Her angel said again to her:—

"Daughter, My Lord Jesus will not take it away from thee till thou hast suffered it twelve days, for He will that thou know thereby whether it is better that God speak to thee, or the devil. And My Lord Jesus Christ is never the wrother with thee, though He suffer thee to feel this pain."

So she suffered that pain till twelve days were passed, and then had she as holy thoughts, as holy memories and as holy desires, as holy speeches and dalliance with Our Lord Jesus Christ as ever she had before, Our Lord saying to her:—

"Daughter, believe now well that I am no devil."

Then she was filled with joy, for she heard Our Lord speaking to her as He was wont to do.

Therefore she said:—"I shall believe that every good thought is the speech of God, blessed may Thou, Lord, be, that Thou deign to comfort me again. I would not, Lord, for all this world, suffer such another pain as I have suffered these twelve days, for methought I was in Hell, blessed may Thou be that it is past.

"Therefore, Lord, now will I lie still and be obedient to Thy will. I pray Thee, Lord, speak in me what is most pleasing to Thee."

1677, 1678 ⊕

The Diary of Christoph Haizmann

The marks of true demonic possession were clear in the minds of medieval authorities. Possessed persons could not pray, take the Eucharist, or look upon the image of Christ without fear. They were prone to bodily convulsions, uncontrollable grimacing and contortion of the face, rolling of the eyes, and uncontrollable rages of cursing and blasphemy in a voice not their own.[1]

The treatment for possession was the ritual of exorcism performed by a priest. By the seventeenth century, the Church had established a standard formula for exorcism, written into the *Rituale Romanum*. First the priest prays to himself, to gather his own strength and confidence. Then he commands, "in the name of him who rules the seas and the winds, the heavens and earth, in the name of him who was crucified by men," that the Devil, "the adversary of all," leave the body of the possessed and return to "the regions from whence he came." Having spoken that command, the priest places his crucifix upon the forehead of the possessed, then upon the heart, and again upon the forehead, stating that the power to heal the possessed comes not from any earthly source, but from God above.[2]

Christoph Haizmann was a painter, a native of Bavaria, staying for a time in the Seignory of Pottenbrunn, near Vienna. On August 29, 1677, while attending church, Haizmann was seized by what a clerical witness described as "certain unnatural convulsions."[3] The seizures continued through that day and into the next until at last Haizmann was taken to the prefect of Pottenbrunn. The prefect asked him

---

[1] Neaman, *Suggestion of the Devil*, p. 32. In the late nineteenth century, Charcot and others began to examine medieval accounts and concluded that the possessed were really suffering from what was soon to be called "schizophrenia." The simple equation of possession and schizophrenia, however, is inappropriate. One suspects that medieval possessions arose from a number of sources, including a recently identified disease known as Tourette's Syndrome, a poorly understood loss of normal inhibitory processes leading to violent tics and loud outbursts including coprolalia (involuntary utterances of obscenities).

[2] Ibid., p. 33.

[3] Haizmann's narrative of demonic possession is the sole account we shall consider in which the central figure was *not* thought to be mad at, or soon after, the time of the experience. Though Kempe had visions of devils and for a time thought she was

"whether perhaps he practised the forbidden arts or was tangled in a pact with the Devil." Haizmann made the following confession.

Almost nine years earlier, while despondent over the death of his father, and troubled about his career as an artist, Haizmann met the Devil in a forest, disguised as a respectable old man. The Devil offered to help him in his life, provided that he would give the Devil power over his soul after nine years. Haizmann refused nine times but at last was persuaded to sign a pact, first in ink, later in blood. With great remorse and fear, Haizmann explained to the prefect that the pact was to fall due within a month, on September 24, 1677. He begged to be sent to the Shrine of the Most Blessed Virgin at Zell—otherwise known as Mariazell—to be exorcised.

The prefect sent him to Mariazell, where for three days and nights the exorcist, Father Sebastian Meitinger, ordered the Devil to appear at the Altar of the Virgin to return the written pact and restore Haizmann. At midnight of the third day, the day of the Feast of the Nativity, Haizmann saw the Devil at the altar, holding the piece of paper on which the first pact was written. Haizmann broke loose from the grasp of the priests around him and tore the scrap of paper out of the Devil's hands.

Immediately after that dramatic midnight event, Haizmann's seizures stopped. In gratitude, he stayed at Mariazell long enough to paint the story of his several encounters with the Devil and his seemingly successful exorcism. At last, sure of his recovery, he left Mariazell and went to Vienna, to live with his sister and her husband.

However, the convulsions and possession returned. Haizmann had several frightening visions of the Devil in Vienna, which he recorded in a diary, and at last, in early May 1678, he returned to Mariazell, asking once again for the rite of exorcism. On May 9, after much priestly invocation, the Devil gave up the second pact, the one written in blood. Thereafter, according to clerical accounts, Haizmann was fully free from demonic bondage. For the rest of his life he was tempted by the Devil to sign another pact, but he never again yielded. In 1700 Haizmann died peacefully.

The account we have comes relatively directly from original sources—Haizmann's diary, his paintings, eyewitness accounts—

---

possessed, simultaneously she was treated for madness. Haizmann, on the other hand, was treated solely for possession—nothing more. However, I think that Haizmann's experience was an experience of what we would call madness, simply seen from a different world-view. Other twentieth century commentators hold the same opinion. Therefore, I include it in this "history of madness."

that were preserved by the religious order guarding the shrine at Mariazell as evidences of a miracle. That material was put together fourteen years after Haizmann's death, transcribed (the paintings copied), and eventually preserved in the Austrian National Library in Vienna. The manuscript then emerged in the early 1920s when the director of the Vienna library discovered it and sent it to Sigmund Freud, thinking the case might have some medical or psychiatric interest. Freud published an analysis in 1923, "A Neurosis of Demoniacal Possession in the Seventeenth Century," in which he argued that Haizmann's possession was in reality a psychiatric problem arising from certain repressed homosexual fantasies.[4] But Freud merely summarized the original material, seeming to favor those portions which supported his theory, while he neglected to reproduce any of the paintings. In 1956, however, Ida Macalpine and Richard Hunter, partly in an attempt to repudiate Freud's analysis, published the entire manuscript in English translation, including plates of all nine of Haizmann's paintings, along with their critique of Freud and their own analysis of the possession, in *Schizophrenia 1677: A Psychiatric Study of an Illustrated Autobiographical Record of Demoniacal Possession.*[5]

Most fascinating are Haizmann's nine paintings of the Devil as he appeared to him at various times. The first painting shows the Devil to be a well-dressed, respectable old man with a black dog; in the second he has become a creature of reddish hue with a bearded man's face, horns, a serpent's tongue, eagle's talons in place of hands and feet, and four pendulous female breasts. In successive paintings, the Devil continues to have female breasts, sometimes two, sometimes four. In the third painting, he is shown also to have a long, snake-like tail and bat-like wings. He becomes more grotesque, sometimes more absurd, progressively more reptilian until, in the eighth and ninth paintings, he is shown to be a scaly dragonlike creature, bathed in fire, with a long serpentine tail and torso. Interestingly enough, the paintings may not be atypical of medieval representations of the Devil. Albrecht Dürer's *Descent into Hell*, for instance, shows a devil with large female breasts, bat wings, and a scaly reptilian torso and tail. Perhaps we ought to be reminded how much perception and fantasy can be influenced by context or environment.

The following excerpts are taken from Haizmann's diary, written in Vienna after his first exorcism. Haizmann first describes a series of visions or hallucinations of several diabolic personages disguised as

---

[4]Freud's analysis here is very similar to his analysis of Schreber's madness (1903).

[5]This work is the source of all my background information on Haizmann.

handsome cavaliers and beautiful women. The general coherence and reasonableness of the experience, compared to most hallucinatory experiences considered in this volume, is striking. The account most resembles Joanna Greenberg's description of her visions in *I Never Promised You a Rose Garden* (1964). Haizmann's second excerpt describes experiences and events which are less coherent and reasonable. He comes to himself, feeling in the midst of flames and "stench." He rolls on the floor until blood pours from his mouth and nose. Later he experiences some unusual tactile hallucinations—the sensations of being tortured by ropes, being pulled apart by devils, having a devil sit on his tongue. Such experiences are similar to Schreber's 1903 account of his own terrifying bodily "miracles."

We may prefer to call Haizmann's experiences "hallucinations," but it is important to remember that *his* perception of them was quite different. For him, they not only seemed real at the time they occurred, as dreams may seem real, but they also seemed real afterward. They remained for him very real, very disturbing encounters with the personal, intelligent force behind all earthly evil.

AFTER I HAD ARRIVED IN VIENNA and had myself received into the Holy Rosicrucian Brotherhood, I lived in peace until 11th October between 11 and 12 at night, when a well-dressed cavalier appeared who spoke to me and asked why I was so simpleminded as to allow myself to be enrolled into the Brotherhood. Of what help would it be to me? I should throw away the scraps of paper as they were useless and nothing but sheer tomfoolery. He added besides: as I was deserted by everybody, what would I do now? But as I did not listen to him, he receded from me and vanished.

On the 12th between 2 and 3 at night, I imagined I was in a beautiful hall which was delightfully furnished, full of silver chandeliers in which candles were burning; the most magnificently dressed cavaliers were dancing round and round me with the most beautiful women. Then one of them said to me, had he only stayed with us he could enjoy these pleasures too; it is all his own fault. The cavalier said I should tear up the drawings of the apparition which I had sketched, and not paint the High Altar, he would then give me a goodly sum of money. But I would not listen to him and knelt down and prayed a rosary. Thereupon I lay down on the floor and prayed five Paternosters, five Ave Marias, and one Credo, and then everything vanished.

On 14th October between 3 and 4 in the morning, I again saw this stately hall and in it a long table covered with the most select delicacies, and adorned with the most beautiful goblets of gold and silver, with gorgeously decked out cavaliers who were eating and drinking well together. Also amongst them sat the cavalier who had originally appeared to me, he called me to him, I was to sit between him and the lady who had the seat next to him; but as I could not get myself to do this he told the lady to get up and try and bring me to them. She got up and came to me. But as often as I screamed: Jesus, Mary and Joseph! she receded. This shouting was heard by my brother-in-law, and it made him together with my sister and other people rush into my room, with a light and a font from which they sprinkled holy-water round the room, until at last they came up against these hellish monsters in disguise who receded step by step, until finally they were driven close to the wall, whence they disappeared.

On 16th October there appeared to me again a still more beautiful hall adorned with precious pieces of silver and decorated with fine golden candlesticks, and in them white candles were burning. In the centre stood a throne made up of pieces of gold and on each side of it stood a guilded lion rampant; each held in the right paw a kingly crown and in the left a sceptre. Various cavaliers stood around them in great numbers who were arguing among themselves and apparently eagerly awaiting the arrival of their king; but as they could not wait for him any longer, the previously mentioned cavalier came up to me saying, that I should be seated on the throne, they would take me for their king and thus honour me to all eternity. Whereupon I screamed Jesus, Mary!—came to my senses again and saw nothing more.

On 20th October in the evening between 6 and 7 o'clock, a radiant light appeared to me: I immediately shouted: Jesus, Mary, Joseph. Then I heard a voice out of the light which said: I am sent by them. It said also I should not be afraid: Arise, o sinner, it said, and love Me Jesus. I saw what great bliss and indescribable pain there was in eternity, and with that I fell into a trance lasting two and a half hours. In it he showed me eternal bliss and eternal pain, neither of which I can put into words, nor describe. After this vision he said to me, that I should go into the wilderness for six years and therein serve God; after that I could go wherever I wanted. With that I awoke again so to speak, and came to myself.

*   *   *

On 26th December I went in the afternoon to Stephen's Cathedral to worship. While I worshipped to the best of my ability there came a strapping maid and a well done up man, and I thought to myself I wish I were he and as well done up as he; after that I went home. In the evening I went to my bedroom to say my prayers there and after I had said them there was a clap of thunder and a bright flame came down on me so that I again fell into a swoon.

Thereupon my sister came and with her a gentleman who called me by my name, and with that I came to myself. Then it seemed to me as if I were lying in nothing but fire and stench, and could not stand on my feet. I rolled out of my chamber into the room, and rolled around the room until the blood gushed out of my mouth and nose. Then my sister did not know what to do with me; so she sent for the priests. After they had come the stench and heat disappeared. As I could not yet stand on my feet I was lifted on to a chair. A quarter of an hour after the priests had left me again, something came to my side and spoke to me: this suffering is given to you because you have such worthless and idle thoughts. I was to comply in the matter and become a hermit, as had been ordained by God. Then I got up from the chair and it was as if nothing had happened.

On the 26th day of December and on 30th December, two evil spirits tortured me with ropes, which I felt on my limbs for two days afterwards. They said the torture would be repeated every day until I joined the hermit Order.

*   *   *

On the 2nd day of January, I returned home towards evening. I paced up and down in the room when a feverish shivering came over me. My sister said to me, I was to sit by the fire and then I would feel better. I had hardly sat down when six evil spirits came and wanted to charge at me and pull me to pieces. I shouted out Jesus, Mary and Joseph! stand by me; so they drew back, but soon moved forward again. The struggle between us lasted for one whole hour. Then the priests came, and as soon as they had come, so they vanished one after the other. Afterwards I got up from the floor.

On 7th January I had my lesson in the Jesus, Mary and Joseph Brotherhood. On the same day I went to the Franciscan Fathers and wanted to confess there and take Communion. When I wanted to confess the priest ordered me to say the confession-prayer. But I could not pray it although I started four times, yet I failed every time until the priest recited it before me; then I could say it and complete the prayer. While I was confessing the Foul Fiend came for me twice and plagued me during confession. After I had confessed I went into the Church and received the High Sacrament from the Altar. Then the priest ordered me to take my lesson in the afternoon, and I went home. After I had eaten the mid-day meal, four evil spirits came and started to torture me terribly. Throughout the whole afternoon and the whole night until the next morning they went for me; one of them sat on my tongue, so I took my hand and tore out the evil spirit.

During this time several people watched over me, who were also so horror-stricken that they became seriously ill and saw visions.

On 13th January while sitting and actually painting my picture, the Foul Fiend came and sat on the table next to me; so I shouted to my sister that the Evil One was present. Then my sister came with holy-water and sprinkled it around the room, at which everything vanished from the table.

1714 ⌐

The Life of the Reverend Mr. George Trosse: Written by Himself, and Published Posthumously According to His Order in 1714

George Trosse was a Presbyterian minister in Exeter during England's century of religious strife. Having refused to take an oath of conformity to certain Anglican practices, Trosse was for a time liable to prosecution. In 1685 he was indeed arrested for participating in an illegal religious gathering and placed in jail for six months, along with four other Nonconformist ministers. But by the time he wrote his *Life*, in the first decade of the eighteenth century, Trosse was a highly esteemed member of the Exeter community, no longer an object of persecution.

In his *Life*, Trosse tells very little about his long, successful career as a minister, instead choosing to focus on events of his rebellious youth, the first twenty-five or twenty-six years of his life in which he remained "in a State of Nature, in a Course of Sin and Folly; and experienc'd it to be brutish, unreasonable, ruinous and destructive to Health, Estate and Name, to Rest and Reason, as well as tending to Horrour, Despair, Rage and Hell."

The mature, reformed Trosse, in telling this story of youthful folly, and madness, serves not only as a kind of moral censor—showing us past events through the screen of his mature judgment—but also as an intellectual or rational censor, always careful to distinguish between appearance and reality. Particularly during descriptions of his experience of madness, he uses such qualifiers as "I fancy'd," or "seemingly." Nonetheless, Trosse the narrator believes that his madness was *both* a possession and a natural illness, brought about by sinful living and, as he puts it, by having "*tempted* the very *Temptor.*" He tells us at one point that the visions and voices of his madness were (like those distracting visions and voices seen and heard by the Papists, leading them to believe in purgatory) brought about by a "disturb'd *Brain*," which was in turn "influenc'd by a *deceitful* and *lying* Devil." But at other points in his description, the Devil seems actually to be present, rather than simply an influence behind the scenes.

26

At length, standing up before the *Window*, I either *heard a Voice*, which bid me, or *had a strong Impulse*, which excited me, to *cut off my Hair;* to which I reply'd, *I have no Scissars.* It was then hinted, that a *Knife would do it;* but I answer'd *I have none.* Had I had one, I verily believe, this *Voice* would have gone from my *Hair* to my *Throat*, and have commanded me to *cut it:* For I have all Reason to conclude, that the Voice was the Voice of *Satan*, and that his Design was, to *humble* me as *low as Hell:* But the Absence of a *proper Instrument* prevented it.

Trosse's characterization of his young self as having *"tempted the very Temptor"* is a particularly interesting expression because it gives us an idea of how complex the issue of responsibility is here. The Devil tempts him, but he is responsible for having made himself vulnerable to the temptation of the Devil. As if to complicate this even further, in at least two places Trosse assures us that God limited the seriousness of his sins as an act of mercy. The unresolved issue of individual responsibility and spiritual manipulation goes much deeper than it did in Margery Kempe's *Book*. Kempe did not consider herself very responsible; from her point of view, most of her thoughts and actions were brought about as a direct result of spiritual influence. But with Trosse, the connection between self and thought, between self and action, is much stronger. Trosse clearly sees his self as capable of acting with free will. And if Trosse is capable of acting with free will (with the Devil waiting at a small distance) then he is indeed capable of sin and depravity. In sum, Trosse's greater freedom leads to greater responsibility, which in turn leads to greater potential for sin and greater potential for guilt (self-censure). It should not be surprising, then, that Trosse's madness seems to be a manifestation of self-hatred and that much of the emotional tone of this *Life* is a tone of self-censure, as the elder Trosse condemns so severely the actions of the younger.

In the following excerpt from the *Life*, Trosse describes his first of three attacks of madness, in which he believes, in part, that the Devil has possessed him. The reader may want to compare this highly dramatic description of madness and possession with John Custance's description of his depressive madness in *Wisdom, Madness, and Folly* (1952).

I REMEMBER, I went into the *Country* (about Twelve Miles from Exon) with my *Mother;* I left *her* there, and one Day return'd to

the *City*, to be a *Surety* for one who had been a *Major* in the
King's Army, but was at that Time very *poor*, and liv'd *obscurely*.
He was thought to be a *dangerous Person* by such as then were in
Authority: Insomuch that an Order coming from the *Protector*,
To secure all suspected Persons, the *Sheriff* of the *County*, suppos-
ing *him* to be *such a Person*, requir'd *him* to give Security in a
Bond, of some Hundreds of Pounds, not to leave the City, or
else to yield himself into their Hands at *all Demands*. I believe,
the *Sheriff* thought none would have *stood bound* for him, since
he was a *single Person*, one who had nothing to engage him to
make his Stay in *Exon*, no Interest to induce him to *keep his
Promise*, and, if he had thought it for his *Advantage*, he, no
Doubt, would have *broken* it. Without Question, *no Prudent
Man*, in *such Circumstances*, would have been *Surety* for him.
But I was a *vain rash Young-Fellow*, throughly devoted to the
Interest of the *Cavaliers*, and extreamly fond of *that Party*.
Hereupon, I would be a *Surety* for him, to keep him from Con-
finement, tho' the *Sheriff* disswaded me, telling me it might
prove of *Ill Consequence* to me: But I *slighted* his Caution and
Advice, and so was actually *bound* for *this Fellow*, that he might
have his *Liberty*.

Hereupon, I went up and down from Place to Place in the
City, prating and *drinking*, 'till at length I was *excessively drunk;*
but yet would ride back again to my *Mother* in the *Evening*,
according to my *Promise*. In my Return back I fell from my
Horse; but how I got on Horseback again I know not. I have
sometimes been apt to believe, but am not positive, *that God*,
who amidst *all my Wickedness* had such Thoughts of *Mercy* towards me, as since has so evidently appear'd, might imploy *his
Angels* for my Preservation. Well! when I was brought *safe* home,
I was fit for nothing but the *Bed*. Just as I was going, I ask'd my
Mother's Blessing, and fell upon my Face, not being able to stand;
and thus leaving my *Mother* sad and griev'd, I was carried to my
Bed, more like an *Hog* than a *Man*. I slept 'till the Morning, a
Serving-man lying with me; who rising about Five of the Clock
left me well in Body and compos'd in Mind, and I talk'd with
him as I had been wont to do: But I was not willing to rise so
early, therefore lay still, and slept an Hour or two more. I then
waking, and being alone in the Chamber, fancy'd I heard some

rushing kind of Noise, and discern'd something at the *Bed's-Foot* like a *Shadow;* which I apprehended to have been a *Spirit.* Hereupon, I was seiz'd with *great Fear* and *Trembling,* rose in Haste, went forth into the *Outer-Chamber* in *great Consternation,* and walk'd up and down in it as one *amaz'd.* As I was thus walking, with *dismal Apprehensions,* my being *bound* for the *Major* came into my Mind, with great Aggravations of the *Folly* and *Danger* of it: fearing that the *Major* either *was gone,* or *would get away;* and *then,* I concluded, I should be *undone. This* greatly perplex'd my Spirit. The *Devil,* who in our Blindness and Presumption hurries us upon *rash* and *foolish Actions,* knows how in a Time of *Trouble* to set *them* home, with such Aggravations, as utterly to sink & distract us.

While I was thus walking up and down, hurried with these worldly disquieting Thoughts, I perceiv'd a *Voice,* (I *heard it plainly*) saying unto me, *Who art thou?* Which, knowing it could be the Voice of *no Mortal,* I concluded was the *Voice of God,* and with Tears, as I remember, reply'd, *I am a very great Sinner, Lord!* Hereupon, I withdrew again into the *Inner-Room,* securing and barring the Door upon me, & betook my self to a *very proper* and *seasonable Duty,* namely, *Secret Prayer;* performing it with some kind of *Conscience* towards *God,* and with Hopes to receive some *Good* at his Hands, (which I *never* did all my Life-time *before*). But it was an *impudent* and *proud Prayer:* For I *pray'd* in *my own Strength,* as tho' I was good enough to have *Communion* with an *Holy God,* and worthy enough to have Access to Him, and Success with him, as to all I *pray'd for.* I look'd not to the *Spirit* to *help* me in Prayer, nor to the *Lord Jesus* to render it *acceptable.* So that altho' I had liv'd a *Sinner* and a *Publican* all my Days, yet now I *pray'd* like a *Pharisee,* with a *carnal Confidence,* which was an infinite Dishonour to God, and could not but be a *great Provocation,* as the Event prov'd.

For while I was praying upon my Knees, I heard a Voice, as I fancy'd, as it were just behind me, saying, *Yet more humble; Yet more humble;* with some Continuance. And not knowing the Meaning of the *Voice,* but undoubtedly concluding it came from God, I endeavour'd to comply with it. Considering that I kneel'd upon something, I remov'd it; and then I had some kind of Intimation given me, that that was what was requir'd. Thus I kneel'd upon the Ground: But the *Voice* still continu'd, *Yet more humble; Yet more humble.* In Compliance with it I proceeded to pluck down my *Stockings,* and to kneel upon my *bare Knees:* But the same *awful Voice* still sounding in mine Ears, I proceeded to pull off my *Stockings,* and then my *Hose,* and my *Doublet;* and as I was thus uncloathing my self, I had a strong internal Impression, that all was well done, and a full Compliance with the Design of the *Voice.* In Answer likewise to this *Call,* I would *bow* my Body as *low as possibly I could,* with a great deal of Pain, & *this* I often repeated: But *all* I could. do was not *low enough,* nor *humble enough.* At last, observing that there was an Hole in the Planking of the Room, I lay my self down flat upon the Ground, and thrust in my Head there as far as I could; but because I could not fully do it, I put my Hand into the Hole, and took out *Earth* and *Dust,* and sprinkled it on my *Head;* some *Scripture Expressions* at that Time offering themselves to my Mind, I thought *this* was the *Lying down in Dust and Ashes* thereby prescrib'd.

At length, standing up before the *Window,* I either *heard a Voice,* which bid me, or *had a strong Impulse,* which excited me, to *cut off my Hair;* to which I reply'd, *I have no Scissars.* It was then hinted, that a *Knife would do it;* but I answer'd, *I have none.* Had I had one, I verily believe, this *Voice* would have gone from my *Hair* to my *Throat,* and have commanded me to *cut it:* For I have all Reason to conclude, that the *Voice* was the Voice of *Satan,* and that his Design was, to *humble* me as *low as Hell:* But the Absence of a *proper Instrument* prevented it.

Thus, pretending the *Worship of God,* I fell, in effect, to the *Worshipping* of the *Devil;* and my Falling on my Knees before *God* issu'd in a Prostration at the *proud Usurper's* Feet. I am perswaded, that *many* of the Quakers formerly were deluded by *such Voices* and *Impulses* from the *Impure Spirit,* which they mistook for the *Holy Spirit of God;* many of them having been grosly ignorant, and so fitted to entertain such Delusions of the *Devil,* as I *then* was. [And I verily believe, that those many Visions and Voices among the *Papists,* which gave the Occasion, and are the Establishment of their *Purgatory,* came from the same Author, or Cause, *viz.* A crack'd Brain, impos'd upon by a deceitful and lying Devil.]

After a while, I began to incline to put on my Cloaths again; and sitting down in order thereto, I was directed by *strange Kinds of Impulses* what Garment first to put on, and so in Order; and then with what Leisure, and with what Awe and Reverence all was to be done. Thus I comply'd with *these Impulses* in putting on several of them, 'till I came to the Putting on One of my *Stockings;* for then, having pull'd it up Half-way, with all Dread and Caution, I apprehended I was not allow'd to draw it higher: But without any *Impression,* or against it, I pluck'd up my *Stocking* about my *Leg;* whereupon I thought I had *greatly offended.* And immediately, in a Corner of the Room, towards which my Eyes were directed, I saw, as it were, a *Breath* coming down from the Roof, about the Bigness of a Man's Thigh, and to look to was somewhat like the *Beams of the Sun* shining into a Window; and by and by, from that *Breath,* I *(seemingly)* heard a Voice, saying with great Anger, *Thou Wretch! Thou hast committed the Sin against the Holy-Ghost.* This *Breath* I then believ'd to have been the *Holy-Ghost;* because I had read, that *Christ breathed* upon the *Disciples,* when He gave them the *Holy-Ghost.* And believing that I had been inspir'd and taught by *Him* in all these *ridiculous Acts* of *Humiliation,* (I am sure they were *so* as done by *me.*) I presently concluded, that I *really* had been guilty of the *Sin against the Holy-Ghost,* and so could not possibly be *pardon'd.* Thus by my careless and prophane Reading and Hearing the *Word of God,* and not endeavouring to *understand* the *Meaning of it,* I gave the *great Deceiver* an Advantage to make me believe, that the *Word* perverted and understood in a wrong Sence was the *Word of God:* For, not *Receiving the Truth* in the *Notion,* much less in the *Love* of it, I was dispos'd to believe every *Falshood* that the *Father of Lies* might impose upon me. But I bless *God* I am well assur'd that *this* was not the *Sin against the Holy-Ghost;* no, nor *all* the *other more horrid* and *aggravated Sins* which I afterwards committed: For I am perswaded, that God hath given me *Repentance* as to *all* my *Sins,* and a *sincere Faith in Christ,* and so a *full Remission.*

From this Perswasion, that I had been guilty of the *Sin against the Holy-Ghost,* I was fill'd with grievous Horrour and Anguish, with great Anxiety and sinking Despair; and then went forth in the *Outward Room* with my *Cloaths* hanging about me, and some of them off. As I was going out, I met an Antient *Servant-Maid;*

(A Sight doubtless frightful to Her.) and in a distracted manner cry'd out, *I have committed the Sin against the Holy-Ghost, and I must necessarily be Damn'd.* I begg'd she would lend me a *Pair of Scissars* to cut off my Hair; but she fearing a *worse Use* (as I suppose) would be made of them than I pretended, refus'd my Request.

Walking up and down in the Room, in a miserable distracted, despairing Condition, I had a Suggestion and Temptation to *curse God and die.* Whatever was the Meaning of *those Words* in the Mouth of *Job's Wife,* I am sure, I *then* apprehended them to be *Literally meant.* This was a Suggestion so *black* and *horrid,* as could be suppos'd to have been from *none* but the *Dark Prince,* that *great Enemy* and *Blasphemer* of God. Whereupon, methought, all was fill'd with Horrour and Confusion about me. And the *whole Creation* might justly have been muster'd up, with all it's Rage and Fury, to *revenge* such an *infinite Indignity* offer'd to it's Creator. It was matter of Wonder that the *Fire* did not burn me, or the *Earth* did not swallow me up, or *Angels* did not fall upon me with all Severity, or that *God* did not Damn me.

A *Brother-in-Law* of mine, standing by, demanded of me whether I would be rul'd and follow Advice; assuring me, that, in case I would, all might be well again. To whom I instantly reply'd I would do so. But, after this, I was full of all manner of *Blasphemies* and *wicked Passions,* and was haunted with horrible distracting Temptations to *Self-Murther,* & with a great many terrifying and disquieting *Visions and Voices;* which tho' (I believe) they had *no Reality* in themselves, yet they *seem'd* to be *such* to me, and had the *same Effect* upon me, as if they had *been really* what they *appear'd* to be. Thus was I disturb'd with silly ridiculous Fancies, and Thousands of unreasonable and non-sensical Delusions. I shall only mention a *few* of them.

Wherever I turn'd mine Eye, for some Time, I fancy'd I saw *my Companion in Wantonness* using some *indecent Gestures,* as heretofore; and this was to my Shame, the Horrour of my Soul, and the Torment of my Conscience. It seem'd to me that I heard her Voice, calling to me with Earnestness and Importunity, which was *worse* to me than *Thunder-Claps.* So that my *impure Paradice* was turn'd into a *dreadful Hell.* I fancy'd that the *Devil* was about to take her, and carry her away, to make her his *Prey;* but she cry'd to me, and ask'd me whether I would suffer it.

I also wickedly fancy'd, that I was able, by my bare willing it, to make God *miserable;* yea, that I could *torment Him* in *devouring Flames:* And as it was in my *blasphemous Mind* to *fancy* it, so it was in my *malicious Will* to *resolve* it; and *this* I took delight in. Thus having liv'd without any due and serious Apprehensions of God, and his Divine Perfections, in my Sinful State, I was dispos'd to entertain *any* the most *unreasonable* and most *dishonourable Conceptions* of Him; and so degraded Him beneath *every other Being,* accounting Him *weaker* than the *weakest of Creatures:* For tho' by *bare Willing* I could not hurt a *Gnat* or a *Flea,* yet was I fully perswaded that by *this Way* I could extreamly torment the *Almighty* and *Unchangable God.* Thus by exerting *Enmity* against the *Image,* the *Ways,* the *Graces* and *Holy Spirit* of God, in my secure and unwaken'd Condition I was now dispos'd to discover Rage and Cruelty against *God himself.* But notwithstanding all this *Blasphemy and desperate Enmity* against God, He did not suffer *Infernal Flames* to kindle upon me.

I strongly fancy'd that God watch'd Opportunities to destroy me; but I also presum'd that God must get in by the Door, or he would not be able to come at me; and I foolishly conceited, that if I did but tie the Door with a particular sort of a Knot, He would be effectually shut out; which I attempted to do, that I might be secur'd from his *Wrath.* Many and constant, for some Time, were my Temptations to *destroy my self.* Sometimes I was sollicited to dash my Head against the Edge of the Board near which I sate; at other times, I was tempted to dash out my Brains against the Walls, as I walk'd. So that between a Desire to do this, and a natural Unwillingness to offer such Violence to my self, I was miserably distracted.

Thus with a Multitude of *blasphemous horrid Thoughts* was I fill'd as I walk'd up and down. But when I was lay'd upon my Bed, where I continu'd for some Time, I was, from the *Devil's Influence,* induc'd not to *look or speak:* So that for several Days, in a Compliance with *this Temptation,* I would neither *open* my *Eyes* nor my *Lips:* And those Words of *Scripture* came into my Mind, and were strongly impress'd upon me, *(viz.) Touch not; Taste not;*

Handle not; which, quite different from the Meaning of the *Holy-Ghost,* were urg'd upon me, to perswade me not to make use of any *Meat.* Hereupon I would neither *touch it,* nor *taste it,* nor *smell to it:* For that was also suggested to me, *Smell not.* So that I refus'd all *Food* whatever which might be offer'd me. I would not endure the *Smell* of it. If it was brought nigh me, I would turn aside with the greatest Indignation and Aversion, as if it had been some abominable Thing. And I make no Doubt but it was the Design of the *Devil* by that Temptation, to seek to *starve me.* Thus I continu'd several Days under the Influence of this Delusion, as tho' the *Starving* of my *Body* was the Way to *save* my *Soul.*

While I thus lay upon my Bed, with such a wild and troubl'd Fancy, Night and Day, I *seemingly* heard many Voices and Discourses; which I attributed to *Fairies,* who, I thought, were in the Wall, and there convers'd and were merry together. And I fancy'd I saw upon the Wall a *great Claw,* for a long while together; but what the Meaning of that was I could not tell. Thus was I continually haunted with Multitudes of such Whimsies.

Being in this miserable distracted Condition, and refusing to make use of any suitable and proper Means, in order to my Recovery, my Friends had Intelligence of a Person dwelling in *Glastonbury,* who was esteem'd very skilful and successful in such Cases. They sent for him. He came; and engag'd to undertake the Cure, upon Condition that they would safely convey me to his House, where I might always be under his View and Inspection, and duely follow his Prescriptions. Hereupon, my Friends determin'd to remove me to his House; but I was resolv'd *not to move out of my Bed;* for I was perswaded that if I removed out of it, I should fall into *Hell,* and be plung'd into the *Depth of Misery.* I likewise apprehended *those about me,* who would have pluck'd me out of my Bed, to have been *so many Devils,* who would have dislodg'd me: Therefore I *stoutly resisted* them, with *all* my *Might* and *utmost Efforts,* and *struggled* with all Violence, that they might not pluck me out of my Bed and cloath me. When *one* of the Persons about me came behind me to hold me up in my Bed, I was under terrible Apprehensions *it was the Devil that seiz'd me.* And the same Thought I had of *all about me,* that they were *murtherous Devils;* and that they exerted *all their Power* to carry me away into a *Place of Torment.* By their concurrent Strength they at length prevail'd against me, took me out of my Bed, cloath'd me, bore me out between them. They procur'd a *very stout strong Man* to ride before me; and when *he* was on Horseback, they by Force put me up behind *him,* bound me by a strong Linnen-Cloth to *him;* and, because I struggled, and did all I could to throw my self off the Horse, they tied my Legs under the Belly of it. All this while I was full of *Horrours* and of *Hell within:* I neither open'd mine Eyes nor my Mouth, either to see what was done about me or to make any Lamentations: for still I look'd upon this as my *necessary Duty.*

Thus, like a miserable, wretched, and *Condemn'd Malefactor,* was I carry'd out of *that Place* and *Country* where I had committed so many *great Sins* against *my God.* As I rode along, I fancy'd *many Devils* flying in the Air just over me, and by my Side as so many Fiery *Flying-Dragons,* expressing their Rage against me.

Upon the Way, the *Men* stay'd a little to refresh themselves, (for I was very troublesome to them by my continual Struggling) and they offer'd me some *Meat;* and altho' I had not *eaten* nor *drunk* for a *long time,* yet then I was perswaded to it. And when they put a Glass into my Hand to *drink* of it, methought I saw in the Glass a *Black Thing,* about the Bigness of a great *black Fly,* or *Beetle;* and *this* I suppos'd to have been the *Devil;* but yet would *drink* it; and, methought, the *Devil* went down my Throat with the *Liquour,* and so *took possession* of me. At which *desperate Madness* of mine, it seem'd to me that all were astonish'd; and I fancy'd, that every Step I stepp'd afterwards, I was making a *Progress* into the *Depths of Hell.* When I heard the *Bell ring,* I thought it to have been *my Doom* out of *Heaven;* and the Sound of every *Double Stroke* seem'd to me to be, *Lower down; lower down; lower down; (viz.)* into the *Bottomless Pit.* This to me *then* was a dismal dejecting Sound. Whatever Noises I heard as I past by, my Fancy gave them *Hellish Interpretations:* For I was now perswaded that I was no longer *upon Earth,* but in the *Regions of Hell.* When we came to the Town, I thought I was in the *midst* of *Hell:* Every House that we pass'd by was as it were a *Mansion* in *Hell;* and it seem'd to me that all of them had their several

Degrees of *Torment*; & as we went forward, methought, their *Torments encreas'd;* and I fancy'd I heard some say, as they stood at their Doors with great Wonder, and somewhat of Pity, *What, must he go yet farther into Hell? O fearful! O dreadful!* and the like.

At last, by God's good Providence, we were brought safely to the *Physician's* House. Methought all about me were *Devils,* and he was *Beelzebub.* I was taken off my Horse, and expected immediately to be cast into *intolerable Flames* and *Burnings,* which seem'd to be before mine Eyes. The Carrying me into the House, and into an Inner and an Under Room appointed for my Lodgings, I thought to be a *Casting* me *into Utter Darkness.*

Here I was committed to a Person who came to be my *Guardian,* to watch me, that I might not *destroy my self.* And in this Room and House I continu'd several Weeks, nay, as I take it, Months. All the while I was full of *Horrour, Delusions, Blasphemy, & c.* and all attended with great Temptations to undo my self. Sometimes I continu'd in the Bed all the Day: Sometimes they put Bolts upon my Hands and Fetters on my Feet, when I prov'd *violent* and *unruly* (which I often did); for I would often *strive* and *fight,* contending with my *utmost Strength,* to get away from them, and so to free my self from that Place, which I thought to have been *Hell,* and from those Persons whom I thought to have been *Tormentors.*

When I was thus *outragious* at any Time, then would they throw me upon the Bed, and thus put Bolts upon me; and there should I lie in great Pain and Weariness 'till I could well endure it no longer; then should I desire to be releas'd and promise to be quiet.

Once, when I was thus manacled and fetter'd, the *Mortifying of the Flesh,* as commanded in *Scripture,* was brought to my Mind; and I was perswaded, that the *Grating* of my *Flesh* from my *Bones,* or the *Putting* of my *Flesh to great Pains,* was the *Mortification* requir'd. Therefore I twisted and wrested my Legs in my Fetters with all the Strength I had, enduring great and grievous Pains, and grating away some of the Flesh of my Legs thereby. I can shew, to this very Day, some of the Marks of that Cruelty I us'd towards my self. Thus I, who would not *mortify* the *inordinate Lusts* thereof, according to God's Command in *Scripture,* was induc'd to *mortify the Flesh* of my *Body* as to the *very Substance* of it, in a Compliance with the Suggestions of the *Devil.*

One Person in the House I fancy'd to be *Jesus Christ:* and every Thing almost that I spoke or did, I thought to have been a *Grief* to him, and a *Crucifixion of Him afresh;* I apprehended him pain'd under it, and complaining to God, and calling for Vengeance to seize and crush me. Sometimes I would go to him, (if not fall down before him) and beg him to be my *Friend,* and to keep off *Wrath* from me. But, methought, he gave me a Repulse, and with some kind of Adjuration, or Oath, ratify'd his Rejection of me. I lay upon my Bed, every Instant expecting to be *rack'd* or *cut in Pieces,* and to have all Manner of *Cruelties* to be us'd towards my Body. Every *Person* I saw seem'd to me to be an *Executioner;* and I thought *every Thing* either an *Instrument* of, or a *Preparation* for, my Misery and Torture. I apprehended *Self-Murther* to be the only wise and charitable Act that I could do for my self, as the only Prevention of all expected and dreaded Torment. In Expectation of a *necessary* and *inevitable Injection* into the *Lake* of *Fire and Brimstone,* I presum'd that the *longer* I was *out* of it, the *deeper* I should at last *sink into* it, and the more *intolerable* would be my *Torment* there; because, I did nothing but Sin continually, and so every Minute of mine Abode on *Earth,* would be a great Increase of the Intenseness of my Misery in *Hell.* Hereupon, I was also fully convinc'd, that there was nothing so *good* and *beneficial* to me as *immediately* to *cast my self into the Burning Lake,* since there was an utter Impossibility of escaping it; and I conceiv'd, that the *sooner* I was in it, the *easier* I should be, and so prevent *greater* Degrees of my *everlasting Burnings* there. Thus the *Murderer* had got the *Assent* of *Carnal Self,* the grand Ruling Principle which had influenc'd me all my Days, and was the Chief Cause of all my *Wickedness* and *Rebellion* against God, prompting me to *Self-Destruction,* and *Self-Damnation:* But my God and Saviour would not permit it to have such a fatal Influence upon me.

When I expected every Moment to be cut off, and cast into *Hell,* and could not but own it would be *just,* I would not so much as *bow* a *Knee,* or *open* my *Lips,* either for the *deferring* or the *diminishing* of my *Torments* there, much less for their *perfect Prevention.* I did not *shed a Tear,* nor *bewail my self;* but, like a *harden'd Sot* and *stupid Wretch*, expected an *Excision*, and a being *thrown* into *Hell*, without the least *Endeavour* to escape it.

If *I* did put on my Cloths, and *ty'd* them about me, then I thought I *bound my self to the Devil:* If *I unloos'd,* and *put them off,* then I fancy'd I *unloos'd my self from God.*

[My awaken'd Conscience muster'd up my secret Sins in order before me. The Terrors of the Lord surrounded me. My darling Sin became my perplexing Misery, and my impure Paradise was turn'd into a confounding Hell. My Buttons, Gold, Silver and the Silk upon my Sleeves lay very heavy on my Conscience, as an intolerable Burthen, as weighty as a World.] For I had been a *foolish Gallant,* and that too against the *Will* of my *Parent.*

1739 ⌐

The London-Citizen Exceedingly Injured; Or, A British Inquisition Display'd, in an Account of the Unparallel'd Case of a Citizen of London, Bookseller to the Late Queen, Who Was in a Most Unjust and Arbitrary Manner Sent on the 23rd of March Last, 1738, by One Robert Wightman, a Mere Stranger, to a Private Madhouse, by Alexander Cruden

In general, mad people in medieval Europe were taken care of privately, within the family. The few who had no family ties might be social outcasts, expelled from cities, at times whipped or beaten. Sir Thomas More, in his *Apologye* of 1533, tells of a madman who had been in Bedlam and who would at times wander into church services and "make many madde toyes & tryfles" during quiet periods of worship. More had the man bound to a tree and whipped before the whole town, and afterward noted that "it appered well that hys remembraunce was good inough" when "it was beten home."[1] At this time, Catholic monasteries and priories occasionally took in the sick and the poor, and provided what little institutional care there was for mad people.

By the seventeenth and eighteenth centuries, large-scale institutional confinement had begun. Beggars of all sorts, including the mad, were put into the *hôpitaux généreaux* of France, the *Zuchthäuser* of the German-speaking countries, and the houses of correction and workhouses of England. All these early institutions housed together quite indiscriminately the unemployed, the homeless, the criminal, and the indigent mad. In the Hôpital Général of Paris, only about one-tenth of the inmates were registered as "insane" or "demented" or of "wandering mind" or "persons who have become completely mad."[2] In the workhouses of England, the same was generally true.

Eventually, these catch-all institutions developed separate quarters for their mad inmates, but whatever treatment they received was, at

---

[1] More, *The Apologye of Syr Thomas More, Knyght*, pp. 132, 133.
[2] Foucault, *Madness and Civilization*, p. 65.

the very best, haphazard. In 1811 the English reformer William Tuke recorded in a diary his observations of the facilities for madwomen in one particular workhouse. He saw several women locked in small wooden cells, with no heat, the ventilation and light provided only by an open iron grate in the door. Their beds were merely wooden platforms. Although the weather was very cold—the temperature had dropped to sixteen degrees below freezing the night before—the women were naked. "One of these forlorn objects," wrote Tuke, "lay buried under a miserable cover of straw, without a blanket or even a horse-cloth to defend her from the cold."[3]

Gradually, institutions solely for the purpose of detaining and treating mad people developed. In the eighteenth century a small number of charitable asylums, supported by public subscription, opened— the earliest, in 1713. Sometime early in the seventeenth century, another sort of institution exclusively for mad people had started: the private madhouse.[4]

The private madhouse was a privately-owned, profit-making establishment for the care of mad people. Possibly the first form of state aid to mad people took the form of a few informal private contracts by local governments to physicians and others to care for some of the indigent mad. Of course, mad people from families of means might also be cared for by people who were paid for their services. And eventually some people began specializing in the care of the mad. They brought them into their own homes, and in some cases expanded or redesigned their homes to prepare for the care of several patients at once.

The conversion of private homes into private madhouses was simple enough. Obviously there were kitchen and sleeping facilities for the patients. There were also probably added means of mechanical restraint—chains, leg locks, and wrist locks—in case of violent or potentially violent patients. Smaller rooms, sometimes outhouses and stables, might have been converted into locked cells for patients who needed to be alone or who wanted to leave.

There was money in madness, and the managers of these institutions presented themselves and their houses with no little flamboyance. James Newton converted an old London manor house into a madhouse and in an advertisement printed in the late seventeenth century made the following claims:

---

[3] Tuke, *Chapters in the History of the Insane*, pp. 126, 127.
[4] A private madhouse may have existed in Wiltshire in 1615, perhaps earlier. The Reverend George Trosse was kept in a private madhouse in 1656.

In Clerkenwell Close . . . liveth one who by the blessing of God cures all Lunatick, distracted, or mad people; he seldom exceeds three months in the cure of the Maddest person that comes in his house; several have been cured in a fortnight and some in less time; he has cured several from Bedlam, and other mad-houses in and about the city, and has conveniency for people of what quality soever. No cure— no money.[5]

For a long time, the status and power of madhouse keepers remained pretty much undefined in the law. A law passed early in the eighteenth century said that two or more justices of the peace could authorize the arrest by local authorities of any person deemed "furiously mad, and dangerous," and could order his or her incarceration, "safely locked up," where chains could be used for restraint if necessary.[6] Whipping was specifically forbidden, but there was no provision for licensing, or inspection, and therefore virtually no control whatsoever over the happenings inside private madhouses during the first three-quarters of the eighteenth century. And as a profit-making institution, rather than a charitable or public-supported institution, the private madhouse was particularly open to charges of abuse and malpractice.[7]

At first the main public fear about private madhouses was not that mad people might be poorly or cruelly treated, but rather that sane people might be wrongfully imprisoned. Apparently in response to public concern, Parliament, in 1763, formed a select committee to investigate this possibility. The committee particularly investigated two London madhouses, in Chelsea and Hoxton, where they found evidence that sane people had indeed been locked up as if they were mad, simply on the authority of friends and relatives. Sane people had been confined for drunkenness or violent tempers, a wife had been imprisoned by her husband because she had been extravagant and indifferent toward him, and two young girls had been locked up by their parents to break off love affairs.

Eleven years later, in 1774, Parliament passed the first significant English legislation concerning the rights of persons accused of madness. The act required that a medical certificate be filled out by a physician, surgeon, or apothecary, before non-pauper patients were

---

[5]Tuke, *Chapters in the History of the Insane*, pp. 92, 93.
[6]Parry-Jones, *The Trade in Lunacy*, p. 7. Most of my information on private madhouses comes from this book.
[7]Ibid., p. 221.

confined. Of course, this had no effect on pauper patients. As for the non-pauper patients, it probably had little real effect on them, since medical certificates were easy to come by and often enough were sloppy, makeshift productions. For example, consider this medical certificate, made out by an apothecary in 1809:

> He^Y Broadway A Potcarey of Gillingham Certefy that Mr. James Burt Misfortin hapened by a Plow in the Hed which is the Ocaision of his Ellness and By the Rising and Falling of the Blood And I think a Blister and Bleeding and Meddesen Will be A Very Great thing But Mr James Burt would not A Gree to be don at Home. March 21, 1809. H^{ay} Broadway.[8]

The act also established the licensing and regular inspection of all private madhouses in England and Wales. There were no requirements for licenses, though; licenses were to be given "to all persons who shall desire the same."[9] And there was no provision for the revocation of licenses or for any other expression of opinion by the madhouse inspectors. The inspection system was patently useless, and so inspection quietly continued for a few years and then faded away.

Toward the end of the eighteenth century and the beginning of the nineteenth, England as well as much of Europe was experiencing sudden and extreme changes in the quality of life. To begin with, this was a time when radical ideas were made manifest in political systems by violent action: the American Revolution of 1775, the French Revolution of 1789. Furthermore, beginning just before the American Revolution and lasting for some sixty years, England was undergoing radical changes of its own, a time that was retrospectively called the Industrial Revolution. Advances in technology and industrial organization brought about a mass influx of people from the countryside to the cities, a half century of great poverty and misery for the working class, and frightening increases in population. During the reign of George III (1760–1820) the population of England increased from seven to twelve million. With that drastic increase in overall population came an even greater increase in the apparent numbers of mad people. An 1807 census recorded 2,248 "lunatics and idiots" in En-

---

[8]Tuke, *Chapters in the History of the Insane*, p. 163.
[9]Ibid., p. 102.

gland and Wales, while a census taken only two decades later, in 1828, recorded 12,547.[10] "Madness, strides like a Colossus in the country," wrote a London physician, John Reid, in 1808.[11] For whatever reason, there was a very real increase in the numbers of people considered to be mad. This was a great economic boom for the private madhouses. At the beginning of the century there were some twenty private madhouses in all of England and Wales. By the middle of the century there were about one hundred.[12]

At the same time, there seems to have been some kind of remarkable change in the attitudes of European society in general toward the mad. In 1789 a Parisian mob stormed the Bastille, for the sake of liberté, egalité, and fraternité. Three years later Dr. Philippe Pinel was appointed director of the Bicêtre, one of the units of the old Hôpital Général, which was by then used exclusively to house madmen. One of Pinel's first acts was to restore liberté, egalité, and fraternité to the inmates of the Bicêtre by striking off their chains and breaking open their cages.

There is no question that mental patients before this time were severely abused as a matter of course. However, life in general before the nineteenth century was often severe. Even in the first quarter of the nineteenth century, theft, forgery, shoplifting, sheep-stealing, and similar crimes could lead to the gallows in England.[13] In the late eighteenth century, an Englishman named John Howard toured institutions of all sorts throughout Europe, and found brutal, crowded, infested, unsanitary conditions to be standard.[14] Beyond the fact of hard conditions in general, however, was a vaguely formulated, centuries-old philosophy that mad people, because of their lack of obvious rationality, were much like beasts and should be treated like beasts. It seemed to some that the mad were oblivious to extremes of heat and cold, in the way that animals might be. It also seemed that the best way to treat, perhaps cure, madness was by using the same coercive methods used to train wild animals. A Frenchman described the Salpêtrière, the unit of the Parisian Hôpital Général for mad women: "Madwomen seized with fits of violence are chained like dogs at their cell doors, and separated from keepers and visitors alike

---

[10]Parry-Jones, *The Trade in Lunacy,* p. 12.
[11]Ibid., p. 11.
[12]Ibid., p. 38.
[13]Ibid., p. 289.
[14]Howard, *The State of The Prisons.*

by a long corridor protected by an iron grille; through this grille is passed their food and the straw on which they sleep; by means of rakes, part of the filth that surrounds them is cleaned out."[15]

By striking off the chains of the patients at the Bicêtre (and later, the chains of the female patients at the Salpêtrière) Pinel declared that henceforth they were to be treated as human beings rather than peculiar beasts.

Similar remarkable changes were taking place, so it seemed, throughout Europe. In England, for instance, a group of Quakers under the leadership of William Tuke founded a Retreat for mental patients at York in 1796, after a fellow Quaker died under suspicious conditions in the public asylum of York. At this Retreat workers were forbidden to use chains, harsh treatment, most medicines, and blood-letting; instead they were supposed to use kindness and reason.

During the first two decades of the nineteenth century, asylum and madhouse reform became an important issue in England, given added impetus by the much-publicized madness of George III, as well as the assassination in Parliament of Prime Minister Spencer Perceval by a madman in 1812. For the first time, Parliament and the public became seriously interested not only in the potential for wrongful imprisonment of sane persons, but also in the possibility of the abuse of the mad. Parliament appointed several investigating committees to consider alleged abuses of patients in various public and private institutions throughout England.

In 1815, for instance, a Parliamentary committee investigated reports of bad conditions in several private madhouses around London. In a Bethnal Green madhouse sometimes known as Dr. Warburton's White House, the committee described seeing several pauper men and women patients chained to their beds, naked, and covered only with rugs of hemp during the cold of January. A former housekeeper testified before Parliament that she had seen an attendant kicking and beating patients; she described a woman patient who was sometimes confined, with chains and manacles, in what had originally been a pig-sty. Other times, this patient had been hobbled with an iron bar between her legs, confined to each ankle, with a chain attaching the iron bar to her handcuffs.[16] The committee concluded that new laws were needed to control such abuses, and in 1816, 1817, and 1818, three bills were passed through the House of Commons, but were then rejected by the House of Lords.

---

[15] Foucault, *Madness and Civilization*, p. 72.
[16] Tuke, *Chapters in the History of the Insane*, pp. 155, 156.

A few years later, in 1827, another Parliamentary committee carried out investigations and reported to Parliament about, among other things, continuing scandalous conditions in Dr. Warburton's madhouse. Partly in response to those reports, the House of Commons passed another reform bill in 1828 which at last was carried through the House of Lords, becoming the first significant reform since 1774. The 1828 act, known as the Madhouse Act, in essence repeated the principles of the 1774 act but with distinctly increased strength.

Then in 1829 a patient in the Lincoln Asylum died because he had been strapped to his bed in a straitjacket all night. The death caused enough of a scandal that the asylum issued a new policy: an attendant would have to stay with any patient on whom mechanical restraints were used at night. Before the patients had been locked up at night and left with only minimal attendance. Under the new rule, the doctors soon discovered that in fact not many mechanical restraints were needed. Most of the patients just went to sleep. And not long after, they found that mechanical restraints could generally be eliminated during the day, too. In 1837, under the direction of Dr. Robert Gardiner Hill, Lincoln Asylum did away with mechanical restraints altogether. This meant more staff, more training, and the occasional physical holding of violent patients were necessary, but the use of mechanical restraints in non-emergency situations had been eliminated.

Dr. John Conolly, director of Middlesex Asylum, studied the new system at the Lincoln Asylum and in 1839 put it to practical use in his institution with impressive results. Upon first assuming direction of Middlesex, Conolly made the following inventory: "Instruments of restraint, of one kind or another, were so abundant in the wards as to amount, when collected together, to about six hundred—half of these being leg-locks or handcuffs." But by 1840 Conolly could observe: "no form of strait-waistcoat, no hand-straps, no leg-locks, nor any contrivance confining the trunk or limbs, or any of the muscles, is now in use. The coercion chairs, about forty in number, have been altogether removed from the wards." [17] Conolly went on to develop a comprehensive system of management based upon the elimination of mechanical restraints and the creation of alternatives, publicizing the system widely with his book, *The Treatment of the Insane Without Mechanical Restraints* (1856).

Although Conolly's system aroused much resistance on the Conti-

---

[17] Conolly, *The Treatment of the Insane Without Mechanical Restraints*, pp. 189, 190, 194.

nent and lasting antagonism in America, in England it profoundly affected the course of asylum management. Where it was employed judiciously it seemed to work. A numerical count of restraints became one of the ways in which the English were to measure the advancement of reform.

The reform movement in England peaked in the 1840s. In 1842 government inspectors went through all private madhouses and public asylums in England and Wales and published a comprehensive report on what they saw. They made recommendations that Parliament put into law through two important acts in 1845. Described by Daniel Hack Tuke as "the Magna Charta of the liberties of the insane," the legislation, among other things, established a permanent inspection committee and gave authority for more frequent and detailed inspections.[18]

Possibly the most important part of the 1845 legislation, however, was that which specifically required counties and important boroughs in England and Wales to build public asylums to take in their indigent mad. Through the first half of the century, those who wanted to reform private madhouses saw at least a partial answer in the construction of new, public institutions: the county asylums. The theory was that county asylums would be easier to observe, supervise, and regulate—since they were owned by the state—and that wrongful imprisonment for mercenary reasons would be impossible.

When legislation was passed dictating that county asylums be built, profound changes were set into motion. An important source of income for private madhouses was diverted into these new public institutions. Private madhouses after 1845 came more and more to serve only the wealthier classes. As legislative control increased and as the nonrestraint philosophy spread, the blatant and severe abuses taking place behind closed doors of private madhouses in the first few decades of the century, became less common.

Although the creation of a massive nationwide public asylum system probably diminished the chances of wrongful imprisonment, as well as covert patient abuse, it may have unwittingly limited the chances of genuine treatment and individual care. The county asylums were larger and more impersonal. As they filled to capacity and beyond, in the 1860s and 1870s, possibilities of treatment were forgotten by new, custodial regimes. Great care had been taken to make

---

[18] Tuke, *Chapters in the History of the Insane*, p. 188.

these county asylums externally attractive, appealing to the Victorian eye. But by 1880 at least one observer remarked on the contrast between the care given the buildings and the care given the patients: "It was simply a larger prison and the inmates sitting listlessly and depressed in the lengthened corridors served only to be mocked by the polished floor and costly furniture to which they had been unaccustomed and of which they took no heed."[19] Nonetheless, the basic direction of reform established in the first half of the century continued unchanged.

Institutions for the mad were built and gradually reformed. At the same time, not surprisingly, the inmates of these institutions began writing about their experiences—at first in small pamphlets, later in books. By the nineteenth century, the most common type of autobiographical writing by mad and allegedly mad people was the protest.

I know of only one piece of protest writing from the seventeenth century, a pamphlet entitled *The Petition of the Poor Distracted People in the House of Bedlam*, which was registered in 1620 but then lost. For all practical purposes, protest writing by English mental patients begins in the eighteenth century, with Alexander Cruden's dramatic call for justice, *The London-Citizen Exceedingly Injured*.

Alexander Cruden (1701–1770) was a London publisher, proofreader, author, and eccentric, probably best remembered as the author of *A Complete Concordance to the Holy Scriptures*, an index so thorough and accurate that it remains to this day an authoritative source. Three times in his life Alexander Cruden was locked up in madhouses. The last two times he published angry, detailed accounts of his experiences as part of his drive for vindication, an attempt to prove and carry charges of false imprisonment through court. The pamphlet considered here is his first, an account of his incarceration in 1738.

He had recently finished the *Concordance* after tremendous and tedious labor. He did the work and publication at his own expense, and he hoped for some recompense from the crown. He presented the completed work to Queen Anne, who smiled and murmured her gratitude but died sixteen days later, before her gratitude could be transformed into cash. Perhaps it was his great disappointment at that failure, combined with a rejected marriage proposal, that precipitated the events leading to his imprisonment in a private madhouse in Bethnal Green.

---

[19] Parry-Jones, *The Trade in Lunacy*, p. 259.

There he was held prisoner for nearly ten weeks at the direction of a certain Robert Whiteman, a merchant, who for unclear reasons chose to involve himself in the case. At times, Cruden was kept in handcuffs, held in a straitjacket and chained to his bed. According to his account, his pockets were rifled, private papers were seized, his mail was intercepted and opened, he was denied visitors, he was beaten by an attendant, he was denied writing materials, his "physick" was prescribed for him by a private physician, Dr. James Monro, six days before Dr. Monro ever saw him, and for the last five weeks he was chained to a bed without any release whatsoever, not even to change his clothes.

Finally, Cruden managed to escape—but his conflict with Wightman and Dr. Monro continued. Cruden believed that Wightman, in concert with Dr. Monro and others, plotted to have him sent to the infamous Bethlehem Hospital. Cruden wrote several angry letters to Wightman and prepared to take Wightman and Dr. Monro to court, asking damages of ten thousand pounds for false imprisonment. Before the case was heard, he wrote and published *The London-Citizen Exceedingly Injured*, probably expecting that the written statement would help his legal position. He hoped for "the recovering" of his own character, that Wightman and Dr. Monro might be made "Examples to deter others from the like crimes," and that "the LEGISLATURE will see the necessity of bringing in a bill to regulate Private Madhouses." Unfortunately, he lost the case.

Even if we were not informed in the pamphlet that Cruden intended to take his adversaries, Wightman, Monro, and others, to court, the style of the pamphlet ought to alert us to that fact. Nearly all persons mentioned in the narration are treated as potential witnesses. Either Cruden recounts their expressed opinions on the issue of his sanity or he carefully describes how very sensibly and rationally he behaved in their presences. As if to assist a courtroom presentation, names of persons are usually followed by occupations and often by places of residence. Minor events that may have some bearing are described in methodical detail (for instance, when his pulse is taken, he notes who took the pulse, what was said about the pulse, and what possible interpretation could be made about what was said).

A closer examination reveals, however, that the pamphlet is not as objective as it pretends to be: the facts are interspersed with a good deal of strong opinion. Cruden is unable, or unwilling, to conceal his rage. Most of his references to Wightman and Dr. Monro are overtly biased: not fact but opinion, and extreme opinion at that. We cannot know how far to trust it. Perhaps the least trustworthy part of the narration is Cruden's account of his original trouble with his neighbors. If we are to follow his version, the only version we have, indeed the whole neighborhood is acting madly, and we are left feeling that information has been withheld.

Nonetheless, the pamphlet remains a moving account of real abuse of a man accused of madness. We cannot know how "sane" Cruden was, we cannot know how deliberately malicious and "barbarous" Wightman and Dr. Monro and the others really were, but we must at last conclude that Cruden was treated arbitrarily, unfairly, and cruelly.

I have selected the following two excerpts for their intrinsic interest. First Cruden describes his seizure as a madman. Then he recounts his remarkable escape.

A SHORT NARRATIVE is here given of the horrid sufferings of a *London-Citizen* in *Wright's* private Madhouse at *Bethnal-Green*, during nine weeks and six days, (till he made his wonderful Escape) by the Combination of *Robert Wightman* Merchant at *Edinburgh*, a stranger in *London*, and others, who had no right, warrant or authority in Law, Equity or Consanguinity, or any other manner whatsoever, to concern themselves with him or his affairs; and yet most unjustly imprisoned him in that dismal place. How unjustly and unaccountably they acted in first sending Mr. C. to *Bethnal-Green*, and how cruel and barbarous they were in their bold and desperate Design to fix him in *Bethlehem*, (after Mr. C. refused to sign their Pardon) that they might screen themselves from punishment, by covering one heinous crime with another more heinous, will appear by the following Journal of Mr. C.'s Sufferings.

*   *   *

Monday, March 20. This morning *Wightman*, without being desired or expected, came to Mr. C.'s room, and advised him not to go to the Printing Office that day, but to be let blood, and stay at home, which Mr. C. at last complied with, tho' with great reluctance. Mr. C. wrote a letter to Mr. *Ragg* the Surgeon, who came and let him blood: He was at home all that day in a quiet and calm manner.

Tuesday, March 21. He called in the morning on his Landlady

Grant's Wife for some of his Papers committed to her care, but she for a great while made no Answer, 'till at last she said they might be about his bed: But while Mr. C. was making diligent search for them, *John Huet* a Blacksmith in the neighbourhood came up with a stick in his hand, in order to seize him as a Madman; which Mr. C. looked upon as the highest Affront and greatest Provocation. Mr. C. took the stick from him, and forced him down stairs: but in a few minutes *Grant* and his Wife alarmed the neighbourhood as if he was a Madman, and so about a dozen of them came in, whom he obliged to go out, and then shut the doors. They rallied by the cellarwindow, particularly a bloody Butcher came from below, who disfigured Mr. C.'s face with several blows: And while he was grappling with this diabolical Butcher, *John Duck* a Blackmore and *John Anderson* a Coachman came up, rescued Mr. C. from the Butcher and seized him. This cruel Butcher soon after gave him a severe blow, to the great effusion of his blood, with a stick on the head, without the least provocation, and then quickly disappeared, and no body can give any account of him. Mr. C. was amaz'd at this uncommon Treatment and asked whether they were all become Madmen?

Duck and *Anderson* went up stairs with Mr. C. where he lay down on a bed, and Mr. *Ragg* the Surgeon came to dress his Wound. He examined if it had fractured the Skull, but happily it had not; for had it been a little deeper, it had been mortal. A Tool of *Wightman's* formerly an Apprentice to a Taylor, but lately a Coffin-breaker and Grave-digger in St. *Andrew's* Burying-ground, and a few months before a pretended Physician of no figure, came in, who with great impudence insulted over Mr. C. but he greatly despised this silly man, and calmly and composedly desired *John Duncan* then in the room, to go to the learned and eminent Physician Dr. *Hulse*, to come and see him; but tho' *Duncan* promised to go, he never went. Mr. C. often called for a Constable, but tho' there was one at hand, he would not come, he not approving of their conduct. This was about twelve o'clock. He saw himself obliged to submit peaceably and patiently to their orders all that day.

Wednesday, March 22. Mr. C. stayed at home all day, cool and sedate, employing his time in reading: But the foolish people would allow none of his Friends to visit him, tho' some particular Friends called both yesterday and to day, and earnestly desired to go up to see him; yet *Wightman* hindered Mr. *Kelsey Bull* and Mr. *Frederick Bull,* two of Mr. *C.*'s particular Friends, from coming up to see him; and *Grant* and his Wife who stood at the door, were so impudent as to refuse Entrance to Mr. *John Cargil* another particular Friend, and made Mr. C. their Prisoner.

Thursday, March 23. Mr. C. sorting his Papers this morning in his room on the table where a candle stood, the foolish people made a great breach in the door, and knocked at it with such Fury, that they made the snuff of the candle to fall upon three loose sheets of paper on the table, and set fire to them; which Mr. C. to prevent any bad consequence, wrapt up together, and put them out at the breach of the door. This is all the ground that the malicious people had to say that Mr. C. designed to set the house on fire; which is abominably false.

This day *Oliver Roberts* a Chairman came, as he said, from one *Robert Wightman* in *Spring-Gardens,* and told Mr. C. that the said *Wightman* wanted to speak with him at his lodgings in *Spring-Gardens;* and *Roberts* taking with him *Anderson* the Coachman, decoy'd Mr. C. into a Hackneycoach; and till the Coach came to *Ludgate-hill* Mr. C. did not fully discover their wicked Design, for the Coachwindows were drawn up: Mr. C. had asked *Roberts* in *Chancery-Lane* which way the Coach was to go to *Spring-Gardens? Roberts* answered Up the *Strand.* And when Mr. C. saw himself thus imposed upon, he expostulated with them in the following manner: "Oh! what are you going to do with me? I bless God, I am not mad. Are you going to carry me to *Bethlehem?* How great is this Affliction! This is the way to put an end to all my Usefulness in the World, and to expose me to the highest Degree! Oh! what shall I do? God help me! I desire to submit to the Will of God." *Roberts* then positively told him that he had Orders from the said *Wightman* to carry him to Country-Lodgings near *Bow,* which proved to be *Wright's* private Madhouse on *Bethnal-Green,* where he delivered him to *John Davis* the Under-Keeper of the said Madhouse, when Mr. C. requested *Roberts* and *Anderson* not to expose him by telling any body of his being brought to so dismal a Place: And *Roberts* particularly remembers that Mr. C. said, he hoped that God would make this great Affliction turn to his Good. *Roberts* also declares that Mr. C. always spoke sensibly, and behaved well, and much like a Gentleman.

The said *Davis* locked Mr. C. up in a room in the Madhouse, who was at first much dejected, but after going to Prayer was greatly comforted; and soon after *Davis, Samuel Wall* the Barber, *and Dorothy Mayleigh* Housemaid came, and spoke very civilly to the Prisoner, who this afternoon asked *Wall* if he saw any sign of Disorder about him? To which *Wall* replied, None at all as yet, but that he did not know how soon as alteration might come, which proved only a groundless suspicion.

That very afternoon the Prisoner desired Pen, Ink, and Paper, but *Davis* refused it to one in his Circumstances; yet the Prisoner acquainting *Davis* with the occasion, relating to his Shop under the *Royal-Exchange*, and promising to shew the Letter to *Davis*, the Housemaid brought him some Paper. This Letter was directed to *John Scot*, who had the care of the Prisoner's Shop, and was acknowledged by *Scot* and others to be a very sensible Letter, and much to the purpose.

Soon after in the evening the said *Scot* with Mr. *Robert Macpherson* and Mr. *John Duncan*, came to visit the Prisoner, who spoke to them very sensibly, and shewed no signs of Madness in his Conversation with them, as had been attested under the hands of the said *Macpherson* and *Duncan*.

After they were gone, *Wightman* and *Duncan* came to the Prisoner, who with very great temper seriously expostulated with *Wightman* about his presuming to send him to a Madhouse, that had no Power over him in Law, Equity or Consanguinity, but was his very slender acquaintance, and a stranger to all his affairs; and asked by what authority he had been so bold as to do so?

Wightman was confounded, and blamed *Grant* and his Wife, who, he said, were very weak silly persons: *Oswald*, like a self-condemned Person, was very silent, especially upon hearing that his Wife had been convicted of a gross Lye she had uttered to *Wright's* Wife in the morning, when she took the room for the Prisoner; and so *Wightman* and *Oswald* went away abruptly and without ceremony, instead of begging Pardon and releasing the Prisoner. *Davis* was present at this Conversation, and told

Wightman, after he went out of the room, that he had not observed any signs of Madness about his Prisoner; but *Wightman*, who pretends to know that a person is made from the Tone of his Voice, replied, that the Prisoner would be ill about three o'clock in the morning, but he proved a false Prophet. When the Prisoner went to bed about eight o'clock, *Davis* came and told him, that seeing he was in a Madhouse, he must allow himself to be used as a Madman, and submit to have the Chain on the bedstead lock'd upon his Leg, which the Prisoner patiently submitted to.

*   *   *

Saturday, May 27. The Prisoner being still chained night and day to his bedstead in this hot season, and being alarmed with being sent to *Bethlehem*, happily projected to cut the bedstead thro' with a knife with which he eat his victuals. He made some progress in it this day. In the afternoon Mr. *Willock* the Bookseller came in *Wightman's* name, desiring to know the state of Mr. *Conon's* account with the Prisoner, for *Wightman* was ready to settle it with him. The Prisoner answered that he had nothing to do with *Wightman*, and would settle no accounts in concert with him, who had no power to meddle in his Affairs, and that therefore he hoped that Mr. *Conon* would wait a little longer.

The *Lord's Day, May 28.* The Prisoner being still chained night and day, made his own bed himself very early to conceal his design, but used not his knife this day upon the bedstead. *Thomas Lindon* Apothecary, with a Friend, came to see him, who declared that he found him in the full exercise of his reason and judgment.

Monday, May 29. The Prisoner being still chained night and day, took Physick by *Monro's* order in the morning; and in the afternoon he again used his knife upon the bedstead.

Tuesday, May 30. The Prisoner being still chained wrote a Letter to Serjeant *Cruden* to send him a hand-saw, doubting of the strength of the Knife, but providentially did not deliver this Letter to his woman-keeper; for if he had, it had certainly fallen into *Wright's* Wife's hands, and been sent to *Wightman*, as other Letters were by that unfaithful woman's means, and so his Escape had been prevented, and he had been most severely used. Therefore he went to work again, prayed hard and wrought hard, till his Shirt was almost as wet as if dipt in water; and as if he had received more than common Vigour and Strength, he finished the great Operation about four o'clock in the afternoon: Upon which he kneeled down and returned God thanks. Then he sent for *Hollowel* to shave him, and began to prepare for his Escape. He prayed at night that he might awake seasonably for his Escape, and he slept some hours that night as sound as ever he did in his life, chearfully and believingly committing this affair to God *who had never left him nor forsaken him.*

Wednesday, May 31. The Prisoner's birth-day, he awoke early, performed his Devotions, held his chain in his hand full fastened to his leg, and deliberately got out at the Window into the Garden, mounted the Garden-wall with much difficulty, lost one of his slippers, and jumped down into the back-way, just before the clock struck two. He went towards *Mile-End*, and his left-foot that wanted a slipper was sorely hurt by the gravel-stones, which greatly afflicted him, and obliged him to put the slipper on his left-foot. From thence he went towards *White-Chapel*, and in his way met with a kind Soldier, who, upon hearing his Case, endeavoured to get him a Coach, but in vain; therefore he and the Soldier walked undiscovered til they came to *Aldgate*, where the Watchmen perceiving a chain, and suspecting him to be a person broke out of Gaol, several Watchmen and the Constable Mr. *Wardly* followed him to *Leadenhall-Street*, and brought him back to *Aldgate* watch-house. He acquainted the two Constables Mr. *Ward* and Mr. *Wardly* with his Case, which did much affect them. They allowed him some refreshment, and promised to carry him before my Lord Mayor, but sent a Watchman privately to *Bethnal-Green*, to know the certainly of the Account; upon which *Davis* and two more of their bull-dogs came to the Watch-house with handcuffs to carry back the Prisoner; but the Constable perceiving his meek and sedate Conversation, would not allow it, but desired *Wright* their master to come before my Lord Mayor, at *Grocers Hall*, about 11 o'clock, where he would see his Prisoner.

The Prisoner after five o'clock desired the Constable to carry him in a coach to *North's Coffee-House* near *Guild-Hall*, where he was much refreshed and heartened about five hours. A Printer at *Aberdeen* in *Scotland* came this morning to the Coffee-house, and artfully insinuated to the Constable, that it would be the best way to deliver up the Prisoner to be confined some time longer. This Printer lodged at *Grant's* in *White's-Alley*, and it is supposed that he was sent thither by *Wightman* and *Oswald*, with whom he became suddenly much acquainted; and it's certain that he falsely said to the Prisoner, that he came to the Coffee-house accidentally without knowing of his being their. He was received kindly by the Prisoner, he being lately come from *Scotland*; but this false man, as the Constable rightly-judged, proved very treacherous in several respects; and particularly upon his going to *Scotland* he greatly injured the Prisoner by poisoning his relations with false reports; and his falshood is attended with great ingratitude, he being some years ago great-ly obliged to the Prisoner, upon his first coming as a Journey-man to *London*, but now *Oswald* is become his Correspondent, and the Printer appears to be a selfish, ungrateful man.

The Prisoner went to *Grocers-hall* about eleven o'clock, with his chains on, for he would not have them taken off till the Lord Mayor should see them. Before he appeared, *Wightman* with some of his friends had been with his Lordship, in order to fill him with Prejudices against the Prisoner: And *Wightman* hear-ing the Constable speak very favourably of the Prisoner, and of his rational Behaviour, gave him half-a-crown, which the Const-able looked upon as a bribe to be silent; and *Wightman* was so base as afterwards to charge it to the Prisoner. The Constable told his Lordship the situation of the Prisoner when he seiz'd him; and the Prisoner gave his Lordship a just and full account of his illegal and barbarous Imprisonment, and demanded that *Wightman* might be immediately sent to *Newgate*, or held to bail. To which his Lordship made no reply.

The Prisoner was several hours in bed at *North's Coffee-house*, and had not time to send for his friends; but *Wightman* was surrounded both with friends and wretched Tools; for *London* the Apothecary and *Grant* of *White's-Alley*, both took their oath before his Lordship that the Prisoner was *Lunatick*, tho' *Grant*, poor Creature, knows no more what is meant by *Lunatick*, than a Child of a year old, and had not seen the Prisoner for nine weeks and six days before. The Prisoner told his Lordship that, if he had complied with *Wightman's* earnest request to pardon him, he had long ago been out of that dismal place, but that he was always resolved to vindicate his own Character, and to have legal satisfaction. For proof of which the Prisoner shewed his Lordship the joint Letter of Dr. *Stukeley* and Dr. *Rogers*, which his Lordship read. His Lordship asked why he appeared before him with his Chain? To which the Prisoner replied, that this chain being put on by illegal power, he was resolved to have it taken off by legal authority; and accordingly the Constable unlocked the chain in the presence of his Lordship. He also told his Lordship that base *Wightman* had intercepted all his Letters, and several to his Lordship, particularly one writ last week, which *Wightman*, like a cat who had lost her tail, sneakingly took out of his pocket, it being opened, and gave it to his Lordship. Vile *Wightman* said to his Lordship, that no body would receive the Prisoner as a lodger: To which the Prisoner answered that it was abominably false, and he named an honest family that would heartily receive him. Then the Lord Mayor said to the Prisoner, Will you submit to Dr. *Monro's* judgment? Which he refused to do with indignation, knowing him to be intirely *Wightman's* Creature from his gross lies and calumnies against him. He offered to refer his Case to Dr. *Stukeley*, but no Physician came. It is supposed, that *Monro*, *Wightman's* Tool, was at hand, ready to assert any thing, right or wrong, to screen guilty *Wightman*.

But when the Prisoner saw *Wightman* endeavouring to have him still under his care, he fell upon his knees before Sir *John Barnard*, and begged most earnestly not to be delivered into the hands of cruel *Wightman*, but rather into the hands of an honest Constable, or any body his Lordship pleased: And rising from his knees he pulled up his courage, and told his Lordship plainly, that he perceived *Wightman* had poisoned him too much, but that if his Lordship, or the greatest subject in *England* should send him to a Madhouse (when he was not mad) he would pursue him to the utmost. Then Providence soon gave a turn to the matter, and his Lordship recommended him to a lodging in *Downing-street*. And so Mr. C. glad to be delivered out of *Wightman's* power, went in a Coach from *Grocers-hall*, to Mr. *Morgan's* Joiner in *Downing-street* near *Hide-park-corner* this 31st of *May*, 1738; and there Mrs. *Morgan* his landlady took great care of him, particularly of his foot that had been greatly hurt this Morning, and was now much swelled. *Wightman* was much chagrined at the Prisoner's Escape, and refused at first to pay *Wright*, saying that he could not answer for his Escape.

1774 ╼╾

One More Proof of the Iniquitous Abuse of Private Madhouses, by Samuel Bruckshaw

Samuel Bruckshaw was a wool merchant in the town of Bourn, near Stamford, in Lincolnshire. In 1769 he bought some property in Stamford and quickly moved in, preparing for business. But soon something went wrong. It appears he overextended his credit and was forced into some kind of bankruptcy in which much of his property was sold, including considerable business stock and his new residence. Bruckshaw was upset about the sale of his home. He insisted that he gave permission only for the disposal of his business stock and refused to sign the note of sale for the property. Finally he went to the new owner, a Mr. Langton, and warned him not to spend any money on improvements because he intended to reclaim the house. Langton was not sympathetic. Eventually, the town sergeant visited Bruckshaw and told him the mayor didn't want him to bother the Langtons any longer. Bruckshaw then asked the mayor to go with him to the Langtons and arbitrate. First the mayor agreed, then he declined. Bruckshaw decided to go on his own, whereupon he was "collared" by two constables, "dragged through the public streets," and locked up. According to Bruckshaw, he was then beaten by two of his jailors and bound hand and foot to a bed. Later he was shackled and transported to a private madhouse some distance north of Stamford, in Yorkshire, under a warrant issued by the mayor.

The private madhouse in Yorkshire was run as a family business by the Wilsons. Bruckshaw says that the Wilsons kept his clothes from him and chained him to a bed for about a month, that he was fed poorly, insulted, threatened with violence, refused medical treatment, and chained a second time to a bed for eighty-two days. In addition, his mail was read without his permission, his journal was taken from him, he was robbed of a ten-pound note, and was not allowed visitors. He was finally released after two hundred and eighty-four days under the Wilson's hospitality.

After his release, Bruckshaw was unable to reestablish his business, due in part to the stigma of having been in a madhouse. He spent a great deal of time and money on two attempts to sue the mayor of Stamford and others for false imprisonment, but the only profit gained was by his lawyers—both times the case was thrown out of court. In 1774, as a last, desperate measure, Bruckshaw wrote and published *One More Proof of the Iniquitous Abuse of Private Mad-houses*, stating his hopes for general public benefit from the exposure of his case and for the advancement of his legal pursuits.

Even more than Cruden's pamphlet of 1739, this pamphlet has all the traits of a legal proceeding. The narrative portion of the pamphlet comprises only slightly half the full length, and is followed by a lengthy, complicated, and rather boring discussion of Bruckshaw's misadventures in the courts, followed in turn by an appendix of pertinent documents and affidavits.

What may seem at first glance to be an unbiased presentation of a legal case, calling upon witnesses both pro and con, in fact contains a good deal of bias and of artful, positive self-presentation. But in spite of his carefully, even artfully presented defense, Bruckshaw may have revealed more of himself than he intended. He was obviously a contentious man, rough, probably humorless, possibly overbearing, and obsessed with getting his just due. For instance, the town constables come to arrest him, but he does not go quietly, meekly, as many might have. Instead, when one of the constables seizes him by the collar, Bruckshaw turns around and seizes *him* by the collar, demanding to know his authority. He was a bristly man, but beyond that, he reveals himself to have been suspicious to the point of pathology. He writes in detail of an extensive conspiracy perpetrated by several Stamford citizens. It was that conspiracy that caused his years of trouble: his financial collapse, his false arrest, and false imprisonment. Not only does he suspect many of the local people, he suspects his lawyer in London as well. And when a physician visits him in jail, Bruckshaw thinks that he is part of the conspiracy as well and that the physician's bottles of "physick" might be some kind of poison. After his financial collapse, not long before his troubles at Stamford, Bruckshaw also fell ill with what he describes as an "anguish disorder," obviously a severe depression, for which he required several months' medical treatment. And twice during his imprisonment, he heard anonymous voices, which may have been hallucinations.

From our distance of two hundred years, it is of course impossible to know whether Bruckshaw was sane or not at the time of his incarceration. We have no other significant documents about the events, nothing other than Bruckshaw's side of the story. Yet we have no reason to doubt his detailed and methodical descriptions of being chained, threatened, tormented, and poorly fed. It seems clear enough that he was locked up by arbitrary authority.

I have chosen to reprint here Bruckshaw's account of his first meeting with the Wilsons and his unhappy residence in their madhouse in Yorkshire. Bruckshaw has carefully tried to reproduce his keeper's Yorkshire dialect. The immediate effect is comic; yet the portrayal of Wilson's insouciance and ultimate brutality reveal a personality more cruel than comic.

JUST BEFORE MY DINNER was brought up, on the 26th of June 1770, two strangers came abruptly into the said garret, and with an air of great familiarity addressed themselves to me thus; "Well, Mr. Bruckshaw, *how doone you*, Com yoo'sen go with us, t'see yoor friends i' Yorkshire." I asked their names; they answered, Wilson. I replied, "I came from thence only a fortnight ago. My business lies in London, requires my immediate attendance, *and I will be there as soon as possible.*" They still importuned me to go with them, to which I answered, *If your business here is to insult me,* I desire you will immediately quit the room, which will save me the trouble of shewing you the way out. If you choose to behave civilly, sit down, and welcome, *my dinner is coming in.*" Upon which they sat down, and after some time said, "Well, Maister, if yoo winnow goo with us ween be getting towards hoom, han-you any messuage that yoo chus'en to send by us to your friends." I thanked them and said, "You may tell them the situation I'm in; *that I have been most barbarously treated:* but these men who are placed in my next room as my guard have repented of what they have done, *and that they were hired to it* by the mayor and his friends; and since that they have behaved to me with some civility. *I expect to be released every minute,* and then they shall hear from me, and *that I am very well.*" To which they answered, "We win, *so fare yoo weell,* they'll be glad to hear fro' yoo;" and immediately withdrew.

In the evening, *to my great surprize,* the aforesaid Wilsons returned into the said garrett, and with the assistance of Clarke the gaoler, Walker, Whittle, and White, seized me, threw me upon the bed, *clapped irons on my hands and legs,* and dragged me into a chaise: In the first stage, Wilson Senior said, *"The mayor wanted us tak yoo with us without his warrant,* but I knew better; I have one i' me pocket, *signed by the mayor and one alderman Exton:* the mayor seemed to sit on thorns when he had ge'en me the warrant." Walker, who went with us the first stage, informed me of two other Persons *who executed the aforesaid bond.*

*   *   *

When Wilson shewed me to bed, he carried me up into a dark and dirty garret, *there stripped me,* and carried my cloathes out of the room, which I saw no more, *for upwards of a month,* but lay chained to this bad bed, *all that time;* this appears to be their breaking in garret; under the ridge-tree is a box for the harbour of pigeons, which they disturb in the night time, to affright their prisoner when he should rest. For this purpose some of Wilson's family are up all night long, sometimes they throw pails of water down under the window, now and then brushing across, with a few small rods, or rubbing with a stone or brick upon the wall, sometimes put a light up to the window, and every now and then make a disagreeable noise, to awake you in a fright. In the day-time the window is darkened, and common necessaries denied; they gave me bad victuals, short allowance, with sour beer, oftener water, and sometimes not that; no attendance, but what was as contradictory and provoking as they could possibly invent, and frequently the most barbarous stripes; and to keep these inquisition-like transactions a secret from the world, Wilson's wife does the office of a barber, but I refused to come under her hands, and by that means got a Barber, who is a very respectable evidence.

At the expiration of about a month, I was permitted to have my cloaths *for a day,* and to walk about the house in irons; when any person was in conversation with me, Wilson made it a rule to interrupt us with "Why maister, yo'r weel us'd, *yoo getten plenty of good victuals and drink,* and rest in your bones, *yoon be fitt for any thing* when yoo gone from here; I'm liken to be the best friend *yoo han';"* which generally had the intended effect of enraging me.

This Wilson never failed to observe to the person who I had been conversing with, adding, *"that I was very subject to rave in this manner,* and that I behaved very audaciously at Stamford; *or the mayor (who is a very good* kind of man) would not *have imprisoned him."*

In this manner I was treated, *(now and then a day below stairs,)* in the said garret, till the beginning of November, when I was reduced to a skeleton; I really thought I must have died with pining, cold, and severity of treatment; Wilson had the like apprehensions, allowed me a fire, but refused me a doctor and nurse, permitted me to come down into the family as soon as I was able to stir about, where Wilson's wife threatened me thus: *"I'll lay yoo o' the head with the poker, if yoo doo make complaint to any body that comes into th' house."*

While I enjoyed this privilege, there came a servant maid out of a respectable family in Manchester, and wanted Wilson to cure her complaint in one week, which he undertook to do; Wilson's family gave it out, *"that her disorder was a dropsey, and lowness of spirits,* which made her incapable of doing her business."—I being of opinion that this woman might have got superior advice in Manchester, and that real dropsies were not to be cured in a week, happened to say, that this woman's disorder must certainly, from her applying to Wilson, be of a nature that required secrecy and the assistance of a rogue, and the next day I was chained up in this second garret, which was exceedingly smoaky; sometimes allowed no fire at all. Here I was confined EIGHTY-TWO DAYS.

I was at length permitted to write letters to my friends, which Wilson promised to send as directed, yet stopped, broke open, and read them; one of which was found by a fellow prisoner and brought to me.

My journal was taken from me, when they perceived I took minutes of their transactions, along with a ten pound bank note, my charge for false imprisonment, and the list of names which I took from the mouths of the ruffians at Stamford, who they confessed executed to them the aforesaid Bond.

On the eighty second day of the close confinement in this garret, Wilson came up and addressed me thus: *"weel maister, as this chimney smooks so, if yoon behave mannerly, yoos'en go down into'ith house;"* and took the irons off my leg. I immediately found that it was through the persuasion of a respectable gentleman, well acquainted with maladies of the nature Wilsons and the magistrates of Stamford publicly reported that I laboured under. When I thanked him for my release from the irons, &c.

he told me he prevailed upon Wilsons, by reasoning with them in these words: "I have spent more than once, some hours with Mr. Bruckshaw, and I find him *no more disordered in his senses,* than any one of your own family, or any person *in this parish;* you are destroying his health, which I find he has been as careful in preserving *as if directed by a physician and called in for that purpose,* you cannot mean any good by such treatment. He is naturally of a strong, healthy constitution, *which requires exercise;* why don't you let him come down into the family, *and take a little air?* I am moreover informed that he never was otherwise than he now is, and that it is unanimously allowed by a number of your own neighbours who saw him get out of the chaise at Lusley, upwards of six months ago, that he was no more disordered in his senses at that time than any person there present, which is well confirmed to me, by what I have seen myself, and been informed by the Barber who has shaved him all the time he has been confined here, and the same is avouched by your neighbours all round you." This gentleman is a surgeon and physician of eminence.

I being thus released, out of the said garret; my friend and I walked out together, and called upon several of the neighbours, who informed me, that my confinement would soon be at an end; for the neighbours took such notice, that Wilsons were very uneasy that they had any concern in the matter, notwithstanding all the money they got from the people of Stamford; which they had reason to believe was a considerable sum, and that they might have had more, if they had asked it, and that they were very poor before they fell into this way, scarce able to keep themselves off the parish. That they had seen my brother come and go several times, seemingly in great trouble, and that Wilson's landlord had taken him to task respecting my confinement, and that Wilson answered him, "I want to know how I'm to be paid before I let him goo'a."

They advised me not to think of running away, as my enemies would gratify their malignaty with observing, that I run away from a madhouse. I answered them, that I would not, and told them of the young woman from Manchester, as aforesaid, to which they answered, that they had heard Wilson accused of the like before, but were always willing to hope it was not true.

When I returned back, I made some enquiry of my fellow prisoners, if they had seen my Brother, to which they answered they had, *he had been several times,* and was very importunate to see me; but that Wilson always put him off, with saying, "it'll be better for him, that yoo don't, he's so bad, that he'll be ready to tear you too pieces; I hardly dar go ney him sometimes mysel, and it all as makes him worse." And that Wilsons had denied many others in the same manner, yet they durst not contradict them, for fear of their cruel resentment; they threatened me with close confinement again, if I dared to call in at any of their neighbours houses. I gave them no answer, but walked out, and importuned the neighbours to make a complaint in my behalf, before a magistrate; some of them promised they would, if I was not released soon; they would speak to Wilson first; as he was a desperate fellow, and their neighbour, they had rather not incur his resentment. On my return, I again demanded their authority for detaining me, whereupon they brought me the aforesaid order of John Hopkins, and John Exton, and after reading it, I put it into my pocket, and Wilson's wife immediately called her husband and son, and gave them orders to take it from me by force, which they obeyed, at the same time promising me thus: "yoo'son hav a copy on't when yoo gune fro here." I also presumed to to arraign their judgment, in the management of pretended Lunatics; to which they answered, "Yoo'en been used just as twas fixt on before we touch't yoo." The neighbours importuned them so closely to release me, that they at length let my Brother know I was recovered, and might be at liberty as soon as he pleased: my brother came over on the 25th of March, 1771, and I was released from the aforesaid imprisonment of *Two hundred and Eighty-four days,* by order of John Hopkins, and John Exton, Magistrates of Stamford, under their aforesaid charge of insanity.

1816 ⊑⊸

Memoir of the Early Life of William Cowper, Esq.

At least four times in his life William Cowper (1731–1800), the English poet and hymnist, experienced severe crises of depression which rendered him irrational and at times even suicidal. In 1773, at the beginning of his third crisis, Cowper had a dream which led him to believe that God had forsaken him. Except for three days of respite, Cowper lived in despair for the rest of his life, briefly diverting himself with gardening, caring for pets, taking walks, indulging in conversation, and writing letters and poems. His first volume of poetry (1782) brought him recognition, while his second volume (1785)—including his best remembered poem, "The Task"—brought him fame. While neither the best nor the most significant poet of his age, Cowper's studies of English village and domestic life remain well worth reading. Around 1765, at the mid-point of his life and after recovering from a major breakdown, Cowper wrote his *Memoir of the Early Life*. The subject of the book is his second crisis, an experience of despair and self-hatred great enough to lead him to an attempt at suicide and a breakdown into madness. But the book was written well before the onset of his permanent state of despair; thus the tone of the narrator is hopeful and religiously orthodox.

As Trosse did before him, Cowper places his story of mental breakdown within the framework of the Puritan spiritual autobiography: a familiar tale of youthful rebellion and final regeneration told through traditional Puritan language. At the age of twelve or thirteen, the poet was taken ill with smallpox, but his young heart was already hardened against God's usual means of chastisement. He was hardly out of his sickbed before he returned with even more intensity to his old sinful ways. By his thirty-second year, he had not a thought "of the things of my salvation."

Unlike Trosse, Cowper does not detail the nature of his early sins, other than to mention that he was skilled in the "infernal art of lying." But the pivotal moral transgression seemed, in his mind, to lie in the explicit wish that a certain clerk in the House of Lords would die, so that Cowper could take his place. The clerk did die, and Cowper was offered the position. To his horror, he learned that the appointment was being contested. He would have to be examined openly before the House of Lords. Public scrutiny in Parliament seemed to Cowper an intolerable prospect, and he resolved on suicide. In his words: "Now came the grand temptation; the point to which Satan had all the while been driving me—the dark and hellish purpose of self murder." He tried suicide in several ways and failed. Until then, he had been unconcerned with spiritual truths, but after his most serious attempt at self murder, he felt that "Conviction of sin took place." He paced back and forth in his room, telling himself, "There was never so abandoned a wretch; so great a sinner!" He began to think he was damned for all eternity. And then it seemed that he was simultaneously attacked by both Satan and madness:

> Satan piled me closely with horrible visions, and more horrible voices. My ears rang with the sound of torments, that seemed to await me. Then did the pains of hell get hold on me, and, before day break, the very sorrows of death encompassed me. . . . If it were possible, that a heavy blow could light on the brain, without touching the skull, such was the sensation I felt. I clapped my hand to my forehead, and cried aloud through the pain it gave me. At every stroke, my thoughts and expressions became more wild and incoherent; all that remained clear was the sense of sin, and the expectation of punishment. These kept undisturbed possession all through my illness, without interruption or abatement.

Cowper was taken to Dr. Cotton's private madhouse in St. Alban's where he stayed from December 1763 until June 1765. Finally, in a moment of spiritual insight, Cowper found relief from his depression through conversion to an evangelical kind of Christianity. Like Trosse, Cowper did not see his madness as an accidental sickness of the mind, but a manifestation of the workings of spiritual forces. The experience of madness was at once attributable to a chastisement by God and a possession by Satan. Cowper's cure came from the experience of conversion and the realignment of personal belief.

I have chosen to reprint here Cowper's description of his most serious attempt at suicide, his attack of madness, and his recovery in Dr. Cotton's private madhouse. This is one of the earliest clear, subjective descriptions of an experience of madness, which Cowper chose to mold into the traditional framework of the Puritan spiritual autobiography.

IN THIS MANNER the time passed till the day began to break. I heard the clock strike seven, and instantly it occurred to me that there was no time to be lost. The chambers would soon be opened, and my friend would call upon me to take me with him to Westminster. "Now is the time," thought I,—"this is the crisis;—no more dallying with the love of life." I arose, and, as I thought, bolted the inner door of my chambers, but was mistaken; my touch deceived me, and I left it as I found it. My preservation indeed, as it will appear, did not depend upon that incident; but I mention it, to show that the good providence of God watched over me to keep open every way of deliverance, that nothing might be left to hazard. Not one hesitating thought now remained; but I fell greedily to the execution of my purpose. My garter was made of a broad scarlet binding, with a sliding buckle being sewn together at the end: by the help of the buckle I made a noose, and fixed it around my neck, straining it so tight, that I hardly left a passage for my breath, or for the blood to circulate, the tongue of the buckle held it fast. At each corner of the bed, was placed a wreath of carved work, fastened by an iron pin, which passed up through the midst of it. The other part of the garter, which made a loop, I slipped over one of these, and hung by it some seconds, drawing my feet under me, that they might not touch the floor; but the iron bent, and the carved work slipped off, and the garter with it. I then fastened it to the frame of the tester, winding it round, and tying it in a strong knot. The frame broke short and let me down again. The third effort was more likely to succeed. I set the door open, which reached within a foot of the ceiling; and by the help of a chair I could command the top of it; and the loop being large enough to admit a large angle of the door, was easily fixed, so as not to slip off again. I pushed away the chair with my feet, and hung at my whole length. While I hung there, I distinctly heard a voice say three times, " 'Tis over!" Though I am sure of the fact, and was so at the time, yet it did not at all alarm me, or affect my resolution. I hung so long, that I lost all sense, all consciousness of existence.

When I came to myself again, I thought myself in hell; the sound of my own dreadful groans was all that I heard; and a feeling like that produced by a flash of lightning, just beginning to seize upon me, passed over my whole body. In a few seconds I found myself fallen with my face to the floor. In about half a minute, I recovered my feet, and reeling, and staggering, stumbled into bed again. By the blessed providence of God, the garter which had held me till the bitterness of temporal death was past, broke, just before eternal death had taken place upon me. The stagnation of the blood under one eye, in a broad crimson spot, and a red circle about my neck, showed plainly that I had been on the brink of eternity. The latter, indeed, might have been occasioned by the pressure of the garter; but the former was certainly the effect of strangulation; for it was not attended with the sensation of a bruise, as it must have been, had I, in my fall, received one in so tender a part. And I rather think the circle round my neck was owing to the same cause; for the part was not excoriated, nor at all in pain.

Soon after I got into bed, I was surprised to hear a noise in the dining-room, where the laundress was lighting a fire. She had found the door unbolted, notwithstanding my design to fasten it, and must have passed the bed-chamber door while I was hanging on it, and yet never perceived me. She heard me fall, and presently came to ask if I were well; adding, she feared I had been in a fit. I sent her to a friend, to whom I related the whole affair, and dispatched him to my kinsman, at the coffee-house. As soon as the latter arrived, I pointed to the broken garter, which lay in the middle of the room; and apprized him also of the attempt I had been making.—His words were, "My dear Mr. Cowper, you terrify me;—to be sure you cannot hold the office at this rate—where is the deputation?" I gave him the key of the drawer where it was deposited; and his business requiring his immediate attendance, he took it away with him; and thus ended all my connexion with the Parliament-House.

To this moment I had felt no concern of a spiritual kind. Ignorant of original sin, insensible of the guilt of actual transgression, I understood neither the law nor the gospel; the condemning nature of the one, nor the restoring mercies of the other. I was as much unacquainted with Christ, in all his saving offices, as if his blessed name had never reached me. Now, therefore, a new scene opened upon me. Conviction of sin took place, especially of that just committed; the meanness of it, as well as its atrocity, were exhibited to me in colours so inconceivably strong, that I despised myself, with a contempt not to be imagined or expressed, for having attempted it. This sense of it secured me from the repetition of a crime, which I could not now reflect on without abhorrence.

Before I arose from bed, it was suggested to me, that there was nothing wanting but murder, to fill up the measure of my iniquities; and that, though I had failed in my design, yet I had all the guilt of that crime to answer for. A sense of God's wrath, and a deep despair of escaping it, instantly succeeded. The fear of death became much more prevalent in me now than even the desire of it had been. A frequent flashing like that of fire, before my eyes, and an excessive pressure upon my brain, made me apprehensive of an apoplexy; an event which I thought the more probable, as an extravasation in that part seemed likely to happen, in so violent a struggle.

*   *   *

Satan plied me closely with horrible visions, and more horrible voices. My ears rang with the sound of torments, that seemed to await me. Then did the pains of hell get hold on me, and, before day break, the very sorrows of death encompassed me. A numbness seized the extremities of my body, and life seemed to retreat before it. My hands and feet became cold and stiff; a cold sweat stood upon my forehead; my heart seemed at every pulse to beat its last, and my soul to cling to my lips, as if on the very brink of departure. No convicted criminal ever feared death more, or was more assured of dying.

At eleven o'clock, my brother called upon me, and in about an hour after his arrival, that distemper of mind, which I had so ardently wished for, actually seized me. While I traversed the apartment, in the most horrible dismay of soul, expecting every moment that the earth would open and swallow me up; my conscience scaring me, the avenger of blood pursuing me, and the city of refuge out of reach and out of sight; a strange and horrible darkness fell upon me. If it were possible, that a heavy blow could light on the brain, without touching the skull, such was the sensation I felt. I clapped my hand to my forehead, and cried aloud through the pain it gave me. At every stroke, my thoughts and expressions became more wild and incoherent; all that remained clear was the sense of sin, and the expectation of punishment. These kept undisturbed possession all through my illness, without interruption or abatement.

My brother instantly observed the change, and consulted with my friends on the best manner to dispose of me. It was agreed among them, that I should be carried to St. Alban's, where Dr. Cotton kept a house for the reception of such patients, and with whom I was known to have a slight acquaintance. Not only his skill, as a physician, recommended him to their choice, but his well-known humanity, and sweetness of temper. It will be proper to draw a veil over the secrets of my prison house; let it suffice to say, that the low state of body and mind, to which I was reduced, was perfectly well calculated to humble the natural vain-glory and pride of my heart.

These are the efficacious means which Infinite Wisdom thought meet to make use of for that purpose. A sense of self-loathing and abhorrence ran through all my insanity. Conviction of sin, and expectation of instant judgment, never left me from the 7th of December, 1763, until the middle of July following. The accuser of the brethren was ever busy with me night and day, bringing to my recollection in dreams the commission of long forgotten sins, and charging upon my conscience things of an indifferent nature, as atrocious crimes.

All that passed in this long interval of eight months, may be classed under two heads: conviction of sin, and despair of mercy. But blessed be the God of my salvation for every sigh I drew, for every tear I shed; since thus it pleased him to judge me here, that I might not be judged hereafter.

After five months' continual expectation, that the divine vengeance would plunge me into the bottomless pit, I became so familiar with despair, as to have contracted a sort of hardiness and indifference as to the event. I began to persuade myself, that while the execution of the sentence was suspended, it would be for my interest to indulge a less horrible train of ideas, than I had been accustomed to muse upon. "Eat and drink, for tomorrow thou shalt be in hell," was the maxim on which I proceeded. By this means, I entered into conversation with the Doctor, laughed at his stories, and told him some of my own to match them; still, however, carrying a sentence of irrevocable doom in my heart.

He observed the seeming alteration with pleasure. Believing, as well he might that my smiles were sincere, he thought my recovery well nigh completed; but they were, in reality, like the green surface of a morass, pleasant to the eye, but a cover for nothing but rottenness and filth. The only thing that could promote and effectuate my cure was yet wanting;—an experimental knowledge of the redemption which is in Christ Jesus.

I remember, about this time, a diabolical species of regret that found harbour in my wretched heart. I was sincerely sorry that I had not seized every opportunity of giving scope to my wicked appetites, and even envied those, who being departed to their own place before me, had the consolation to reflect, that they had well earned their miserable inheritance, by indulging their sensuality without restraint. Oh, merciful God! what a tophet of pollution is the human soul! Wherein do we differ from the devils, unless thy grace prevent us?

In about three months more (July 25, 1764), my brother came from Cambridge to visit me. Dr. C. having told him that he thought me greatly amended, he was rather disappointed at finding me almost as silent and reserved as ever; for the first sight of him struck me with many painful sensations, both of sorrow for my own remediless condition, and envy of his happiness.

As soon as we were left alone, he asked me how I found myself; I answered, "As much better as despair can make me." We went together into the garden. Here, on expressing a settled assurance of sudden judgment, he protested to me, that it was all a delusion; and protested so strongly, that I could not help giving some attention to him. I burst into tears, and cried out, "If it be a delusion, then am I the happiest of beings." Something like a ray of hope was shot into my heart; but still I was afraid to indulge it. We dined together, and I spent the afternoon in a more cheerful manner. Something seemed to whisper to me every moment, "Still there is mercy." Even after he left me, this change of sentiment gathered ground continually; yet my mind was in such a fluctuating state, that I can only call it a vague presage of better things at hand, without being able to assign a reason for it. The servant observed a sudden alteration in me for the better; and the man, whom I have ever since retained in my service, expressed great joy on the occasion.

I went to bed and slept well. In the morning I dreamed that the sweetest boy I ever saw came dancing up to my bed-side; he seemed just out of leading-strings, yet I took particular notice of the firmness and steadiness of his tread. The sight affected me with pleasure, and served at least to harmonize my spirits; so that I awoke for the first time with a sensation of delight on my mind. Still, however, I knew not where to look for the establishment of the comfort I felt; my joy was as much a mystery to myself as to those about me. The blessed God was preparing me for the clearer light of his countenance by this first dawning of that light upon me.

Within a few days of my first arrival at St. Alban's, I had thrown aside the word of God, as a book in which I had no longer any interest or portion. The only instance, in which I can recollect reading a single chapter, was about two months before my recovery. Having found a Bible on the bench in the garden, I opened it upon the 11th of St. John, where Lazarus is raised from the dead; and saw so much benevolence, mercy, goodnes, and sympathy with miserable man, in our Saviour's conduct, that I almost shed tears even after the relation; little thinking that it was an exact type of the mercy which Jesus was on the point of extending towards myself. I sighed, and said, "Oh, that I had not rejected so good a Redeemer, that I had not forfeited all his favours!" Thus was my heart softened, though not yet enlightened. I closed the book, without intending to open it again.

Having risen with somewhat of a more cheerful feeling, I repaired to my room, where breakfast waited for me. While I sat at table, I found the cloud of horror, which had so long hung over me, was every moment passing away; and every moment came fraught with hope. I was continually more and more persuaded, that I was not utterly doomed to destruction. The way of salvation was still, however, hid from my eyes; not did I see it at all clearer than before my illness. I only thought, that if it pleased God to spare me, I would lead a better life; and that I would yet escape hell, if a religious observance of my duty would secure me from it. Thus may the terror of the Lord make a Pharasee; but only the sweet voice of mercy in the gospel, can make a Christian.

But the happy period which was to shake off my fetters and afford me a clear opening of the free mercy of God in Christ Jesus was now arrived. I flung myself in a chair near the window, and seeing a Bible there, ventured once more to apply to it for comfort and instruction. The first verse I saw, was the 25th of the 3d of Romans: "Whom God hath set forth to be a propitiation through faith in his blood, to declare his righteousness for the remission of sins that are past, through the forebearance of God." Immediately I received strength to believe, and the full beams of the Sun of Righteousness shone upon me. I saw the sufficiency of the atonement he had made, my pardon sealed in his blood, and all the fulness and completeness of his justification. In a moment I believed, and received the gospel. Whatever my friend Madan had said to me, so long before, revived in all its clearness, with demonstration of the Spirit and with power.

Unless the Almighty arm had been under me, I think I should have died with gratitude and joy. My eyes filled with tears, and my voice choked with transport. I could only look up to heaven in silent fear, overwhelmed with love and wonder. But the work of the Holy Spirit is best described in his own words, it is "joy unspeakable, and full of glory." Thus was my heavenly Father in Christ Jesus pleased to give me the full assurance of faith; and, out of a strong, unbelieving heart, to "raise up a child unto Abraham." How glad should I now have been to have spent every moment in prayer and thanksgiving! I lost no opportunity of repairing to a throne of grace; but flew to it with an earnestness irresistible and never to be satisfied. Could I help it? Could I do otherwise than love and rejoice in my reconciled Father in Christ Jesus? The Lord had enlarged my heart, and "I ran in the way of his commandments."

For many succeeding weeks, tears were ready to flow, if I did but speak of the gospel, or mention the name of Jesus. To rejoice day and night was all my employment. Too happy to sleep much, I thought it was but lost time that was spent in slumber. Oh that the ardour of my first love had continued! But I have known many a lifeless and unhallowed hour since; long intervals of darkness, interrupted by short returns of peace and joy in believing.

My physician, ever watchful and apprehensive for my welfare, was now alarmed, lest the sudden transition from despair to joy, should terminate in a fatal frenzy. But "the Lord was my strength and my song, and was become my salvation." I said, "I shall not die, but live, and declare the works of the Lord; he has chastened me sore, but not given me over unto death. O give thanks unto the Lord, for his mercy endureth for ever."

In a short time, Dr. C. became satisfied, and acquiesced in the soundness of my cure; and much sweet communion I had with him concerning the things of our salvation. He visited me every morning while I stayed with him, which was near twelve months after my recovery, and the gospel was the delightful theme of our conversation.

No trial has befallen me since, but what might be expected in a state of welfare. Satan, indeed, has changed his battery. Before my conversion, *sensual gratification* was the weapon with which he sought to destroy me. Being naturally of an easy quiet disposition, I was seldom tempted to anger; yet, that passion it is which *now* gives me the most disturbance, and occasions the sharpest conflicts. But Jesus being my strength, I fight against it; and if I am not conqueror, yet I am not overcome.

1818 ⊷

The Interior of Bethlehem Hospital, by Urbane Metcalf

Bethlehem Hospital, one of the earliest European asylums, began as a priory, St. Mary's of Bethlehem, in 1247. It was officially recorded as a "hospital" in 1329, but not until 1403 was it noted that Bethlehem had mad patients. It was never very large. In 1403 there were only six mad patients. Toward the end of Elizabeth's reign, the last years of the sixteenth century, Bethlehem had only about twenty mad patients.[1] There were a few other similar institutions in Europe during that time, but until the seventeenth century, Bethlehem—known colloquially as Bedlam—was the only significant asylum in England.

During England's great period of reform in the first half of the nineteenth century, government committees investigated Bethlehem several times. An investigation in 1815 reported to the House of Commons that patients were often chained to the walls as well as manacled and that one of the female patients had been chained without release for eight years. They also reported the case of a patient named Norris who had been chained for twelve years. Artist's prints, depicting Norris's confinement, were exhibited before the House. An iron collar, attached by a chain to a pole at the foot of his bed, restrained him by the neck. His ankles were chained to the foot of his bed, and an iron frame enclosed his torso. The governors of Bethlehem, however, defended his treatment insisting that his confinement appeared "to have been, upon the whole, rather a merciful and humane, than a rigorous and severe imposition." At the same hearing, Dr. Thomas Monro, one of Bethlehem's physicians, testified on the medical treatment of Bethlehem patients: routing bleeding, vomiting, then purging. Said Dr. Monro: "it was handed down to me by my father, and I do not know any better practice."[2]

Those 1815 hearings caused little immediate change at Bethlehem. A report in 1837 noted that some patients were still chained and that hospital funds were being misused by employees. The reform acts of 1845 specifically excluded Bethlehem (as the only asylum legally belonging to the City of London, Bethlehem was always in a unique

---

[1]Tuke, *Chapters in the History of the Insane*, pp. 52, 63.
[2]Ibid., pp. 80, 153.

position), and as late as 1851 investigations showed unsatisfactory conditions. In 1853, however, Parliament at last officially directed that Bethlehem be subject to legislation, thus placing it under the jurisdiction of a permanent inspection and licensing committee. By 1877 an investigation by the House of Commons into all types of institutions for the mad, including Bethlehem, found nothing seriously wrong.[3]

Urbane Metcalf, however, wrote *The Interior of Bethlehem Hospital* over half a century before, when Bethlehem was without question a very unpleasant place. His account may well be the single surviving patient's description of the inside of the oldest existing asylum in the world. Metcalf tells almost nothing about himself in the pamphlet, except that he had been a patient at Bethlehem at that time and several years earlier, between 1804 and 1806.

Bethlehem began keeping case notes on its patients a short time before Metcalf's second admission, and most of the information I have about this obscure man comes from those notes.[4] He was admitted to Bethlehem for the second time on October 16, 1817, at which time he considered himself to be the son of Matilda, sister to the king of Denmark, and therefore an heir to the throne of Denmark. He was put into the "incurable Gallery," according to a note of November 1, 1817, where he remained for about a year. The following case notes describe the official view of his progress during the last five months of his stay at Bethlehem:

> June 1: This patient is extreamly orderly . but seems somewhat depressed in spirits . his appetite . digestion and sleep is good . he is frequently engaged in the occupation of a Tailor . but I am informed that he gets his living out of Doors as a Hawker and Pedlar.
>
> July 1: I am informed by Thomas Rodbird the Keeper of N° 4 in which Gallery this patient has constantly resided . that he has now ceased to consider himself as heir to The Throne of Denmark—and I observe that he does not seem so depressed.
>
> July 3: A yellowness of the countenance is remarkable and his digestive organs are a little out of order.
>
> August 1: Notwith standing his having given up the idea of being The Son of Matilda and Altho the depression is not so manifest still there is something peculiar in his manner . as there is abundance of evidence of his having been frequently deranged I cannot help thinking that there is some latent disorder existing—he continues his medicine.

---

[3]Ibid., p. 197.
[4]From Bethlem Royal Hospital Archives.

September 1: This patient appears rather irritable at this period and has complained to me about the badness of the provisions and of the ill treatment which some of the patients have endured from their respective keepers . he has also made the complaints to Dr. Munro—but I cannot ascertain any fact upon which his accusations are grounded—his health is improved and he continues to take the Pills.

September 4: Upon my return from Bridewell this morning I found that Urban Metcalf had made the same complaints to Dr. Tuthill that he had told to Dr. Munro and myself but as I was not present I do not conceive that any entry of his narrative upon that occasion needs any comment from me . Dr. Tuthill desired that he might be confined to his room.

September 7: His health is good . but he is irritable and full of complaints respecting the economy of the Hospital as well as against the Keepers.

October 15: Dr. Tuthill considered him well enough to have a months leave of absence . it was this day granted him by The Committee.

November 12: Discharged Well.

Metcalf may well have been an ordinary patient in many ways. But, from the entries made on September 1 and after, we see he was also a troublemaker. Although cooperative up to the point of taking his pills, he tended to be "irritable." He was "full of complaints," without justification. "I cannot ascertain any fact upon which his accusations are grounded," says the note-taker. A note on September 4 informs us that Metcalf was confined to his room, though it does not tell us why, or how long.

Metcalf's pamphlet, published very soon after his release, may explain that mysterious confinement:

About the end of August last I mentioned most of these abuses to the physicians, apothecary, and steward, who treated them with indifference and neglect, and to three gentlemen who visited the house on the first Thursday in September, who I think belonged to the Committee of the House of Commons, I attempted to acquaint them with the cruelties and abuses . . . for this attempt I was confined to my room by Dr. Tothill's orders till the 20th of October, 1818, the day I was discharged, during that time they refused my friends admittance to see me, though they applied several times.[5]

---

[5]The discrepancy of dates may be more apparent than real. On October 15 he was granted a "leave," which may have taken effect a few days later; in any case, to Metcalf it must have seemed equivalent to a "discharge."

Perhaps the confinement was simply a deliberate attempt to control a troublesome malcontent: they confined him then quickly released him, hoping that he would return to the matrix of anonymous humanity from which he had emerged a year earlier. Instead, Metcalf wrote *The Interior of Bethlehem Hospital*, selling it all over London for three cents a copy.

Like Alexander Cruden before him, Metcalf attempts to present himself as a reliable narrator, describing briefly who he is and how he obtained his information about Bethlehem. He tells of a past propinquity, during his first stay at Bethlehem, to the patient Norris, whose peculiar chaining caused serious scandal in 1815: "Part of the time, I occupied the next room to that occupied by the truly unhappy Norris, (whose case is already before the public,) the iron bar to which he was fastened stood at the foot of my bed, O what a disgrace!" How the iron bar to which Norris was fastened could have been at the foot of Metcalf's bed when Norris was in another room is a mystery, and perhaps a bit of self-dramatization by the author. But certainly—whether the situation actually occurred or not—Metcalf is trying to establish an image of himself as a narrator who *was there*, who has experienced firsthand the awful truth of the interior of Bethlehem.

Except for the discussion of his confinement at the end, Metcalf speaks of himself only as a witness to the cruelties and abuses practised against others. He says: "I myself have not cause to complain as I was generally treated with great civility, but I am, from a sense of humanity, pleading the cause of the unfortunate." And it is probably the lack of a central figure, a central "I," that accounts for the lack of coherence in this pamphlet. Metcalf gathered all information possible, but he was unable to organize that information effectively. The result is a slightly confusing survey which moves with equal emphasis from Dr. Munro's neglect of his patient Lloyd, to Blackburn's murder of the patient Fowler, to Rodbird's inattention to the patient Stockley's dirty socks. At times, the writing resembles a blurred photograph. Nonetheless, this pamphlet's historical position as one of the earliest protests against the abuse of the mad, as well as its interest as a rare survey of Bethlehem's interior, make it well worth reading. It is reproduced here in its entirety.

IT WILL BE NECESSARY to say something of myself, that it may appear how I obtained my knowledge of the cruelties and abuses that are daily practised in the first establishment of the kind in Europe. During the years of 1804, 5, and 6, I spent twenty-two months in that dreary abode, Old Bethlehem Hospital; not more I believe than six weeks during that time I was incapable, through indisposition, of judging of the occurrences that daily took place. From the supineness of the then physician, the cruelty of the apothecary, the weakness of the steward, and the uncontrouled audacity of the keepers, such scenes passed, that if the hospital had stood in a solitary place, where only six sensible and humane persons could have access in the course of a year, it would even then have been astonishing that they remained unexposed; but what was the fact? it stood in the midst of the most populous city in Europe, and was under the management of governors, some of them men the most humane and respectable in their private characters that Britain could boast; had officers that bore respectable characters, and keepers that passed for honest men: and was almost daily visited by some of the most exalted characters in the country, as well as by foreigners. Part of the time, I occupied the next room to that occupied by the truly unhappy Norris, (whose case is already before the public,) the iron bar to which he was fastened stood at the foot of my bed, O what a disgrace! I was under a keeper of the name of Davies; far be it from me unnecessarily to rake up the ashes of the dead, but this I must say, he was a cruel, unjust and drunken man, and for many years as keeper secretly practised the greatest cruelties to those under his care; he was some time previous to his death, porter, and when he died the committee had the goodness, thinking he had been a good servant, to give a handsome sum towards the expences of his funeral, but they were greatly deceived.

I, on the 16th of October 1817, became again a patient in the New Bethlehem Hospital, and am happy to be able to state that I found many alterations in the provisions, and in other things that greatly added to the comfort of the patients, and to the honour of those governors through whom those alterations were effected. I found there were four galleries, and that the patients in one gallery had seldom access to those in another, except when in the green yard, and the establishment to be considerably larger, but not so many patients. I became Dr.

Tothill's patient, and was put in the upper gallery, Thomas Rodbird keeper, I wish to observe that I have read the printed rules of the establishment, and their principle is good, the comforts of the patients are secured in every respect, but these regulations are departed from and the keepers do just as they please.

	Dr. Tothill, Dr. E. T. Munro, }	PHYSICIANS.
	Mr. Wallett,	–APOTHECARY.
	Mr. Humby,	–STEWARD.
	Simmons	–PORTER.
	{ Allen and Goose }	*First gallery or basement.*
KEEPERS,	{ Dowie,	*Second gallery.*
	Blackburn,	*Third gallery.*
	Rodbird,	*Fourth gallery.*
CUTTER,	Vickery.	

It is to be observed that the basement is appropriated for those patients who are not cleanly in their persons, and who, on that account have no beds, but lay on straw with blankets and a rug; but I am sorry to say, it is too often made a place of punishment, to gratify the unbounded cruelties of the keepers.

The present physicians, I think too supine: providence has placed them in situations wherein they have it in their power greatly to add to, or diminish from the comfort of the unfortunate; I have known patients make just complaints to them, which have been received with the utmost indifference, and not at all attended to; one instance, to Dr. Tothill, Mr. Parker, in my hearing, in the green yard, told him that he had been used very ill by another patient, and conceived that Dowie the keeper, in his gallery had set him on, likewise that Dowie had three shillings of his, which he had in his pocket when he first came there; why Dowie had kept it so long I cannot conceive, for no doubt during nearly twelve months, Mr. Parker would often have been glad to have made use of it to purchase snuff and other little articles, but my opinion is, that if Mr. Parker's memory had been bad, Dowie's would not have been much brighter on the subject; I myself, at my first admittance, twice applied to Dr. Tothill to allow me butter instead of cheese, but in vain, it would not have been setting a precedent as some other patients had that indulgence, but whether it failed Dr. Tothill's memory in the hurry of business, or whether I ought to have got Rodbird to interest himself in the affair by giving him 5s. I leave to their better judgment.

I well remember on Saturday, the day after Good Friday, a patient of the name of Lloyd, Dr. Munro's patient, was in the green yard, no other patient being there, during two or three hours excessive rain, Dr. Munro going through the upper gallery with a friend with him, came to the window of the keeper's room, I was standing by, he observed to his friend that that was the airing ground, I opened the window hoping that he would see Lloyd in the green yard, but he took no notice of him, though he, Lloyd, appeared to me to stand in full view.

I will allow that Mr. Wallett the apothecary is a very pleasant man in his deportment, but I think he is very negligent as being the resident apothecary, a great deal depends on him with regard to the management of the house, and the comfort of the patients.

Mr. Humby the steward, in my humble opinion acts with great injustice, he admits provisions of the worst quality; the beer during the twelve months that I speak of was exceedingly bad, not fit in general, for any person to drink, the cheese was very bad; the butter was very often bad; the meat in general very bad; the potatoes very bad; none of the provisions fair upon an average but the bread, and I have understood that is not under his management. Though I have known that repeated complaints have been made to him, I believe that the governors contract with the tradesmen for good wholesome provisions, and if Mr. H. admits inferior he is doing the patients an injustice, and no doubt is a gainer by it.

With regard to the beds, I think there is great mismanagement, there are beds which frequently get wetted; those flocks are taken into an upper room, emptied out of the ticks, the ticks washed and mended, but the flocks never thoroughly dried, so that when they are put again in the ticks they are still damp and of course very dangerous for any person to sleep on, though I believe that every clean patient on going into the house is allowed a new bed. I myself had a damp bed given me which I laid on for some time, and fear I shall feel the effects of it through my future life, as I have for some months past been subject to a pain in my loins, which I never had before. That economy in every establishment is necessary I will allow, but to be carried to such lengths as to deprive the unfortunate of comforts, to fill the pockets of an individual is an act of the most cruel injustice; another thing, Mr. H. has snuff and tobacco at his disposal, to give to any patient who stands in need of them, but I have observed that there are but few individuals who obtain it, and those whose real wants do not warrant an application on their parts, while the poor and friendless go without: Mr. Humby's injustice as steward, has very bad effects, not only as far as it is carried on by himself, but setting an example to the servants under him, who never fail to make the amplest use of it in plundering the unfortunate, when any man placed in the same situation, by acting with integrity could produce the most incalculable benefit to the unfortunates under his charge.

Rodbird, keeper of the fourth gallery.

The gallery I was in, there is a patient of the name of Samuel Breeze, he and fourteen more were in the old house when I was there, in the year 1804; last February, for a trifling affair he was locked up in his room for four days, and I know that during that time he had no breakfasts nor suppers, but only a dinner each day; another patient, Charles Saunders, had in the old house, though as inoffensive as a child, had been kept chained for years, that the keeper might have his clothes to sell. On the sixteenth of October, when I went in, his age was nearly 70 years, he appeared dropping into the grave through the decays of nature, and gradually got worse; I three distinct times remember him asking Dr. Munro his physician, to put him on the sick mess, as his appetite was so bad he could not eat the regular provisions, but his request was disregarded, he was not put on the sick mess till two days before he died: he died on the last day in the year. Another patient of the name of Leonard, is in general a very quiet man, I have known Rodbird the keeper, abuse him repeatedly and set the other patients on to do it: I remember well I was once at the pump and Rodbird came to rinse out a drinking horn, Rodbird said he had been giving Leonard physic, and there were two doses of it, and damn the B-gg-r he wished it was poison. And though it was Dr. Tothill, his physician's order that he should go to chapel when he chose, he used to hinder him whenever he pleased. Another patient of the name of Brown, some months back it was thought necessary to keep in a strait jacket, but afterwards he was allowed in the day time to have it off. On Tuesday's, Thursday's and Saturdays, the evenings that Rodbird went out, he would put the jacket on before Brown had had his supper, and I have seen him put to the greatest difficulty to contrive to eat his supper as he had not the use of his hands, and this was done merely to save Blackburn, who on those evenings supplied Rodbird's place, the trouble of putting the jacket on at bed time. Another patient of the name of Nugent, a quiet, well behaved man, from what cause except Rodbird's cruel manners, I cannot tell, he would abuse in a very shameful manner. Another patient of the name of Rophy, who is a man of mild manners, and has moved in a respectable sphere in life, and has a great aversion to obscene language, I have known him often to insult in that way in a very gross manner; once I remember Rodbird had been out, and when he came in he told Mr. Rophy that his, Rophy's son was sitting under the wall with a fiddle, begging, and as it rained at the time, he observed, that he was very wet; O what cruelty! I well remember on new year's evening four of us were playing at cards, William Kendal and Freeman got quarrelling and at last to fighting, the keeper Blackburn was present, Rodbird being out that evening; though he Blackburn might have prevented them from fighting if he had pleased, they went to bed in the greatest perturbation of mind against each other; in the morning Rodbird opened another patients room door and returned to bed leaving that patient to open the other doors, in a short time Kendal and Freeman got again to fighting, Freeman with a broom cut Kendal's head; Rodbird had to get again out of bed to part them, they were each confined to their rooms, and as the greatest blame fell to Freeman's share, he was sent down into the basement to sleep on straw for two or three months, this appeared all fair to the officers, but there was an under plot to be carried on; at that time and for some time previous, Freeman had had a shilling a week and most of Rophy's provisions for waiting on him, but Rodbird thought this a fair opportunity to get it out of his hands into his own, and which he has ever since retained, this is the way in which patients are used, and the officers deceived to gratify the avarice of cruel keepers. I humbly imagine that when the alarm bells were put up they were thought necessary, but during the summer months they are entirely useless in the gallery I was in, as Rodbird is scarcely ever in the gallery and his room door is kept shut, so that whatever accident might happen they are useless; there is another thing I wish to mention, the tray in which the suppers are brought, instead of being brought into the dining room, and each patient having his supper given him, it is set by Rodbird outside the gallery door, and the patients are called to get their suppers, any poor confused patient that neglects to go for his supper, Rodbird in his great kindness forgets too, but no doubt he does not forget to make use of the victuals another way. There is a patient of the name of William Stockley, who is a poor confused creature, he is a strong young man, but he is entirely made a slave of by the keeper and by any other patient that pleases in the gallery, and not only so, but he is sent a great deal of his time down into the laundry to be made a drudge of there, and this with Mr. H. the steward's knowledge and leave; and very often is sent to bed without his supper through Mr. Rodbird's kindness, and I know that he has not a clean pair of stockings more than once in three months, though his friends and the governors no doubt, think he is made comfortable. I myself have not cause to complain as I was generally treated with great civility, but I am, from a sense of humanity, pleading the cause of the unfortunate, this I will say of Rodbird, that he is an idle, skulking, pilfering soundrel, and during the time I am speaking of, he was not upon an average, in his gallery three hours in the day and this could not be without the stewards knowledge and connivance. Another circumstance, about four months back when the patients that were at Hoxton belonging to the sick and hurt office were removed to Hasler Hospital, there were six men who came to Bethlehem, four were put in Rodbird's gallery, and two in the basement, one of the four named Coates, had been disordered, he had some ways with him that Rodbird thought troublesome, and wished to get him in the basement, and I believe spoke to the officers on the subject, but not succeeding in the first instance he had the artifice to empty another patient's night bowl in Coates' shoes, and shewed that to Dr. Munro and Mr. Wallett, who had him removed to the basement: O what a scoundrel! the best proof I can give of the existing abuses is the continuance of such servants in the establishment for any length of time, Rodbird has been there six years. William Stockley, Samuel Breeze, and U. Kantlin three patients in Rodbird's gallery had their flannel waistcoats and draws withheld from them during last winter, whether it rests with Mr. Humby the steward, or Rodbird the keeper, I cannot pretend to say, be that as it may, an investigation is loudly called for.

Blackburn, keeper of the third gallery.

This man possesses an improper control over the officers, and no doubt stands high in the estimation of some governors, I will endeavour to unmask him. In the Old House there was a patient of the name of Fowler, who one morning was put in the bath by Blackburn, who ordered a patient then bathing, to hold him down, he did so, and the consequence was the death of Fowler, and though this was known to the then officers it was hushed up; shameful! Likewise a patient named Popplestone, I believe he came from Cornwall, during a severe winter was so long chained in his room that the iron round his leg literally eat into his flesh, in this dreadful state he lay unattended, until Blackburn became accidentally acquainted with his situation, the lock was clogged with dirt so that he Blackburn, was obliged to borrow an awl of Truelock to clear it; a short time afterwards Popplestone's leg rotted off and he died in the house, this should have been sufficient to provoke an investigation, but it was hushed up; shameful neglect!

New House

The case of Kemp, a patient now in the house, a man of good education, and who has lived in respectable circumstances, who has not only the misfortune of being disordered, but of being poor; on his admittance he was put in Blackburn's gallery, but not suiting him, he contrived to get him removed into the basement by the following means: he (Blackburn) complained to Dr. Tothill (Kemp's physician,) that he of a night made so much noise that he disturbed the other patients and prevented their recovery and got other patients to corroborate his assertion, for this he was removed into the basement, but I know if he had money, or been a good cleaner all would have been well, and he might have remained there, as there are patients who make far more noise now in his gallery; the villian without any provocation had the cruelty to say to Kemp, had *I a dog like you I would hang him.* Another patient named Harris, for the trifling offence of wanting to remain in his room a little longer one morning than usual, was dragged by Blackburn, assisted by Allen, the basement keeper, from No. 18, to Blackburn's room, and there beaten by them unmercifully; when he came out his head was streaming with blood, and Allen in his civil way wished him good morning.

The case of Morris; this man had some pills to take, which he contrived to secrete in his waistcoat pocket, this Blackburn discovered, and by the assistance of Allen, they got him to his room and there beat him so dreadfully for ten minutes as to leave him totally incapable of moving for some time, Rodbird was looking out to give them notice of the approach of any of the officers; they are three villians. A man by the name of Baccus, nearly eighty years of age, was this summer admitted into the house; one very hot day he had laid down in the green yard, another patient named Lloyd, very much disordered, trod on the middle of his body purposely, this Blackburn the keeper encouraged by laughing, and Lloyd would have repeated it, but something diverted his attention: Baccus is since dead.

Coles, a patient of Blackburn's, one day, for refusing to take his physic, was by Blackburn and Rodbird beat and dashed violently against the wall several times, in the presence of the steward, though from the general tenor of this man's conduct it is probable a little persuasion would have been sufficient to induce him to take the medicine quietly, Coles is since put upon the long list, and is now in the upper gallery.

This keeper has held his situation seven years and from his attention to his business out of the hospital and the care of his birds and his cage making, and his being so much out, his place is almost a sinecure; as to his being out that cannot be without the steward's permission which is too often the case, I will give one instance, this summer the day that Allen the basement keeper was married to a woman keeper, Blackburn was out the whole day, which was Tuesday, the following Thursday after the Committee had left sitting; he again asked the steward to let him go out, but was refused on account of his having five new patients in that day; the next day he went out; I will allow that his gallery is kept very clean, but how is it done? by rousing his patients by five o'clock in a morning, to get all in order that he may attend to his private concerns, which are by far greater objects of solicitude with him than his public duties.

Dowie, keeper of the second gallery.

He has a patient named Clarke, not long since being very much disordered, it was thought necessary to handcuff him; this man was in the habit of picking grass, putting it in his pocket; one day in the green yard, Dowie in my hearing told a patient of the name of Locke if he saw him do amiss to give him a blow or two, Clarke moving to another part of the yard avoided Lock's notice, who seeing another patient act as he thought improperly gave him several violent blows.

Some time ago, Dowie had a patient by trade a tailor who earned money by working for the servants, this man not finding the house allowance sufficient paid Dowie 5s. per week, to let him have as much as he could eat, this would have been fair if Dowie had disposed of what belonged to himself, but instead of that he robbed the other patients of part of their allowance; what honesty!

Mr. Sutherland, a patient under Dowie's care was occasionally visited by his sister, they were too poor to see Dowie, and the consequence was the following act of inhumanity; one Monday morning while conversing with her brother she fainted (I believe from privation,) we who were in the room afforded her every assistance to recover her, Dowie came in and very rudely said "I don't know why you come here at all, you never *bring* anything, I dare say you have come without your breakfast," the manner of expressing these words was sufficient to mark the brutality of his disposition.

Allen and Goose, basement keepers.

From being in the upper gallery, I was necessarily precluded from obtaining a knowledge of the abuses practised by the keepers of the basement, but from the ready assistance Allen gave Blackburn and others in ill-using their patients, it is fair to conclude that his own fared no better; Goose by nature is unqualified for maltreating the patients personally, but he possesses all the appetites of a tyrant, and what nature has denied him in bodily strength he makes up by petty artifice to discomfort the patients under his charge, and rewards himself by pilfering.

And I believe that there is not more humanity or regularity exercised in the criminal part; if I had spent a month in it I should have known more, but this I know, that two of the keeper, Hooper and Webster have been in Allen's room for two hours together at cards, and little Goose's employment at the time was to look out that none of the officers surprised them, and of course Wooten the other keeper was in the criminal part by himself.

With respect to the green yard, I humbly think, it never, when the patients are in it, ought to be without a keeper, which very frequently is the case; there is a number of loose stones which any patient may throw at each other, the danger of their remaining is obvious, where there are so many persons who are disordered.

It is well known to those of the establishment that I had an opportunity part of my time of seeing the women's green yard, and I know that there are great irregularities and neglect in the management of the women's side, if elegant dressing and keeping gay company are qualifications for a matron of Bethlehem Hospital, the present one is well qualified.

There is now in Bethlehem Hospital a young lady named Clarke, (daughter of Alderman Clarke, Chamberlain of the City of London, and *treasurer of Bethlehem*,) who is a private patient to the matron; from my heart I declare I am not actuated or influenced by malice, I disclaim all intentions of wounding the feelings of the worthy Alderman, but I do think that a greater abuse cannot exist than the permission extended to the servants of the institution, to take in private patients, setting aside the injustice of making a public establishment subservient to private interest; they cannot if they are occupied by the care of private persons devote their time to the exercise of those duties they are hired to discharge. During the last summer, Miss Clarke and the matron went to Worthing, and were absent for a fortnight; Miss Clarke's liberty is indisputable, but surely the matron ought not to absent herself, at any time, it is a gross violation of her duty, and calls for the severest reproof if not a total dismissal.

Mr. Wallett, the resident apothecary, whose pleasant manners we before noticed, frequently has it in his power to exercise the natural humanity of his disposition; his kindness never sleeps, or if it should dose now and then, it is too sensative to resist the touch of gold: The following circumstance speaks for itself; three patients came into the criminal part during the last summer, one of them the French gentleman who cut the catholic priest; this person was fortunately too *rich* to be thought *mischievous*, and on that account was permitted to walk in the back garden for some time every afternoon with a private attendant; the crime for which this patient was tried, was an attempt to murder, surely the person to whose charge he was committed should have felt it his duty to watch him more narrowly, it ought to have been remembered that the perturbed state of mind which doubtless this patient was in, might have occasioned serious mischief, but every fear vanishes before gold, gold makes the coward brave, and madman sane, or if Mr. Wallett has so far forgotten his experience in these matters as to suffer such a patient to use his own discretion may we not say, "surely the affairs of the world are at a fine pass when the fool is desired to take care of the madman."

Truelock having discovered some of the malpractices of Simons, Blackburn, and Dowie, servants of the establishment, obtained their permission to leave the house when he pleased, I saw him myself in Hadland's shop, corner of Fetter Lane, Holborn, and supposed he was entirely discharged, Truelock told me Simmons let him out because he, Simmons, sold the meat and coals which should have been appropriated to the use of the patients; this honest servant has been 16 years in the establishment: Blackburn was fearful of exposure with respect to his treatment of poor Popplestone, whose case has already been detailed: Dowie in taking in some stores at the old establishment, made free with a bundle of flannel waistcoats, one dozen in number; Truelock perceived him in the act, and Dowie to bribe him into silence promised to wink at his leaving the house when he had the key. These honest men still hold their situations!

Mr. Vickery the cutter, has it in his power to defraud the patients in many instances, and he never suffers an opportunity to pass without gratifying his disposition to pilfering, this cutter cuts down the allowances to some purpose, for instance, there are two hundred patients in the house, and supposing he restrains his theft to one ounce per head, in the meat he takes 36 lb. per week as his own perquisites, bread in proportion; these perquisites he sells and manages to live comfortably by depriving the patients of part of the food intended for their sustenance.

Vinegar is allowed by the establishment, but excepting Rodbird's gallery, I believe it is sold by the keepers for their benefit, and many other comforts which are intended for the patients, by the villainy of these wretches is appropriated to their own use. If the patients received the governors allowances in quality and quantity, there situation would be considerably mended, and there would be no cause of complaint.

In each of the galleries the keepers pick out one of their patients whose strength fits him for the situation of bully, and when it is not convenient to be at the patients themselves, they cause him to do it, this is a great abuse.

Another existing evil is the prevention of patients friends from seeing them, when it is their pleasure to say he is so much disordered that they cannot possibly bring him to the visiting room, there is now in Dowie's gallery one Owen, whose mother has informed me that she was not permitted to see him during 16 weeks, from no other cause than to gratify the cruel disposition of the keeper. I have suffered confinement in the establishment, and am fully acquainted with the practices of the keepers, and advise such persons as have friends confined to insist on seeing them, if they leave any thing it is a matter of chance whether it is given them, the porter takes what he pleases in the first instance, and the keeper the remainder in the last, but the patient invariably comes off with short commons. It is impossible under the existing circumstances that the governors committee should arrive at the knowledge of the various abuses practised by casual examinations of persons whom they meet in different parts of the building, the steward and officers have men on each gallery whom they bribe, for the purpose of deceiving those gentlemen who benevolently use their exertions to discover the malpractices carried on in our public institutions, it is only by sheer accident that a solitary case now and then comes before the public, which by threatning an exposure, procures an amelioration in the condition of those persons confined through indisposition.

It would extend far beyond the limits of this little work to pourtray the villainies practised by the Jacks in office, bribery is common to them all; cruelty is common to them all; villainy is common to them all; in short every thing is common but virtue, which is so uncommon they take care to lock it up as a rarity. Like other establishments this appears to be erected too much for the purpose of making lucrative places; the apartments appropriated to the use of the officers are elegant in the extreme, every thing which luxury can covet is at their command; they eat, they fatten, while the poor creatures under their charge are left to all the miseries which confinement and privation can inflict; good God; in England, in this country, so famed for its munificence, surely the miseries of the wretched inmates of this humane institution are totally unknown to the exalted characters who support it, they should not sleep till the abuses are altogether removed; their supiness is the villain's security, their activity alone can prevent the new establishment falling a prey to the miseries and cruelties which disgraced Old Bethlehem.

About the end of August last I mentioned most of those abuses to the physicians, apothecary, and steward, who treated them with indifference and neglect, and to three gentlemen who visited the house on the first Thursday in September, who I rather think belonged to the Committee of the House of Commons, I attempted to acquaint them with the cruelties and abuses practised, Mr Humby was with them, who said I was a troublesome discontented person, but Mr. Humby knew I attempted to speak the truth, to which he is no friend, as it would probably soon un-steward him if spoken to his superiors; for this attempt I was confined to my room by Dr. Tothill's orders till the 20th of October, 1818, the day I was discharged, during that time they refused my friends admittance to see me, though they applied several times; I was at a loss to discover by whose authority Mr. Humby acted; I know his cruel and inhuman disposition too well to suppose he would wait for any when he had his victim within his power; I fully appreciate the kindness of my friends in coming to visit me in my confinement, they are people who earn their livelihood by labour, and if Mr. Humby from experience could form an idea of "honest industry" he surely would not have caused them to lose day after day when on their first visit he might have informed them the time I should be liberated, for I am too well acquainted with this "knot of villains" to suppose their conduct in confining me was not a stretch of deliberated cruelty. The institution in itself is an honor to humanity, and purged of the villains who oppress its unfortunate inmates would reflect a lustre on the individuals who support it by their fortunes. Our country has been famed throughout the world for the splendour of her charitable institutions, remedy their abuses her fame will be just; at present, however laudable the intentions of its supporters may be, the unfortunate who are compelled to claim their protection finds virtuous establishments prostituted to vicious purposes by wretches whose least crime is a total abuse of humanity.

1838 and 1840 ⊶

A Narrative of the Treatment Experienced by a Gentleman, During a State of Mental Derangement; Designed to Explain the Causes and the Nature of Insanity, and to Expose the Injudicious Conduct Pursued Towards Many Unfortunate Sufferers Under That Calamity,
by John Perceval

John Perceval (1803–1876) was the fifth son of six sons and six daughters in an English family of some distinction. His father was prime minister until 1812 when he was assassinated in the House of Commons by a madman. Perceval's early career was in the military. He served for a time in Portugal without seeing battle. In 1830 he resigned his commission and entered Oxford. Soon after, he traveled to Scotland to witness a particular evangelical revival known as the "Row Heresy," whose members sought communion with God through submission to spontaneous impulse. They often spoke in spontaneous gibberish that they believed to be a mystically received language of the Pelew Islands. Perceval passed some days on the fringes of this group and began himself yielding up to impulse, but his behavior was even too spontaneous for his fellow Row evangelicals. He left for Dublin, a spiritually charged man. There he yielded to the enticements of a prostitute and eventually underwent treatment for syphilis. Shortly thereafter, spontaneous impulses began to take over. Perceval saw visions and heard voices that told him to do strange, often contradictory things. His behavior was erratic enough that a "lunatic doctor" was called in. The doctor had him strapped down to his bed, hand and foot, and gave him broth and medicine. A few days later Perceval's brother arrived and took him back to England, to a private madhouse near Bristol run by a Dr. Fox. Perceval was an inmate of that madhouse during the most severe phase of his madness, from January 1831 to May 1832, and then was taken to Mr. C. Newington's private madhouse in Sussex where he remained until early 1834. Soon after his release, he married and in 1835 went to Paris where he began writing about his experiences as a patient, publishing two volumes in 1838 and 1840 of *A Narrative of the Treatment Experienced by a Gentleman, During a State of Mental Derangement*.[1]

A few pages into the first volume Perceval apologizes for the "irregularity and abruptness of style, and change of manner," whereby a loosely chronological narrative is interspersed with analysis, opinion, and tirade. The second volume is further complicated by a seemingly random selection of diary entries and letters. The disorganization may have to do in part with Perceval's difficulty in recalling this obviously painful material, with simple impatience and lack of editing, and perhaps in part—as one authority believes—with the result of a schizophrenic process.[2] Nonetheless, the disorganization is to be found only on a larger scale; on the smaller scale, sentences and paragraphs almost always possess a coherence of thought and clarity of style.

The purpose of the *Narrative* seems to be very clearly stated in a preface to the second volume: to reform the laws regarding the alleged mad, the management of asylums, and the treatment of patients by their relatives.[3] To achieve its purpose, as a work of protest and part of a campaign for reform, Perceval's *Narrative* operates on the principle of empathy. Early in volume I, the author asks readers to put themselves in the place of the mad person: "In the name of humanity, then, in the name of modesty, in the name of wisdom, I intreat you to place yourselves in the position of those whose sufferings I describe." With unusual candor, Perceval proceeds to describe his experiences as a madman, his point of view, his often naive and

---

[1] Additional biographical information is taken from Bateson's introduction to *Perceval's Narrative* and MacAlpine and Hunter, "John Thomas Perceval."

[2] Macalpine and Hunter, "John Thomas Perceval," p. 394.

[3] Taking these statements at face value we must conclude that Perceval's *Narrative* is above all a serious work of protest, another call for reform. The intensity and persistence of Perceval's post-patient career as a reformer ought to reinforce that conception. In 1838 Perceval worked for the freedom of Richard Paternoster, patient in a Kensington madhouse, later author of the protest work, *The Madhouse System* (1841). In 1839 he tried, without success, to introduce reform legislation in Parliament, and began his twenty-year letter-writing campaign for reform. In 1841 he became interested in the case of Dr. Pearce, a patient in the criminal section of Bethlehem, and ten years later published Dr. Pearce's *Poems. By a Prisoner in Bethlehem* to raise funds for the ensurance of Dr. Pearce's comfort in Bethlehem. In 1844 and 1855 Perceval wrote and published two short accounts of the unjust treatment of patients. In 1845 he and a group of acquaintances founded the Alleged Lunatic's Friend Society; he became honorary secretary in the following year. In 1859 and 1860 he and other members of the society appeared before an investigative parliamentary committee, where he described himself as "the attorney-general of all Her Majesty's madmen." See ibid., p. 394.

confused awareness, and his own errors in response to his keepers, as well as their errors in response to him.

Without digressing from a mad perspective, he describes in careful detail the physical abuse that took place in Dr. Fox's madhouse: beatings, excessive restraints, forced cold baths, and forced medical treatment. Without leaving a mad perspective, he also depicts the constant psychological abuse, the treatment of himself "as if I were a piece of furniture, an image of wood, incapable of desire or will as well as judgment." He was treated with a complete disregard for his social status, seldom introduced to people, needlessly confused by the absence of simple explanation and direction, spoken to condescendingly, humiliated by lack of attention to his ordinary daily needs, never consulted in decisions affecting him, and given no warning before medical treatment and no explanation after.

In the preface to volume II, Perceval lists as his third purpose for writing the book "to teach the wretched and affectionate relations of a deranged person, what may be his necessities, and how to conduct themselves toward him, so that they may avoid the errors which were unfortunately committed by the author's own family." In actuality one final result of the work, one other intention, may have been the destructive exposure of his family. In spite of his occasional insistence on love and serious concern for the welfare of his family, Perceval often bitterly condemns them. Not only does he repeat his reasons for feeling ill-treated by his mother and family, he even publishes and comments on personal letters between himself and his mother and other family members. The Narrative becomes at times a blunt weapon in a family feud, wielded by Perceval to embarrass and humiliate his mother and the rest of his family.

The full title of Perceval's Narrative suggests still another purpose: "to explain the causes and the nature of insanity." Completely interwoven with descriptions of Perceval's external experiences and his contact with other persons, places, and situations, the book gives an immensely lucid description of the ephemeral dreamlike current of his abnormal perceptions. Perceval must have felt his work was also important as a rare documentary look into the interior of a mad person's mind, a contribution to early psychiatry. Especially in volume II, where the narrative is much more digressive, there are frequent gratuitous self-analyses that seem wholly irrelevant to the purpose of protest.

At times his self-analyses and theories seem a little absurd, but other times he often strikingly anticipates modern psychiatry. At one point Perceval describes in unmistakable terms what Freud would later call "the psychopathology of everyday life," and in the same passage he anticipates Freud's theory of the unconscious:

> Now all or nearly all the phenomena which I have narrated, strange as they may appear, are to some degree or other familiar to all men. . . . For instance, the power of a spirit to control the utterance is daily experienced, though not remarked, in what we call a slip of the tongue. . . . The degree of error is not the same, but the phenomenon is the same—the organs of speech are made use of without the volition or rather intention of the person speaking. This is remarkable, because it would prove the residence in the temple of the body, of two distinct powers, or agents, or wills.

Approximately one hundred and twenty years after its original publication, Perceval's *Narrative* was republished as a "psychiatric autobiography," valued for its wealth of clear, careful psychological detail, and edited and introduced by Gregory Bateson. Bateson has left out much of the protest material in his edition and in an introduction presents an interesting interpretation of Perceval's illness. However, Bateson sometimes presents conjecture as if it were fact. He suggests that the contradictory voices Perceval hears echo the contradictory "double-bind" communications of his parents during his childhood, while in reality we know nothing of Perceval's childhood.

As the voices become quieter and less threatening during the process of Perceval's madness, Bateson says that a spontaneous self-healing transition from "double-bind" hallucination to "freedom of choice" hallucination is occurring. But certainly the process and meaning of Perceval's madness cannot be so easily circumscribed. Like a dream, it can be analyzed by a variety of systems, yet it remains only partly comprehensible, retaining an edge of the fantastic and the mysterious.

The first two excerpts were taken from the narrative portions of volume I where Perceval recounts his stay at Dr. Fox's private madhouse near Bristol. Those excerpts describe hallucinations, distorted perceptions and delusions, and the perverseness of madhouse treatment. Perceval is confused and helpless. He has little sense of where he is, who he is, or who his attendants and fellow patients are. Instead of helping to orient him the entire system of management seems designed to confuse him even more and to humiliate him in the bargain. The last excerpt is an effective tirade about the problems and abuses that concerned him most. He was frequently struck by

attendants, but he was much more upset by being spoken to condescendingly, as if he were a child.

WE TURNED to the left through some gates by a porter's lodge, a
few miles on the road to London, and we drove up to a door of a
house on the right hand side; we alighted, and I was ushered
into a small room on the left hand side of the passage, and
shortly after a young man came in, and then an old man, a very
old man. I do not recollect being introduced to either. My
brother went out and came in again. A man servant came and
occupied himself in taking away the portmanteaus, and in
laying the cloth for my dinner, he afterwards waited on me; He
had a black coat on, and my spirits told me his name was
ZACHARY GIBBS. All was in a mystery to me; only I understood
that on certain conditions I was to go home, which *was all I
desired*, whilst on certain other conditions I was to be left here.
The spirits told me this.

After the meat, a raspberry tartlet or two were brought to
table; they appeared to be very large, clean, and beautiful, and I
was told they were sent to me from heavenly places; that I was
to refuse them; that they were sent to try me; that if I refused
them I should be doing my duty, and my brother would take me
to E——. The same humour came on me to eat them all the
quicker, under the idea that they had given me nothing but
slops and physic for a fortnight or more, and now, if they are
such fools as to bring me up into heavenly places, I'll make the
best of it. My brother again went out, and I did not see him
enter any more; this pained me exceedingly; I thought he would
at least have bid me adieu; but the spirits told me that he was so
disgusted at seeing me eating the tarts, when he knew that if I
could only have refused one I should have been allowed by the
Almighty to return to my mother and family, and that I knew it,
that he had resolved to leave me without bidding adieu, and
had given me up into the hands of the Almighty. I imagine now
that his abrupt departure was preconcerted for fear of any
opposition on my part.

Well, my brother went, and I was left amongst strangers.

If I had had any introduction to Dr. F. at least I was unconscious of it. I was left to account for my position in that asylum, for I was in Dr. F.'s asylum, to the working of my own, and be it recollected, a lunatic imagination?

My spirits told me that I was in the house of an old friend of my father's, where certain duties were expected of me, that I knew what those duties were, but I pretended ignorance because I was afraid of the malice and persecution of the world in performing them. I persisted nevertheless in inwardly maintaining my ignorance and in divining what could be the meaning of these words. What ensued the evening my brother went away I do not recollect. I went to bed in a small, narrow, disconsolate looking room with stuccoed floor, over part of which was a carpet, bare white walls, a fire place and fire in the corner, on the right hand side by the window: the window opposite the door, the sill about the height of a man's waist, white window blinds, a table, a wash-hand-stand and a few chairs: on the left hand side, two beds, occupying more than one third the breadth of the room, the one nearest the window with white bed hangings on a slight iron frame, the other nearer the door, made on the floor or very low: on this my attendant slept.

I was put to bed with my arms fastened. Either that night or the next, the heavy leathern cases were taken off my arms, to my great delight, and replaced by a straight waistcoat. The night brought to me my usual torments, but I slept during part of it sounder and better than before. In the morning I recollect observing a book of manuscript prayers, and a prayer book or bible bound in blue morocco; the impression on my feelings was very dreary, and as if I had been imprisoned for a crime or for debt; but I was occupied as usual with the agony of mind occasioned by the incomprehensible commands, injunctions, insinuations, threats, taunts, insults, sarcasms, and pathetic appeals of the voices round me. Soon after I awoke, Zachary Gibbs made his appearance with a basin of tea and some bread and butter cut in small square pieces, about the size of those prepared for the holy sacrament. He staid in my room by my bed side, whilst I eat my breakfast.

I was not now aware that I was lunatic, nor did I admit this idea until the end of the year. I knew that I was prevented from discharging my duties to my Creator and to mankind, by some misunderstanding on my part; for which, on the authority of my spiritual accusers, I considered that I was wilfully guilty; racking my mind at the same time to divine their meaning. I imagined now that I was placed in this new position as a place of trial, that it might be seen whether I would persist in my malignant, or cowardly, or sluggish disobedience to the last. I imagined at the same time, that I was placed here *"to be taught of the spirits,"* that is, (for they all spoke in different keys, tones, and measures, imitating usually the voices of relations or friends,) to learn what was the nature of each spirit that spoke to me, whether a spirit of fun, of humour, of sincerity, of honesty, of honour, of hypocrisy, of perfect obedience, or what not, and to acquire knowledge to answer to the suggestions or arguments of each, as they in turn addressed me, or to choose which I would obey.

For instance, whilst eating my breakfast, different spirits assailed me, trying me. One said, eat a piece of bread for my sake, &c., &c.; another at the same time would say, refuse it for my sake, or, refuse *that piece* for my sake and take *that*; others, in like manner, would direct me to take or refuse my tea. I could seldom refuse one, without disobeying the other; and to add to my disturbance of mind, at these unusual phenomena, and at the grief of mind—and at times alarm, I appeared to feel at disobeying any, Zachary Gibbs stood by my bed-side observing me in a new character. I understood that he was now no longer Zachary Gibbs, but a spiritual body called HERMINET HERBERT, the personification, in fact, of that spirit which had attended me in Dublin, so intimately united with my Saviour; indeed in my mind almost identified with Jesus.

I understood that as a seal to the information I now received from my spirits, he had put on a nankeen jacket, in order by that colour to remind me of the dream, in which the Holy Ghost, who was his mother, had appeared to me, promising never to desert me. That he knew all my thoughts, and all I was inspired to do, and could not be deceived. He had come to aid me; but that at the same time, to prove my faith, that he would act as if he were a man in plain circumstances, if he saw I doubted.

Whilst therefore I was hesitating about each morsel I put into my mouth, he stood by, encouraging me to eat, and pressing me to finish my breakfast, or he would leave me and come back, saying, "What! have'nt you done yet?" Persuaded that he knew and commanded what was going on in my mind, I did not believe his encouragements sincere; but intended also to try me. I could not stand the ridicule I met with from my spirits, or to which I exposed myself in reality: I forced my conscience, wounding my spirits; teased, tormented, twitted, frightened, at times I was made to dupe my spirits by humor. Thus, it appeared to me that, whilst standing on the very threshold of heaven, eternal hell yawned at my feet; through my stupidity and impatience.

For about three mornings, my breakfast was brought to me in this manner; after breakfast, I was dressed, and for two or three days taken down to a small square parlour, with two windows opposite the entrance, looking over some leads into a court, thence over a garden to a flat country terminated by hills, about two or three miles off. The windows had iron Venetian blinds before them; looking through them, I saw snow on the leads; I was still under the impression that this was the effect of a dismal winter sent upon my country for my disobedience. There was a round mirror between the windows; in the left-hand side of the room, an iron fire-place with a fire in it. At the bottom of the grate, over the arch under which the cinders fall, a hideous face and mouth appeared moulded in the iron. At the end of the year, when I examined it again, I saw my eyes also had been deluded, unless the grate had been changed, for the ornament was a basket of flowers, not a face. Besides this, there was a horsehair sofa opposite the windows, against the wall; some chairs and a table; also a table against the wall in the centre of the room.

When I came into the room, there was a mild old rheumatic man there, who had on a white apron. He was of low stature, and in countenance resembling my father very strongly. My spirits informed me it was my father, who had been raised from the dead, in order, if possible, to assist in saving my soul. He was also in a spiritual body. Every thing in short, had been done to save me by quickening my affections, in order to overcome my torpor, and ingratitude, and fear of man. The chairs in the room, resembling those I had seen when a child in my father's dining-room; the very trees in the distance, resembling others in the prospect round my mother's house; almost all that I saw had been brought by the Almighty power, or infinite goodness of the Lord, and placed around me to quicken my feelings! If a man can imagine realizing these ideas, in any degree, awake, he may imagine what were my sufferings.

I asked now what I was to do. There was a newspaper lying on the table, but I could not read it, because, before I had been taken unwell in Dublin, when looking for guidance from the Holy Spirit, I had been diverted from reading the papers, except here and there, as if it were unwholesome to the mind. I thought it ungrateful now to have recourse to them for amusement, and for that reason, or "by that reply," in the language of my invisible companions, I decided my resolution, without quite satisfying them.

What was I to do? I was told it was necessary to do something "to keep my heart to my head, and my head to my heart," to prevent "my going into a wrong state of mind," phrases used to me. I was told, at length, to "waltz round the table, and see what I should see." I did that—nothing came of it. My attendant requested me to be quiet; at last, my dinner was brought. I had, if I recollect accurately, two dinners in this room—one was of a kind of forced meat; the other had bacon with it: both meals were very light, and although I did not refuse them, I recollect feeling that I could have eaten something more substantial, and also being nauseated at the forced meat and bacon, which, I considered, could not be exactly wholesome for me.

My dinner in this room was served on a tray, with a napkin, silver forks, decanters, &c. &c., and in these respects, such as was fitting for a gentleman.

Unfortunately, the second day I think after my entrance into this asylum, having no books, no occupation, nothing to do but to look out of window, or read the newspaper, I was again excited by my spirits to waltz round the room; in doing this, or at a future period, I caught the reflection of my countenance in the mirror, I was shocked and stood still; my countenance looked round and unmeaning: I cried to myself, "Ichabod! my glory has departed from me," then I said to myself, what a hypocrite I look like! So far I was in a right state of mind; but the next thought was, "how shall I set about to destroy my hypocrisy;" then I became again lunatic. Then I resumed my waltzing, and being directed to do so, I took hold of my old attendant to waltz with him; but at last, deeming that absurd, and finding him refuse, the spirits said, "then wrestle with him if you will." I asked him to wrestle; he refused. I understood this was to try me if I was sincere; I seized him to force him to wrestle; he became alarmed; an old patient in the asylum passing by the door, hearing a struggle, entered, and assisted in putting me into a straight waistcoat: I was forced down on the sofa. He apologized to me for it many months after, saying it was in the afternoon, when all the other assistants were out walking with their respective patients.

Thus commenced my second ruin; and the history of an awful course of sufferings and cruelties, which terminated in my recovery from my delusions about the beginning of the next year, and was followed by my confinement as a madman, for nearly two years in a sound state of mind; because I entered into dispute with my family on their conduct to me, and the nature of my treatment, determined to bring them to account at law, for the warning of others, and to satisfy my excited sense of wrong. I can no longer, after arriving at this period of my trials, call Dr. F—'s house by any other name than that it deserves, *mad-house*, for to call that, or any like that, an *asylum*, is cruel mockery and revolting duplicity!

I have already stated, that when I came to this house, I did not know that I was insane. And my insanity appears to me to have differed in one respect from that of many other patients; that I was not actuated by *impression* or feeling, but misled by audible inspiration, or *visible*, rather than *sensible* guidance of my limbs. To the voices I heard, and to these guidances, I surrendered up my judgment, or what remained to me of judgment, fearing that I should be disobeying the word of God, if I did not do so. When I first came to Dr. F—'s madhouse, my health was somewhat restored, my mind somewhat confirmed; yet my attendant informed me at the close of the year, I looked so ill when my brother left me, that he thought I could not live. I was like a child in thought and will, so far as my feeling were directed to those around me. I knew no malice, no vice. I imagined that they loved me, and were all deeply interested in the salvation of my soul, and I imagined too that I loved them dearly. Yet I wrestled with the keepers, and offered to do so with others, and struck many hard blows; sometimes, as one informed me, making it difficult for three strong men to control me, yet whenever I did this, I was commanded to do so. I was told that they knew I was commanded, that they wished me to do so, to prove my faith and courage, but that they were commanded to prove both till they were satisfied of my sincerity. I may safely say, that for nine entire months, if not for the whole of the period of my confinement in Dr. F—'s charge, I never spoke, hardly acted, and hardly thought, but by inspiration or guidance, and yet I suppose that never was there any one who so completely contradicted the will of the Almighty, or the desires of those around him, and I could not help laughing now at the delusions which made me constantly choose that conduct which was most disagreeable and terrifying to my doctor and his keepers, as in the reality the most agreeable to them, if I were not overcome by a sense of the cruel state of abandonment and exposure to their malice and ignorance in which I was left.

After being fastened in the straight waistcoat, I was taken down stairs to a long saloon or parlour, to the left of the little parlour I had been as yet confined to, and on the ground floor. There was a long table in the middle of the room, allowing space to pass round it, a fire on the left hand side, and a glass bow window and door at the further end. I was fastened in a niche on a painted wooden seat between the fire and the glass window, in the curve in the wall forming the bow at the end of the room; another niche opposite to me was occupied by a trembling grey headed old man; there were several other strange looking personages on the chairs about the room, and passing occasionally through the glass window door which looked out in the same direction as the windows of the room I had quitted, into a small court yard. I think I hear the door jarring now, as they slammed it to and fro. I marvelled at my position; my spirits told me that I was now in a mad-house, and I was told that it only remained for me to pray for the inmates, that they might be restored to their senses, and that they should be restored, but that I must then forego certain advantages. I attempted to pray, though I did not quite believe that I was in a mad-house, being unconscious of my own melancholy state, or imagining that I was placed there for convenience, not from necessity. There was an appearance of wretchedness and disorder amongst my associates, and I felt happy to be taken up to my bed-room after tea had been served in the evening.

The next morning my breakfast was brought to me as before in bed. I was dressed up stairs, and Herminet Herbert conducted me down to the seat I occupied the night before. There was an appearance of more cleanliness, order, and composure in the persons of the wretched individuals around me. Now I was told by my spirits that my prayer had been heard, that they had been restored to a sound state of mind, that they were in consequence among the redeemed of the Lord and knew that I had prayed for them, that they had in their turn desired to be allowed to remain with me one year as guides to me, and as a species of jury, to wait until I became obedient to the Almighty, and to judge me whether I was sincere in my difficulties or not; this delusion lasted for more than six months with this difference, that sometimes I conceived it my duty to recognize in their persons, relations, and friends, sometimes ministers and officers of the king.

*   *   *

The next morning after my entrance into the lunatics' common room, I observed three men, apparently *servants* or attendants of the gentlemen there. One was Herminet Herbert, whom in a black coat I was to address as Zachary Gibbs, and who I was afterwards told, on seeing him in a blue coat, was Samuel Hobbs; but under all these appearances he was one and the same Jesus. I used to call him Herminet Herbert, the simple and Jesus Christ. He was a short, active, fair, witty, clever man. The other was a tall, spare, aquiline nosed gawky man, from Devonshire, like a groom. The voices told me to call him at times Herminet Herbert Scott, at times, Sincerity; at times, Marshall; *that was his name.* The third was a stout, jovial, powerful man, like a labourer. The voices told me he was Herminet Herbert, the simple, God Almighty, and that I was to call him SIMPLICITY; his name was Poole. Besides this, a very stout, powerful dark man, like a coach-man, with a very small voice and gentle manners, was occasionally occupied in attending on me and other patients. I called him by order Herminet Herbert the Holy Ghost, or Kill-all. I understood these were incarnations or manifestations of the Trinity. A stout benevolent old gentleman, a lunatic, who was dressed in a suit of blue, and had been handsome, was I was informed, the Lord Jehovah, supremely omnipotent, the trinity in unity, who had taken upon himself the form of an old writing master who used to teach me when a child, and whose name was Waldony, by which name, and by that of Benevolence, I was at times desired to address him. Likewise I understood Herminet Herbert Scott, or Marshall, to be a favourite servant of my Father's, who had lived in our family at Hampstead, and had been raised from the dead with my father and my eldest sister to attend on me. And Herminet Herbert the simple, or Samuel Hobbs, I was told had lived in my mother's family after my father's death, and had been very fond of me and my brothers, and familiar with us; that my brothers had known at the time that he was Jesus, but that I had not; that during an illness I had had when young, he had wrestled with me in the school-room, it being necessary for my health, and he had come now in hopes of winning me to wrestle with him again, which was continually enjoined to me for the salvation of my soul, and the keeping me in a right state of mind. Several persons about the asylum, I was told, were my father, Dr. F., a Dr. L., and two aged keepers, one of whom I called Honesty; the other, my real father, because he most resembled him. Now, when I did not recognize any of these facts or any of these people, I was told it was on account of my ingratitude and my cowardice. That I feared to acknowledge objects as they were, because then I knew I must prepare to endure my awful torments.

Now all these persons, and each person around me, wore a triple character, according to each of which I was in turns to address them. Samuel Hobbs, for example, was at times to be worshipped in the character of Jesus, at times to be treated familiarly as Herminet Herbert, a spiritual body, at times to be dealt with as plain Samuel Hobbs. The stout old patient was at times knelt to as the Lord Jehovah; at times he was Mr.

Waldony, a spiritual body; at times a gentleman. So with the rest: and these changes took place so instantaneously, that I was completely puzzled as to my deportment towards them. I saw individuals and members of the family of Dr. F—, approach me in great beauty, and in obedience to a voice, my inclinations sprang forward to salute them, when in an instant, their appearance changed, and another command made me hesitate and draw back. In the same manner, when books, pencils, pens, or any occupation was presented to me, I turned from one page and one object, to another, and back again, usually ending in a fit of exasperation and inward indignation, against the guidance that so perplexed me.

*   *   *

Now with regard to my treatment, I have to make at first two general observations, which apply, I am afraid, too extensively to every system of management yet employed towards persons in my condition. First, the suspicion and the fact of my being incapable of reasoning correctly, or deranged in understanding, justified apparently every person who came near me, in dealing with me also in a manner contrary to reason and contrary to nature. These are strong words; but in the minutest instances I can, alas! prove them true. Secondly, my being likely to attack the rights of others gave these individuals license, in every respect, to trample upon mine. My being incapable of feeling, and of defending myself, was construed into a reason for giving full play to this license. Instead of my understanding being addressed and enlightened, and of my path being made as clear and plain as possible, in consideration of my confusion, I was committed, in really difficult and mysterious circumstances, calculated of themselves to confound my mind, even if in a sane state, to unknown and untried hands; and I was placed amongst strangers, without introduction, explanation, or exhortation. Instead of great scrupulousness being observed in depriving me of any liberty or privilege, and of the exercise of so much choice and judgment as might be conceded to me with safety;—on the just ground, that for the safety of society my most valuable rights were already taken away, on every occasion, in every dispute, in every argument, the assumed premise immediately acted upon was, that I was to yield, my desires were to be set aside, my few remaining privileges to be infringed upon, for the convenience of others. Yet I was in a state of mind not likely to acknowledge even the justice of my confinement, and in a state of defencelessness calculated to make me suspicious, and jealous of any further invasion of my natural and social rights; but this was a matter that never entered into their consideration.

Against this system of downright oppression, enforced with sycophantish adulation and affected pity by the doctor, adopted blindly by the credulity of relations, and submitted to by the patients with meek stupidity, or vainly resisted by natural but hopeless violence, I had to fight my way for two years, wringing from my friends a gradual but tardy assent to the most urgent expostulations: not from the physicians; their law is the same for all qualities and dispositions, and their maxim to clutch and hold fast.

The first step adopted towards me by my friend, Captain——, in Dublin, was injudicious and indelicate. If I had been incoherent, I had hitherto only rendered myself ridiculous; and if, by one act, I had run the risk of injuring my person, it was also evident that I had relinquished my purpose at the request of his family. I trace my ruin to the particular trials, to the surprise, the confusion, the puzzle, which the sudden intrusion of a keeper brought upon me. But at that time, unfortunately, I did not consider my dignity so much as my relationship to the Almighty, as his redeemed servant, bound in gratitude, and from self-abasement, to exercise forbearance and humility. If it be replied, My ruin might have been brought about another way; I answer, I do not know what might have been, but I know what did take place.

The first symptoms of my derangement were, that I gazed silently on the medical men who came to me, and resolutely persisted in acts apparently dangerous. No doubt there were also symptoms of bodily fever. But from that moment to the end of my confinement, men acted as though my body, soul, and spirit were fairly given up to their control, to work their mischief and folly upon. My silence, I suppose, gave consent. I mean, that I was never told, such and such things we are going to do; we think it advisable to administer such and such medicine, in this or that manner; I was never asked, Do you want any thing! do you wish for, prefer any thing? have you any objection to this or to that? I was fastened down in bed; a meagre diet was ordered for me; this and medicine forced down my throat, or in the contrary direction; my will, my wishes, my repugnances, my habits, my delicacy, my inclinations, my necessities, were not once consulted, I may say, thought of. I did not find the respect paid usually even to a child.

1849 ᘓᐳ

Five Months in the New-York State Lunatic Asylum, Anonymous

In colonial America and well into the nineteenth century many mad people were kept and cared for at home. Families who could afford to might hire a physician. Unfortunately, home care was never an assurance against ignorant treatment or abuse. Mad people who were confused, violent, or difficult might be chained or locked up in the cellar, outhouse, or attic by their families. In 1849 reformer Dorothea Dix described one extreme instance of such family "care." An Illinois woman had kept her brother locked up in a rough, open pen, approximately eight feet square. Every one or two weeks she would clean the area by having neighbors tie him down while they threw buckets of water into the pen. One winter the man's feet froze, crippling him. Still, the woman refused to send her brother to an institution, saying, "We had rather take care of him, than leave him to strangers, because we are kinder, and treat him much better than they would."[1]

Mad people without families were not likely to be much better off. In colonial times, welfare was strictly the responsibility of the local community. Sometimes, the results of this welfare were reasonable acts of charity. In 1721, for example, New York City voted to give a woman "commonly called Mad Sew" the following assistance: "a good pair of Shoes & Stockings & other Necessary Warm Clothing. She being Very Old Poor & Non Compos Mentis & an Object of Charity." Providence, Rhode Island, in 1655 voted to pay a man named Pike fifteen shillings and promised further financial assistance of up to ten pounds or more "for helpe in this his sad condition of his wife's distraction." New Haven in 1645 paid their town marshal to care for the Goodwife Lampson "so far forth as her husband is not able to do it." And for at least a decade after 1607 the town of Braintree, Massachusetts, paid for the boarding out of Abigail Neal into the homes of several physicians, hoping to cure her madness (pp. 47–50).

Often local governments simply placed their indigent mad in jail. Sometimes they built special cells. In 1789 a court at Upland, Pennsylvania, made the following order:

---

[1]As quoted by Deutsch, *The Mentally Ill in America*, p. 167. Hereafter cited in the text.

Jan Vorelissen, of Amesland, Complayning to ye Court that his son Erik is bereft of his naturall Senses and is turned quyt madd and yt, he being a poore man is not able to maintaine him; Ordered: yt three or four persons bee hired to build a little block-house at Amesland for to put in the said madman.

Braintree, Massachusetts, voted in 1689 "That Samuel Speere should build a little house 7 foote long & 5 foote wide & set it by his house to secure his Sister good wife Witty being distracted & provide for her." The New York State legislature in 1824 learned that the town of Danville had built a small house in the public square "for the express purpose of containing" an indigent mad person. And in the 1840s Dorothea Dix told of the way a small Rhode Island town had chosen to care for Abram Simmons, a mad pauper. The town had constructed a stone vault, some six to eight feet square, with an iron door and no window or ventilation. Simmons slept on wet straw thrown across an iron bed frame, covered only by two quilts. Frost coated the inside walls in winter, and Simmons' outer quilt was so wet and frosted it resembled a sheet of ice (pp. 42, 43, 125, 169).

Because local responsibility for welfare also meant local expense, the usual result was community resistance to welfare. In a report made in 1686 Governor Dongan of New York colony described the situation in these terms: "every Town and County are obliged to maintain their own poor, which makes them bee soe careful that noe Vagabonds, Beggars, nor Idle Persons are suffered to live here" (p. 44).

Early American communities were able to "bee soe careful" in a number of ways. By maintaining strict settlement laws they could deny residence to potential welfare cases. Strangers arriving in town were immediately scrutinized to determine their financial status; sometimes they had to furnish bond in order to remain. Usually a newcomer would not be an accepted member of a town until a respectable residency of three months to a year had been maintained. If at some time during that probationary period the person's financial welfare seemed to be precarious, he or she would be "warned out" of town. A historian of Roxbury, Massachusetts, notes that until the end of the eighteenth century "Indian stragglers and crazy persons" were frequently asked to leave town. Even persons who once held positions of high respectability might be subjected to this treatment. In 1742 Boston voted to warn out a former chaplain who had become "in a Distracted Condition & very likely to be a Town Charge" (p. 45). In some colonies a person faced a public whipping if he or she should dare to return. In New York, according to a law of 1721, the penalty for returning was thirty-six lashes on the bare back for a man and twenty-five for a woman.

Continuing well into the nineteenth century, local governments would "bee soe careful" about potential welfare cases by "dumping" them—that is, transporting them in the dark of night to another town. An official of Franklin, New York, described one instance of the cruel dumping of an indigent mad person. An elderly stranger traveling through Franklin became ill and "partially deranged." Incoherent, he was unable to tell anyone who he was or where he was from. Franklin town officials decided he was probably from the town of New Berlin so they dumped him in New Berlin. New Berlin did not want him and took the case to court. Eventually the old man was returned to Franklin. Finally, the fathers of Franklin decided he must be from Williamstown, Massachusetts, so they took him across the state border in the middle of the night and left him in the streets of Williamstown (p. 124).

Rural communities often took care of potential welfare cases by auctioning them off as farm labor. Usually the town would pay for the care of the pauper to the lowest bidder, but occasionally the indigent person appeared to be a good enough prospect for labor that a farmer would actually pay the town to take him in. Sometimes families were torn apart at the auction block. According to the town records of Gardner, Massachusetts, such was the fate of the Upton family in 1789:

> Oliver Upton and wife bid off by Simon Gates, at ten shillings per week. Oldest child bid off by Simon Gates, at one shilling per week. Second child bid off by John Heywood at ten pence per week. Third child bid off by Andrew Beard, at one shilling, two pence per week. Fourth child bid off by Ebenezer Bolton, at one shilling, nine pence per week. (P. 119)

For more than half a century after the American Revolution this bidding-out system was the dominant form of welfare throughout the nation.

One result of these practices was that some indigent persons, including the mad, simply wandered. An order of the General Assembly of Connecticut Colony in 1756 described one such drifter, "a strolling woman that has been sometime wandering from town to town, calling herself Susannah Roberts of Pennsylvania, who is so disordered in her reason and understanding that she passeth from place to place naked, without any regard for the laws and rules of decency." The assembly instructed the town of Wallingford to clothe this Susannah Roberts and to put her under the care of "some discreet person that she may labour for her support" (p. 46).

In America, as in Europe, the earliest establishments housing the indigent mad were simply catchall institutions for the needy. In France the *hôpitaux généraux* were founded early in the seventeenth century for this purpose, while the workhouse emerged in England somewhat later. The American counterpart was the "almshouse" or "poorhouse," which began in the late seventeenth century, but was not in general use until the end of colonial times. Like the *hôpitaux généraux* and the English workhouse, the American poorhouse eventually developed separate facilities for mad people, but the treatment was solely custodial.

The first poorhouse in America was built in Boston in 1662. As early as 1791 Delaware made mandatory the erection of a poorhouse in each county. But it was during the 1820s that for a brief time the poorhouse was seen as a panacea for the problems of the poor. In 1820 the Massachusetts legislature created a committee to carry out the first statewide study of the existing patterns of indigent relief. The committee presented its findings in 1821 and strongly recommended the establishment of a system of county-run poorhouses. The legislature quickly followed that recommendation. In 1800 Massachusetts had only thirty-five poorhouses within its borders. Mostly as a result of the 1821 recommendation the number by 1830 had more than tripled. After a similar statewide survey in 1824 the New York state legislature mandated that each county build and maintain its own poorhouse. Other states soon followed the leads of Massachusetts and New York. According to the idealized visions of the decade the poorhouse system would give the needy food, shelter, dignity, and occupational skills, and would give the taxpayer the cheapest form of relief—a sort of nineteenth-century WPA.

In some instances these early poorhouses fulfilled the hopes of the 1820s. Many actually had infirmaries to care for the sick and the mad, and in some cases these infirmaries evolved into great hospitals. New York's Bellevue, the Philadelphia General Hospital, and the New Orleans Charity Hospital all began as poorhouse infirmaries. In general, however, the experiment was a failure. It had perhaps been doomed from the beginning for two reasons: constant increases in population assured perpetual overcrowding, and the heterogeneity of the poorhouse inmates brought about disorganization, confusion of goals, and inadequate treatment.

By the 1840s and through the rest of century one of the principal goals of the various reform movements became the transfer of mad people from their wards in the poorhouse to the wards of the public asylums. In 1890 this was mandated by law in New York. But still, in 1926, a national survey showed that mad inmates were kept—sometimes under vile conditions—in many poorhouses throughout the country. As late as 1933 one midwestern poorhouse chained its mad inmates to trees during the day.

A few hospitals and asylums were opened between 1752 and 1830. In theory these were a radical change from the poorhouse: the difference lay in the goal of therapy, treatment, and cure. In practice, unfortunately, the difference was not always so great. But even at the very worst, when these new institutions degenerated to mere places of confinement, the existence of the therapeutic ideal held at least a promise for the future.

In 1750 Benjamin Franklin and a group of prominent Philadelphia Quakers proposed the creation of the first public American hospital, to be called Pennsylvania Hospital. Two years later two patients, one of them mad, were taken into temporary quarters while the permanent edifice of Pennsylvania Hospital was under construction. The following blacksmith's bill to the hospital may give us some idea of what the new building was to be like: "John Cresson, blacksmith, against ye hospital 1 pair of handcuffs, 2 legg locks, 2 large rings and 2 large staples, 5 links and 2 swifells for legg chains" (p. 61). By 1756 the building was finished and patients began moving in. Upon admission mental patients were bled, purged, shaved to the scalp, and then given a cell in the basement where they were chained by the waist or ankle to the walls. The basement cells were about ten feet square, half underground, and unheated. They were constructed of solid stone walls with a barred window at one end and a heavy door at the other; through an opening in the door, food and other necessities might be passed. The patients were often restrained with handcuffs, ankle-irons, chains, and a form of straitjacket known as the "madd-Shirt." During the first few years the keepers carried whips and used them. The whips were soon phased out, however, and by 1796 mental patients were taken out of those cold, damp basement cells and settled into a new wing.

By 1830 thirteen hospitals and asylums had been constructed as far west as Kentucky and Ohio but mostly along the eastern seaboard. Perhaps the most important thing to realize about these institutions is that their impact was not great. Although a few were built and maintained according to enlightened principles, most were rough establishments where care was crude and inadequate. The nation's population was small in comparison to what it is today, but these early hospitals were still ineffectual in their numbers and size. By the end of the 1820s, for instance, Massachusetts' one asylum, McLean Asylum, had room for only 23 patients. The Maryland Hospital had space for 40 mental patients. The Eastern Kentucky Lunatics Asylum was filled to capacity with 200 patients and the Ohio Lunatics Asylum with 160. Despite the fact that every one of these early state institutions provided for some indigent patients, few local governments ever sent their paupers to them. Hospital and asylum care was simply more expensive than the usual local systems of care. An indigent patient, for example, could stay at New York's Bloomingdale Asylum for $2.00 a week, but local governments could keep their welfare cases in jails and poorhouses for a mere $.50 to $1.00 per week.

Before 1830 no state other than Virginia had wholly provided for its mad; but by 1873, every state in America except Delaware and one or two western states had built at least one asylum. Between 1840 and 1870, while the overall population of the United States increased only three and one-half times, the number of mad and allegedly mad people in state-run institutions increased from twenty-five hundred to seventy-four thousand (p. 232).

In the most general terms this trend toward state care was part of a larger transition in America from a loosely organized, rural, and agricultural society to a more centrally organized, urban, and industrial society. The trend toward specialized care—from the poorhouse to the asylum—was part of an overall change in ideas about the appropriate treatment of mad people taking place throughout the western world. Over the century the patients of the *hôpitaux généraux* of France, the workhouses of England, and the poorhouses of America were gradually transferred into institutions specializing, or claiming to specialize, in psychiatric care.

In America there was also the "cult of curability" and its own peculiar and fascinating influence. Certain physicians early in the century had been making extraordinary claims about the curability of madness, given proper institutional care. By mid-century the fashion of easy curability had become so powerful that many superintendents of American institutions doctored their statistics to suggest cure rates of 90 percent or higher. In 1843 Dr. William Awl of the Ohio State Lunatic Asylum was able to claim a one hundred percent cure rate—by considering only the patients who had been discharged. He became

known as Dr. Cure-Awl (p. 153). The substance of such claims may
have been the stuff of dreams and wishes, but their effect was quite real
and even perhaps beneficial. The concept of easy curability with proper
treatment tremendously stimulated the development of American asylums in the 1830s and 1840s.

Perhaps the single most important inspiration for asylum construction
in nineteenth century America was Dorothea Lynde Dix (1802–
1887), a retired schoolteacher from New England. In the winter of 1841
Dix taught a Sunday school class in a jail in East Cambridge. There
she saw several deranged people locked in cells without heat. She
asked the jailer to give them heat and he refused, saying, "The insane
need no heat." Dix took the issue to the East Cambridge court and
won: the mad inmates of the jail were provided heat. She was
touched by the incident and went on for the next two years touring
the entire state of Massachusetts and seeing for herself the treatment
of mad people in that state.

With the results of her two-year survey Dix addressed the Massachusetts legislature giving the following inventory. In Lincoln one
madwoman was caged. In Medford one retarded person was
chained, another had been kept in a closed stall for seventeen years.
In Concord a woman was kept in a cage in a poorhouse. In Savoy one
man was caged. In Lenox, two mad persons were kept in the town
jail. And so proceeded her list. From town to town, county to county,
she gave her evidence of inhuman treatment of the mad and mentally
retarded to the state legislature. The opposition was immediate and
noisy, but by a large majority the legislature voted to enlarge Worcester
State Hospital to take in the indigent mad from the jails and the poorhouses of the state.

From there Dix went to Rhode Island, then to New Jersey. During
the next decade she went through every state in the union east of the
Rockies. In each case she exposed the treatment of the mad and
proposed a single solution—the construction and expansion of state
asylums. By the end of her career in 1881 she was directly responsible
for the creation or expansion of thirty-two asylums in the United
States and abroad.

The tendency for the rest of the century was toward the creation of
more and more similar institutions. But it seemed that as soon as an
institution was built, it was filled to capacity. Furthermore, the asylums themselves were often not much better than the poorhouses
they were meant to replace. Reformists had tended to see the state
asylum as an end in itself. Conditions in the poorhouses and jails
were so bad, and the advocates of easy curability had made such
enticing promises, that many reformists attributed almost a magical

curative aura to the mere edifices of these new public psychiatric institutions. The urgency and faith with which these nineteenth-century public institutions were created produced a nationwide system of specialized institutional buildings, but it did not produce a nationwide system of specialized treatment. With few exceptions these American asylums were characterized more by their lack of treatment than by treatment. At best they had discarded some of the old regimen—bloodletting, excessive coercion—but seldom made significant replacements.

We know little about the anonymous narrator of the early American protest, *Five Months in the New-York State Lunatic Asylum* (1849). He was a fourteen-year resident of Buffalo, New York. He may have been a businessman. He may well have been the same person who registered the work in 1848, a Mr. W. Hotchkiss. At any event, in 1847 the narrator experienced "a very high fever in [his] head" and became "very much deranged." He describes that experience of derangement in this way: "My brain seemed like a liquid mass, throbbing, rolling, tumbling, foaming and evaporating. My imagination roamed over wild creation in wild and eccentric flights. Thoughts rushed in rapid succession into my mind, and as rapidly rolled from my lips, independent of my own volition. I had no more control over my thoughts words and actions, than I have now over the raging tempest." Someone bound him hand and foot and sent him by carriage to the recently opened state asylum in Utica where he stayed five months.

Soon after his release he published *Five Months in the New-York State Lunatic Asylum*, a "plain statement of facts" to the public and an "execution of . . . duty." The work is interesting partly because it gives some unusually vivid descriptions of what we would now call "mania." It is even more interesting as a rare inside view of the great institutional hope of the nineteenth century: the state asylum.

During the 1800s New York was a leader in social and institutional reform. The Utica Asylum, which opened in 1843, was New York's first state asylum and the most costly asylum in the entire country. It was the first to have steam heat. It was also the first asylum to adopt, in 1846, a form of restraint known as "the crib," sometimes called the "Utica crib": a wooden structure like a baby crib with a lid on top in which the patient could be pinned. The first superintendent of Utica, Dr. Amariah Brigham, was one of the best and most prominent psychiatric physicians of his time. He was one of the founders of what is now the American Psychiatric Association and originated *The American Journal of Psychiatry*. Utica fell woefully short of providing for all the indigent mad in New York (an 1855 survey counted 2,123 indigent mad, with only 296 at Utica). Nonetheless, it was hoped that the enlightened system of treatment would be a model for the state asylums opening up across the country.

Given such a rosy official view, it is only reasonable to examine in detail this anonymous unofficial insider's view of the same institution. The narrator himself quickly suggests that there will be a conflict between the external and internal views of Utica: "When people visit or take friends to the Asylum, they are invited into the office or sitting room, which is carpeted and furnished in good style. The doctors are very polite; and perhaps speak eloquently of their wonderful success in treating the insane." And his own view indeed contradicts the optimism of the times. In spite of the modern setting and expensive construction, the narrator describes the crowding and herding of patients into large halls, the inadequate portions of food, and scrambling and conniving for food among patients. The superintendent, Dr. Brigham, is certainly a prominent psychiatric physician but the writer seldom sees him. Most of the time he remains under the control of a handful of untrained and vicious attendants who beat him, force medicines down his throat, choke him, and sometimes throw him to the floor and jump on him. One attendant threatens him with a knife. The narrator concludes with this comment on the new, developing state asylum system: "The different counties of this state can provide a home for their insane, as well and as cheap, as they can support them at the Asylum, and save the expense of travel."

In his preface the writer promises "a plain statement of facts." Occasionally he resorts to strong, simple metaphor: "My blood throbbed like a boiling pot; my tongue was parched with a raging fever." But his style is generally straightforward, with surprisingly little intrusion of opinion or emotion. Nonetheless, there is a selectivity and collapsing of events that at last floods us with images of cruelty and brutality, leading finally to a Dantesque vision of hell. The narrator concludes his work with this fervent statement: "Is it thus to be treated like swine, that you send your friends from their own houses to the asylum? That Institution professes to the world to be a home for the suffering insane, but to them it is a *hell!*"

ON THE SEVENTH DAY of November, 1847, I was taken from the city of Buffalo and carried to the New York State Lunatic Asylum at Utica. I had a very high fever in my head; it may have been the inflammation on the brain, but I know not what it was. I was very much deranged, and had been for two days previous to my removal from Buffalo. Until that time I had regularly attended to my business. I was bound hand and foot, and fastened to the bottom of the car; I knew not whither I was going. When I reached Utica I was much worse from the effect of my ride. My head felt like a ball of fire; I was in constant fear of those who attended me. But one of them, in whom I had the most confidence, after I was taken from the cars at Utica and placed in a carriage to be conveyed to the Asylum, saw that I was afraid of my attendants. He placed his cold hand on my cheek and assured me that I should not be injured; this greatly quieted me, for I believed what he said. In apprehension that I might escape, they placed a rope around my breast; this exceedingly increased my fear, supposing the Thugs of India had me in tow; but when he soothed me with kind words, my fear to a great extent was removed. While on our way to the Asylum there fell a refreshing shower of rain. I held my head uncovered out of the carriage window; the rain cooled very much my brain. I supposed it was a breeze from the ocean, and passing a cottage which resembled one I had seen in New Haven, Connecticut, I imagined I was in that city, and that the Asylum was Yale College. I cannot tell precisely where I was taken from the carriage, but I think it was in the inclosure in the rear of the Asylum. An attendant supported my weak frame on either side. At the door we met Dr. Brigham. He asked me if I remembered a person (calling his name) who had been an inmate in the Institution, from Buffalo. I think I made no reply. The doctor's countenance made an impression upon my mind which will never be effaced. It was full of kindness and sympathy. Had he then taken me by the hand and conducted me to a good bed, I think I should have secured some rest; and by such a manifestation of regard for me, he would have so completely gained my confidence that he could have controlled me as he pleased. But there are too many inmates in the Asylum, to receive such attentive treatment. I did not stop, but was hurried onward. I do not recollect who were by my side. I had but one glance at Dr. Brigham. We passed through a long hall in the basement, which had rooms on either side. There were potatoes in one room, and bricks were scattered along the hall, which made an unfavorable impression upon my mind. We soon passed into another hall in which there were some lunatics, who looked worse to me than bricks and potatoes. I was placed in a cell eight or ten feet square. A door which had open-work at the top, was locked after me; a batten door closed upon the outside of the jamb-casing of the inside door, so that I could not see into the hall. There was one window in the room, with iron bars on the outside of the sash. A wooden shutter made like a picket gate, opened on the inside of the window, but it was kept locked to secure the window from the inmate of the room. When I was conducted into the room, I was exhausted and fell to the floor. I did not again see those who, a few moments before, had promised me that I should not be injured. My confidence in all human beings was fast failing. I imagined the floor I was on was hung on hinges, and served for a trap-door to let persons through into a dissecting room, which I supposed was under it. I thought those who came with me to the Asylum, had sold me to the Doctor for dissection, and that one of them had gone below to unfasten the floor and let me down. I fancied the floor moved; I sprung to the window; held on to the shutter till I supposed they had given me up, or some one had come to my rescue. The floor did not fall, and I conjectured the reason why it did not, was that it wanted my weight to carry it down. Concluding that some one had made it fast, I let go my hold on the shutter and ventured myself again upon the floor. Soon after this, Dr. Brigham, with two other persons, opened my door, and took me to a room on the opposite side of the hall. They took a sketch of my features with a pencil as I supposed. They then returned me to the side of the hall whence they had taken me, but to a room, I believe, next below the one in which I was first placed. It was of the same size of my first room. When the door was closed on me, I saw that it was gnawed half through in some places. On the wall was marked or drawn the form of a man lying horizontally, with the head of a nail or screw in each joint. This figure produced great fear in my mind.

From the window of my room I looked into an enclosed yard, in which were kept a large buck and doe, and where the patients in the summer season are let out to play ball. Had it been in my power, I would have given worlds to a kind friend, who would have taken me from that dismal place, and given me a comfortable room. Some doves flew past my window—I was delighted with the sight, for they seemed harmless. I imagined they were the ones that Noah had in the Ark; and the buck having branching horns, I fancied was the beast with ten horns mentioned in Holy Writ.

In a short time, the batten door to my cell was opened, and a piece of bread was handed me through the open-work of the inner door. My taste was bad, but I took the bread, and it tasted like dung. I threw it back, and told the attendant that it was dung. The moment it struck the floor, a half a dozen or more patients scrambled after it, as though they had been without food for a week. One black imp, whom, upon first sight, I had considered an Egyptian mummy and incapable of motion, won the prize and instantly swallowed the bread. I believed the inmates had just risen from the dead and were shut up for a season in prison with the spirits of the damned. My outer-door was soon closed, and I saw no more of them for some time.

It now began to grow dark. I looked out of my window; a brick wing erected at right angles to the stone or front building was in full view. They were lighting up in the different halls, which greatly pleased my fancy. I thought there was some one who would rescue me soon. I thought my wife had risen from the dead, and would help me as soon as she could. I raised myself up to my window by holding on to the inside shutter, and talked pretty loud of victory and of never giving up until the last breath of life was taken from me. I fell from my window three times exhausted, and the fourth time I clung with a deadly grasp, determined never to let go my hold while life lasted, and not to stop talking as long as I could move my tongue. It is impossible to describe my feelings. I knew not what I had done to deserve such treatment. Two beings bearing the forms of men, then entered my cell and laid hold of me, one on each side. They drew me from the window and said it was enough, and I thought it was finished as they threw me headlong upon the floor. The back of my head struck the floor, and I lay senseless, I know not how long. I suppose I lay thus until morning. Whether I had a bed of straw that night or not, I do not know.

There was no bed of any kind when I entered the room, nor a seat to sit upon. The next I recollect it was daylight. Two men were holding me with a gag in my mouth, pouring in medicine of some kind which I thought was aqua fortis.

*   *   *

There were, I think, between thirty and forty patients in this hall. There were five negroes; and two or three whites, who, I was told, had committed murder. Some were from the State Prisons, and others from the poor houses of the several counties. In this hall most of the patients were together during the day, but at night were locked up in seperate rooms. During the day some were up for office, running for president, some pleading law, some preaching, praying, cursing and swearing; others were lying and fighting, hallooing murder, having fits, and others still were dancing and crying; some were naked, and some were doing nothing. I can only give a description of this hall for one or two days; and I think that will satisfy all who may read these pages. I was informed that the name of the first attendant in this hall was WARREN POTTER; the name of the second attendant, I believe, was HUNT or HUNTER. I thought the first attendant was MOHAMMED, and the second half an aligator or man eater. At three or four o'clock in the afternoon, each day, POTTER places himself at the head of the hall, and cries at the top of his voice, "pots." At the sound of his voice all the patients rush from different parts of the hall, under full headway, for the pot-room, each one straining his nerves and lungs, and crying "pots," "pots," "pots;" and from the confusion one would think there was nothing left in the world except pots; but when his room is unlocked at five o'clock in the morning, and each one sets his pot out side of the door and in the hall, all who have the sense of smelling find there is something left besides pots. Some of the pots are not large enough, and consequently run over; some get broken; some patients are pulled out of bed, and in the affray their pots are turned over, which leaves the contents running upon the floor, mixed with tobacco juice, which altogether makes a good job. Don't it? And now all is hurry and bustle—some carrying pots to the washroom; some running for the water closet with pail, mop, and water, and others dressing, and some swearing—I generally went to the veranda to obtain fresh air. POTTER soon comes in with medicine for some of the patients. I took it three times each day while I was in this hall, which was between three and four months. When he finds that I have the window up, he would order it down, and order me to take a dose of something out of a mug similar to those Deacon GILES' workmen carried when in his distillery, and not to raise the window again under penalty of being shut up in a dark room, as they call it. But I loved fresh air at this time, and talking out of the window, so well, I could not obey, and up went the window; and then in came two attendants and a watchman. They would sometimes strap the mittens on so tight that it made me faint. They would throw me headlong upon the floor, then one would take hold of my shoulders and one hold of my legs. Sometimes one would catch hold of my cravat and nearly choke me, and would almost stop my breath; but if the mittens were not on, perhaps I could get two fingers between my cravat and throat in order to keep my windpipe from being broken.

Now commences the chase. They run the length of the hall in this manner, pouncing me at every jump upon the floor with all their might, at the same time endeavoring to loosen my hold of my cravat, for fear it would not choke hard enough to suit their purpose. Then I am pressed into the room, excited and feeling bad that any thing in the form a man could treat a human being in such a barbarous manner. My shattered and fevered brain becomes heated and my mind enraged. I curse the attendant and bid him defiance, that he can not kill me, although I never raised a hand to injure him or to defend myself, yet he is enraged at my talk. Two stand and look on while I lie upon my back on the bare floor, and POTTER jumps with his knees some half dozen times into my breast with all his might, then leaves me locked up until breakfast; perhaps all day. I have no seat to sit upon nor bench on which to recline; my hands sometimes made fast by the mittens; if I lie on the bare floor my head is too low; if I am on my back, the lock or staple cuts the bones and flesh; the mittens secure my hands so that below my elbows my arms are at right angles with the part above, and when I turn upon my side it brings my elbows under the short ribs; if I turn upon my breast the staples cut my hands; so that in no position could I enjoy any ease. Many a night I lay in this torturing manner while in the basement. If I am left all day, HUNT comes with bread and water or coffee, feeds me and at the same time remarks; "that he is feeding the animal." It enrages me; I reply that the beast is doing it. If I am lying down when the attendant comes to the door, he orders me up; but he never assists me. I have to turn on my knees and elbows; my knees being covered with sores, the blood spirting out and running quite freely, sometimes filled my shoes half full; when it dries up it sticks my drawers fast to the sores, so that all is pain.

1868 ⇥

The Prisoner's Hidden Life, or Insane Asylums Unveiled: As Demonstrated by the Report of the Investigating Committee of the Legislature of Illinois. Together with Mrs. Packard's Coadjutors' Testimony, by Elizabeth Parsons Ware Packard

In 1860 the Reverend Theophilus Packard committed his wife, Elizabeth, to the Illinois State Asylum at Jacksonville. In fact very little in Elizabeth Packard's appearance or behavior suggested madness. Her greatest offense seemed to be openly disagreeing with her husband on religious matters within his church. She insisted that she was locked up "for simply expressing religious opinions in a community who were unprepared to appreciate and understand them," but according to the Illinois commitment law of 1851 Packard's sanity or madness did not matter: married women could be held in an asylum indefinitely, solely on the authority of their husbands with the concurrence of the asylum superintendent.

Though she was usually denied writing materials Packard kept a journal, hiding the pages behind her mirror, in false liners of her hatbox and satchel, and inside her bonnet. Released in 1863, after three years' confinement, Packard proceeded to publish a number of protests partly based on that asylum journal. At the same time she lobbied to change state commitment laws and in 1867 persuaded the Illinois legislature to pass into law a "personal liberty bill" requiring trial by jury before a person could be committed. In 1872, due to Packard's influence, Iowa passed a similar law. Other states followed suit.

The concept of jury trial commitments, however, was doomed to fail. For various reasons, Illinois repealed its "personal liberty" law in 1892, after Packard's death. In the twentieth century many states still had jury trial commitment procedures, but the liberal psychiatric movement became progressively convinced that such commitments were bad. It was argued that jury trials caused unnecessary public embarrassment to the patient, suggested criminality, were slow, and were liable to be unfair due to the medical naïveté of jurors. In 1930 the First International Congress of Mental Hygiene recommended the abolition of all such laws, and the American Psychiatric Association soon echoed that sentiment. By the middle of the twentieth century nearly all commitments were taking place without appeal to a jury. Any person could be imprisoned indefinitely, essentially on the word of one or two psychiatric experts.

In *Insane Asylums Unveiled,* Packard describes severe beatings, chokings, forced cold baths (a therapy of the time), and subtler forms of abuse, but she is most absorbed by the broader issues of the civil rights of mental patients and of women. She notes that an 1867 investigation of the Illinois Asylum at Jacksonville found some 148 women detained "without the proper legal evidence of their insanity." She also describes the situations of individual women incarcerated by their husbands. Finally, she attaches at the end of her own narrative the testimonies of five other female patients at Jacksonville three of whom insist they were never mad.

In the following excerpts, Packard describes her seizure and transportation to the Illinois asylum; in the final scene we are left with the image of her four younger children, broken-hearted at the separation from their mother. Packard's habits of melodrama tend to weaken the pathos of the actual event. The exclamation points lose their effect after a while, as do the rhetorical "O's." Packard's description of her son, George, running down the track after the train loses much of its effect when we realize that she could never have witnessed that event; at best, it is dramatized after hearsay. Nonetheless, through all the reconstruction and dramatization of this story, there is a moving real event. The basic scenes and dramatis personae are true-to-life. With exaggeration and melodrama stripped away, the picture remains of a hard, authoritarian husband, a firm yet rational and dignified wife, a family torn apart. In another time, under different laws, this might have been the story of a simple marital breakup. As it stands, it is the story of a husband dreadfully abusing a wife with the full cooperation of his community and the State of Illinois.

AND NOW THE FATAL HOUR had come that I must be transported into my living tomb. But the better to shield himself in this nefarious work, Mr. Packard tried to avail himself of the law for commitment in other cases, which is to secure the certificate of two physicians that the candidate for the Asylum is insane.

Therefore at this late hour I passed an examination made by our two doctors, both members of his church and our bible class, and opponents to me in argument, wherein they decided that I was insane, by simply feeling my pulse!

This scene is so minutely described in the "Introduction to my Three Years Imprisonment," that I shall not detail it here. The doctors were not in my room over three minutes, conducting this examination, and without asking me a single question, both said while feeling my pulse, "she is insane!"

My husband then informed me that the "forms of law" were now all complied with, and he now wished me to dress for a ride to Jacksonville Insane Asylum. I complied, but at the same time entered my protest against being imprisoned without a trial, or some chance at self-defence. I made no physical resistance however, when he ordered two of his church-members to take me up in their arms, and carry me to the wagon and thence to the cars, in spite of my lady-like protests, and regardless of all my entreaties for some sort of trial before commitment.

My husband replied, "I am doing as the laws of Illinois allow me to do—you have no protector in law but myself, and I am protecting you now! it is for your good I am doing this, I want to save your soul—you don't believe in total depravity, and I want to make you right."

"Husband, have I not a right to my opinions?"

"Yes, you have a right to your opinions, if you think right."

"But does not the constitution defend the right of religious toleration to all American citizens?"

"Yes, to all citizens it does defend this right, but you are not a citizen; while a married woman you are a legal nonentity, without even a soul in law. In short, you are dead as to any legal existence while a married woman, and therefore have no legal protection as a married woman." Thus I learned my first lesson in that chapter of common law, which denies to married woman a legal right to her own identity or individuality.

The scenes transpiring at the parsonage, were circulated like wild-fire throughout the village of Manteno, and crowds of men and boys were rapidly congregating at the depot, about one hundred rods distant from our house, not only to witness the scene, but fully determined to stand by their pledge to my son, I.W., that his mother should never leave Manteno depot for an Insane Asylum.

The long two-horse lumber wagon in which I was conveyed from my house to the depot, was filled with strong men as my body guard, including Mr. Packard, his deacons, and Sheriff Burgess, of Kankakee city among their number. When our team arrived at the depot, Mr. Packard said to me, "now, wife, you will get out of the wagon yourself, won't you? You won't compel us to lift you out before such a large crowd, will you?"

"No, Mr. Packard, I shall not help myself into an Asylum. It is *you* who are putting me there. I do not go willingly, nor with my own consent—I am being forced into it against my protests to the contrary. Therefore, I shall let you show yourself to this crowd, just as you are—my persecutor, instead of my protector. I shall make no resistance to your brute force claims upon my personal liberty—I shall simply remain a passive victim, helpless in your power." He then ordered his men to transport me from the wagon to the depot in their arms.

*   *   *

As soon as I was landed in the cars, the car door was quickly locked, to guard against any possible reaction of the public, manly pulse, in my defence. Mr. Packard, Deacon Dole, and Sheriff Burgess seated themselves near me, and the cars quietly moved on towards my prison tomb, leaving behind me, children, home, liberty and an untarnished reputation. In short, all, *all*, which had rendered life desirable, or tolerable.

Up to this point, I had not shed a tear. All my nervous energy was needed to enable me to maintain that dignified self-possession, which was indispensably necessary for a sensitive womanly nature like my own, to carry me becomingly through scenes, such as I have described. But now that these scenes were past, my hitherto pent up maternal feelings burst their confines, and with a deep gush of emotion, I exclaimed, "O! what will become of my dear children!" I rested my head upon the back of the seat in front of me, and deliberately yielded myself up to a shower of tears. O! thought I, "what will my dear little ones do, when they return to their desolate home, to find no mother there! O their tender, loving hearts, will die of grief, at the story of their mother's wrongs!"

Yes, it did well nigh rend each heart in twain, when the fact was announced to them, that they were motherless! My sons, I. W., and George were just about this time returning from their prairie errand, and this fact was now being communicated to them, by some one returning from the depot, whom they met near the same. When within speaking distance, the first salutation they heard was, "Well, your mother is gone."

"What?" said I. W., thinking he had misunderstood.

"Your mother is gone!"

Supposing this was only an old rumor revived, he carelessly replied, "No she isn't, she is at home; where I just left her, and I am now on the way there to take her to ride with me."

"But she *has* gone—I just came from the depot, and saw her start."

Now, for the first time, the terrible truth flashed upon his mind, that this is the reason George and I have been sent off on this errand, and this accounts also, for the attentions so lavishly bestowed upon us this morning by my groom, by my father, and by Mr. Comstock. Yes, this awful fact at last found a lodgment in his sensitive heart, when he, amid his choking and tears could just articulate, "George! we have no mother."

Now George, too, knew why he had been so generously treated to sugar-plums that morning, and he too burst into loud crying, exclaiming, "they shall not carry off my mother."

"But they have carried her off! We have no mother!" said I. W. Here they both lifted up their voices and wept aloud, and as the team entered the village, all eyes were upon them, and others wept to see them weep, and to listen to their plaintive exclamations, "We have no mother! We have no mother!" As they drew near the front of Mr. Comstock's store, seeing the crowd settling there, I. W. felt his indignation welling up within him, as he espied among this crowd some of his volunteer soldiers in his mother's defence, and having learned from his informant that no one had taken his dear mother's part, he reproachfully exclaimed, as he leaped from his wagon, "And this is the protection you promised my mother! What is your gas worth to me!"

They felt the reproaches of a guilty conscience, and dared not attempt to console them. Mr. Comstock was the only one who ventured a response in words. He said, "You must excuse me, I. W., for I did what I thought would be the best for you. I knew your father was determined, and he would put her in at any rate; and I knew too, that your opposition would do no good, and would only torment you to witness the scene. So I had you go for your good!" "For my good!" thought he, "I think I should like to be my own judge in that matter!" He spoke not one reproachful word in reply, but quickly sought his mother's room, where he might weep alone.

But George, knowing the direction the cars went with his mother, ran on the track after them, determined he never would return until he could return with his mother rescued from prison! He was not missed until he was far out of hearing, and almost out of sight—he only looked like a small speck on the distant track. They followed after him; but he most persistently refused to return, saying, "I will get my dear mamma out of prison! My mamma shan't be locked up in a prison! I will not go home without my mother!"

He was of course forced back, but not to stay—only until he could make another escape. They finally had to imprison him— my little manly boy of seven years, to keep him from running two hundred miles on the track to Jacksonville, to liberate his imprisoned mother!

But O, my daughter! no pen can delineate thy sorrow, to find thy mother gone! perhaps forever gone! from thy companionship, counsel, care and sympathy! She wept both night and day, almost unceasingly; and her plaintive moans could be heard at quite a distance from her home. "O! mother! mother! mother!" was her almost constant, unceasing call. Her sorrow almost cost her her reason and her life. And so it was with I. W. He grieved himself into a settled fever, which he did but just survive; and during its height, he moaned incessantly for his mother, not knowing what he said! His reason for a time was lost in delirium.

But my babe, thank God! was too young to realize his loss. *For him*, I suffered enough for two human beings.

Here we leave these scenes of human anguish, to speak one

word of comfort for the wives and mothers of Illinois. Conscious that there had already been innocent victims enough offered in sacrifice on the altar of injustice, in consequence of these cruel laws of Illinois against my own sex, I determined to appeal, single handed and alone, if necessary, to their Legislature, to have them repealed, and thereby have the personal liberty of married women protected by law, as well as by the marital power. Consequently, in the winter of 1867, I came alone, and at my own expense, from Massachusetts to Illinois, and paid my board all winter in Springfield, Illinois, trying to induce the Legislature to repeal the barbarous law under which I was imprisoned, and pass in its stead a "Bill for the Protection of Personal Liberty," which demands a fair jury trial of every citizen of the State, before imprisonment in any Insane Asylum in the State. The Legislature granted my request. They repealed the barbarous law, and passed the Personal Liberty Bill, by an unanimous vote of both houses. So that now, no wife or mother in Illinois need fear the re-enacting of my sad drama in her own case; for, thank God! your personal liberty is now protected by just laws.

1869 ᴈᴇ

The Trial of Ebenezer Haskell, in Lunacy, and His Acquittal Before Judge Brewster, in November, 1868, together with a Brief Sketch of the Mode of Treatment of Lunatics in Different Asylums in this Country and in England, with Illustrations, Including a Copy of Hogarth's Celebrated Painting of a Scene in Old Bedlam, in London, 1635

A photograph of Ebenezer Haskell on the frontispiece of his book shows him to be middle-aged, portly, and generally dignified. He is formally dressed, wearing a black coat, white shirt, and a loose black cravat. His eyes are dark and not very expressive, his nose is broad. Most notably, he sprouts a full, curly white beard. The white hair of his head is thin, receding, and combed forward at the temples. His expression is almost blank, with no social smile, just the trace of a slightly quizzical frown and a pensive lowering of the brow.

In a preface he describes himself in positive terms. He had been a resident of Philadelphia for over forty years; he "won by honest industry a fair name and fame in business circles." Like many other protest writers before him, Haskell tries hard to project a persona of sobriety, promising "simply to speak a few plain unvarnished truths." But there is almost no other information about his life before he became a patient.

In May 1866 a police officer interrupted Haskell's breakfast and took him to the Philadelphia Almshouse, not explaining why. At the almshouse, forty-three dollars in cash and a gold watch were taken from him, his beard was shaved, his hair was cropped, and he was placed in a yard with some five hundred other patients in the Almshouse Insane Department. A few days later he was removed to the Pennsylvania Hospital for the Insane where he remained until June when his wife removed him against the advice of hospital physicians. Over the next two years authorities took him back to the almshouse three times but he escaped each time—once by sawing through a barred window. During his final escape he broke his leg and was captured and taken to the Pennsylvania Hospital (different from the Pennsylvania Hospital for the Insane). In November 1868 he had to appear before court, apparently in an attempt to establish a long-term commitment, but the court ruled in his favor.

Was he mad? Physicians at the trial insisted he was. Dr. S. P. Jones, a physician from the Pennsylvania Hospital for the Insane, described Haskell as unusually loquacious, excitable, and hostile toward his family, accusing them of conspiring to lock him up over the issue of an inheritance. Jones went on to say that symptoms of mania often included: "enmity towards family, aversion to relatives." On the other hand Jones noted that in madness "excretions from the skin are often offensive," and such was not the case with Haskell. Nonetheless the physician concluded that the man had been mad. Dr. S. Butler, a physician from the almshouse, concurred with Dr. Jones: "I saw Haskell and believed him at that time, insane, he manifested every appearance of it." The judge and jury, however, disagreed and set Haskell free. Soon after, he wrote and published *The Trial of Ebenezer Haskell*.

The book opens with a long transcript of the trial, proceeds to Haskell's disappointingly short narrative of his experiences as a patient, then finishes with some brief sketches of conditions in other asylums Haskell observed as a visitor. Of consequence are the several ink drawings in the original, some of which portray asylum conditions and various abusive treatments of patients. Two of the drawings show Haskell in the act of escaping; and these particular images add impact to the work as a whole. One drawing depicts his first escape in November of 1866. Formally dressed, wearing a top hat, his white beard flowing, Haskell descends by a rope or knotted bedsheet from the third-story window (bars sawed open and bent back) of a massive prisonlike building. A second drawing shows his escape in September 1868. He dangles by the fingertips of one hand from the top of a stone wall more than twice his height, about to drop on the free side—and as we know from the trial manuscript—about to break his leg.

One wishes that Haskell had included accounts of his several escapes to accompany these drawings. He did not, however, and we must rest content with his brief but clear and absorbing narrative of life inside the Philadelphia Almshouse and the Pennsylvania Hospital for the Insane (which he sometimes calls "Kirkbride's" after the prominent superintendent of that institution). Included here is all of that narrative and sections containing his description of one of the

water-shock treatments of the time, the "spread-eagle cure" with
"douche bath."

ON THE MORNING of May 24th, 1866, while sitting at breakfast I
was kidnapped by a policeman and forcibly taken to the Philadelphia Almshouse. It never occurred to me that a charge of
insanity was preferred against me, causing the outrageous
arrest.

The questions put to me by the keeper, were as follows, viz:
"Where is your native place?"
"How old are you?"
"What is your occupation?"
After that my pockets were searched, and forty-three dollars
in money, and my gold watch, worth one hundred dollars
more, were taken from me.

Next I was ordered to take off my clothes, then the barber
came to shave off my beard and hair close to the skin, and a
straight jacket was close at hand to be placed on me instead of
the clothing removed. After a short consultation with the keepers or managers I was directed to follow a rough looking fellow
with a bunch of keys in his hand, through several doors. At last
one opened into the outer ward, which contained upwards of
500 black and white males of every grade one can imagine.
Some of them half naked and full of sores, and diseases of all
sorts and kinds, half of them were lying on the ground, some
were standing on their heads, others were singing, while some
were dancing. Forty or fifty of them had leather mittens on their
hands strapped close to their bodies, others had straight jackets
on, which are a kind of shirt pulled down over their bodies,
their arms inside pinioned close to their bodies. Such frightful
objects of misery are indescribable. From what I have said the
reader may form a faint idea of human beings huddled together
within the sound of church bells of the City of Philadelphia,
with a Christian population of several hundred thousand, living
in affluence, ease and comfort as unconcerned as though no
such place of torture was allowed in the country. The whole
present Almshouse system of management would be a disgrace

to any heathen nation on the face of the earth. Death is far preferable to the misery endured in the Blockley Almshouse of Philadelphia; in short it is a living sepulchre. The few days I was there sickened my heart at the cruelty practiced by those monsters in human shape called nurses. I have seen poor sick and feeble old men kicked and knocked down, hit in the face and on the head with a large bunch of keys, their eyes blackened, noses bleeding, lips cut and swollen, which all added to make life a burden. There is a great want of proper attendants; nearly all the nurses are without education, and brute force used continually upon all under them. The day the committee propose to visit a public or private institution should not be made known in the institution. When it is known everything is cleaned up in good order to deceive, so that the report will read "in excellent condition," and such like. To prevent abuse the authorities should send committees once a week, made up from outside the institution and in no way connected therewith.

I have seen marks of thumb and finger nails on the throats of the poor victims, being choked by the rough nurses, remain for two weeks. While I was locked up in the seventh ward in Kirkbride's mad house I have witnessed a struggle on the floor with a poor victim and his keeper over half an hour; the poor fellow had his hands strapped close to his body and fought with desperation; he was finally conquered by choking until he was black in the face, his tongue protruding from his mouth and his eyes nearly strained from their sockets, the froth and blood oozing from his mouth; he was then taken off from the floor by two stout keepers, and put into a dungeon naked, with a bundle of straw for his bed. I was confined during the night for over three months in a dungeon which joined this poor victim's; at first his yelling and howling kept me from sleeping. We are all creatures of circumstances and soon become reconciled; when he stopped it awakened me, the same as the howling did at first. In the day time about thirty of us were let out of our cells and dungeons with the liberty of going up and down the corridors and into a small yard off the ground floor. It is necessary if you want to place a human creature in this mad house to pay thirteen weeks' board in advance. As soon as payment of his board bill is discontinued the person remains there for three months more free of charge; after that time he is removed to the

Almshouse or some other Poor House and supported at the expense of the county or State treasury.

The Spread Eagle Cure

It is a term used in all asylums and prisons. A disorderly patient is stripped naked and thrown on his back, four men take hold of the limbs and stretch them out at right angles, then the doctor or some one of the attendants stands up on a chair or table and pours a number of buckets full of cold water on his face until life is nearly extinct, then the patient is removed to his dungeon cured of all diseases; the shock is so great it frequently produces *death*.

If all the persons in this commonwealth found intoxicated and not able to govern themselves in a proper manner should by LAW RECEIVE SUCH MEDICAL TREATMENT, say four buckets full of cold water applied in that way for the first offence, and for the second two more added and so on until the desired reform is accomplished, it would do more to prevent crime and INTEMPERANCE than any other means. The tax payers would save a vast amount of money collected now to support the paupers of every grade in this community. Let a steady stream of water seven or eight feet in height fall down directly on the face of the patient, it will have the same effect as if he was held under water the same number of feet for the same time; a person cannot breathe when the water is falling down directly in his mouth any better than he can ten feet under water; it is a shock to the whole nervous system, and it drives the blood from the brain, which has been forced up there in many ways, which causes the patient to lose his proper balance of mind.

*   *   *

I speak from my own observation on the spot. I have witnessed the most cruel and barbarous treatment by a nurse in the hospital at Pine street that could be inflicted on a human being. The person was brought to the hospital with the mania a potu, and put into a cell, strapped on an iron bedstead, with a hard mattress under him—the term familiarly used in the hospital, *made into a spread eagle*. The person is stretched out flat on his back, with a strap around the bedstead, up over the breast of the victim, and buckled under the bedstead; his legs are pulled wide apart and strapped to each corner at the foot of the bedstead, the arms are pulled out straight from the body, and strapped down under the bedstead, leaving his head scarcely room to turn one quarter around; in that position a person was kept three days and three nights; on the fourth night, at 9 o'clock, death relieved him of his agony.

1903 ⊷

Memoirs of My Nervous Illness, by Daniel Paul Schreber

The last of the great exorcists in the medieval tradition was Father Johann Joseph Gassner (1727–1779).[1] Born in a mountain village of western Austria in 1727, and ordained in 1750, Father Gassner began his career as a country priest in 1758 in a small village in eastern Switzerland. After a few years of ministry Gassner fell ill with severe headaches, dizziness, and other symptoms, which became aggravated during preaching, confession, or performance of the Mass. He believed he was possessed by the Devil and treated himself with prayer and traditional Catholic exorcism.

When the symptoms disappeared Gassner assumed the exorcism had worked and soon he began to practice it on his parishioners. His reputation as an exorcist developed rapidly and members of other parishes began coming to him to be exorcized. In 1774, after the successful treatment of Countess Maria von Wolfegg, Gassner acquired international fame and notoriety. Count Fugger, the prince bishop of Regensburg, invited Father Gassner to take an honorary office in his court. The priest consented and left his country parish to take residence in the town of Ellwagen under the count's patronage. There he became something of a tourist attraction. Crowds of Europeans, both well and ill, came to see and be treated by Father Gassner. He exorcized out in the open, for everyone to see, before church authorities, physicians, nobility, persons of all rank. A notary public recorded every word and act, and the records were countersigned by the highest ranking members of the witnessing crowds. In Germany, Austria, Switzerland, and France, dozens of pamphlets were published arguing both for and against his veracity.

In retrospect Gassner can be seen as an important representative of a dying medieval world view. Scientific advances since the late Renaissance seemed to prove that the world could be understood, perhaps even manipulated, by reason. This new world view—which we call the Enlightenment—affected not only the intellectual life of Europe, but the political, social, economic, and religious life as well.

---

[1]Information about Father Gassner is taken from Ellenberger, *The Discovery of the Unconscious,* pp. 53–57.

136

The Church itself was anxious to put away some of its most egregious superstitions and errors. The practice of witch-hunting was nearly over. In England the last execution for witchcraft took place in 1716 when a woman and her child were hanged in Huntington.[2] On the Continent such executions had become quite rare, though a woman was executed for witchcraft as late as 1782 in Switzerland. The Church, meanwhile, had made the order of Jesuits a scapegoat for past inquisitory excesses and suppressed the order in 1773. Talk of demons, possession, and exorcism had become an embarrassment to the Church and was generally shunned as a vestige of medieval superstition.

Gassner's protector, Count Fugger, was apparently forced to order a formal inquiry in 1775 after which he advised the priest to select his patients more carefully. In Munich another inquest was undertaken by the prince elector Max Joseph of Bavaria. The commission of this trial invited a young Viennese physician, Anton Mesmer, for consultation. Mesmer claimed Gassner's successes had nothing to do with exorcism but that Gassner had mistakenly stumbled on the new scientific principles of "animal magnetism." He demonstrated this concept to the commission, causing various symptoms, including convulsions, to appear and disappear in subjects merely by the touch of a finger. The imperial court at Vienna asked Count Fugger to dismiss Gassner, which he did, and Gassner retired to the isolated village of Pandorf. Meanwhile the Pope had ordered his own investigation of Gassner after which he issued an oblique disclaimer stating that while the Church still sanctioned exorcism in certain instances, it had to be performed discreetly and strictly according to established ritual.

"Animal magnetism," otherwise known as Mesmerism and later known as hypnotism, was in certain respects Mesmer's own creation. He used the same healing modality previously associated with exorcism—authoritarian suggestion—but he described it in secular, seemingly-scientific terms, in accord with the intellectual demands of the Enlightenment.[3] He theorized that the stars passed their influence down to earth through a fluid which pervaded everything

---

[2]Deutsch, *The Mentally Ill in America*, p. 23.

[3]Ellenberger, *The Discovery of the Unconscious*, pp. 55–57, 62, 63. According to Ellenberger, the traditions and techniques of the great modern systems of dynamic psychotherapy (non-somatic healing which involves interaction with unconscious processes) have been in existence since ancient times: "a continuous chain can be demonstrated between exorcism and magnetism, magnetism and hypnotism, hypnotism and the great modern dynamic systems" (p. vi).

animate and inanimate. One form of the fluid was magnetism, another electricity, and a third animal magnetism. He spoke of the third form of this fluid in terms analogous to the recent scientific theories of electricity: it had poles, streams, discharges, positive and negative potential, conductors, isolators, and accumulators.[4] Equilibrium of the animal magnetic fluid insured health, but disequilibrium was sure to bring illness; Mesmer claimed that he, as a magnetizer, had the power to restore equilibrium. He went to Paris in 1778 and created a sensation by producing miraculous cures of psychological and psychosomatic ailments.

Mesmer would stare into a patient's eyes, grasp the thumbs, then pass his hands along the limbs, realigning the invisible magnetic fluid. He would repeat the process two or three times until the patient typically went into a "crisis"—of laughing, crying, minor convulsions, or unconsciousness. For group sessions he invented a magnetizing machine which he called the *baquet*. Based on the design of the recently invented Leyden jar, the *baquet* was a circular tub filled with magnetized iron filings that had several projecting iron rods which his subjects could easily grasp. Mesmer would appear and produce curative motions of the invisible fluid emanating from the tub by waving his hands and moving his eyes, adding to the intensity of the situation with large mirrors that reflected the fluid and with music from magnetized instruments. From time to time he would play a few ear-splitting notes on his glass harmonica, a newly invented musical instrument perfected in America by Benjamin Franklin.

After Mesmer had been in Paris about six years the Académie des Sciences, the Académie de Médicine, and the Société Royale appointed committees of prominent scientists to investigate. Included on the committees were the American ambassador Benjamin Franklin, the chemist Antoine Lavoisier, the astronomer Jean Sylvain Bailly, and the physician Joseph Guillotin. Both Lavoisier and Bailly were beheaded a few years later by a machine that Dr. Guillotin had introduced in France, but of course no one could foresee that at the time of the investigation. As it was, there seems to have been little disagreement among the gentlemen of the investigating committees. They observed the work of Mesmer's disciple, Dr. D'Eslon, and found serious flaws in Mesmer's claims. When Mesmer and D'Eslon prompted their subjects to go into crisis by touching magnetized trees, the doctors noticed that many patients were touching un-

---

[4]Ibid., p. 63.

magnetized trees and still going into crisis. The committee reported that it had "demonstrated by decisive evidence that imagination without magnetism produces convulsions and that magnetism without imagination produces nothing," and hence that "animal magnetic fluid . . . does not exist and therefore cannot be useful."[5]

The rejection of the theory of animal magnetism by those scientific gentlemen is of some interest because it illustrates an attitude of the time regarding the "imagination." The scientists did not reject animal magnetism because it had no effect but rather because its effect was the result of imagination.

The transition from exorcism to magnetism marked the end of medieval, spiritual psychiatry, but modern psychiatry had not yet arrived. The nineteenth-century scientific community was preoccupied with the study of matter and appeared oblivious to the importance of the non-material imagination. Not until the end of the century did the scientific establishment finally show some curiosity about animal magnetism, by then called hypnotism, thus finally embracing the imagination and the mind as entities open to scientific investigation.

Psychiatry as a science began in the nineteenth century. Although that particular word was not used until about 1846, the first European schools of psychiatry were opened early in the century in Paris—at the Salpêtrière in 1817 and at the Bicêtre in 1818. Science was the study of physical matter; medical science was the study of human matter, the body; so, logically enough, psychiatric science became the study of gray matter, the brain. There were exceptions: in the first half of the century four prominent German psychiatrists published theoretical works emphasizing the significance of psychological factors in certain forms of madness or mental imbalance as well as the importance of psychological treatment.[6] But by the 1850s German psychiatry had fallen almost wholly under the dominance of positivism, which followed the models of physics and chemistry and rejected speculation in favor of factual knowledge gained by experimentation.[7]

German psychiatry focused on the anatomy of the brain and thus a somatic view of madness. In France the isolation and description of general paresis as a disease of the central nervous system in which

---

[5]As quoted by Zilboorg, *A History of Medical Psychology*, p. 345.
[6]Ellenberger, *The Discovery of the Unconscious*, pp. 211–14.
[7]Ibid., p. 225.

purely somatic changes could be seen under a microscope and in which the origin was found to be in a comprehensible physical event— the contraction of the syphilitic spirochete during sexual intercourse— lent a good deal of weight to the somatic beliefs of both French and German psychiatry. The French physician Jean Pierre Falret, who made major discoveries regarding general paresis, stated what seems to have been the majority opinion in 1822:

> I believe firmly that in all cases, without exception, one could find in the mentally sick appreciable lesions in the brain or its membranes; these lesions are sufficiently marked and sufficiently constant to account satisfactorily for all the various intellectual and affective disturbances in insanity.[8]

Typically the "mind" was considered to be accessible to scientific study only when it was linked to the brain and spinal cord and nerves, only when it was a segment of the body, the soma, and could be looked at through a microscope or cut with a scalpel. That portion of the mind which could not be located in the brain or spinal cord or nerves might be the "soul" or psyche, but whatever it was, it was not interesting to official psychiatry.

In philosophy and literature, however, the theme of the "unconscious" was gradually emerging. Lancelot Law Whyte has shown that during the two hundred years between 1680 and 1880, well over fifty important figures of the European intellectual community contributed to a cumulatively developing concept of the unconscious.[9] By the end of the nineteenth century Nietzsche's vision of man as a self-deceiver, driven by instinctual, irrational forces of the unconscious, was commonly accepted. Freud remarked in 1925 that for a long time he had avoided reading Nietzsche to keep his mind clear of external influences but that he at last recognized Nietzsche as a philosopher "whose guesses and intuitions often agree in the most astonishing way with the laborious findings of psychoanalysis."[10]

While official psychiatry was turning increasingly toward a somatic view of madness, and while the mysteries of the unconscious continued to be a subject for the "guesses and intuitions" of philosophers, a few physicians and lay healers continued to practice the form of dynamic psychotherapy known as magnetism and later called

---

[8]Zilboorg, *A History of Medical Psychology,* p. 398.
[9]Whyte, *The Unconscious Before Freud,* p. 63.
[10]Freud, *An Autobiographical Study,* p. 114.

hypnotism. But what the philosophers of the unconscious lacked, and what the early hypnotists lacked, was a sense of scientific methodology: the application of measurement, quantification, and systematic analysis. Freud's statement about Nietzsche makes the difference clear: Nietzsche's "guesses and intuitions" are in amazing agreement with the "laborious findings" of psychoanalysis. Whether Freud's sense of superiority for his own theory is wholly justified is not the point. The point is that while Nietzsche and other philosophers speculated, Freud began the tradition of the systematic, quasi-scientific analysis of the products of the imagination.

Freud received his earliest professional training in neurophysiology. His first work was in Ernst Brücke's physiology laboratory studying the spinal cord of the ammocoetes petromyzon and later studying the medulla oblongata of the human brain. After leaving Brücke's laboratory Freud worked at the Institute of Cerebral Anatomy of Vienna and published several papers on the system and nuclear origins of the medulla oblongata. He gradually established a reputation in Vienna as a diagnostician of organic nervous diseases and in the spring of 1885 was appointed lecturer on neuropathology in Vienna.

Up to this point Freud's interests and studies were not so different from his scientific peers. Then he became interested in hypnotism. His first serious interest may have been brought about by discussions with a prominent colleague, Dr. Josef Breuer, who seemed to have unusual success with the treatment of a young female patient, Bertha Pappenheim, later known in a published account as "Anna O." In the autumn of 1885 Freud left for Paris to attend Charcot's lectures on hypnotism and hysteria at the Salpêtrière. Upon returning to Vienna in 1886 he settled down to private practice as a specialist in "nervous diseases," relying on hypnotism as his principal therapeutic technique. Even though the psychiatric establishment was at the time contemptuous of hypnotism, Freud found "something positively seductive" about working with it.[11] In 1889 he went to Berheim's school at Nancy—the only other school of hypnotism in Europe. He was later to recall: "I was a spectator of Berheim's astonishing experiments upon his hospital patients, and I received the profoundest impression of the possibility that there could be powerful mental processes which nevertheless remained hidden from the consciousness of men."[12]

---

[11]Ibid., p. 29.
[12]Ibid., p. 30.

Freud continued using hypnotism until one of his most responsive hysteria patients came out of hypnosis and spontaneously threw her arms around his neck. For Freud the incident seemed to reveal the real nature of hypnotism "in the crudest light."[13] He abandoned the technique and began using a new one that he called psychoanalysis. He insisted that the only vestigial remnant of hypnotism was the couch. But, in fact, he also maintained the central technique he had developed in hypnotherapy: the exploration of the unconscious. Only now he made the patient do more of the work by no longer suggesting the direction of the unconscious exploration but rather allowing the patient to investigate unconscious material freely by what he called free association.

Freud insisted that psychoanalysis was a science and that his discoveries, therapy, and theories were made by using scientific methods. "I have always felt it as a gross injustice that people always refused to treat psychoanalysis like any other science," he wrote in 1925.[14] But his science was, for the first time, a science of the psyche. The "imagination" that those illustrious scientific gentlemen of Paris chose to dismiss in 1784 now became impossible to ignore.

The development of psychiatry in the nineteenth century spawned its own specialized journalism. Between 1818 and 1893 nearly fifty psychiatric journals appeared, and for the first time scientific works of all sorts began to be written in the vernacular, which greatly expanded the potential audience.[15]

Case histories have been a part of medical literature since the time of Hippocrates, but it was not until Freud and psychoanalysis that case histories and autobiographical material containing manifestations of the unconscious became important as documentation—and open to scientific scrutiny and analysis. Charcot had been the first to try to analyze art in psychological terms. Freud continued that concept and also turned to literature, biography, autobiography, and mythology. Further, through the popular dispersal of psychoanalysis, Freud made such analyses a common intellectual exercise in the twentieth century.

Around the turn of the century Freud published several case histories including his analyses of psychiatric patients. In 1911 he published

---

[13]Ibid., p. 49.
[14]Ibid., p. 111.
[15]Zilboorg, *A History of Medical Psychology*, p. 383.

the first analysis of an autobiographical account of madness, "Psycho-Analytic Notes on an Autobiographical Account of a Case of Paranoia (Dementia Paranoides)." The autobiography on which Freud's article was based, Daniel Paul Schreber's *Denkwürdigkeiten eines Nervenkranken* (1903), translated as *Memoirs of My Nervous Illness* (1955), was originally conceived by its author partly as an attempt at self-justification but mostly as a work of prophecy, a kind of spiritual autobiography. It aroused, however, much psychiatric interest. Reviewers at the time of its publication described the book as "valuable from the scientific medical point of view." Others said it "must be called perfect by the well-informed physician," and should be "recommended to all psychiatrists." [16] Freud's 1911 essay insured the preservation of the *Memoirs*, and perhaps helped create a demand for similar subjective descriptions of madness. Schreber's *Memoirs* is the first autobiographical account of the experience of madness regarded as psychiatric documentation—the earliest "psychiatric autobiography." [17]

Daniel Paul Schreber was *Senatspräsident*, or presiding judge, of the supreme court of the kingdom of Saxony, in Germany, at a relatively early age. He was a man of superior intellect and education. He came from a prominent—indeed, famous—German family. Aside from reports and descriptions of almost a decade spent in an asylum, however, there is actually very little information about his life. He was born around 1842. He married but was childless. And, according to an unconfirmed report, he died in 1911.

---

[16]Daniel Paul Schreber, *Memoirs*, p. 6. Unless otherwise noted, background information on Schreber has been taken from introductory notes by Macalpine and Hunter.

[17]Definition: the psychiatric autobiography is an authentic autobiographical account by a mad person or a person who was formerly mad that has as its main purpose the depiction of inner experience during a state of madness. In some basic ways the psychiatric autobiography might be considered merely a modern continuation of the earlier tradition of the spiritual autobiography. Often, of course, the spiritual autobiography deals with supposedly "normal" inner experience, while the psychiatric autobiography, by definition, deals with "abnormal" inner experience. The crucial difference lies in reference and terminology: the psychiatric autobiography deals with inner experience from a psychiatric rather than a spiritual frame of reference, using psychiatric terminology. The *Memoirs*, however, differs from the typical psychiatric autobiography in some important ways. For one thing, most psychiatric autobiographies have had a large lay audience, while the *Memoirs* has had mostly a professional audience. Also, unlike authors of typical psychiatric autobiographies, Schreber himself thought of his work as a prophetic spiritual autobiography. Perhaps it is best to consider the *Memoirs* as a historical turning point.

He was hospitalized for "severe hypochondriasis" in 1884 at the Psychiatric Clinic of the University of Leipzig under the care of Dr. Paul Flechsig, but he quickly recovered and was discharged in June 1885. In 1893 he became ill again, but this time the illness quickly became more serious and soon developed into what Schreber said was a "nervous illness" combined with unusual contact with the supernatural world. His physician thought the illness was a "paranoid form" of "hallucinatory insanity."[18] For several months he was again under Dr. Flechsig's care at the University Clinic in Leipzig, but in June 1894 Dr. Flechsig had taken him to Sonnenstein Asylum, Germany's first public asylum, near Dresden, where he remained for almost a decade. For the last three years of his confinement Schreber worked on legal proceedings for his own release. After two appeals, and an excellent self-defense in court of his right to freedom under the law, Schreber finally won his freedom. He left Sonnenstein Asylum in 1903.

Dr. Weber, the superintendent of the asylum, had reported in 1899 that at the beginning of Schreber's madness the patient had complained of hypochondriacal symptoms, but had quickly developed ideas of persecution. Upon his transfer to Sonnenstein he was stiff, unmoving, and stared into space with a frightened look. He did not respond to questions and demanded to be left alone. By November 1894 he seemed more accessible, moved around a little, and began speaking, "although in an abrupt and somewhat staccato manner." Gradually Schreber became more active. He still complained of various pains and bodily ailments, but at the same time he became increasingly noisy and prone to attacks of laughter, shouting, "bellowing," and pounding on the piano. He would stand in the asylum garden for long periods of time staring directly into the sun, grimacing, and raving threats at it. Sometimes he raved while in his room, calling out that Dr. Fleschig, his first physician, was a "soul murderer." He shouted abuse so loudly from the window of his room, even late at night, that the townspeople finally met and complained. In June 1896 it was decided to have him sleep in a padded isolation cell at night. During this period another habit began: he was often seen in his room half-undressed, insisting that he was developing female breasts. Gradually his nocturnal outbursts diminished so that in December 1898, after two and a half years of sleeping in a padded cell,

---

[18]Schreber, *Memoirs*, p. 271.

Schreber was allowed to sleep again in his own room. Although some of this behavior continued, Dr. Weber was able to remark one year later that "President Schreber now appears neither confused, nor psychically inhibited, nor markedly affected in his intelligence." Nevertheless, according to Weber, Schreber remained severely mad. His noticeable symptoms had simply become internalized: "the patient is filled with pathological ideas, which are woven into a complete system, more or less fixed." [19]

Dr. Weber went on to describe Schreber's "pathological ideas" in some detail, but much of his information he simply took from Schreber's writings. Dr. Weber, after all, had firsthand knowledge only of Schreber's outer behavior. Schreber alone knew what was happening in his "pathological" internal world. Unfortunately his *Memoirs* emanate a great bubbling incoherence, consisting basically of descriptions of hallucination, confusion, and hypochodriasis, and Schreber's interpretations of these experiences.

When Schreber was beset by hallucinations of voices and visions, he witnessed alternations of the sun and stars, mysterious illuminations in the sky, a bright halo around his head, and the spontaneous generation of insects. He constantly heard voices, usually disembodied, though sometimes apparently coming from birds. Especially in the first year, his ordinary time sense vanished, and in its place he had a sense of living in greatly expanded time. The passage of a few months seemed like centuries.

Schreber referred to his numerous hypochondriacal symptoms as "bodily miracles." And they do indeed have the aura of the miraculous about them. Once he was given a different heart. His lungs were often subjected to violent attacks, his ribs were sometimes smashed, and at times his whole chest would be compressed, destroying his ability to breath. His stomach could be taken away entirely, and his gullet and intestines were often torn or "miracled" away. Pain was directed at his seminal cord, and his abdomen seemed to be putrified so badly that he feared his entire body might rot away. All of his muscles were subject to attacks: when he wanted to play the piano or write there were attempts to paralyze his fingers. When he wanted to walk, there were miracles against his knee-caps. There were miracles against his eyelids, causing them to open and close at inopportune moments, and very threatening miracles were directed against his

---

[19]Ibid., pp. 269–86.

head, as well as his spine, which he felt were mainly meant as attacks on his ability to reason. There were attempts to draw the spinal cord out of his body and attempts to draw the nerves out of his head. His skull was continually sawed apart in various directions. The vibratory ability of the nerves of his brain was attacked, and even his private thoughts were manipulated miraculously: not allowed the "natural right of mental relaxation," he was driven to think compulsively. Finally there was the terrifying "bellowing miracle," the uncontrollable attacks of crying out.

The one miracle that seems to have been quite crucial to Schreber's experience was the "unmanning," or being transformed into a woman. Twice in the early days of his madness, Schreber was certain that he had received a "female genital organ, although a poorly developed one." His body began to look more and more feminine, and his skin began to take on a feminine softness. Some hairs of his beard and mustache were being removed by miracle. His body was becoming smaller. And at times, his penis actually began to retract. For almost two years he desperately fought the unmanning: "I suppressed every feminine impulse." By November 1895, however, the change seemed impossible to ignore. Schreber at last gave in and chose to cultivate femininity. By 1900 the transformation seemed to him so near completion that Schreber offered to submit his body to a medical examination to prove to others the truth of his experience.

That menagerie of voices, visions, and bodily miracles was terrifying and confusing to Schreber, especially during the first year or two. It was probably a great relief to him when he eventually began to sort out some meaning from it all, to develop what others would call a "delusional system." The voices seemed to give him information, sometimes straightforward, but often oblique and cryptic. He listened closely to the voices, and tried to make sense out of them.

He concluded that the voices and visions were indications of a contact with the spirit world and with God and that he had been singled out to have a special relationship with God. He concluded that the various miracles directed against his body and mind were part of a systematic cosmic program of persecution that began when Dr. Fleschig, or perhaps an ancestor of Dr. Fleschig, had tried to commit "soul murder" against him or one of his ancestors. Schreber realized that Dr. Fleschig's soul had raised itself up to the level of God, without the death and purification process that ordinary souls go through. Fleschig's soul entered into a conspiracy with many of the souls near God to commit soul murder, to destroy Schreber's soul and use it selfishly, against the intended order of the world. Instead of succeeding at soul murder, however, Fleschig's soul caused a "nervous illness" that brought Schreber into unusually close nerve contact with the world of souls. Souls who were in God's proximity were so attracted to Schreber's abnormally excited nervous system—caused by his nervous illness—that they were actually being pulled away from God and drawn toward Schreber's head and body. He could hear their cries of "Help! Help!" hundreds of times a day as they were swept into the powerful currents of his nerves, drawn fatally toward him, striking him in the form of little men just before they dissolved into his head and body. Stolen from God, taken over by Schreber, they added even more nervous attraction to his system. Eventually Schreber's nervous system reached such a high state of excitement that God himself was in danger of being pulled apart. God was being drawn into the vicinity of the earth, looming dangerously close. Schreber had for a time anticipated the end of the world, due to the growing attraction between himself and God. That catastrophic situation quickly degenerated into a war between God and Schreber—with most of the aggression coming from God. God was compelled to stop the seepage of his nerves into Schreber's body, and so he attacked, raining down on Schreber those numerous painful miracles designed to be attacks "on my life, my bodily integrity, my manliness and my reason."

Schreber considered the most serious of the attacks to be the assault on his "manliness," the repeated attempts at "unmanning." Schreber had first assumed that God meant to transform him into a woman for the ignominious purpose of sexual abuse, "to hand over my body in the manner of a female harlot." But when, in November 1895, the transformation was almost complete, Schreber developed a new theory: "But now I could see beyond doubt that the Order of the World imperiously demanded my unmanning . . . and that therefore it was *common sense* that nothing was left to me but reconcile myself to the thought of being transformed into a woman." Schreber concluded that in his transformation lay the hope of doomed humanity. Once he was at last changed into a woman, God would be able to impregnate him and thus renew the human race with a nation of Schrebers.

Schreber's *Memoirs* have probably stimulated more discussion and analysis than any other autobiographical account of madness. Eugen Bleuler read the *Memoirs* and made several references to it in his 1911 study of schizophrenia. Freud also became interested in the *Memoirs* and in 1911 published a psychoanalytic interpretation of Schreber's madness.

Freud based his analysis upon the contents of the delusional system. He considered that the madness was simply a psychic reaction to homosexual feelings at a time of crisis. At a basic and unresolved infantile level the original object of Schreber's homosexual love may have been his father, but by the time of his madness the love object had become his first physician, Dr. Fleschig. Since those homosexual feelings were forbidden, he had to try to repress the feelings, to hold them back from conscious awareness. When the attraction became too obvious to ignore, he used a second technique for defending himself from the forbidden impulse: he projected his attraction for Dr. Fleschig. That is, he assumed that the attraction was not originating from within himself but from an exterior source—namely from Dr. Fleschig. He further defended himself by assuming the attraction was hate, rather than love. Rather than having to cope with the intolerable message "I love him," he was able to assume the far more comfortable message "he hates me." That maneuver may have worked for a time, but the forbidden homosexual interest continued. At last it was necessary to erect yet another defensive system: since the interest could no longer be ignored, Schreber at last admitted it to conscious awareness, then denied the most threatening part. Making a leap into further depths of fantasy, Schreber convinced himself that homosexual impulses, which would in ordinary circumstances be degrading and wrong, in certain extraordinary circumstances could be not only acceptable but necessary. Schreber reasoned at last that his feminine impulse, his homosexuality, was fully consonant with the order of things, was due to his special situation in the universe, and was after all not really love for a man but uncontrollable attraction for God. It was demanded from him—as a duty for the good of the universe and mankind.

Freud, it is important to recall, never actually worked with the most severely disturbed patients. Patients who came to his office were generally troubled or neurotic but were never asylum inmates. In fact Freud felt that mad people were inaccessible to psychoanalysis because they were incapable of "transference." Nonetheless, many psychoanalysts accepted his 1911 essay as the classic explanation of paranoia, and some later analysts upheld the essay as the definitive explanation of madness in general.[20] Not until 1953 did anyone pub-

---

[20]Ibid., pp. 10–11.

lish serious criticism of Freud's analysis of Schreber. In that year Ida Macalpine and Richard Hunter pointed out that although Freud seemed to explain the structure of the delusional system, he ignored the original symptoms: the fantastic hypochondriasis and the massive hallucinations. They concluded that those original symptoms were in fact at the heart of the madness and were somatic in origin. What Freud considered to be conflict over homosexuality was really a reaction to the emergence of "archaic asexual procreation fantasies with . . . loss of sex differentiation."[21]

In 1955 Macalpine and Hunter published the first English translation of the *Memoirs*. The appearance of that translation inspired several new analyses of Schreber's madness, including Morton Schatzman's *Soul Murder*, which contains material about Schreber's father.

The father, Dr. Daniel Gottleib Schreber, was a famous physician and a lecturer at Leipzig University. He published several books on pediatrics and social reform, promoted the therapeutic use of gymnastics and athletics, and came to be considered the founder of therapeutic gymnastics in Germany. His influence was significant and lasting. By 1958 over two million German people belonged to societies for exercise and gardening known as Schreber Associations, and small allotment gardens in Germany are called *Schrebergärten*, after him.[22] His book, *Medical Indoor Gymnastics*, went through nearly forty editions and was translated into seven languages.

He saw as the purpose of child-rearing the higher development of the human race. He believed in strict discipline, control and extermination of bad impulses, unconditional submission to authority, absolute mastery over emotion, and absolute control of sexual impulse. In his writings he recommended cold baths for children over six months to induce physical toughness, cold sleeping quarters for children beyond six or seven years old, visual exercises to improve the eyes, and rigid posture while sitting, standing, or sleeping. He felt that in order to learn self-control, children should not eat between meals and should adhere to a strict diet and time schedule, while children under the age of seventeen must be forced to eat all the food given them. He recommended posture exercises to be done twice a day, before breakfast and supper. The parent and educator, he advised, should closely watch the child for any signs of unwanted

---

[21]Macalpine and Hunter, "The Schreber Case," p. 368.
[22]Schatzman, *Soul Murder*, p. 16.

traits, and spontaneity should be kept within narrow limits. The child should not be allowed to play with more than one toy at a time. Even babies could be taught self-control by being forbidden food while their nurses are eating.

Dr. Schreber wrote that children should learn to use their limbs equally, to prevent "one-sidedness." He devised several means to insure good posture such as his exercise to fight stooped head and shoulders in which the child practices "bridging" his body between two chairs, feet on one, head on the other. "Schreber's straight-holder," forced children to sit properly: an iron crossbar clamped to a table or desk, serving as a sort of fence at the upper chest to prevent leaning forward. He invented a spring-tensed shoulder strap to habituate good posture in children. A "head-holder" attached the child's hair to his underwear so that if he did not keep his head straight his hair would be pulled. Schreber's unique chin band, attached by straps around the head, ensured the correct growth of jaw and teeth.

The father's ideas of child-rearing were, of course, practiced on his children—with less than optimal results. Although little is known about his three daughters, it is known that both Dr. Schreber's sons went mad. Daniel Paul's only brother, Daniel Gustav, was said to have suffered a "progressive psychosis." He shot and killed himself at the age of thirty-eight. Schatzman concludes that Schreber's "nervous illness" was nothing but a direct symbolic response, late in life, to the remembered tyrannies of his father.

The following excerpts from Schreber's *Memoirs* were chosen for their general interest and for their significance to the theoretical controversies about the book. First, Schreber likens the origin of his nervous illness to a soul murder committed some time in the past. Next, he describes one battle in the continuous war between himself and the hostile cosmos: playing the piano enables him temporarily to ward off the "nonsensical twaddle" of the souls' voices, but hostile souls and "rays" from God rain down curses. Once the original absurd premises are expressed, the discussion that follows conveys a perfect sense of the rules of logic and rationality. In the third excerpt, Schreber faces a crucial moment of decision: he concludes that his unmanning is not part of a malevolent design but is instead consonant with the "Order of the World." That conclusion is, of course, central to Freud's analysis of the madness. Finally, Schreber describes an aspect of his experience which has been ignored by the theorists: the appearance of thought disorder, the "compulsive thinking" and especially the "system of not-finishing-a-sentence." The passage is the clearest description found to date of an experience Bleuler called the "disorder of association" present in schizophrenia.[23]

THIS "MIRACULOUS STRUCTURE" has recently suffered a rent, intimately connected with my personal fate. But it is impossible even for me to present the deeper connections in a way which human understanding can fully grasp. My personal experiences enable me to lift the veil only partially; the rest is intuition and conjecture. I want to say by way of introduction that the leading roles in the genesis of this development, the first beginnings of which go back perhaps as far as the eighteenth century, were played on the one hand by the names of Flechsig and Schreber (probably not specifying any individual member of these families), and on the other by the concept of *soul murder*.

To start with the latter: the idea is widespread in the folk-lore and poetry of all peoples that it is somehow possible to take possession of another person's soul in order to prolong one's life at another soul's expense, or to secure some other advantages which outlast death. One has only to think for example of Goethe's Faust, Lord Byron's Manfred, Weber's Frieschütz, etc. Commonly, however, the main role is supposed to be played by the Devil, who entices a human being into selling his soul to him by means of a drop of blood, etc. for some worldly advantages; yet it is difficult to see what the Devil was to do with a soul so caught, if one is not to assume that torturing a soul as an end in itself gave the Devil special pleasure.

Although the latter idea must be relegated to the realm of fable because the Devil as a power inimical to God does not exist at all according to the above, yet the wide dissemination of the legend motif of soul murder or soul theft gives food for thought; it is hardly likely that such ideas could have been formed by so many peoples without any basis in fact. The voices which talk to me have daily stressed ever since the beginning of my contact with God (mid-March 1894) the fact that the crisis that broke upon the realms of God was caused by somebody having *com-*

---

[23]See Appendix II.

mitted soul murder; at first Flechsig was named as the instigator of soul murder but of recent times in an attempt to reverse the facts I myself have been "represented" as the one who had committed soul murder. I therefore concluded that at one time something had happened between perhaps earlier generations of the Flechsig and Schreber families which amounted to soul murder; in the same way as through further developments, at the time when my nervous illness seemed almost incurable, I gained the conviction that soul murder had been attempted on me by somebody, albeit unsuccessfully.

*   *   *

Playing the piano in particular was and still is of immense value to me; I must confess that I find it difficult to imagine how I could have borne the compulsive thinking and all that goes with it during these five years had I not been able to play the piano. During piano playing the nonsensical twaddle of the voices which talk to me is drowned. Next to physical exercises it is one of the most efficient forms of the so-called not-thinking-of-anything-thought; but again one wanted to deprive me of it by introducing the "musical-not-thinking-of-anything-thought" as it was called in the soul-language. The rays always at least have a visual impression from my hands and from my reading the score, and every attempt at "representing" me by the "creation of a false feeling" and suchlike is doomed to end in failure because of the real feeling one can put into piano playing. Piano playing therefore was and still is one of the main objects of curses.

The difficulties which were put in my way defy description. My fingers are paralysed, the direction of my gaze is changed in order to prevent my finding the correct keys, my fingers are diverted on to wrong keys, the tempo is quickened by making the muscles of my fingers move prematurely; all these were and still are daily occurrences. Even the piano itself was frequently the object of miracles and strings were broken (luckily much more rarely in recent years). In 1897 alone the bill for broken piano strings amounted to no less than 86 Marks.

This is one of the few instances which I believe furnishes sufficient proof to convince other people of the reality of the miracles which I maintain happen. Superficial judgment might lead some to assume that I myself have caused the piano strings to snap by senseless banging on the piano; this was for instance my wife's repeatedly stated opinion, possibly having heard it from the physicians. In reply I maintain—and I am convinced that every expert will support me in this—that it is *altogether impossible* to snap the strings of a piano merely by banging on the keys, however violently. The small hammers linked with the keys only lightly touch the strings, and could never strike them sufficiently hard to break them. Let anyone try to hit the keys as hard as he likes, even with a hammer or a log of wood; the keyboard may perhaps be broken to pieces but he will never be able to break a string. Strings have broken much less frequently in recent years—it still happens occasionally—because the rays' (God's) intent towards me has become less unfriendly (more about this later) owing to my constantly increasing soul-voluptuousness; the rays were also forced by still more unpleasant conditions (even for them) in particular by the so-called "bellowing", to consider piano playing the most congenial pasttime for all concerned.

*   *   *

The month of November 1895 marks an important time in the history of my life and in particular in my own ideas of the possible shaping of my future. I remember the period distinctly; it coincided with a number of beautiful autumn days when there was a heavy morning mist on the Elbe. During that time the signs of a transformation into a woman became so marked on my body, that I could no longer ignore the imminent goal at which the whole development was aiming. In the immediately preceding nights my male sexual organ might actually have been retracted had I not absolutely set my will against it, still following the stirring of my sense of manly honour; so near completion was the miracle. Soul-voluptuousness had become so strong that I myself received the impression of a female body, first on my arms and hands, later on my legs, bosom, buttocks and other parts of my body. I will discuss details in the next chapter.

Several days' observations of these events sufficed to change the direction of my will completely. Until then I still considered it possible that, should my life not have fallen victim to one of the innumerable menacing miracles before, it would eventually be necessary for me to end it by suicide; apart from suicide the only possibility appeared to be some other horrible end for me, of a kind unknown among human beings. But now I could see beyond doubt that the Order of the World imperiously demanded my unmanning, whether I personally liked it or not, and that therefore it was *common sense* that nothing was left to me but reconcile myself to the thought of being transformed into a woman. Nothing of course could be envisaged as a further consequence of unmanning but fertilization by divine rays for the purpose of creating new human beings. My change of will was facilitated by my not believing at that time that apart from myself a real mankind existed; on the contrary I thought all the human shapes I saw were only "fleeting and improvised", so that there could be no question of any ignominy being attached to unmanning. It is true however that those rays which were intent on "forsaking" me and which for that purpose wanted to destroy my reason, did not fail to make a hypocritical appeal to my sense of manly honour; some of the phrases, since repeated innumerable times whenever soul-voluptuousness appeared, were: "Are you not ashamed in front of your wife?", or still more vulgarly: "Fancy a person who was a *Senatspräsident* allowing himself to be f....d." But however repellent these voices, however often I had occasion to air my just indignation in one way or another during the thousand-fold repetition of these phrases, I did not allow myself to be diverted from that behaviour which I had come to recognize as essential and curative for all parties—myself and the rays.

Since then I have wholeheartedly inscribed the cultivation of femininity on my banner, and I will continue to do so as far as consideration of my environment allows, whatever other people who are ignorant of the supernatural reasons may think of me. I would like to meet the man who, faced with the choice of either becoming a demented human being in male habitus or a spirited woman, would not prefer the latter. Such and *only such* is the issue for me. The pursuit of my previous profession, which I loved wholeheartedly, every other aim of manly ambition, and every other use of my intellectual powers in the service of mankind, are now all closed to me through the way circumstances have developed; even communication with my wife and relatives is denied me apart from occasional visits or exchange of letters. I must follow a healthy egoism, unperturbed by the judgment of other people, which prescribes for me the cultivation of femininity in a manner to be described more fully later. In this way only am I able to make my physical condition bearable during the day and at night—at least in some measure—and obtain the sleep necessary for the recuperation of my nerves; *high-grade voluptuousness eventually passes into sleep*—maybe this is even known to medical science. Conducting myself in this manner I serve at the same time the express interest of the rays, that is God Himself.

*   *   *

In the previous chapters I described the changes in my outward life during the past years and the forms the battle of annihilation assumed which divine rays led against me. I will now add some more about the forms—also vastly changed—of the constant *compulsive thinking*. Compulsive thinking has been defined in Chapter V as having to think continually; this contravenes man's natural right of mental relaxation, of temporary rest from mental activity through thinking nothing, or as the expression goes in the basic language, it disturbs the "basis" of a human being. My nerves are influenced by the rays to vibrate corresponding to certain human words; their choice therefore is not subject to my own will, but is due to an influence exerted on me from without. From the beginning the *system of not-finishing-a-sentence* prevailed, that is to say the vibrations caused in my nerves and the words so produced contain not mainly finished thoughts, but unfinished ideas, or only fragments of ideas, which my nerves have to supplement to make up the sense. It is in the nature of nerves that if unconnected words or started phrases are thrown into them, they automatically attempt to complete them to finished thoughts satisfactory to the human mind.

The system of not-finishing-a-sentence became more and more prevalent in the course of years, the more the souls lacked own thoughts. In particular, for years single conjunctions or adverbs have been spoken into my nerves thousands of times; these ought only to introduce clauses, but it is left to my nerves to complete them in a manner satisfactory to a thinking mind. Thus for years I have heard daily in hundredfold .repetition incoherent words spoken into my nerves without any context, such as "Why not?", "Why, if", "Why, because I", "Be it", "With respect to him" (that is to say that something or other has to be thought or said with respect to myself); further an absolutely senseless "Oh" thrown into my nerves; finally certain fragments of sentences which were earlier on expressed completely; as for instance

1. "Now I shall",
2. "You were to",
3. "I shall",
4. "It will be",
5. "This of course was",
6. "Lacking now is",

etc. In order to give the reader some idea of the original meaning of these incomplete phrases I will add the way they used to be completed, but are now omitted and left to be completed by my nerves. The phrases ought to have been:

1. Now I shall resign myself to being stupid;
2. You were to be represented as denying God, as given to voluptuous excesses, etc.;
3. I shall have to think about that first;
4. It will be done now, the joint of pork;
5. This of course was too much from the soul's point of view;
6. Lacking now is only the leading idea, that is—we, the rays, have no thoughts.

The rather tasteless phrase about the joint of pork (number 4) is due to myself having used years ago the figure of speech "done like a joint of pork" in the nerve-language. This phrase was seized on and became a constantly recurring part of the speech-material. The "joint of pork" I was to refer to myself: it was meant to express that I was done, i.e. that my power of resistance against the attacks on my reason by the rays must by now be exhausted.

The purpose of not-finishing-a-sentence is consistent with God's attitude to me throughout: to prevent dissolution in my body which would necessarily result from its attraction. While conditions prevailed which were at least somehow in consonance with the Order of the World, that is before tying-to-rays and tying-to-celestial-bodies was started (compare Chapter IX), a momentary uniform *feeling* was enough to make the freely suspended souls jump down from the sky into my mouth, thus ending their independent existence; an event, as mentioned in Chapter VII, page 83, I actually experienced repeatedly. But mere "intellectual deliberation" had the same effect; whenever expressed in a grammatically complete sentence, the rays would be led straight to me, and entering my body (though capable of withdrawing) temporarily increase its soul-voluptuousness. Not-finishing-a-sentence has apparently the effect that the rays are, as it were, held up half way, and could therefore withdraw before having added to soul-voluptuousness in my body; but even this does not permanently prevent the attraction completely; it only shows it down.

It is hard to give a picture of the mental strain the compulsive thinking imposed on me particularly after it had become so much worse, and what mental torture I had to suffer. During the first years my nerves indeed seemed irresistibly compelled to continue each started clause to the satisfaction of the human mind, much as in ordinary human intercourse an answer is regularly given to somebody's question.

I will give an example to illustrate how such a need is inherent in the nature of human nerves. Consider the case of parents or teachers being present during a school examination of their children. If they follow the examination attentively they will automatically answer every question in their mind, perhaps only in the form: "I am not at all sure whether the children will know this". Of course there is no mental compulsion for parents or teachers, they have only to divert their attention from the proceeding examination towards something else in their environment to spare their nerves this strain. This is the essential difference between this example and my case. The questions or querying particles spoken into my nerves compel my mind to work by setting the corresponding nerves in vibration, in a way that they cannot possibly escape the impulse to think. I must leave undecided whether the expression I chose of my nerves being set in corresponding vibrations by the rays, covers the circumstances correctly; what I directly feel is that the talking voices (lately in particular the voices of the talking birds) as *inner voices* move like long threads into my head and there cause a painful feeling of tension through the poison of corpses which they deposit.

In contradistinction to these inner voices I hear outer voices particularly spoken by birds, which come to me from outside, from the birds' throats. However, in both cases my nerves cannot avoid the sound of the spoken words; the stimulation of my nerves follows automatically and compels me to think on when I hear questions or incomplete thoughts. In earlier years my nerves simply had to think on, to answer questions, to complete broken-off sentences etc. Only later was I gradually able to accustom my nerves (my "basis") to ignoring the stimulation which forced them to think on, by simply repeating the words and phrases and thus turning them into not-thinking-of-anything-thoughts. I have done that for a long time now with conjunctions and adverbs which would need a full clause for their completion. If I hear for instance "Why, because I", or "Be it", I repeat these words for as long as possible without attempting to complete the sense by trying to connect them with what I thought before.

I proceed in the same manner when attempts are made with the words "If only my" to compel my nerves to develop ideas of fear, not really present in my mind but falsely imputed to me. I know what can be "expected" to follow—because as a rule the corresponding miracle happens simultaneously and I feel it on my body; the intended continuation is sometimes "If only my voluptuousness were not disturbed", sometimes "If only my boots were not removed by miracle", sometimes "If only my nose, my eyes, my knee-cap, my skull, etc., would not be affected by miracles."

Since my nerves have become accustomed to suppress the corresponding stimulation, I no longer elaborate in words the nonsense to which these falsified ideas lead; I am satisfied to keep on repeating the same words "If only my" without adding anything to them. In ordinary conversation of course everybody would simply counter "If only my" with "What do you really mean", or perhaps would use abusive language in self-defence. This is very difficult for me because the rays regularly answer "We have had this before" (with the effect mentioned in Chapter IX). It would in any case be unendurable in the long run to submit nerves all day long to the counter question "What do you really mean", or to abusive language.

The infringement of the freedom of human thinking or more correctly thinking nothing, which constitutes the essence of compulsive thinking, became more unbearable in the course of years with the slowing down of the talk of the voices. This is connected with the increased soul-voluptuousness of my body and—despite all writing-down—with the great shortage of speech-material at the disposal of the rays with which to bridge the vast distances separating the stars, where they are suspended, from my body.

No one who has not personally experienced these phenomena like I have can have any idea of the extent to which speech has slowed down. To say "But naturally" is spoken B.b.b.u.u.u.t.t.t. n.n.n.a.a.a.t.t.t.u.u.u.r.r.r.a.a.a.l.l.l.y.y.y, or "Why do you not then shit?" W.w.w.h.h.h.y.y.y d.d.d.o.o.o...........; and each requires perhaps thirty to sixty seconds to be completed. This would be bound to cause such nervous impatience in every human being, not like myself more and more inventive in using methods of defence, as to make him jump out of his skin; a faint idea of the nervous unrest caused is perhaps the example of a Judge or teacher always listening to a mentally dull witness or a stuttering scholar, who despite all attempts cannot clearly get out what he is asked or wants to say.

Playing the piano and reading books and newspapers is—as far as the state of my head allows—my main defence, which makes even the most drawn-out voices finally perish; at night when this is not easily done or in day-time when the mind requires a change of occupation, I usually found committing poems to memory a successful remedy. I learnt a great number of poems by heart particularly Schiller's ballads, long sections of Schiller's and Goethe's dramas, as well as arias from operas and humorous poems, amongst others from Max and Moritz, Struwelpeter and Spekter's fables, which I then recite in silence on the quiet verbatim. Their value as poetry naturally does not matter; however insignificant the rhymes, even obscene verses are worth their weight in gold as mental nourishment compared with the terrible nonsense my nerves are otherwise forced to listen to.

Even while reciting poems I have to combat difficulties which at times reduce their effectiveness; miracles aimed at scattering my thoughts act on my nerves and make it impossible to find the continuation of a poem learnt by heart; or when the most persistent inner voices have at last been silenced by the recital of longer poems and I have reached a state of great soul-voluptuousness through union of all rays, the lower God starts the bellowing miracle until I am so breathless that I cannot continue reciting the poems even softly. I am therefore forced to change the systems much in the same way as externally new systems are continually started (by God's omnipotence) to slow down the attraction of rays and prevent the union of all rays necessary for sleep or complete soul-voluptuousness. Recently I found counting aloud up to a large figure of great help, but this is naturally very boring for any length of time. When severe bodily pain sets in or persistent bellowing occurs, the last remaining remedy is swearing aloud which I have to do occasionally, but which I sincerely hope will become less and less necessary in future.

1908 ⸺

A Mind That Found Itself, by Clifford Beers

After Clifford Beers graduated from Yale in 1897 he embarked on a promising business career with a life insurance firm on Wall Street. Eventually, a tendency toward shyness, combined with a morbid fear that he might succumb to seizures and a brain tumor—as his older brother had—left him incapacitated. He came to see suicide as the only solution and on June 23, 1900, jumped from the fourth story window of his home in New Haven. He survived and was hospitalized with broken bones in his feet. In the hospital, for reasons not clear, he became delirious. Lying in the hospital bed, he watched an attendant put bars in the windows to keep him from trying another jump. Beers mistakenly thought that he was being held prisoner and concluded that he was going to be tried for the crime of attempting suicide. He became scared and suspicious. Speaking to no one, he slowly began to imagine he was being held for crimes far more serious than suicide. He eventually believed that he was at the center of all evil and crime, that he had committed numerous horrible crimes, written about daily in the newspapers. He was afraid that the public at large hated him for these crimes and that he was a disgrace before the world. He returned home for a short while but then was sent to a private sanatorium, still mute. Beers soon decided that this sanatorium was set up by the government, that the nurses, the attendants, and the patients were really detectives trying to gather information about the many crimes he had committed. He was careful about all his actions, trying not to communicate anything, in any way, to all the detectives around him. His food tasted odd and he assumed it was poisoned. After a year, he was sent to another private institution, then, finally, to a large state institution. His family visited him at times, but he refused to speak to them, believing that his real family had been taken away by the government, and that the people visiting him were "doubles" sent to obtain information from him.

During the first two years Beers remained depressed, secretive, and mute. His brother visited him regularly, but Beers always regarded him as a double—not his actual brother at all. Beers desperately fixed upon suicide as his only escape from persecution, but as a last resort sent a letter to his brother. When the "agent," the person Beers thought was posing as his real brother, returned the next day with the letter, Beers realized he had been wrong all along and at last the "Gordian knot" of his faulty belief system was cut. He was so pleased to have made contact with his real brother, he talked for two hours almost without pause. His vocal cords were very weak from two years of silence, so he often had to whisper. After he left his brother he went back to his ward and talked to the patients as much as he could during the next two weeks—only pausing to sleep two or three hours a night.

Beers had previously written only one letter—the fateful letter to his brother—during the full two years of his hospitalization. Now he began to make up for that lapse. He wrote letters until he ran out of stationery and then used wrapping paper, tearing strips a foot across and four feet long. Most of his letters were composed of several of these strips fastened together, sometimes twenty or thirty feet in length. One letter stretched the full length of his ward corridor, one hundred feet.

He became manic: aggressive, brash, extremely talkative, sleeping little, and filled with impossible energy and grandiose schemes. First, he believed he had invented a way to defy gravity. Then he believed he would create a worldwide movement to reform mental hospitals. Little by little, however, his mania subsided and by 1903 he was well enough to resume his business affairs.

Beers persisted in his grandiose schemes for reform, however. He wanted to start a patients' rights movement to change the treatment of American mental patients. To establish his own credentials in this venture, he wrote an autobiographical account of his experiences as a mental patient, *A Mind That Found Itself*. Beers lucidly describes his unusual mental experiences, his multiple hallucinations, and the logic that held together his delusions. The book gives one of the clearest descriptions of abnormal mental experience, but it may be principally significant as a protest. Almost unpunctuated by commentary, judgment, or emotionalism, Beers's direct and vivid accounts of ward life at the turn of the century remain a particularly disturbing reminder of what can happen when people are given almost unlimited power over others.

In the private sanatorium where he first stayed, the owner made some $100,000 a year, by "economies." Attendants were untrained, usually ignorant, rough, and poorly paid. In the next institution Beers was kept in a cold, unventilated cell for three weeks and not permitted to bathe. In the state institution he was severely assaulted by attendants—knocked down, kicked, beaten, choked—and the attendants were never reprimanded. He saw attendants kicking and beating some helpless patients daily; he watched vicious beatings of elderly patients which resulted in injuries and, in one case, death.

Beers outlined serious plans for a reform movement and—sending out *A Mind That Found Itself* as his calling card—won the support of several influential people, including William James and Adolph Meyer. In 1908 he founded the Connecticut Society for Mental Hygiene and, a year later, the National Committee for Mental Hygiene to promote the "humane and scientific institutional care of mental disease." The Connecticut Society expanded and became the model for nearly thirty state societies. The National Committee also grew, attracted philanthropic support, and was the prototype for several national organizations, including the Canadian National Committee for Mental Hygiene founded in 1918. In 1928 Beers established the American Foundation for Mental Hygiene which was mainly a money-raising organization designed to generate continuous financial support and distribute it to important projects. In 1930 he organized the First International Congress in Mental Hygiene, which met in Washington: a gathering of representatives from fifty countries. One result of that conference was the creation of a permanent international organization known as the International Committee for Mental Hygiene. During this time the National Committee, founded by Beers in 1909, endured—promoting research, legislation, hospital care studies, information programs, and community guidance centers. In 1950 it merged with two other groups to form the National Association for Mental Health, the one organization of its kind still active.

Clifford Beers, former mental patient, created the greatest psychiatric reform movement of this century, the "mental hygiene movement." Eventually Beers was awarded an honorary degree from Yale, a medal of honor by the French, a gold medal from the National Institute of Social Sciences, and was made an honorary member of the American Psychiatric Association.

In the first excerpt, Beers describes the incidents following his first suicide attempt in 1900; in the hospital, then in his own home, Beers begins to suspect a plot as his familiar world drifts into a world of visions and hallucinations. The beatings by attendants are depicted next. Beers then portrays the "Bull Pen," a row of isolation cells in a state institution for 2300 patients.

NATURALLY I WAS SUSPICIOUS of all about me, and became more so each day. But not until about a month later did I refuse to recognize my relatives. While I was at Grace Hospital, my father and eldest brother called almost every day to see me, and, though I said little, I still accepted them in their proper characters. I remember well a conversation one morning with my father. The words I uttered were few, but full of meaning. Shortly before this time my death had been momentarily expected. I still believed that I was surely about to die as a result of my injuries, and I wished in some way to let my father know that, despite my apparently ignominious end, I appreciated all that he had done for me during my life. Few men, I believe, ever had a more painful time in expressing their feelings than I had on that occasion. I had but little control over my mind, and my power of speech was impaired. My father sat beside my bed. Looking up at him, I said, "You have been a good father to me."

"I have always tried to be," was his characteristic reply.

After the broken bones had been set, and the first effects of the severe shock I had sustained had worn off, I began to gain strength. About the third week I was able to sit up and was occasionally taken out of doors. But each day, and especially during the hours of the night, my delusions increased in force and variety. The world was fast becoming to me a stage on which every human being within the range of my senses seemed to be playing a part, and that a part which would lead not only to my destruction (for which I cared little), but also to the ruin of all with whom I had ever come in contact. In the month of July several thunder-storms occurred. To me the thunder was "stage" thunder, the lightning man-made, and the accompanying rain due to some clever contrivance of my persecutors. There was a chapel connected with the hospital—or at least a room where religious services were held every Sunday. To me the hymns were funeral dirges; and the mumbled prayers, faintly audible, were in behalf of every sufferer in the world but one.

It was my eldest brother who looked after my care and interests during my entire illness. Toward the end of July, he informed me that I was to be taken home again. I must have given him an incredulous look, for he said, "Don't you think we can take you home? Well, we can and will." Believing myself in the hands of the police, I did not see how that was possible. Nor did I have any desire to return. That a man who had disgraced his family should again enter his old home and expect his relatives to treat him as though nothing were changed, was a thought against which my soul rebelled; and, when the day came for my return, I fought my brother and the doctor feebly as they lifted me from the bed. But I soon submitted, was placed in a carriage, and driven to the house I had left a month earlier.

For a few hours my mind was calmer than it had been. But my new-found ease was soon dispelled by the appearance of a nurse—one of several who had attended me at the hospital. Though at home and surrounded by relatives, I jumped to the conclusion that I was still under police surveillance. At my request my brother had promised not to engage any nurse who had been in attendance at the hospital. The difficulty of procuring any other led him to disregard my request, which at the time he held simply as a whim. But he did not disregard it entirely, for the nurse selected had merely acted as a substitute on one occasion, and then only for about an hour. That was long enough, though, for my memory to record her image.

Finding myself still under surveillance, I soon jumped to a second conclusion, namely, that this was no brother of mine at all. He instantly appeared in the light of a sinister double, acting as a detective. After that I refused absolutely to speak to him again, and this repudiation I extended to all other relatives, friends and acquaintances. If the man I had accepted as my brother was spurious, so was everybody—that was my deduction. For more than two years I was without relatives or friends, in fact, without a world, except that one created by my own mind from the chaos that reigned within it.

While I was at Grace Hospital, it was my sense of hearing which was the most disturbed. But soon after I was placed in my room at home, *all* of my senses became perverted. I still heard the "false voices"—which were doubly false, for Truth no longer existed. The tricks played upon me by my senses of taste, touch, smell, and sight were the source of great mental anguish. None of my food had its usual flavor. This soon led to that common delusion that some of it contained poison—not deadly poison, for I knew that my enemies hated me too much to allow me the boon of death, but poison sufficient to aggravate my discomfort. At breakfast I had cantaloupe, liberally sprinkled with salt. The salt seemed to pucker my mouth, and I believed it to be powdered alum. Usually, with my supper, sliced peaches were served. Though there was sugar on the peaches, salt would have done as well. Salt, sugar, and powdered alum had become the same to me.

Familiar materials had acquired a different "feel." In the dark, the bed sheets at times seemed like silk. As I had not been born with a golden spoon in my mouth, or other accessories of a useless luxury, I believed the detectives had provided these silken sheets for some hostile purpose of their own. What that purpose was I could not divine, and my very inability to arrive at a satisfactory conclusion stimulated my brain to the assembling of disturbing thoughts in an almost endless train.

Imaginary breezes struck my face, gentle, but not welcome, most of them from parts of the room where currents of air could not possibly originate. They seemed to come from cracks in the walls and ceiling and annoyed me exceedingly. I thought them in some way related to that ancient method of torture by which water is allowed to strike the victim's forehead, a drop at a time, until death releases him. For a while my sense of smell added to my troubles. The odor of burning human flesh and other pestilential fumes seemed to assail me.

My sense of sight was subjected to many weird and uncanny effects. Phantasmagoric visions made their visitations throughout the night, for a time with such regularity that I used to await their coming with a certain restrained curiosity. I was not entirely unaware that something was ailing with my mind. Yet these illusions of sight I took for the work of detectives, who sat up nights racking their brains in order to rack and utterly wreck my own with a cruel and unfair Third Degree.

Handwriting on the wall has ever struck terror to the hearts of even sane men. I remember as one of my most unpleasant experiences that I began to see handwriting on the sheets of my bed staring me in the face, and not me alone, but also the spurious relatives who often stood or sat near me. On each fresh sheet placed over me I would soon begin to see words, sentences, and signatures, all in my own handwriting. Yet I could not decipher any of the words, and this fact dismayed me, for I firmly believed that those who stood about could read them all and found them to be incriminating evidence.

I imagined that these visionlike effects, with few exceptions, were produced by a magic lantern controlled by some of my myriad persecutors. The lantern was rather a cinematographic contrivance. Moving pictures, often brilliantly colored, were thrown on the ceiling of my room and sometimes on the sheets of my bed. Human bodies, dismembered and gory, were one of the most common of these. All this may have been due to the fact that, as a boy, I had fed my imagination on the sensational news of the day as presented in the public press. Despite the heavy penalty which I now paid for thus loading my mind, I believe this unwise indulgence gave a breadth and variety to my peculiar psychological experience which it otherwise would have lacked. For with an insane ingenuity I managed to connect myself with almost every crime of importance of which I had ever read.

Dismembered human bodies were not alone my bedfellows at this time. I remember one vision of vivid beauty. Swarms of butterflies and large and gorgeous moths appeared on the sheets. I wished that the usually unkind operator would continue to show these pretty creatures. Another pleasing vision appeared about twilight several days in succession. I can trace it directly to impressions gained in early childhood. The quaint pictures by Kate Greenaway—little children in attractive dress, playing in old-fashioned gardens—would float through space just outside my windows. The pictures were always accompanied by the gleeful shouts of real children in the neighborhood, who, before being sent to bed by watchful parents, devoted the last hour of the day to play. It doubtless was their shouts that stirred my memories of childhood and brought forth these pictures.

In my chamber of intermittent horrors and momentary delights, uncanny occurrences were frequent. I believed there was some one who at fall of night secreted himself under my bed. That in itself was not peculiar, as sane persons at one time or another are troubled by that same notion. But *my* bed-fellow—

under the bed—was a detective; and he spent most of his time during the night pressing pieces of ice against my injured heels, to precipitate, as I thought, my overdue confession.

The piece of ice in the pitcher of water which usually stood on the table sometimes clinked against the pitcher's side as its center of gravity shifted through melting. It was many days before I reasoned out the cause of this sound; and until I did I supposed it was produced by some mechanical device resorted to by the detectives for a purpose. Thus the most trifling occurrence assumed for me vast significance.

*   *   *

On the night of November 25th, 1902, the head attendant and one of his assistants passed my door. They were returning from one of the dances which, at intervals during the winter, the management provides for the nurses and attendants. While they were within hearing, I asked for a drink of water. It was a carefully worded request. But they were in a hurry to get to bed, and refused me with curses. Then I replied in kind.

"If I come there I'll kill you," one of them said.

"Well, you won't get in if I can help it," I replied, as I braced my iron bedstead against the door.

My defiance and defences gave the attendants the excuse for which they had said they were waiting; and my success in keeping them out for two or three minutes only served to enrage them. By the time they had gained entrance they had become furies. One was a young man of twenty-seven. Physically he was a fine specimen of manhood; morally he was deficient— thanks to the dehumanizing effect of several years in the employ of different institutions whose officials countenanced improper methods of care and treatment. It was he who now attacked me in the dark of my prison room. The head attendant stood by, holding a lantern which shed a dim light.

The door once open, I offered no further resistance. First I was knocked down. Then for several minutes I was kicked about the room—struck, kneed and choked. My assailant even attempted to grind his heel into my cheek. In this he failed, for I was there protected by a heavy beard which I wore at that time. But my shins, elbows, and back were cut by his heavy shoes; and had I not instinctively drawn up my knees to my elbows for the protection of my body, I might have been seriously, perhaps fatally, injured. As it was, I was severely cut and bruised. When my strength was nearly gone, I feigned unconsciousness. This ruse alone saved me from further punishment, for usually a premeditated assault is not ended until the patient is mute and helpless. When they had accomplished their purpose, they left me huddled in a corner to wear out the night as best I might—to live or die for all they cared.

Strange as it may seem, I slept well. But not at once. Within five minutes I was busily engaged writing an account of the assault. A trained war correspondent could not have pulled himself together in less time. As usual I had recourse to my bit of contraband lead pencil, this time a pencil which had been smuggled to me the very first day of my confinement in the Bull Pen by a sympathetic fellow-patient. When he had pushed under my cell door that little implement of war, it had loomed as large in my mind as a battering-ram. Paper I had none; but I had previously found walls to be a fair substitute. I therefore now selected and wrote upon a rectangular spot—about three feet by two—which marked the reflection of a light in the corridor just outside my transom.

The next morning, when the assistant physician appeared, he was accompanied as usual by the guilty head attendant who, on the previous night, had held the lantern.

"Doctor," I said, "I have something to tell you,"—and I glanced significantly at the attendant. "Last night I had a most unusual experience. I have had many imaginary experiences during the past two years and a half, and it may be that last night's was not real. Perhaps the whole thing was phantasmagoric—like what I used to see during the first months of my illness. Whether it was so or not I shall leave you to judge. It just happens to be my impression that I was brutally assaulted last night. If it was a dream, it is the first thing of the kind that ever left visible evidence on my body."

With that I uncovered to the doctor a score of bruises and lacerations. I knew these would be more impressive than any words of mine. The doctor put on a knowing look, but said nothing and soon left the room. His guilty subordinate tried to appear unconcerned, and I really believe he thought me not absolutely sure of the events of the previous night, or at least unaware of his share in them.

*   *   *

Like fires and railroad disasters, assaults seemed to come in groups. Days would pass without a single outbreak. Then would come a veritable carnival of abuse—due almost invariably to the attendants' state of mind not to an unwonted aggressiveness on the part of the patients. I can recall as especially noteworthy several instances of atrocious abuse. Five patients were chronic victims. Three of them, peculiarly irresponsible, suffered with especial regularity, scarcely a day passing without bringing to them its quota of punishment. One of these, almost an idiot, and quite too inarticulate to tell a convincing story even under the most favorable conditions, became so cowed that, whenever an attendant passed, he would circle his oppressor as a whipped cur circles a cruel master. If this avoidance became too marked, the attendant would then and there chastise him for the implied, but unconscious insult.

There was a young man, occupying a cell next to mine in the Bull Pen, who was so far out of his mind as to be absolutely irresponsible. His offence was that he could not comprehend and obey. Day after day I could hear the blows and kicks as they fell upon his body, and his incoherent cries for mercy were as painful to hear as they are impossible to forget. That he survived is surprising. What wonder that this man, who was "violent," or who was made violent, would not permit the attendants to dress him! But he had a half-witted friend, a ward-mate, who could coax him into his clothes when his oppressors found him most intractable.

Of all the patients known to me, the one who was assaulted with the greatest frequency was an incoherent and irresponsible man of sixty years. This patient was restless and forever talking or shouting, as any man might if oppressed by such delusions as his. He was profoundly convinced that one of the patients had stolen his stomach—an idea inspired perhaps by the remarkable corpulency of the person he accused. His loss he would wofully voice even while eating. Of course, argument to the contrary had no effect; and his monotonous recital of his imaginary troubles made him unpopular with those whose business it was to care for him. They showed him no mercy. Each day—including the hours of the night, when the night watch took a hand—he was belabored with fists, broom handles, and frequently with the heavy bunch of keys which attendants usually carry on a long chain. He was also kicked and choked, and his suffering was aggravated by his almost continuous confinement in the Bull Pen. An exception to the general rule (for such continued abuse often causes death), this man lived a long time—five years, as I learned later.

Another victim, forty-five years of age, was one who had formerly been a successful man of affairs. His was a forceful personality, and the traits of his sane days influenced his conduct when he broke down mentally. He was in the expansive phase of paresis, a phase distinguished by an exaggerated sense of well-being, and by delusions of grandeur which are symptoms of this form as well as of several other forms of mental disease. Paresis, as everyone knows, is considered incurable and victims of it seldom live more than three or four years. In this instance, instead of trying to make the patient's last days comfortable, the attendants subjected him to a course of treatment severe enough to have sent even a sound man to an early grave. I endured privations and severe abuse for one month at the State Hospital. This man suffered in all ways worse treatment for many months.

I became well acquainted with two jovial and witty Irishmen. They were common laborers. One was a hodcarrier, and a strapping fellow. When he arrived at the institution, he was at once placed in the violent ward, though his "violence" consisted of nothing more than an annoying sort of irresponsibility. He irritated the attendants by persistently doing certain trivial things after they had been forbidden. The attendants made no allowance for his condition of mind. His repetition of a forbidden act was interpreted as deliberate disobedience. He was physically powerful, and they determined to cow him. Of the master assault by which they attempted to do this I was not an eyewitness. But I was an ear witness. It was committed behind a closed door; and I heard the dull thuds of the blows, and I heard the cries for mercy until there was no breath left in the man with which he could beg even for his life. For days, that wrecked

Hercules dragged himself about the ward moaning pitifully. He complained of pain in his side and had difficulty in breathing, which would seem to indicate that some of his ribs had been fractured. This man was often punished, frequently for complaining of the torture already inflicted. But later, when he began to return to the normal, his good-humor and native wit won for him an increasing degree of good treatment.

The other patient's arch offence—a symptom of his disease—was that he gabbled incessantly. He could no more stop talking than he could right his reason on command. Yet his failure to become silent at a word was the signal for punishment. On one occasion an attendant ordered him to stop talking and take a seat at the further end of the corridor, about forty feet distant. He was doing his best to obey, even running to keep ahead of the attendant at his heels. As they passed the spot where I was sitting, the attendant felled him with a blow behind the ear; and, in falling, the patient's head barely missed the wall.

Addressing me, the attendant said, "Did you see that?"

"Yes," I replied, "and I'll not forget it."

"Be sure to report it to the doctor," he said, which remark showed his contempt, not only for me, but for those in authority.

The man who had so terribly beaten me was particularly flagrant in ignoring the claims of age. On more than one occasion he viciously attacked a man of over fifty, who, however, seemed much older. He was a Yankee sailing-master, who in his prime could have thrashed his tormentor with ease. But now he was helpless and could only submit. However, he was not utterly abandoned by his old world. His wife called often to see him; and, because of his condition, she was permitted to visit him in his room. Once she arrived a few hours after he had been cruelly beaten. Naturally she asked the attendants how he had come by the hurts—the blackened eye and bruised head. True to the code, they lied. The good wife, perhaps herself a Yankee, was not thus to be fooled; and her growing belief that her husband had been assaulted was confirmed by a sight she saw before her visit was ended. Another patient, a foreigner who was a target for abuse, was knocked flat two or three times as he was roughly forced along the corridor. I saw this little affair and I saw that the good wife saw it. The next day she called again and took her husband home. The result was that after a few (probably sleepless) nights, she had to return him to the hospital and trust to God rather than the State to protect him.

Another victim was a man sixty years of age. He was quite inoffensive, and no patient in the ward seemed to attend more strictly to his own business. Shortly after my transfer from the violent ward this man was so viciously attacked that his arm was broken. The attendant (the man who had so viciously assaulted me) was summarily discharged. Unfortunately, however, the relief afforded the insane was slight and brief, for this same brute, like another whom I have mentioned, soon secured a position in another institution—this one, however, a thousand miles distant.

Death by violence in a violent ward is after all not an unnatural death—for a violent ward. The patient of whom I am about to speak was also an old man—over sixty. Both physically and mentally he was a wreck. On being brought to the institution he was at once placed in a cell in the Bull Pen, probably because of his previous history for violence while at his own home. But his violence (if it ever existed) had already spent itself, and had come to be nothing more than an utter incapacity to obey. His offence was that he was too weak to attend to his common wants. The day after his arrival, shortly before noon, he lay stark naked and helpless upon the bed in his cell. This I know, for I went to investigate immediately after a ward-mate had informed me of the vicious way in which the head attendant had assaulted the sick man. My informant was a man whose word regarding an incident of this character I would take as readily as that of any man I know. He came to me, knowing that I had taken upon myself the duty of reporting such abominations. My informant feared to take the initiative, for, like many other patients who believe themselves doomed to continued confinement, he feared to invite abuse at the hands of vengeful attendants. I therefore promised him that I would report the case as soon as I had an opportunity.

All day long this victim of an attendant's unmanly passion lay in his cell in what seemed to be a semi-conscious condition. I took particular pains to observe his condition, for I felt that the assault of the morning might result in death. That night, after the doctor's regular tour of inspection, the patient in question was transferred to a room next my own. The mode of transfer impressed itself upon my memory. Two attendants—one of them being he who had so brutally beaten the patient—placed the man in a sheet and, each taking an end, carried the hammocklike contrivance, with its inert contents, to what proved to be its last resting-place above ground. The bearers seemed as much concerned about their burden as one might be about a dead dog, weighted and ready for the river.

That night the patient died. Whether he was murdered none can ever know. But it is my honest opinion that he was. Though he might never have recovered, it is plain that he would have lived days, perhaps months. And had he been humanely, nay, scientifically, treated, who can say that he might not have been restored to health and home?

The young man who had been my companion in mischief in the violent ward was also terribly abused. I am sure I do not exaggerate when I say that on ten occasions, within a period of two months, this man was cruelly assaulted, and I do not know how many times he suffered assaults of less severity. After one of these chastisements, I asked him why he persisted in his petty transgressions when he knew that he thereby invited such body-racking abuse.

"Oh," he said, laconically, "I need the exercise."

To my mind, the man who, with such gracious humor, could refer to what was in reality torture deserved to live a century. But an unkind fate decreed that he should die young. Ten months after his commitment to the State Hospital he was discharged as improved—but not cured. This was not an unusual procedure; nor was it in his case apparently an unwise one, for he seemed fit for freedom. During the first month of regained liberty, he hanged himself. He left no message of excuse. In my opinion, none was necessary. For aught any man knows, the memories of the abuse, torture, and injustice which were so long his portion may have proved to be the last straw which overbalanced the desire to live.

Patients with less stamina than mine often submitted with meekness; and none so aroused my sympathy as those whose

submission was due to the consciousness that they had no relatives or friends to support them in a fight for their rights. On
behalf of these, with my usual piece of smuggled led pencil, I
soon began to indite and submit to the officers of the institution,
letters in which I described the cruel practices which came
under my notice. My reports were perfunctorily accepted and at
once forgotten or ignored. Yet these letters, so far as they related
to overt acts witnessed, were lucid and should have been convincing. Furthermore, my allegations were frequently corrobo-
rated by bruises on the bodies of the patients. My usual custom
was to write an account of each assault and hand it to the doctor
in authority. Frequently I would submit these reports to the
attendants with instructions first to read and then deliver them
to the superintendent or the assistant physician. The men
whose cruelty I thus laid bare read with evident but perverted
pleasure my accounts of assaults, and laughed and joked about
my ineffectual attempts to bring them to book.

1909 ⊞

The Maniac: A Realistic Study of Madness from the Maniac's Point of View, by E. Thelmar

The Maniac is an autobiographical story of a journalist's acute madness, characterized by continual auditory hallucinations, occasional visual and tactile hallucinations, and strange "out of the body" experiences. Most of the time, E. Thelmar believed that she was possessed by demons of "fiends" and that she was in communication with the spirit world. Only when she began to recover did she renounce, at least partially, the various demons, fiends, spirits, and telepathic contacts and conclude that they were unreal and that she had been mad.

In some ways this account of "demonic possession" is reminiscent of Margery Kempe's fifteenth-century spiritual autobiography, especially the account of the time when she "went out of her mind and was wondrously vexed and laboured with spirits" and thought she saw "devils opening their mouths all inflamed with burning waves of fire." The difference between the two works has to do mostly with presentation. Both women had severe hallucinatory experiences that appeared to be the workings of spiritual forces; both were treated for madness. Yet Margery Kempe only once describes herself as being "out of her mind," while the speaker of *The Maniac*, as she describes retrospectively her unusual experiences, never completely leaves the psychiatric perspective: even though at the time of her mad experiences she often felt that she was communing with spirits, in telling about them she completely accepts the psychiatric opinion that the spirits were products of her own mind and that she was experiencing an "attack of madness." The publishers of *The Maniac* in 1909 presented it as a psychiatric rather than a spiritual study, as the title and the subtitle, *A Realistic Study of Madness from the Maniac's Point of View*, indicate. Various reviewers called it "an affair for psychologists and alienists and other scientific people" which "should be studied attentively by the student of medicine," "should be in the hands of every doctor and every nurse who has to attend to the mentally sick," and "should . . . be given a place in the libraries of all mental hospitals, for the perusal of both the medical staff and the attendants."[1]

---

[1]Thelmar, *The Maniac*, introductory page.

The excerpts included here portray the progression of the journalist's "possession." The speaker describes her first hallucination, which she experiences as a casual, pleasant telepathic conversation with a well-known artist whom she calls Ray Hall. In the next excerpt she relates her second meeting with Hall, during which time she momentarily projects her awareness outside her body. After these initial pleasant encounters the situation rapidly changes. In the last two excerpts, the narrator is seduced by a "fiend" and a hallucinatory crowd of people appears, while threats of attacks by "fiends" and "thousands of mad voices" ring in her ears. By now the hallucinations and strange experiences have taken over her world; she is in some fashion "possessed," and the rest of the book concerns itself with her internal adventures and agonies.

I WENT TO BED EARLY, being so tired.

On referring since to the calendar in my diary, I see that the day and hour at which I did get into bed that night are down in the calendar as being the exact day and hour of the new moon.

Is there really, as superstitiously believed by all nations, any connection between Luna and lunacy?

I did not read in bed, but blew out the candle immediately. My head had scarcely touched the pillow when a man's voice— a very pleasant baritone voice—proceeding apparently from the large armchair by the fireplace, asked clearly and aloud—

"Are you awake?"

I raised myself on my left elbow, and facing the direction whence the voice came, and feeling suddenly no longer tired, but brisk and most alert, I answered—

"Yes, wide awake. Who are you?"

(I have never in my life heard any "voices," and should have been extremely startled at hearing one then had I been in my right senses. As it was, I was no more startled than one is startled by dreams, when the most astonishing and unlikely things seem quite natural and ordinary.)

The "voice" ignored my question and went on—

"Are you not the author of '——'?" (mentioning a book which, five years previously, had taken me six months' incessant labour to write. It was of inordinate length and dealt largely with occultism.)

"Yes!" I exclaimed in surprise. "But how can you possibly know of that? It never was published."

"Well, to prove to you that I do know it, is not the motto to the book '——'?" (The voice quoted in full the three lines of poetry which I had put as a motto.)

"Perfectly correct! But how can you know? Are you——?" (I mentioned a publisher who had offered to publish the book if I would cut it.)

"No, I am not."

"Are you one of his 'readers'?"

"No."

"Are you a 'reader' at any other publisher's?"

"No."

"Well, then, how on earth can you have read my book at all?"

"I did not say that I had read it."

This rather nonplussed me.

"Ah! Then you haven't read it?" I remarked, after a pause.

"Yes, I have—at least, extracts from it. The fact is, a friend of mine read it."

"Oh? Is he a 'reader' anywhere?"

"No."

"Then where could he have read it?"

"At ——'s."

"But if he isn't a 'reader' there, I don't understand how he could have read the thing at all."

"He isn't a 'reader' there, but he works there. He read the book because they told him it was such an extraordinary one. It is he who told me about it, and showed me extracts he had copied from it."

"What is your friend's name?" I asked.

"He might not like me to tell you."

"Oh! I beg your pardon—I did not mean to be rudely inquisitive—but the whole thing seems to me so inexplicable. What did your friend think of the book?"

"It made the greatest impression on him—it changed his whole views of life."

("Now I wonder if it changed them for the better or the worse," I thought to myself: "I am rather curious to know that, but I am not going to court a second snub by asking for any further information whatever about that friend.")

"Yes, it changed his whole life. It made him join such-and-such a community."

Again I longed to inquire whether joining that community had enabled that friend to find what he sought; but again, for the same reason as before, I refrained, and merely remarked—

"Oh?"

"Yes. He tells me everything, you know."

"So it appears." (I was determined not to evince the smallest further curiosity about that friend.)

In my room I had a copy of the work of art of a celebrated living artist—a man who is completely unknown to me personally, but for whose genius as an artist I have always had the greatest admiration.

The voice said to me—

"The young man depicted in such-and-such a position in that work of art in your room is this friend of mine about whom we have been speaking. He was the model from which that figure was drawn."

This statement interested me very much. I said quickly—

"If you know so much about the creation of that work, you must be the artist? You must be ——?" (I named the artist's name—which for the remainder of this history I will alter to the fictitious one of "Ray Hall.")

The voice did not deny this indictment, and throughout the entire remainder of my attack of madness I was fully convinced that this man's voice continually holding converse with me was the voice of that artist. I see now, on carefully reviewing the whole thing, that this voice never once actually admitted to being that artist; it merely never denied it, and always answered instantly to that name whenever I summoned it.

How long exactly the conversation lasted that night, I cannot tell, but when the voice ceased talking to me I dropped quietly off to sleep.

The next morning I was, apparently, perfectly normal, in every respect except one: I clearly remembered the conversation of the previous night, and it still seemed to me the most ordinary occurrence. I merely thought how pleasant it was to be able thus to hold converse with someone so entirely congenial to me in tastes, and that now I should never feel lonely any more in that lodging-room, as the voice had said we should always be able to talk to each other as we had done the previous night, whenever we wished—we were so completely *en rapport*.

I felt disinclined to commence the new story I had intended starting that morning, but I occupied myself with a variety of other usual occupations—lunched out at a restaurant (but quite forgot to order any food to be sent to my lodging for that evening and for Sunday, as I should have done). No "voices" whatever talked to me that day. Again I went to bed early.

Again immediately I blew out the light the same man's voice which had been conversing with me the previous evening recommenced. It asked gently—

"Darling, are you afraid?"

I raised myself in bed and looked in the direction whence the voice seemed unmistakably to proceed—namely the large table in the centre of the room—but I could see nothing. (The streetlights would have enabled me to see objects in my room.) It sounded exactly as if the speaker were seated on the edge of that table nearest to my bed. I felt most wide-awake.

"No," I answered, "I am not in the least afraid; why should I be afraid? But who are you?"

Again the voice evaded any direct reply. Again, when I asked him point-blank if he was "Ray Hall" he did not deny it. What he said was, that we were "twin souls," as was proved by our being able to communicate like this when any distance apart, and that in less than three months' time we should infallibly be united. He said it would be impossible for anything on earth to come between people who could converse direct with each other as we could, no matter what distance separated us. He then began talking about the Medium at the office. He said he wished, for a particular purpose, to engage her as his secretary. He asked me if I thought she would accept the billet?

I said I thought she would.

He then said I was to speak to her on the subject and offer her the appointment.

I said I would when next I saw her. Afterwards I said to him—

"You aren't here bodily, I know. It sounds as if you were sitting on the edge of the big table in my room. Where are you really?"

"In the easy-chair, smoking, in my own room. That is where I am bodily, and I am merely sending my thought to you. But shall we try an experiment?"

"What experiment?" I asked.

"Shall I try if I can send my spirit to you?" inquired the voice.

"Yes. That will be a most interesting experiment," I exclaimed. "Try it."

It seemed to me as if I were divided up into three distinct *layers* of being—layers that should, normally, interpenetrate each other, but now were arranged in three separate, superimposed strata. On the bed lay my physical body, fully awake and conscious. Directly over it, at the distance of a few feet up, was poised in mid-air my human soul, consisting of a replica of my physical body made of a substance like flame. Above that again, at about an equal distance up, was my spirit, which seemed to be composed of cold white light—more like electric light than anything else.

Almost immediately after the preceding remarks, I experienced a vivid and most distinct sensation; not in my physical body at all, but high up near the ceiling in my "top layer." As I have never felt any sensation in the least like it, I cannot describe it. It seemed as if two electric lights—my own spirit and another's—had merged into one light, with a sort of electric shock.

Directly I felt it I exclaimed excitedly (for I was most interested in the experiment)—

"You have managed it! I can feel you here!"

The voice answered—

"I feel absolutely nothing."

"Oh, what a pity!" I exclaimed. "You don't know what you are missing! Evidently you must be unconscious in your spirit. That is most unfortunate. If you are unconscious, you might as well not be here at all, as far as you are concerned. Try to send your soul, and see if you are conscious in that, apart from your body."

The next instant I felt another, totally different sensation; this time in my "second layer." It was a warm, magnetic sort of sensation, and seemed caused by the mingling of two fiery flames.

"I can feel that!" exclaimed the voice. "This is good enough for me!"

"Ah! that is because you were unconscious in your spirit," I said. "That utterly surpassed this! However, it is useless trying spirit experiments if you are unconscious in the spirit—you had better just stay here in your soul."

He stayed, talking for some time, and then remarked—

"Are you aware that I am still up and dressed, in my smoking-room, and that it must be between two and three in the morning now, I should think? I am afraid I shall have to leave and go and get into bed."

"Very well," I said. "Good-night. Try this experiment again to-morrow night—but go to bed first, as I have done."

"All right. Good-night."

"Good-night," I answered, and went off to sleep.

*   *   *

"Kneel down and pray," said the voice.

"Where shall I kneel?"

"There, in the sunlight by the fireplace. Be sure to kneel in the sunlight."

I deposited the brush on the mantelpiece, and knelt down as directed.

"Lean more forward into the sunlight," ordered the voice.

I obeyed.

"Bend your head lower."

Again I obeyed; and my hair, which was hanging loose, fell all over my face.

"Push back your hair from off your face," the voice commanded.

"Oh, what *does* it matter where my hair is when I am praying?" I exclaimed impatiently, for all these elaborate preparations were beginning to annoy me. However, I pushed back my hair as directed, but as my head remained in the bent position ordered, my hair immediately tumbled once more over my face, shutting out all view of everything except what was directly beneath my eyes. This happened to be a small black coal-shuttle.

Reflected in this shiny surface I saw quite distinctly a picture of a very well-known woman occultist. (She is unacquainted with me, but I am acquainted with her both through her books and her lectures.)

"Oh," I thought, "this is all right. She understands all about these things. Evidently this is part of some occult experiment, and when the fiend appears she means to tackle it."

I did not feel in the least afraid, and was racking my brain to think what prayer would be suited to this most unusual occasion, when suddenly I experienced a violent, physical sensation inside my body. It did not in the least hurt me, but it was so violent and unaccountable it frightened me. I could not understand what was happening to me. (I neither saw nor heard anything.)

I thought to myself, "Has this perhaps something to do with that fiend that they were warning me against?" And instantly the voices confirmed this fear, saying that the fiend had now got inside my body; that the explanation of this whole mysterious sensation was that I had been seduced by a fiend, and that I should therefore have a fiend-child.

*   *   *

This sent me off into a perfect frenzy.

I fully believed it to be the true explanation of the unaccountable sensation I had experienced.

I began calling on God, and everything and everyone I could think of, in heaven and on earth, to come to my rescue. I sobbed and cried and wrung my hands in agony of terror and despair. I got up off my knees and rocked myself to and fro on the arm of the big armchair, exclaiming—

"O God! What *have* I done, that such an awful thing should have happened to me? O God! O God! O God! O God!"

While I was going on thus, like the demented creature that I was, the wall of the room facing me seemed suddenly to fade away before my eyes, and up near the ceiling—but as if far away in the dim distance—I saw a crowd of people seated in what looked like a very large box at a theatre. They seemed to have been observing, from that great way off, all that had been taking place in my room. They seemed to be the people who had been conducting the experiment which had resulted in this awful catastrophe to me.

Seated in the centre of the box, I could distinguish the woman-occultist whose reflection I had seen in the japanned coal-shuttle, and I could hear her sobbing; whilst beside her, turning towards her so that his face was hidden from me, was a man standing up and denouncing her and these infernal experiments in a voice that I instantly recognised as Ray Hall's.

He said, "Mrs.——, you are a fiend, and this is your doing!"

I stopped sobbing, and exclaimed, "Ray Hall! Take care what you say! I am quite certain that Mrs. —— would never have harmed me intentionally. It may be nobody's fault, but I am simply done for," and I recommenced sobbing.

He said, "I am going to drag all these fiends of people, with their infernal experiments, to justice! I swear I will denounce them and their practices, publicly, to the whole world! If I die for it, I will have vengeance on them for the fiendish wrong they have committed!"

"What is the use of vengeance?" I moaned. "It will help nobody. Stop their experiments, to save other victims—not for any vengeance. As for me, anything now is too late to save me; I am done for!" And I sobbed and sobbed.

"No, you are not done for!" he exclaimed; "you are my wife and I will never desert you!"

"Oh, no!" I sobbed, "I am not fit now to be the wife of any decent man; but I call God to witness that I am a perfectly innocent woman!"

"You are! And you are my wife, and I will never desert you, but stand by you through all this, and get to the bottom of this whole thing. I swear it!"

"Oh!" I said, "you have spoken like a true man, Ray Hall. I can never be your wife now; but I will live, and not kill myself, in order that you and I together may get to the bottom of this whole awful affair."

I went on sobbing uninterruptedly, and moaning—

"Oh! why didn't you jump down from that gallery, Ray Hall, into the arena, to help me and save me from the fiend? Now all help is useless, and what am I to do? O God! What am I to do?"

I walked across to my bed and flung myself face-downwards upon it, sobbing ceaselessly. I paid no further attention to the crowd in the gallery, which seemed to vanish in the same manner in which it had appeared.

Presently some voice exclaimed excitedly—

"Another fiend is coming!"

I started up in terror from the bed, and said—

"Where shall I pray?"

"There, in the sunlight by the sofa," answered the voice.

I threw myself upon my knees in the spot indicated, and was just about to commence frantic prayers, when suddenly I thought, "No! Why should I pray? Prayer is utterly useless! I prayed before, and nobody helped me. I am perfectly innocent. I will not pray: I demand justice! Besides, what does it matter how many fiends come now? I have nothing more to lose!"

I got up from my knees, burst into a wild laugh, and quoting, "'Come one, come all!'" I sat myself down on the sofa and gazed round the room, feeling that if I caught sight of any approaching fiend I would not wait for it to attack me, but would attack it with the courage and fury of despair, and frighten it a good deal more than any fiend whatever would now be able to frighten me.

I neither saw nor felt anything.

Finding nothing was coming, I got up, and was walking across the room to throw myself again upon the bed to sob, when suddenly thousands of mad voices commenced yelling in my ears.

What those voices are like defies description. No human being who has not actually experienced it can imagine such hell-torment.

The voices seemed to be legion, and each separate voice felt like a charge of dynamite exploding in my head, rending and shattering the living substance of my brain.

I stopped dead-short in the centre of the room, held my head between my hands (for my very skull felt as if being blasted), and said aloud, quite quietly and slowly, these exact words—

"My God! This awful thing that has happened to me has sent me stark, raving mad! This is unmistakable madness. And yet I am sane enough to know that I *am* mad, and I shall do nothing that these voices are yelling at me to do. I shall go and have a good square meal, for it is my belief that one-half of this is sheer starvation."

It was midday, and I had not had a morsel of food.

In a perfect agony of mind and body, and with those screaming voices still shattering my brain, I finished my dressing. I hastily twisted up my hair and pinned it; I put on my dress, and hunted about for a lace tie and a brooch to finish it off. I thought—

"I must compose myself and dress myself properly; if I go out looking as wild as I am feeling, I shall attract everyone's attention, and perhaps be taken up in the street as a madwoman before I have had time to get to the bottom of all this. I mean to live and get to the bottom of this."

1910 ⊸⊟⊸

Legally Dead, Experiences During Seventeen Weeks' Detention in a Private Asylum, by Marcia Hamilcar

The British reform legislation of 1845, as we have seen, was aimed both at maintaining a careful system of inspection and control over existing private madhouses (and other institutions), and at reducing their numbers—by establishing a network of public county asylums. It partly succeeded in those aims. Certainly the number of madhouses continued to diminish into the twentieth century.

Several serious protests by English mental patients have been written during this century. *The Lost Days of My Life*, Jane Simpson's 1958 account of a childhood spent in English homes and asylums, is probably the most alarming. But Marcia Hamilcar's *Legally Dead* is one of the last written protests by a private madhouse patient.

In December 1907 Marcia Hamilcar, a fifty-seven-year old unmarried English schoolteacher, became severely depressed. During the Christmas holiday she went to stay at the house of a relative and quite suddenly, as she explains it, "the proportion of things" became distorted. She believed she had committed many serious crimes, that she was liable to be arrested at any moment, and suspected that the police were already at her home, waiting for her. Trembling, unable to sleep, she at last decided to return home. Back at home her sister and a physician urged her to go to a private nursing home for what she expected to be a short rest. She agreed to go.

Though Hamilcar was not yet officially certified as mad, the woman running the nursing home, with the apparent collusion of Hamilcar's sister, held her prisoner for five weeks, taking away her clothes, cutting off her hair, strapping her to the bed, and keeping her bound in some kind of straitjacket. They forced drugs upon her and fed her only a pint of milk a day. After five weeks Hamilcar had lost twenty-five pounds and was covered with bruises that the director of the nursing home said were "self-inflicted." By then she probably did look quite mad, or, at the very least, peculiar, with her hair shaven to the scalp, unnaturally thin, trembling, frightened, and occasionally lapsing into a delirious state that was probably drug-induced. Two physicians examined her and signed a commitment order; the order was countersigned by a local magistrate who was too busy actually to see her for himself.

With the commitment properly signed Hamilcar was taken away to a private madhouse, where she was beaten and force-fed. Though she was never treated well there she was detoxified from the drugs given her at the nursing home and allowed to eat full meals. She gained weight and improved enough that within five weeks the superintendent told her she could leave, provided her sisters would agree. Her sisters did not agree, and Hamilcar remained imprisoned in that institution for an additional seven weeks.

During her stay in the private madhouse, Hamilcar took notes in preparation for *Legally Dead*. Like many protests this book opens by calling attention to the author's sincerity and veracity, insisting that hers will be a "true, plain, unvarnished tale, untouched by the glamour of imagination." It is true that during much of her early experience in the nursing home she was delirious, and there is an almost pathological bitterness that touches virtually all her descriptions (the asylum water tastes terrible, the tea is always too strong, and so on). But we have no reason really to doubt the major issues of her story. Hamilcar insists that, once accused of madness, any person's civil rights vanish. And her own experiences seem to support this disturbing thesis. Legitimate complaints of false imprisonment and physical assault went unheeded. Requests for release were ignored. She claims she had only "lost the proportion of things," but whatever her mental condition, she was pronounced "insane" by those around her—which meant that she was "legally dead."

In the following three excerpts we witness some of Hamilcar's experiences as a legally dead person. In the first excerpt, her hair is cut off, without her permission or cooperation. In the second, she is beaten and force-fed. Finally, she tries to plead her case before a visiting inspector, who seems barely aware of her existence.

BUT THE CROWNING ACT of this fiend's cruelty was the cutting off of my luxuriant head of hair. And this was accomplished under circumstances of wanton cruelty. As a child I had a wealth of natural curling hair, my father's pride, and which my mother had always tended with great care. I had throughout my life continued to give it the same attention, with the result that my tresses were unusually abundant for my age. As my hair was of a curly nature, it was perhaps difficult to keep in plaits, unless tied at the ends, and as I was unable to attend to it myself, it may have given some little trouble. Although she was well-paid, the woman was too lazy to give any attention to it, and I remember opening my eyes one day and finding my sister standing near my bed. My hair was lying on the pillow, and the woman was complaining of the trouble it caused her. "I should cut if off," remarked my sister.

Some hours later I was awakened by violent tugging of my hair, which, as I have always had a very sensitive scalp, caused me cruel pain. Looking at the head of the bedstead, I saw the woman with a pair of scissors in her hand. Putting my hand instinctively to one side of my head, I encountered only the ends close to the scalp. As I lay on one side the woman had found no difficulty in clipping my hair on the other. I had got down at least two feet from the head of the bed, and the intense pain I felt was caused by the woman pulling my remaining locks through the bars of the bedstead, and dragging me bodily up to the bars by this means. When my head touched the iron, fearing, I imagine, my resistance, she cut my hair through or rather against the ironwork, in spite of my cries and entreaties, and the slight resistance I was able to make. With all her strength she pulled at my hair, dragging me, at the same time shouting and commanding me to lie still, and to give her no trouble, or I should suffer for it. I put my hands up to save my hair, in which I had taken a natural pride, and these narrowly escaped being cut, too. My very natural resistance was called "violence," and I was represented as a dangerous maniac, because I had tried as far as excessive weakness permitted to prevent this abominable outrage.

I have since been told that when the doctor next visited me he expressed his indignation that such an extreme measure had been adopted without his authorization or knowledge; but my sister, whose locks have always been of the scantiest, had accomplished her double purpose—she had robbed me of my abundant tresses, and done all in her power to secure for me the severest treatment, when I should arrive at the asylum, to which she had from the outset of my illness determined to consign me. The woman also was freed from a daily duty she found irksome, *my* feelings were far too insignificant to be considered by either.

What the loss of my hair cost me in mental suffering I can never express. I was completely disfigured. What right had that woman to cut off my hair? Would she have dared to do so had I not been a mental patient? Why should this difference be made in the sane and insane? The latter does not cease to feel, simply because the mind is deranged. It may seem an exaggeration to say that I felt the loss of my hair almost as much as that of my home; I dreaded to go again into the world, fearing ridicule; besides, my shorn head completely altered my appearance. As an instance of the daily annoyance to which I was subjected, the night before I left the "Home" the woman showed me the hair she had so ruthlessly cut from my head. The tresses were laid on an open newspaper. "Give them to me!" I cried. "They are mine! You have no right to keep my hair!"

"I have a perfect right," she replied. "You will never have your hair, for I shall keep it. It belongs to me."

I tried to take it, but I was too weak to rise from my bed, and the woman triumphantly bore off my locks, and placed them in her own room. Months after, a few wisps, about a quarter of the amount cut off, were sent me. What was done with the remainder I do not know.

*   *   *

About midnight I heard voices and steps near my cell. I presume that some one had remembered that I had, so far, had nothing to eat, for two attendants appeared, one bearing a tumbler of some liquid, the other a lantern. Before I could speak, one, a tall, very strong, coarse, swearing woman, whose name I discovered afterwards was Stiles, had seized me roughly, and in a moment I was lying flat on the unsavoury mattress (I had for an hour or two sat up, with a blanket—or piece of blanket—round me, vainly trying to get some warmth into my frozen feet by weakly rubbing them). The other attendant sat upon my trembling legs, whilst she pinioned my shaking arms. Then Stiles roughly opened my mouth and thrust a tube down my throat, causing me intense pain. The choking sensation was indescribably horrible. To swallow was impossible, and a sickening sensation of suffocation almost robbed me of consciousness. How long the pipe was in my mouth I cannot say; it seemed, from the agony it caused me, quite half an hour. When the pipe was withdrawn the woman turned—or so it seemed to me—my mouth inside out. As I have before stated, I have no natural teeth, and all my life my gums have been very sensitive. What she really did, was to deliberately thrust her big, coarse fingers around my gums. She may have considered my mouth a curiosity, and so a desire to examine it led her to cause me the pain she did. As her rough fingers went round and round my mouth they lacerated the gums in every direction, and a stream of blood followed them as she removed them. Before I could protest she struck me a heavy blow on my left cheek-bone, which protruded from the skin alone that covered it. This was followed by some half dozen blows on my head—a twentieth century method of "settling the brains." Then, getting up from the floor, she gave me a parting kick, and with a vile word never before addressed to me, she left me more dead than alive.

The intense pain in my throat, the smarting of my mouth and face, the pain in my head from the blows alone prevented me from relapsing into unconsciousness.

When, later on, I was able to get up I recounted to the matron what happened on that first night, exactly as I have given it here, but she made no remark whatever, nor was any report made to the doctor. Such brutal attacks were too common to be noticed.

Some hours later I was taken by a woman into the bath-room. She threw a towel at me with which to wipe my bleeding mouth.

Looking at her, I said, as I showed her the large discoloured patch, "You will hear of this again. You have no right to treat me like this."

Knowing her power, the woman only laughed and mocked. I was too impotent, she well knew, to bring a rebuke on her head.

*   *   *

As the spring advanced the patients began to talk of the visit of the commissioners, which usually took place at this time of the year, and I questioned everybody as to their powers of pro-

cedure. Could they discharge me? I was answered in the negative; only the doctor could do that. But I determined that I
would get speech with these gentlemen. I knew that a private
interview would be useless. Doctors, matron, or nurses were
always within hearing, where all doors were kept open, even if
the interview were supposed to be private; but I would do my
best to be heard, and I would ask for my release.

The "Temple" underwent a thorough purification in anticipation of the visit, which, from the anxiety of the matron and
attendants to have everything in order, was evidently regarded
by them as a matter of very considerable importance. The patients regarded it, however, with indifference; nothing appeared
to them important. Their sombre, dreary days brought no event
that concerned them nearly, they had left events outside the
walls of their graves, nothing occurred now to quicken the slow
beat of their languid pulses, and they looked on at the sweeping, cleaning and garnishing with unconcern.

But I looked forward with eagerness to a conversation with
these arbiters of my fate, as I meant they should be. This visit is
supposed to be a surprise, but it is nothing of the sort. The
evening before I was seated in the garden with Miss Devise
when the Superintendent came up to her, and said—she was a
voluntary patient—"I suppose you do not wish to see the commissioners. I have just heard at the club that they will be here
to-morrow morning at eleven, and if you like, you can go for a
walk at that time," which she did, and one of the gentlemen
was sent out at the same hour with an attendant.

The morning for which the staff had made such extensive
preparations was, for that cold season, bright and spring-like,
and the peremptory attendant ordered those patients who were
in the convalescent ward even more peremptorily than usual
into the garden much earlier than usual. We obeyed, but in a
quarter of an hour here again peremptorily ordered to return to
the lounge. There we found Miss Hares, who did not as a rule
appear until after eleven, and the fat old lady, who had been
induced to hasten her toilette, and was being made happy with
one of the hard cakes left over from Sunday. The lounge looked
its best, as the two elderly gentlemen entered it, and there were
about eighteen patients in it. Curiously enough, as the former

entered, the matron asked me if I would fetch her something she had left in another part of the house, and I was away quite five minutes, for I could not find the article which, I believe, was not there at all. For some reason best known to the authorities it was evidently deemed advisable that I should see as little as possible of the proceedings and the commissioners—hence my errand.

When I got back to the lounge, the younger of the two men, who was well over sixty, was questioning a patient. This operation lasted perhaps ten seconds, then he passed on to another. The elder was apparently in an advanced stage of senile decay, and, standing with his hands under his frock-coat tails, gazed vacantly about him. If he attempted to approach a patient the younger man bade him return to his side, which he obediently did; nor did he address any of the patients whilst I was in the room. As the interviews were of but a few seconds' duration with each patient, these were half over when I got back to the lounge; but I meant to speak to one, if not both; so I approached the younger man, who held a note-book in his hand, to which he frequently referred.

"What is your name?" he inquired.

I gave it, and he referred to his book and verified my statement.

"I am very anxious to leave this asylum," I said. "I am not mentally ill. I have no delusions, nor am I suffering from any form of insanity."

The Superintendent here heard my voice, and turning round, placed his hand on my shoulder.

"This was a very bad one," said he in a tone expressive of the evident credit he took to himself for my cure, which he was the last person in the world to deserve. Yet to me individually he did not devote more than one half hour of his precious time throughout the seventeen weeks of my detention.

"Ah, let me see," replied the latter, "I think we have already had some correspondence with reference to this lady. Well, she seems much better." The doctor drew me away from the commissioner, who was already addressing another patient, and my opportunity vanished, my hopes sank to zero. In a few minutes the gentlemen had left the lounge.

1918, 1919 ᴇ⃝

The Diary of Vaslav Nijinsky

Born in Kiev in 1890 Vaslav Nijinsky was of the fifth generation of a family of dancers.[1] His father, Thomas Nijinsky, traveled with his own troupe of dancers through Russia, and at the age of three Vaslav made his first public appearance in his father's troupe. At the age of nine he was accepted into the Imperial School of St. Petersburg, one of the greatest ballet schools of the world. There, students and teachers alike recognized him as a prodigy. Two years before scheduled graduation his teachers declared they could teach him nothing more and suggested he graduate early—a unique event in the school's century and a half history. Even though he declined early graduation and continued his studies, Nijinsky was at the same time given increasingly prominent roles in the St. Petersburg's Mariinsky Ballet.

In 1909 Sergei Pavlovitch Diaghilev, a Russian aristocrat and patron of the arts, formed the Russian Ballet which was to tour Europe. Diaghilev acquired some of Russia's best dancers from both the Mariinsky Theatre of St. Petersburg and the Bolshoi Theatre of Moscow. Nijinsky was included. In September of that year the Russian Ballet gave its first performance, in Paris. The ballet was an enormous success, and Nijinsky was the star.

Aside from being a genius at characterization and a brilliant choreographer, Nijinsky was perhaps the greatest dancer of the century. He was the only dancer who could do an *entrechat dix*, a movement in which the dancer, while in the air, crosses the feet back and forth ten times. His leaps were tremendous. He was said to rise unusually high, almost floating at the peak of his leap, and then appear to descend twice as slowly as he rose. At the end of one dance, Nijinsky would cross an entire stage, front to back, in a single leap, to be caught by a human net behind the stage.

One of the great artists of Europe before the war, Nijinsky counted among his friends Debussy, Ravel, Cocteau, Stravinsky, Picasso, Rodin, and Charlie Chaplin. In spite of his universal recognition, Nijinsky remained a modest, self-effacing man of simple tastes, who

---

[1] All biographical information on Nijinsky is taken from *Nijinsky*, by Romola Nijinsky.

had been protected from childhood on. There was at once a personal, social, sexual, and artistic relationship between Diaghilev and the young dancer. Diaghilev allowed Nijinsky to express his genius fully in dance and choreography at the same time that he isolated him from others. In 1912, however, the Russian Ballet performed in Budapest, and a young Hungarian woman, Romola Markus, the daughter of Hungary's greatest stage actress, saw Nijinsky and fell in love. Remarkably, even though she had no training as a dancer, the young woman persuaded Diaghilev to let her travel with the ballet as a student. She and Nijinsky were married the following year.

Upon hearing of the marriage Diaghilev dismissed Nijinsky from the company and vowed to destroy his career. Nijinsky tried to form his own group but without success. When war broke out in Europe Nijinsky and his wife were in Hungary. Because he was a Russian, the Hungarian authorities took him and his family prisoner; they were allowed to stay with Romola's parents in Budapest but were forbidden to travel. In 1916, after repeated requests from various aristocratic and political figures of Europe, as well as the pope, the Austro-Hungarian government agreed to "lend" Nijinsky to the United States for an extended tour.

Upon returning to Europe with his wife and child in 1917 Nijinsky retreated to St. Moritz, Switzerland, to await the end of the war. During this time Romola began to notice disturbing changes in his behavior. He became more solitary, preferring to take long walks by himself. He began to write obsessively in his diary in Russian, working many nights until dawn. He seemed to be more impulsive and once—in an act wholly foreign to his nature—pushed Romola down a stairway. At one point he performed a highly unusual dance in St. Moritz, a violent, spontaneous, symbolic depiction of the horrors of the war and afterward told Romola he had become married to God. At last, deeply troubled by Nijinsky's behavior, his wife persuaded him to see the psychiatrist, Eugen Bleuler, in Zurich. Bleuler interviewed Nijinsky for ten minutes and then told Romola he was "incurably insane."

Hearing of this pronouncement Romola's parents rushed to Zurich and arranged to have Nijinsky locked up. His hotel was surrounded by firemen, in case he should try to jump out a window; police came to the door and seized him. "What have I done? What do you want of me? Where is my wife?" he asked. He was taken to the state asylum at Zurich, where he lapsed into a catatonic stupor. Although Romola consulated all the great psychiatrists—Freud, Jung, Bleuler, Kraepelin, Ferenczy—Nijinsky spent most of his remaining years in an asylum. It is said that he became hallucinatory and sometimes even violent, but mostly he was withdrawn and blankly indifferent to the rest of the world.

Nijinsky wrote his diary in 1918 and 1919 while in St. Moritz. At times he tells us his words are the words of God, a spiritual message to humankind. Though it was not published until 1936 (and then at the direction of Romola) it seems as if Nijinsky had intended his diary to be the preliminary study for a later, more finished piece. Intentions aside, however, it is clear that the diary also served as a private confessor, a way of dealing with his troubling thoughts, fantasies, and experiences, a way of separating and examining them.

Taken as a whole, the diary is a rambling combination of philosophy and anecdote. The philosophy resembles a Tolstoyan Christian mysticism. Nijinsky is seeking God, seeking the God in himself, and somehow he associates the human connection to God with a dominance of spontaneous feeling over the reasoning mind. At times, his search for God seems almost to become a deliberate and willful acquisition of madness: "I want the death of the mind," he says.

His identity is precarious. He tells us he is Nijinsky. Then he is God in Nijinsky. Other times, he says he is Christ, Buddha, and so on.

> I am a *moujik*, a workman, a factory worker, a servant, a master, an aristocrat, the Tsar. God. I am God. I am God. I am all, life, infinity. I will be always and everywhere. I can be killed but will live because I am all. I want infinite life, not death. I also have faults, but I shall have no more faults when people begin to help me. I want to see people and therefore my doors are always open, my cupboards and trunks always unlocked. Should you find my door locked, ring the bell and I will open it if I am at home.

But this expansiveness and fluidity of ego is no more remarkable than the words of a host of artists, prophets, or visionaries. America's greatest poet, Walt Whitman, said the same things; the above passage is certainly reminiscent of sections of *Leaves of Grass*. But where Whitman resolves his mystical journey, his loss of ego, his travel beyond the world of time and space and self, Nijinsky cannot. Beyond the mystical vision and the marked wisdom of a great man, we can see a pathology, a sorrow, and a renunciation of human life. As with Margery Kempe, Nijinsky's relationship to God at times becomes petty, absurd, and self-limiting. Ironically, the "marriage" to God described in the last excerpt is not a liberation but an imprisonment, figuratively and literally.

What was the cause and meaning of this madness, this alteration in thinking and personality that so suddenly overcame the dancer? Perhaps there was a hereditary predilection to madness. Nijinsky's oldest brother was an asylum inmate in Russia, but his illness may in fact have been caused by a childhood head injury. Or perhaps Nijinsky's divine marriage was an escape from difficult human marriages and entanglements—with Diaghilev, with Romola and her family, and with a Europe at war. Nijinsky himself said, "I retired into myself. I retired so far that I could no longer understand people."

Nijinsky was an extraordinary being. An American journalist called him "the human bird," an image that represents both his physical and mental being: a person too sensitive and uncompromising to endure life intact. The following three excerpts explore his relationship with God. The first is a positive, hopeful statement of mystical identity. The second depicts just how absurd and debilitating that relationship has become. The last excerpt is a dialogue between Nijinsky and God, just before he is taken away to the asylum.

I AM FEELING THROUGH the flesh and not through the intellect. I am the flesh. I am the feeling. I am God in flesh and feeling. I am man and not God. I am simple. I need not think. I must make myself felt and understood through feeling. Scientists think about me and break their heads, but their thinking will not give any results. They are stupid. I speak simply without any tricks.

The world was made by God. Man was made by God. It is impossible for man to understand God, but God understands God. Man is part of God and therefore sometimes understands God. I am both God and man. I am good and not a beast. I am an animal with a mind. I am flesh but I do come from flesh. God made flesh. I am God. I am God. I am God. . . .

*   *   *

Once I went for a walk and it seemed to me that I saw some blood on the snow. I followed the traces of the blood and sensed that somebody *who was still alive* had been killed. I went in another direction and more traces of blood were visible. I was afraid but I followed the tracks; there was a precipice. I realized that the traces were not of blood but manure. Walking in the snow, I noticed the marks of skis which had apparently stopped near the traces of blood. I thought that someone had buried a man in the snow, having knocked him down and killed him. I got frightened and ran back. Later I returned again and felt that God wanted to see whether I was afraid of Him or not. I said aloud: "No, I am not afraid of God: He is life and not death." Then God made me walk towards the precipice, telling me that He had been hurt and should be saved. I was afraid. I thought that the devil was tempting me, the same way as he did Christ. He was saying: "Jump down, then I will believe you." I was afraid and stood there for a little, then I felt that I was being drawn towards the precipice. I approached its edge and slipped, but some branches I had not noticed before stopped my fall. I was amazed and thought it was a miracle. God had wanted to try me. I understood Him. I tried to push the branches away but He did not allow me. For a long time I held on to them, then became terrified. God told me that I would fall if I let the branches go. Finally I disentangled myself from the bushes but did not fall. God said to me: *"Go home and tell your wife that you are insane."* I realized that God wanted to help me, and went home to bring this news to my wife.

On the way back again I saw the traces of blood, but no longer believed in their existence. God had shown me these in order that I should feel Him. I felt His presence and returned. He told me to lie down in the snow. I did so. He made me lie there for a long, long time. My hands began to get cold, to freeze. I took my hand off the snow and said that this could not be God's wish, as my hand was hurting. God was pleased, but after I had taken a few steps He ordered me to go back and lie down near a tree. I got hold of the tree, then slipped. God again commanded me to lie in the snow. I was lying there for a long time. I did not feel the cold any more—then God made me get up. I got up. He told me to go home. I went home. God said to me: *"Stop!"* I stopped. I again saw the traces of blood. He told me to return, I did. He said: *"Stop!"* I stopped.

*　　*　　*

I offended my wife without realizing it—then I asked her forgiveness; my faults were continuously being brought up at a suitable moment. I am afraid of my wife; she does not understand me. She believes that I am insane or wicked. I am not wicked, I love her. I write about life, not death. I am not Nijin-sky as they think. I am God in man. My wife is a good woman. I told her in secret all my plans, then she told the doctors every-thing, believing this would help me. My wife does not under-stand my object; I did not explain it, not wanting her to know. I will feel and she will understand. She will feel and I will under-stand. I do not want to think, thinking is death. I know what I am doing. *"I do not wish you ill. I love you. I want to live and therefore I will be with you. I spoke to you. I do not want intelligent speech."* The doctors speak with intelligence, so does my wife. I am afraid of them. I want them to understand my feelings. *"I know that it hurts you. Your wife is suffering because of you."* I do not want death to come and therefore I use all kinds of tricks. I will not reveal my object. *"Let them think you are an egoist. Let them put you in prison. I will release you because you belong to me. I do not like the intelligent Romola. I want her to leave you. I want you to be mine. I do not want you to love her as a man loves. I want you to love her with a sensitive love. I know how to simplify and smooth everything that has happened. I want the doctors to understand your feelings. I want to scold you because the doctors think that your wife is a nervous woman. Your cross has done so much harm that you cannot disentangle it all. I know your faults because I have committed them."* I put on a cross on purpose: *"She understood you. The doctor came in order to find out what your intentions are and does not understand anything at all. He thinks and therefore it is difficult for him to understand. He feels Romola is right and that you are right too. I know how to understand."* I think better than doctors. *"I am afraid for you, because you are frightened. I know your habits. Your love for me is infinite; you obey my orders. I will do everything to make you understand, I love your wife and you. I wish her well. I am God in you. I will be yours when you will understand me. I know what you are thinking about: that he is here and is staring at you. I want him to look at you."* I do not want to turn round because I can feel him looking at me. *"I want to show him your writing. He will think that you are ill because you write so much. I understand your feelings. I understand you well. I am making you write with a purpose because he will understand your feelings too. I want you to write everything I am telling you. People will understand you because you are sensitive. Your wife will understand you also. I know more than you and therefore I ask you not to turn around. I know your intentions. I want to carry out our plans but you must suffer. Everybody will feel and understand only when they see your sufferings."*

I want to write about my conversation in the dining room with my wife and the doctor. I pretended I was an egoist because I wanted to touch him. He will be offended if he finds this out but I do not care. I do not divide love. I wrote that I loved my wife better than anybody—I wanted to show how I feel about my wife. I love A. just as much. I know her tricks. She understands my feelings because she is going away in the next few days. I do not want her presence. I want my mother-in-law to come because I want to study her and help her. I do not study people's character in order to write about them. I want to write in order to explain to people their habits—which lead them to death. I call this book "Feelings." I love feeling and will write a big book about it. There will be a description of my life in it. I do not want to publish this book after my death. I want to publish it now. *"I am afraid for you because you are afraid for yourself. I want to say the truth. I do not want to hurt people. Perhaps you will be put in prison for writing this book. I will be with you because you love me. I cannot be silent. I must speak. I know you will not be put in prison; legally you have not committed an offense. If people want to judge you, you shall answer that everything you said is God's word. Then they will put you into an asylum, and you will understand insane people. I want you to be put in a prison or into an asylum. Dostoievsky went to the gallows and therefore you also can go and sit somewhere. I know people whose love is not dead and they will not allow you to be put anywhere. You will become as free as a bird when this book is published in many thousands of copies. I want to sign the name of Nijinsky—but my name is God. I love Nijinsky not as Narcissus but as God."* I love him because he gave me life. I do not want to pay any compliments. I love him. He loves me because he knows my habits. *"Nijinsky has faults, but Nijinsky must be listened to because he speaks the words of God."* I am Nijinsky. *"I do not want Nijinsky to be hurt and therefore I will protect him. I am only afraid for him because he is afraid for himself. I know his strength. He is a good man. I am a good God. I do not like Nijinsky when he is bad."* I do not like God when he is bad. I am God, Nijinsky is God. *"He is a good man and not evil. People have not understood him and will not understand him if they think. If people listened to me for several weeks there would be great results. I hope that my teachings will be understood."* All that I write is necessary to mankind. Romola is afraid of me, she feels I am a preacher. Romola does not want her husband to be a preacher, she wants a young, handsome husband. I am handsome, young. She does not understand my beauty, I have not got regular features. Regular features are not like God. God has sensitiveness in the face, a hunchback can be Godlike. I like hunchbacks and other freaks. I am myself a freak who has feeling and sensitiveness, and I can dance like a hunchback. I am an artist who likes all shapes and all beauty. Beauty is not relative. Beauty is God, He is in beauty and feeling. Beauty is in feeling too. I love beauty. I feel it and understand it. Those people who think write nonsense about beauty. One cannot discuss it. One cannot criticize it. I am feeling beauty. I love beauty.

I do not want evil—I want love. People think that I am an evil man. I am not. I love everybody. I have written the truth. I have spoken the truth. I do not like untruthfulness and want goodness, not evil. I am love. People take me for a scarecrow because I put on a small cross which I liked. I wore it to show that I was Catholic. People thought I was insane. I was not. I wore the cross in order to be noticed by people. People like calm men. I am not. I love life. I want it. I do not like death. I want to love mankind. I want people to believe in me. I have said the truth about A., Diaghilev, and myself. I do not want war and murders. I want people to understand me. I told my wife that I would destroy the man who would touch my notebooks, but I will cry if I have to do it. I am not a murderer. I know that everyone dislikes me. They think I am ill. I am not. I am a man with intelligence.

The maid came and stood near me, thinking that I was sick. I am not. I am healthy. I am afraid for myself because I know God's wish. God wants my wife to leave me. I do not want it, I love her and will pray that she may remain with me. They are telephoning about something. I believe they want to send me to prison. I am weeping, as I love life, but I am not afraid of prison. I will live there. I have explained everything to my wife. She is no longer afraid, but she still has a nasty feeling. I spoke harshly because I wanted to see tears—but not those which have been caused by grief. Therefore I will go and kiss her. I want to kiss her to show her my love. I love her, I want her, I want her love. A. has felt that I love her too and she is remaining with us. She is not leaving. She has telephoned to sell her ticket. I do not know for certain but I feel it.

My little girl is singing: "Ah, ah, ah, ah!" I do not understand its meaning, but I feel what she wants to say. She wants to say that everything—Ah! Ah!—is not horror but joy.

1938

The Witnesses, by Thomas Hennell

Although *The Witnesses* begins in sanity and ends in sanity, the body of the work is about the experience of madness. Parts of London, the interiors of a room or an asylum ward are described, but usually the events are not events of the material world. For the most part, the book relates a mental adventure, a travel through the extraordinary universe of a madman's mind.

The author-narrator, Thomas Hennell, opens by describing his experiences as a poor, overly sensitive young artist who falls in love and is rejected by the woman he loves, a Miss Clarissa Firestone. He introduces the reader to the mundane concerns of the artist—his need to make a living, his poverty and failure, the success of a friend, his lack of self-confidence. But he is obsessed by his love for Clarissa—and troubled. He seeks out a psychiatrist. He goes to a religious counselor. At last, he decides to make a pilgrimage to the grave of his mentor, Bishop Raven. So he sets out from London in the middle of the day, walking out on the Great West Road.

By now the world of ordinary time and space and rationality has begun to collapse. There are distortions in the appearance of things. Evening comes. Outside of London now, as Hennell walks along a country road, the entire world seems on the verge of a horrible transformation or collapse. The stars in the sky are moving inexplicably, new constellations are being formed. A van pulls up out of the darkness. Three men in long coats and helmets, who seem to be pimps disguised as policemen, tumble out, seize him, and roll him into the van amidst large lumps of cloth-wrapped meat and take him to jail. From there he is taken to a mental hospital, is five weeks later discharged, placed in another, escapes twice, is transferred, and is at last discharged.

The narrator's inner world is characterized by dreams, visions, fantasies, hallucinations, which all have the strength of reality. But beyond that, his perceptions of what we would consider to be ordinary objective reality, are at times drastically altered. Ordinary time and space are gone: "all things were whirled out of time and space." Solids can alter shape in fluid fashion: "the walls of the chamber again changed form and aspect: becoming elongated and cylindrical, then tunnelling irregularly upwards as though through the earth."

People appear differently, sometimes exalted, as saints or kings, sometimes degraded or subhuman. And at the end of his stay in the first asylum, Hennell describes his mental experiences as having been "distinguishable states of consciousness, like rooms which open one into another." The visions and hallucinations Hennell experiences are fascinating, a kind of travelogue. Even more interesting are his descriptions of altered time and space and his claim to have entered "distinguishable states of consciousness."

William James, father of American psychology, publicly announced as early as 1901 his conviction that unusual states of awareness or consciousness were indeed real phenomena:

> Some years ago I myself made some observations on . . . nitrous oxide intoxication, and reported them in print. One conclusion was forced upon my mind at that time, and my impression of its truth has ever since remained unshaken. It is that our normal waking consciousness, rational consciousness as we call it, is but one special type of consciousness, whilst all about it, parted from it by the filmiest of screens, there lie potential forms of consciousness entirely different. We may go through life without suspecting their existence; but apply the requisite stimulus, and at a touch they are there in all their completeness, definite types of mentality which probably somewhere have their field of application and adaptation. No account of the universe in its totality can be final which leaves these other forms of consciousness quite disregarded.[1]

Sleeping, dreaming, day-dreaming, and our ordinary waking consciousness are several states of awareness that we all pass through in our daily lives. But there are other states of awareness that are less common—for example, those achieved through meditation, drugs, or mystical experience. Some Eastern civilizations have elaborate systems to describe unusual states of awareness. And there are some twenty nouns in Sanskrit to describe what we know in English as "consciousness" or "mind."[2]

Certain unusual states of awareness or consciousness have an adaptive function. Certain trance states, for instance, have traditionally been important in the healing arts. States induced by pharmacological agents such as CO_2, insulin, amytal, and LSD-25, have

---

[1]James, *The Varieties of Religious Experience*, p. 298.
[2]Tart, *Altered States of Consciousness*, p. 3.

been used widely to facilitate psychotherapy. Mystical experience has often appeared to have religious or ethical functions. And some unusual states of consciousness have been said to enhance creative insight, problem solving, and aesthetic learning.[3] However, we must look at the negative side of all this: there are certain apparent nonordinary states of awareness or consciousness which seem to be maladaptive and pathological. At least some experiences of madness, some times, involve experiences of non-ordinary states of consciousness.

In the early 1950s Dr. Humphry Osmond, a young British psychiatrist, began experimenting with mescaline. It soon occurred to him that his mescaline experiences were very much like the experience of madness described in *The Witnesses*. He felt that it would be "almost perverse to ignore such remarkable similarities."[4] Jointly with a Dr. John Smythies he published a paper in 1952 describing in great detail the similarities, also noting that mescaline has a distinct chemical resemblance to adrenalin, the hormone related to emotion. Osmond and Smythies hypothesized that in certain stress situations when the adrenalin system is overworked, a failure of metabolism might take place which could produce some mescalinelike derivative of adrenalin—as an yet unknown substance which they called the "M-substance."

Osmond, Smythies, and another colleague, Dr. Abram Hoffer, then set out to find the M-substance. Within six months they had discovered a derivative of adrenalin which could be produced in the human body, and which did, like mescaline, bring about certain experiences resembling Hennell's descriptions of his madness. The derivative, a dark crystal which forms in water a brilliant red solution, was called "adrenochrome." They determined the toxicity of adrenochrome on animals, and then began testing it on humans—themselves, their wives, and a volunteer. They noticed some unusual perceptual changes even after small doses which seemed quite similar to the perceptual changes described in *The Witnesses*.

Of course, their experiment did not prove much. But it did add an important element to the theoretical model of schizophrenia, suggesting that altered perception or altered consciousness might be another important sign of schizophrenia and that the origin lay in somatic biochemical processes. Throughout their work Hennell's *The Witnes-*

---

[3]Ludwig, "Altered States of Consciousness," in ibid., pp. 19–21.
[4]Osmond, intro. to Thomas Hennell, *The Witnesses*, pp. 21, 22.

ses was used as a basic source, a model for understanding the experience of madness. Osmond writes of Hennell: "His vivid and moving account of his illness spurred on our enquiries at times when they might otherwise have flagged, suggesting new lines of attack which we might not have considered and gave us reassurances that we were on the right track at times when most of our contemporaries and seniors were certain that we were on a wild goose chase."[5]

Osmond never naïvely supposed that schizophrenia was merely an extended mescaline intoxication. He insisted that mescaline and LSD would merely help us understand some parts of the schizophrenic experience. He eventually objected to calling LSD and mescaline "psychoto-mimetic" (psychosis-mimicking) and instead coined the more benevolent term "psychedelic" (mind-expanding). It was clear that the psychedelic drugs did produce dramatic alterations of consciousness that sometimes seemed identical to perceptual changes in schizophrenia, but there were too many differences between the two types of experience which could not be explained in a direct comparison. For one thing, schizophrenia produces a thought disorder, which does not appear in the psychedelic experience. For another, the few genuine hallucinations experienced with the psychedelic drugs are usually visual (such as seeing geometric patterns), while the hallucinations of schizophrenia are usually auditory (such as hearing voices). Finally, the human nervous system has a remarkably rapid accommodation to the psychedelic drugs, so that continuous intoxication of that sort seems to be impossible beyond a few days.

Nonetheless, Osmonds' experiments were tremendously important and provocative. In essence, they added one more dimension to those classical descriptions of schizophrenia given by Emil Krapelin and Eugen Bleuler at the turn of the century.[6] From now on the ideal theory of schizophrenia would have to account for the symptoms described by Kraepelin and Bleuler and would also have to include the kinds of pervasive, subjective experiences of altered consciousness as described in this psychiatric autobiography, *The Witnesses*.

Obviously, Dr. Osmond considered *The Witnesses* to be a document of great significance. Beyond that, it is a finely wrought work of art. The book has a marvelous symmetry. The madness grows slowly, emerging gradually out of mundane experience, evolving into a tor-

---

[5]Ibid., p. x.
[6]See Appendix II.

nado of chaotic sensations, confused perceptions, extraordinary awareness, and at last gradually returning to the experience of everyday life. The transitions from sanity to madness and back again are not marked by changes in style and distance—and the final effect is powerful.

In the following excerpts from *The Witnesses*, the speaker's ordinary world is collapsing and the reader is transported to a drastically altered experience. As the first passage opens, the narrator is in jail. Across from his cell he sees a man in a uniform, whom he calls variously "the Adversary," "the Principal," and "the Transfigured Man," and whose face goes through remarkable changes. Then the narrator describes his experiences inside an asylum. The patients appear to him in an exaggerated, perhaps archetypal aspect, either as "glorified" into recognizable historical figures and "kings and saints," or as "sinister figures" and "a strange rout of subhuman beings." We may be struck by the accuracy and evocative power of the descriptions. Here are the marks of Hennell's training as a painter: strong details of form and color, a powerful visual sense, a quick and easy leaping to visual comparison, to metaphor. Finally, Hennell's madness appears to be a positive, aesthetic experience as much as it was painful and disturbing. There is awe, humor, fear, pleasure, chagrin, but little agony—mostly an acceptance of a remarkable transfiguration of aesthetic fascination. It is this attitude that gives the work its particular style and color. *The Witnesses* is an amazing document and a remarkable Bosch-like prose painting.

SPEECH SEEMED TO RETURN with primitive rudimentary sounds. Then standing on my feet, I saw through the grate of the cell-door that a man was seated opposite me in the guard-room, across the passage. His elbows were upon the table, his head rested forward upon them, and for a moment it seemed that he was asleep, or rather that he was sightless. His hair was golden or corn-coloured—a long lock of it hung over his brow. He wore the Air Force uniform, with bright silver buttons, and two narrow silver stripes on his right breast, beside the badge of wings.

At almost the same instant a man appeared in the passage between my Adversary and myself: a negro who looked at me and waggled his head sideways, so that it left an instantaneous suggestion of lapping water, seen in a round mirror. I waved him violently away; he withdrew leftwards, by the way he had come; then, as though with several voices at once, I shouted the Name. His eyes opened, and his head moved slowly over from left to right, mine following it from right to left, as if it meant to twist off from my shoulders. "O my dear ———, I *wish* I could have done it."

Between the Principal and the door, a burly, baldheaded man in a dark blue uniform, with upright collar, was also sitting, at that side of the table. An ink-bottle and some papers were by him. He seemed intent on them. His knees were crossed under the table, and his boots were round-ended and intolerably brightly polished—they seemed symbols of the Bully.

"Take away that boot, take away that damned boot!" I yelled at him. At first he seemed purposely to remain mostly out of sight, the door-jamb of the guard-room intervening.

"How long have you been here?" inquired the Adversary in a light and beautiful voice.

"All the time."

"Can you swim?"

"Yes!"

"How far?"

"Oh, twenty miles." Indeed, in his presence, the feat seemed possible.

He then stood before the cell-door (my eyes being fixed on him) and inclined his forehead towards me, first the right part, then the left. These became instantly changed in form and appearance, they brightened to pure pale gold and assumed classical form; his other features changed, so that, for an atom of time, he was perfectly Apollo: the change went past this, he grinned, became more burning and terrible, and was Jupiter.

It seemed that the guards stampeded rather, for there were three loutish heads at the grate: the Adversary standing back so that I could still see him, one of them spoke hastily:

"What's your belief? You've got some creed or other. Say it."

I began to say the Apostles' Creed in the loud and clear intonation in which Bishop Raven had formerly been used to say it, and it seemed with the same voice which then spoke it.

"That will do, that's enough," one of them said, when I had

got no further than "suffered under Pontius Pilate". "Now sing some song or other."

The Transfigured Man seeming to assent, I thereupon sang (with more good-will than judgment) "So early in the morning, the sailor likes his bottle, O". (Archer being very fond of chanties, we had practised them together.)

Then all three bundled into the room together, one holding a tin cup, which he gave me to drink. It was boiling tea, and felt like boiling lead, but I gulped it down to the last. The guards began to struggle with me, but the inspiration was very strong; two of them were thrown down, and the third, who just then had assumed the likeness and actual presence of the Bully of Central Europe (he whose boot I had cursed), was grappling with me and trying to look me out of countenance. He neither did this nor threw me down. It was as though sparks went out from my eyes into his, so that he flinched at last and looked away. The beaming Being upon the other side of the door clapped his hands and laughed. It was instantaneous and complete as an astronomical figure.

When the guards were outside again and had slammed the door on me, he spoke again to them: "Does he drink any water?"

"No!"

He laughed again. One of them asked me: "What would you like to eat?"

"A poached eye."

This was about the limit of our understanding.

I sang again, by request, and this time another unforeseen thing happened. I was aware of a small movement in the ceiling, about two-thirds across the room towards the door, and three-quarters of the width towards my left; the movement became defined as a round depression, wide as a saucer, reverberating and increasing to a regular cylindrical hole three inches deep, and about eight in diameter. Scarcely aware of what I did (still madly excited), I pitched my voice higher, and then whistled, whereat the floor of this hole deepened and narrowed gradually to a long, slightly twisted cone: whether or not there was a pinhole opening to the daylight I could not tell.

During this time my Adversary was seated again, close before the door. He looked up at what was happening, and though no longer regarding him directly, I was partly aware of his appearance now.

It was supernatural, no longer like Apollo, Moses or Jove: he looked up and I was aware of the extraordinary quality of his eyes, of the rich colour of his mouth, now no longer smiling. His hair seems to have become flame-like and standing up. There was something more ancient in this aspect than Israel, Greece, Egypt, perhaps Assyria, yet divine in all these ages, and of them: to which the word "magical" does not seem irreverent.

Presently the guard-room filled with other men. They seemed police, army sergeants and officers in plain clothes; there were many of them, and with them went out the man who had been transfigured. And after that I saw him no more in the flesh, but many times had the encouragement of his speech and magnificent laughter.

*   *   *

The Temple

The day grew late: food was neither offered nor desired; but there seemed to increase amongst us a certain sense of disappointment, as though the thing we looked for was still deferred. A strong after-current of emotion swept through my mind, preventing it from seeking to rationalize its experience: bearing images which still appeared anticipatory. There were half-shaped ideas of resurrection: the croakings and mutterings sounded as voices of almost extinct intelligence, murmurs of departed spirits awaiting, yet not expecting release. A figure from some book recurred to my mind in vivid form: a train of successive generations of prophets and seers, heroes, poets, martyrs; which cycle was renewed, with soaring armies of ghosts, who trod and re-trod the paths of their earthly adventures in the ebb and flow of time. This intensified till it was dreadful, and yet with a nightshade splendour: among our latter generations, those who lived still were the writers, who marched in the guise of characters which they had realized.

A great library was now to be built: friend Baker had designed it, a great structure of steel, having many galleries which radiated to a central domed and circular hall. In this place there would be statues and names inscribed of many famous men; even now, as its geometric plan crystallized in my brain, I seemed to lie in the midst, and yet this place was loaded and dangerous: somewhat as a bundle of fireworks, or set-piece waiting to be touched off. Were there not Gothic churches and chapter-houses, all of catherine-wheels and rockets, at many celebrations in Queen Victoria's honour? So this might typify a great woman's apotheosis; what projections of stars had been those of last night! Now I was within doors, and a strong sense of calamitous danger had returned, though I was not physically affected by fear; but rather in a spiritual apprehension.

When all grew dark, the religious atmosphere was still maintained; and yet there entered and passed before me some sinister figures; who wore a false air, as of comedians who have failed to amuse, and desperately strive to be easy and self-possessed. One may have had some account of me from the taxi-party, for he spoke jeeringly, using words which are not allowed among polite people. Here were some presences which intended me no good, but now I scarcely marked them. So I fell asleep, as it were, under the shade of wings.

During this night twice or thrice I was awoken by momentary brilliant flashes, and for an instant, at each occasion, people stood near. Here again some were jokers; some as bystanders at a road accident; others stood as if in the presence of a spiritual event, or speaking in hushes whispers: and I seemed to discern several whom I knew.

"The Immaculate Conception," said one.

Next morning, as if through wooden bars, were seen many people in shirt-sleeves and coarse trousers sweeping out a large airy room, and some in white night-shirts crossed the floor. There was such a parlour in the House of the Interpreter, full of dust, but, water being sprinkled, the room was swept and cleansed with pleasure. And there too was a wall where a fire burnt, which one man would quench with water, and another, standing at the back of the wall, fed the flames with oil. So some similar thing was here: for now I entered a brick tower or corner-chamber, through the opening in whose door was seen a long, beautiful room whose further end or head had three walls, with windows. The early sunlight glorified the faces of some who lay upon the beds, their heads near the windows. They seemed to be lifeless but waiting to be reanimated, and there were several whom I knew as my friends. So I shouted and sang as loudly as possible, to wake them up, and an increasing heat surged through this place where I was, so that I was filled with the agony of the fire but yet could endure it: the white flame made rings on my head and body. It was an intensification of that white spirit which had been apparent to my mind when I departed from London. These coruscations passed as sparks into the room and into the faces of three or four newly resurrected men who sat close by. Two of these were well known by appearance, for one was a poet and the other a revolutionary; both honoured in their funerals according to the public taste and economy of their respective nations. So they seemed to be here as kings. The earth-shaker looked puzzled and was silent; his grey hair bristled. But the poet's hair was long and white—part stood erect, and part streamed out towards the door, as if struck by the mingled influences of Phosphor and Saturn. If ever amazement and incredulous delight shone in a face, they were seen in his countenance at this moment. A confusion of historical speeches boiled together in my wits, finding fragmentary utterance:

"Sugar, Mr Speaker!" I shouted at the likeness of Lenin. "Sugar, sugar, sugar! Who will now dare to laugh at sugar!"

But he of the dissected brains looked, if possible, still more puzzled at this text from the elder Pitt. A peak-capped guard gave a wink, and asked:

"What is the name of your sweetheart?"

And five or six times the name "Clarissa Firestone! Clarissa Firestone!" was hurled across the room. The old man seemed to catch a live spark from each repetition of this name, and to throw it round the room from eye to eye of all his companions, till it passed out by a passage to the left, where two women stood in silence at a locked gate of iron, painted red. One of these women was in dark clothes; the other in a white garment seemed to be Jane Shore. They were the only women I ever actually saw in this place. This gate was the entrance to a garden, behind the left wall of our long room: and through the windows could be seen other gates and trees; so that there seemed to be successive heavens, each more strange and immaterial, and their gates yet more impossible to open.

And later this momentary glimpse was grown into by fancies and dream-mirage. The further landscapes were discerned to be rocky and barren, yet intensely desirable: and upon the other hand, in the open black gate, where the poet sat, a winter church-yard was seen, its porch overgrown with cotoneaster, and an open grave thereby. There had surely been a key upon the table where the Adversary sat asleep.

There was a roaring and howling sound as of wild beasts, round a double corner at the rear, as though some men had been transformed into wolves and bears, for presently a strange rout of subhuman beings came crowding across the room and moved out by the steps to the left. As they went they laughed and gibbered uncouthly, with curious antics, as though they were betting and laying odds: some were "borogoves", spotted newts or devil's-dice. It was shocking that they were let into the presence of these kings and saints.

There were openings in the brick wall above the door, and these seemed, with the fire and the shouting, to have been changed in form and increased in number, somewhat as if it were a pigeon-cote through whose openings the birds could fly.

"Quite hopeless, I'm afraid," said the very old poet.

The door being now opened, I followed the unruly rout into a long and mean passage which was crowded with such a disorderly, shocking rabble as I never saw; worse than any beggars or ruffians. It was like an underground refuge full of people demoralized and dehumanized by an air-raid. Seeing some stewards or officers pushing them hither and thither into their places, I was willing to lend assistance—but they treated me as if I were red-hot, and by no means to be closely approached. A large safe or strong-room was opened: it was managed that I should enter, and this door was instantly shut fast.

1944 ⤶

Brainstorm, by Carlton Brown

In an introductory chapter, Carlton Brown says that *Brainstorm* is a true story but that he has ghostwritten it for a friend who went through an experience of "manic-depressive psychosis" and was unable to transform his own notes, reminiscences, and letters into a final coherent account.[1] Actually, that "friend" was Brown himself.

Brainstorm is a compelling journey of mood and imagination, beginning with simple exuberance and progressing into higher and higher levels of elation until at last the ordinary world takes on extraordinary significance, and the narrator believes himself to be at the very center of that new world—a new Messiah. The book contains some of the clearest descriptions in existence of a particular type of madness marked by mood elevation, heightening of the senses, loss of inhibition and guilt, and exaggerated feeling of self-reference.

In the following representative chapter from *Brainstorm,* "Michael Kelley Jones" takes a trip out of New York City into the countryside to visit his daughter. He examines a Chinese scroll painting on his wall, takes a taxi and has a conversation with the driver, buys a new suit, has a haircut, takes the ferry to Jersey City, has lunch, talks to the waiter, boards the train, remembers his old girl friend Dina, observes his fellow passengers, has a conversation with one, then at last steps off the train at his destination. The events are held together with a tight and compelling coherence told through a mood of abnormal elation. The haircut is not just an ordinary haircut—it feels like a priestly initiation. The lunch in Jersey City is a feast of "nectar and ambrosia." The reader is transported from one event to the next with a sense of urgency and destination. When Jones finally boards the train, the motion and rhythm of the passage seem inexorable. At last, on the last train ride, we are swept helplessly along in a powerful current of consciousness and event and rhythm, of point and counterpoint: Michael's happy expectations, his urgency, the conductor's cries of "Going home! Going home!" and the quickening and intensifying pulse of the train whistle: more than four times the whistle blows, first a "great sad-happy shout," then a "mounting exultant

---

[1]Carlton Brown, *Brainstorm,* pp. 3, 4.

cry," then crying "victoriously," and finally "crowing like a Gargantuan rooster awakening the universe to its glory."

HANGING ON THE KITCHEN WALL of my apartment was a Chinese scroll painting, some four feet high, of a middle-aged woman, seated, her hands tucked into the sleeves of her richly brocaded robe of vermilion, pink, green, ultramarine blue and gold, patterned with dragons, waves, suns, a bird, clouds and flowers. She wore a long necklace, jade earrings and an elaborately beaded headdress. Except for her face, everything about the portrait was formalized. I had bought a number of portraits of this sort in China more than ten years before, and in all of them the costumes might have been laid in with stencils, their details varying according to the caste of the sitter, but all being serious, formalized and extravagant Oriental versions of the props of an amusement-park photographer, enabling the artist to attach the poser's head to any one of a number of stereotyped bodies.

One day in July I discovered that the features of the Chinese lady had become suffused with the absolute semblance of life. As soon as I had accustomed myself to the surprise of this discovery, I consulted her eyes for verification of each of my enraptured and increasingly convincing intimations of immorality, or for condemnation of the thoughts and actions that still marked me as a mortal, and found what I sought in their vibrant, eloquent depths. Our communion was wordless but complete. She was at once Judy's mother, my own, and Ann, the friend with whom my daughter was staying in the country, a warm, capable woman with two lovely children of her own. Her eyes mirrored the soul of the eternal Madonna whose son I was in the process of becoming, and from them I received implicit instructions in the filling of my new role. She regarded me now with melting compassion and love, now with some of the wrath of God, now with warm tolerance, now with despair. She was the reflection of my own conscience, miraculously externalized.

She looked down in loving approval on the day that I set out to visit my daughter and her playmates in the country. I packed a lot of things to amuse them with—paper, pencils, crayons to draw with, presents for each from the collection of curios I had been assorting and arraying around the apartment, and, for my daughter, a green sweater with red hearts on it, a cap to match, and a little silver ring with tinkling bells hanging from it.

Children figured prominently in all my fantasies. They were the only good people on earth, the only ones whose hearts were pure and emotions unsullied. I felt that I was entering into a childlike state, equipped with the wisdom of an adult but divested of every trace of adult cynicism and world-weariness. I was being reborn in the image of my own childhood ideal. After "seven years of the locust," I was finally to be admitted to a heaven on earth inhabited by a fancied aristocracy of mind and spirit. After bitter years of wandering in search of the key to it, the door to my true home among the noblemen of earth and sky was swinging wide to welcome me. One by one, the secrets of the universe were being disclosed to me, and their possession would secure peace and joy abundant beyond man's most hopeful imaginings, not to me alone but to the whole world.

By now I was imbued with the idea that the timing of my movements was somehow being supervised from on high. If I did a thing when it occurred to me, I would arrive on time for appointments, catch trains, get telephone calls at just the right time, and so on. If I didn't—well, the cosmic schedule didn't mean me to, and I would serenely wait for what it had in store. My concept was infallible because of its allowance for change without notice.

Thus it didn't disappoint me when, setting out to visit Sheila, I missed an appointment for noon with the lawyer who was arranging my divorce. Getting into a taxi on Seventh Avenue, I told the driver to go uptown, and that I would tell him where to turn off in the Forties. I didn't remember the lawyer's address, but I knew the building. On the way, I gave the driver an exuberant line of jabber about my being in on the secrets of the universe.

"I'm playing a winning streak today, and I'll let you in on it. It's a Seven day, see? It's the seventh month and the eighteenth day. Take that eighteen and subtract one from eight and you get seven. Then if you add up the numbers in 1940 you get fourteen;

divide that by two and you get seven again." This sort of lightning numerology went on in my mind constantly, and was applied to telephone numbers and street addresses and all figures
that came into my ken.

"Hey!" I exclaimed when I had guided the cab to my destination. "That's the building and it's Number Seventy. And look at
your meter!" It registered seventy cents.

The lawyer's office was on the seventh floor and its number
was Seven Hundred. He had left fifteen minutes before, but my
trip had served to reinforce my numerological concept with an
amazing string of coincidences. I describe it exactly as it happened, but what I now see as a freakish run in the laws of
chance then gave absolute conviction to my oracular train of
thought. The taxi driver also was amazed, and gladly took my
name and address and agreed to play the extra dollar I gave him
on Number 700 in the Harlem policy drawing, plus an equal
amount of his own.

To garb my rejuvenated self suitably, I had bought a suit of
light-brown tweed and the gayest of accessories. I had had my
hair cut short, too, and after missing the lawyer, on my way to
get the ferry, I stopped at a barbershop on the lower west side
for a trim and a shave. The moment I entered the shop, I was
impressed by its unworldly quality. It had a somehow regal,
sanctified, ceremonial air about it. White marble washstands
with brass spigots stood along one wall, and in a cut-glass case
were shaving mugs with ornate gilt lettering on their surfaces.
Far more than a barbershop, it was a temple erected in the
previous century to the high, traditional tonsorial art. Here, I
thought, they would know how to apply leeches and practice
other lost arts of the days when barbers were chirurgeons. Dark,
mellow mahogany, cut-glass mirrors, shaving soap, lotions,
powders, steaming towels—it was altogether the celestial barbershop, and its atmosphere was luminous, electric.

I asked the bald, old German who attended me for a crew cut,
and was furious when he gave it a Dutch effect, as though a
bowl had been put on my head and clipped around. He apologized abjectly and went on to shave me with what seemed a
touch of pure reverence. I felt that I was being anointed in the
religious sense; this old member of heaven's household staff

knew I was a golden boy-deity and handled me accordingly. As I lay back in the chair and his too-gentle hands worked over my face, a beatific feeling flowed over me and, I felt, transfigured my expression. I sensed that my serene visage was meeting the regard of a greater being than that which shone through the eyes of the Chinese painting, and that He was finding me good to look upon. But then, as the old man massaged me deftly, too-tenderly, murmuring now and then, I became irritated by what struck me as a cloying, fondling attention, as though he did not want to let me out of his hands. I thought of him as a monk or member of the priesthood assigned to preparing neophytes for entry into the inner circle, and, now that he was fairly finished with these preparations, I cut short his lingering pattings and left.

I boarded the ferry and stood at the front of the lower deck, in the exact center and further forward than the other passengers and the cars. I was whistling a continuous blues hymn to the poignant joy of living, a medley of tunes that had been the emotional language of various eras of my life, and it all sounded awfully good to my keenly self-appreciative ears.

As the boat put out into the Hudson toward Jersey City, I was standing in a limber, springy stance, my weight shifting easily, imperceptibly from one foot to the other, when I made the delightful discovery that I was walking on the water. I was infused with a supremely buoyant, bodiless feeling; I was in perfect balance, with the motion of the boat rippling up through me, becoming a part of my own inner rhythm. No—the boat was no more than a magnetic field through which my energy penetrated downward. I stood on nonmaterial stilts, like beams of electric current or columns of atoms extending vertically between me and the water, and connected laterally with the pistons that drove the boat. The action was something like that of riding a bicycle, down with the right and up with the left, down with the left and up with the right, and with each stroke came that light, bodiless, very real junction with the tides of the river. I had no illusion that I had become physically elongated, no hallucination that my supernatural stilts were there in any tangible form. Rather, the phenomenon told me that the miracle of walking the waves was not intended to be taken literally. Anyone could accomplish it if he understood that it meant just this: putting himself into transcendental harmony with the element of water—a harmony, I was to discover, which could be established with all the elements if one knew how to do it.

I danced effortlessly over the waves, directing currents of motive power down through the boat's vitals and up to its helm, leaving the captain powerless to buck my magnetic will. Several times, by a delicate tension of my muscles, I squeezed the boat past other craft in the river by a matter of inches. Several times, the whistle screamed in tumultuous exultation, as though the boat were crying, "You're running away with me and I'm scared silly but I love it!" It was alive like some great whale whose nose I rode and whose churnings through the water I guided with a firm rein attached to a ring in its snout. Luckily for the captain and all aboard, I was headed for the Jersey shore in a happy hurry, rather than for Albany or the open sea. As I swung her safely into the slip, I looked down and saw that the water was covered with an iridescent film of oil, and as I looked, someone on the upper deck cast onto the water a half a loaf of Italian bread.

As you enter the railroad station at Jersey City, there is an enclosed bar and lunchroom to the left of the waiting room. Here, after walking across the Hudson with the ferry in my wake, I lunched on nectar and ambrosia, cunningly disguised, to forestall the envy of ordinary mortals, as ham and eggs, lettuce, French frieds, bread and milk.

The Negro boy who served me immediately recognized my divinity, which was apparent to initiates in my beatific gestures, if in no other way. His eyes were round with awe as he gazed at the halo I had just had burnished and trimmed in the celestial barbershop on Liberty Street, and his face lit up with a reflection of my own seraphic countenance. Clearly he had been prepared for my coming. The restaurant, like the barbershop, was part of the heavenly chain of hotels that was welcoming a new guest of honor. He observed reverently that I did not desecrate the pure ingredients of my meal with catsup, mustard or butter; he scrupulously obeyed my injunction against French or Russian dressing on my lettuce; and noted with beaming approval that I ate my bread dry and used just a little salt for seasoning. In return for this recognition, and because he was my brother and himself a saint, I motioned the waiter closer to me and spoke to him in low, impassioned tones.

"Tomorrow is The Day," I told him, and read complete faith and understanding in his expression. "You are going to be set free—really free. All the good people, the humble people, the beaten people, are coming into their own. You're going to see miracles tomorrow—one big miracle that will sweep over the whole world and change the face of it."

I can reproduce no more than this faint echo of my evangelical speech, but such was its tenor. I explained to my enrapt listener the numerical significance of the day, and gave him the same tip on the number that I had given the cab driver. By some system that I do not recall, I now figured that perhaps 701 rather than 700 might turn up in the next drawing, and that it should be played in combination, assuring winnings on 017, 071, 170, 107, 710 or 701.

As I gave the waiter this tip, I was careful to caution him that it was not infallible. I made an abbreviated explanation of the Rule of Three that had recently come to me by supernatural inspiration. You played a hunch once, and if it didn't hit the first time, you tried it a second and a third time. If it didn't hit by the third time, you might give it up, or you might try it in two more sequences of three times each, making a total of nine tries. Or you might consider that the first hunch, tried three times, was no good because it was the first of three hunches, of which only the third, after it was tried three times, would pan out.

I did not elaborate my system to quite this confusing degree to the waiter, but I indicated its elasticity so that he would be spared any serious disappointment. It might even be that tomorrow was not The Day, but merely a sort of dress rehearsal for it. I gave him a dollar to play for himself and ten cents to play for me, and left a fifty-cent tip besides. I also gave him one of the patriotic lapel pins I had bought at the five-and-ten on my way from the lawyer's office, for by now it was my conviction that America's Christian soldiers would soon reinforce the world-wide anti-Fascist resurrection with arms.

Before leaving to catch my train, I cautioned the waiter against telling more than three people about Number 701. I wasn't quite sure about the importance of this injunction. Perhaps it would be all right to tell everybody; perhaps telling too many would spoil the spell. At any rate, I felt that it should be given out only on the basis of personal friendship; if any commercialization entered in, the whole thing would be called off. On the way to the train, unable to abide by my own rules, I stopped a porter and told him about the number, but did not finance his playing of it. A moment later, I was sorry I had been so impulsive; this last tip might be the one that would jinx the thing.

My train left at some such significant time as 2:20—the influence and position of the sun were represented in the clock's hour and minute hands. I had some time to wait but I didn't want to spend it in the waiting room. I remembered the hour Dina and I, having missed the train on the way out to visit my father, had spent there one winter day shortly after I got back from France.

"I want to kiss you till you're black and blue," I said. "I want to make love to you right here."

"I'll call the cops!" Dina laughed. I put an arm around her and tried to kiss her, but she pulled away.

"I love you, Dina," I said.

"Honest, Mike? I don't believe you do. You wouldn't have gone away if you'd loved me."

"Listen, can't we forget all that? Let's start all over, as though we'd just met—shall we? I did come back, didn't I? And I am going to marry you, aren't I?"

"I d'know, Michael." She was silent for some time, her eyes turned down and one eyebrow raised in that old austerely quizzical expression, half real and half affected, that she may have used because I'd told her it made her look like Garbo. When she spoke again she didn't look at me, and her voice was low and plaintive.

"Mike," she said, "I've got a confession to make. I don't know what you'll think, but I can't go on pretending. I got married while you were away—but, darling," she went on quickly, still avoiding my eyes, "I didn't love him. I dunno what happened—I was just so damn blue, and this fellow came along, and I liked him pretty well, and I thought, well, I'll just show that Jones louse I don't care about his old Michelle, or whatever you call her, so we drove up to Greenwich and got married. It

was a horrible mess. We were tight, or I never would have done it. It was right after you'd written me about that French girl of yours, and nothing seemed to matter very much. We went down to Washington that weekend for our honeymoon, and when I came back Mamma raised holy hell, and I told her all about it and she promptly had the thing annulled. Oh! It was such a mess, Mike! I don't know how I ever did such a crazy thing."

"Didn't you love him, Dina, really?"

"I swear to God I didn't, Michael. It was just a crazy mess, darling, but don't be too hard on me. I'm just getting over it now."

"How do you mean?"

"You're going to think I'm a terrible slut. But it wasn't my fault, honest. I was so damned drunk I didn't know what I was doing. You remember the night we spent at Bunny's, how I wouldn't let you kiss me or anything? Well, I was just after having an abortion."

I couldn't say a word. I stared ahead, shivering, the dirty, inhuman aspect of the waiting room giving me a sinking feeling. I drew close to Dina.

"I love you very much, Dina," I said, looking steadily down at the cement floor. "Dina, let's get married—now, today—let's not put it off this time."

"That goddamned lousy bastard! I didn't know there was any guy in the world so damned dumb!" That wasn't what was in my mind, but that was all I could manage to say. "Who was he, Dina?" The only thing I wanted to know was why it hadn't been myself, why I had been cheated out of my fourth of July. . . .

I left the ghosts of Dina and a defunct me sitting in the waiting room (*pouring gin into paper cups full of Coca-Cola, the gin making the cups soft around the bottom*), and walked out into the big glass-covered shed where the trains pull in and stand behind high iron gates. The lights came down in dusty geometric patterns formed by the framework above, and the dreamlike atmosphere was heightened by the station's hush, clang, chug, sound of feet and quiet voices and occasional oratorical call of the train announcer.

The train I took was a streamliner appropriately called The Crusader ("Clad in Shining Armor"), and though my ticket was for coach travel, I made myself at home in a luxurious, air-conditioned club car, with deeply upholstered lounge chairs, and ordered a Tom Collins. I had bought a bag each of white grapes, cherries and dates at the station, and I arrayed them on a smoking stand at my elbow and ate them in rotation, with a sense of high ritual and with great relish for their color, consistency, flavor and symbolism. Even the bleak, gray, smoke-hung outskirts of Jersey City were a pleasant sight to me—factories doing the world's work with a will, cheerfully making things for man's enjoyment and well-being. As we rolled through suburban towns, I enjoyed every detail of their life that my eyes could take in—the ornate, old-fashioned houses, the trim, standardized new ones, the people strolling the streets on lively errands, the cemeteries waiting to tuck them lovingly in. I saw poetry and art in the very billboards, with their promise of a more abundant life which I knew was about to come true. I waved to kids watching the train go by, sharing their wonder and excitement . . .

Dina and I had gone along these tracks that day when we went to visit my father. The sky was gray and smoky then, night just coming on, and the train chugged out slowly, with factories and rubbish heaps on either side, and desolate hovels along the tracks. Looking off into the gloomy twilight, I was filled with nostalgia for every place in the world but New York. Just to be off and away, to some new environment that would hold no reproach for the self-cheating I had done, where there lurked no reminders of past, seemingly happier days.

Tears of self-pity had welled in my eyes. I told myself that I was incapable of winning the warm and enduring love that was part of the life of normal people; and then I told myself that I was a sickeningly sentimental fool. If I had stayed in New York and worked, worked at no matter what, I would now have a decent position, my asking Dina to marry me might be something other than fantastic. But I hadn't wanted security and a safe, dull job, and I wasn't sure I wanted them now. . . .

But that was long ago, and those wraiths barely clung to the blinds of the heavenly express that now hurtled me through the suburbs of Nirvana.

Across the aisle, three portly well-dressed men of upper middle age and a young man who, from his uniform, might have been a steward of the car, were talking about horse racing. I wanted to tell them about Number 701, but something forbidding, or at least imposing, in their joint façade held me off. I glanced frequently in their direction, until as though by tacit consent they all turned their club chairs around to face away from me and out the window of the car. I was a little piqued at this foursquare snub, but philosophically decided that they were among the life-denying forces which were opposed to such ebullience as I showed in my expressionistic eating, drinking and looking.

I had bought one and then a second Tom Collins, and had been enjoying the cushioned ease of the club car for perhaps a half hour when the conductor came by to punch my ticket and told me that I would have to move to one of the day coaches, unless I wanted to make up the difference in fare. I was approaching that point in my mental excursion at which I decided to see how far I could get without money. I had been spending too much on friends and strangers; now I would see what they would do for me. I did not realize how barely Ann, my kid's foster mother, as I regarded her, managed to meet expenses, in spite of the urgent appeal she had made to me a few days before for ten dollars, apart from the weekly payment I sent her. If I had realized the extent of Ann's poverty, it might have seemed to me a blessed state, but I wouldn't have complicated it by arriving penniless at Medlow Farm, as I did.

I declined to pay the additional tariff to the conductor, and though I was a little disappointed that he did not recognize my sovereign right to ride in the club car at coach rates, I took it with tolerant good grace. I picked up my small suitcase, my camera, and my suit coat, which I had taken off and now carried as though it were a ceremonial robe, and also my bags of fruit and magazines. (I had just discovered how really glorious magazines were, how they meant much more than they had seemed to mean, how significant their very names were and every bit of their contents. Now that I was a member of the universe's directorate, they had become wonderfully illustrated bulletins of what was going on in my domain, guides to its beauties, wonders, strategies and campaigns.)

Carrying my unwieldy and conspicuous burden back to the smoking car, I chose a seat next to a rather villainous looking Negro wearing a dirty yellow suit, and stowed my things in the luggage rack. I found in him an eager disciple for my Messianic jabber and a ready taker of my tip on Number 701. He ate some of my dates and grapes and cherries, and I was thankful for his acceptance of my ritual generosity. As we talked, we found ourselves in general agreement in broad philosophic concepts—the whole subject of how to live. I had some slight sense of self-consciousness, unusual for me now that my introversions were turned almost completely inside-out, but I outstared the adjoining passengers, who seemed disapprovingly curious about our conversation. Like most of my talks with strangers at this time, this one was considerably one-sided. My companion agreed with me that all things came to him who was patient and good, but he said almost angrily that he wished his share would hurry up and come.

The last lap of the journey was to have been by bus, but I had misunderstood the ticket seller's instructions and took it that I was to change to another train that would take me to my destination. Therefore I missed the bus on which my ticket would have been valid, and I had a long wait for a train that did not go as far as I wanted to go. I had to pay another fare, which left me with three pennies in my pocket—three pennies and three golden keys to the contest at the Fair where cars were given away every day.

It was a poky train of prestreamline build that I boarded next. I took the last seat on the right-hand side in the front car, the smoker. It was a hot day, and all the windows were opened wide. In the short flights between stations, we passed through beautiful country, stretches of pasture alternating with deep woods, with occasional glimpses of rocky streams, cattle and barns. I leaned back in the sooty plush seat and let the landscape roll in over me in a tide of lush color and air that was like balm for every woe of the world.

At one station, a boy in overalls, carrying a lunch pail, got on and took the seat in front of me. When he leaned his head back I could see the uplifted visor and crown of his cap, with a sheen of grease and grime completely covering the smooth fabric it was made of. A couple of times the boy looked around. He had a sad, emaciated face, with a bulging forehead and grieving eyes.

Across the aisle and several seats ahead, sitting backward and facing me, were a man and woman of vague middlè age and a sporty aspect not confined to their clothes. The man wore a jaunty checkered cap and coat, vest and trousers that did not match, and a horseshoe tiepin. The woman's hat had feathers rising gaily out of it. The couple gave the impression of being on a clandestine trip. I fancied them checking into some rural boardinghouse as Mr. and Mrs. John Smith, walking through the woods gingerly so as not to get their city shoes wet, the man pulling up his trousers to avoid bagging the knees when they sat down in some secluded spot, spreading out his handkerchief for the woman to sit on.

Their happiness was of the sort that cannot contain itself, and we exchanged what seemed to me loving, compassionate glances. One minute their heads were together in intimate talk, the next they were flung back in mirth that verged on hysteria, and then they would look at me with their eyes confessing their helpless happiness.

The train passed a grove growing close to the track on the left, and all at once there wafted in a warm fragrance more ethereally lovely than any I have ever known. The woods it seemed to issue from were primeval, paradisaical; looking into them I was lost in vibrant, misty green of endless depth and variety. Yet the fragrance was not alone of wood or blossoms. It was a compound, as nearly as I can describe it, of the perfume Judy wore, the smell of finger tips after smoking many cigarettes, the fragrance of the celestial barbershop, my new suit and clean clothes, all diluted in the green-black-yellow, sunlit, shade-cooled air of the summer woods. It was light but rich, complex, heady, evanescent; sweetly simple as new-mown hay but with sophisticated, musky overtones, and a suggestion of something aromatic having been burnt—not the smoke itself but the essence left behind it. It made me so happy that I could hardly keep from crying. My mouth opened and as though to give utterance to what it could not express, the great sad-happy shout of the train's whistle sounded to the skies and shook the earth and made the trees dance.

With my eyes swimming and my ears wincing and my throat tight and my nostrils flaring for more of that unearthly fragrance, I looked at the couple ahead. They were laughing in quiet convulsion, the woman dabbing at her eyes with a hand-kerchief, the man with his head thrown back, unashamedly letting the tears course down his face, his expression trans-figured with excruciating bliss. He was like a man who, long blind and deaf, has had his sight and hearing suddenly restored. The couple looked at me with the open sharing of helpless joy that roller-coaster riders exchange when, weak with fearful plea-sure, they reach the end of a ride. I held back my tears no longer. I had never been so happy—never anywhere nearly so happy. I was filled with an ether that, if it did not escape somehow, would waft me right out the window and up into the blue blue sky. The boy in front of me turned and stretched his head up over the back of the seat. His eyes were red and weepy, his expression un-stable, precariously balanced between fear and delight, and he looked at me as though searching for the source of some influ-ence he felt but could not understand. A wave of tremulous, awe-inspiring gladness flowed like a tangible fluid through the car, like the sweet breath of the world's love made palpable.

The whistle gave another mounting, exultant cry. Again and again it sounded, and each blast seemed to arise from my heart and give expression to the great love of the world that welled up within me. The wheels of the train sang the song of the world, beat like the feet of a runner winning a race in a burst of super-human energy. Again the whistle cried victoriously.

"Going home! Going home!" the conductor sang out, coming into the car from the rear. He was an elderly man with gold-rimmed glasses and an expression of happy benevolence, as though he thoroughly understood and approved, but was a little aloof from, the phenomenon that was taking place in the car. A daily rider on the Heavenly Local, I thought, he would naturally be less affected than those taking the trip for the first time.

"Last stop!" he called, announcing the name of the town. Again the whistle sounded, calling the countryside to celebrate our arrival, crowing like a Gargantuan rooster awakening the universe to its glory.

As the train pulled into the last station on the line, I gathered up my things and led the way to the door, followed by the red-eyed boy, who was now sniffling sharply, and the happy couple, who were murmuring to one another and looking at me with, I thought, complete admiration and love. Against the pitch and roll of the train, I walked with a confident swagger, a rhythmic, light-footed roll, as befitted a favorite son of the Lord of Creation.

"Mmm! *Mmm!*" the conductor exclaimed as I bounded to the platform. "Somebody's going to pick some potatoes tonight!"

1945 ✇

I Question, Anonymous

Nearly all the autobiographical accounts of madness that have been published in this century were influenced by a secularization of the language and metaphor and concept of inner experience brought about by psychoanalysis and modern psychiatry. *I Question* may be an exception. It is a small, confusing book, written by an anonymous patient in a Tennessee asylum and published in 1945 without copyright. It opens with a foreword by psychiatrist Dr. Frank Luton, who says, with some irony, "I can recommend these interesting pages as a faithful record of the beliefs of a man who is sincerely looking for truth." Dr. Luton obviously expects the reader to consider *I Question* a psychiatric document; at the same time he tries tactfully to avoid contradicting the author, who clearly considers his work to be something of a philosophical treatise, a study of his own continuing contact with the spiritual world.

Like the pre-twentieth-century spiritual autobiographies considered earlier in this history, *I Question* has as its central purpose the portrayal of the connection between the human individual and certain intelligent powers of the cosmos. In places the work echoes Margery Kempe's description of her contact with spirits:

> Sometimes she heard with her bodily ears such sounds and melodies that she could not well hear what a man said to her at the time, unless he spoke the louder. . . . She saw with her bodily eyes many white things flying all about her on every side, as thick, in a manner, as specks in a sunbeam.

In the anonymous questioner's words:

> At the time of writing this, I have known of the spiritual world through their voices, seeing their faces, and having certain spiritual feelings for about two years. I am aware at times of seemingly thousands of souls leaving the world. I get this not only in speech from them but also a feeling of thickness in the air, either in an area below, above, or in some other direction from me. Frequently there is within my own body an area that seems thick like soup which leaves me with a feeling as one might have after a dive in a pool followed by a cool sensation.

The questioner's last sentence is particularly interesting because it contains some striking, poetic imagery that is slightly illogical. We might assume that the author meant to describe the cool sensation of diving into a pool, but the sentence does not quite say that. Perhaps the sense of that sentence has less to do with a logical association between "pool" and "cool sensation," than it has to do with an association of sound between "pool" and "cool." This kind of illogical association occurs throughout the book and, in fact, the book is immensely difficult to read, confusing and disorienting in the extreme. Not only is the author apparently an unskilled word-manipulator, not only does he string together words and phrases in some highly idiosyncratic combinations, but, as he informs us, often his thoughts are disturbed by the constant interruptions of voices from the spirit world.

Like Kempe, Haizmann, Trosse, and Cowper before him, the questioner persists in believing that he maintains some special contact with the spiritual world. He differs from them (particularly from Trosse and Cowper) in that his special relationship with the cosmos is wholly unorthodox and idiosyncratic. More than his predecessors, the questioner's self-importance verges on grandiosity: they are priests, while he is a prophet. In the following excerpts, grandiosity and confusion abound. Often there appears to be a thread of theme, but just as often that thread snaps, and the subject changes abruptly. Yet for all its incoherence, this spiritual autobiography remains immensely interesting, drawing us closely into the thoughts and processes of a mind not quite of this world.

I HAVE MANY EXPERIENCES to relate in this book that are made possible by my daily communication with the spiritual world. For the past two years I have been able to converse with spiritual voices through my own thought and am able to actually see persons in the spiritual world. In view of this special capacity I often become aware of many things not known to the average person. I do not know the reason for this, but I do know that these perceptions are real to me. I hope that you will believe much of what I tell you when these things occur.

*   *   *

Law of the Universe

There is a law of the universe. This law of the universe is the law of God and the law of the Goddess. There are undoubtedly three Goddesses just as there are three Gods; it follows then that you are known to God if you are a male and to the Goddess if you are a female.

It has been the will of God and the Goddess that at death one's spirit leaves this world instantly. If they refuse to do so, their penalties mount rapidly and they become more embittered. Those that have anything on the right side lose it rapidly.

At the time of writing this, I have known of the spiritual world through their voices, seeing their faces, and having certain spiritual feelings for about two years. I am aware at times of seemingly thousands of souls leaving the world. I get this not only in speech from them but also a feeling of thickness in the air, either in an area below, above, or in some other direction from me. Frequently there is within my own body an area that seems thick like soup which leaves me with a feeling as one might have after a dive in a pool followed by a cool sensation. This feeling of coolness at a distance seems strange. I also have a sensation of pain at a distance.

Personal Experiences

My trouble first started back about 1919 when I had a physical breakdown. That is when Communism started in Russia, too. Communism struck fear into my soul because it meant not only destruction of all our ideas of economic life but it also meant destroying our faith in God and offering nothing but beastliness in exchange for it. I went down to Florida with my family on a vacation at the time. I had a breakdown there. It lasted about thirty days or so—my heart raced and beat heavily.

About eight years ago, while on a pleasure trip to North Carolina, a remarkable experience occurred. On one of our side trips we seemed to drive into the end of a rainbow—a small one that looked as if it might be two or three hundred feet long. It appeared to end just in the road ahead of us a little to the right. I stopped the car, as a matter of fact, with the radiator parked right in the end of the rainbow.

About two days after this, a friend of mine, a doctor, told me without any apparent reason that I was getting ready to go through a serious change. I feel that he really got it from the other world although he was not aware of it. My reply was:

"Well, Doctor, I hope to take it in its stride." Possibly two years prior to that time he had told me that I was a type similar to Pasteur and some others who, after deep thought or work, would ask to be voluntarily confined. He told me that my type of personality is one which is productive of great achievement and tends to keep the world from standing still. At another time he had told me of his belief in immortality. He looked upon it as a kind of living through our children and not through ourselves. My reply was that if we are worthy of immortality through our children, then why not ourselves as well.

I returned to Nashville about August of that year. One day while playing golf my heart suddenly started racing, skipping and pounding to the point that it felt as if it might jump out of my body. Shortly after that I went to a hospital for observation and a check-up. I stayed there about three weeks and my heart again went through the same similar experience, following which I went to Madison Sanitarium. During my two weeks stay there I was filled with an overwhelming depression.

I want to describe a peculiar incident that happened while I was at Madison. I noticed that a tree on the grounds seemed to shed rain. On examination of the tree, the side I stood under did not seem to have any rain coming down, but I could see it on the other side, and finally could feel a few drops on my side. This so upset and puzzled me that I looked for a pipe up the side of the tree, thinking water might be coming down through that. I noticed the same phenomenon later when my wife and I were sitting out under a tree in the back of our home. It also rained, but not to the extent of the other one.

On a later occasion while in Florida I had something like a breakdown. On the advice of a physician I went to Johns Hopkins in Baltimore for observation. The journey was made by train and when we passed by the Indian River I saw two rainbows that symbolized the existence of both Gods and Goddesses. The reason they give me for our ignorance of a Goddess is of heavy sins in the soul world as all suffered to live perfectly on earth.

When I got to Johns Hopkins I walked into the doctor's office and everything suddenly went black and I knew nothing more for about two weeks or so. I remember just for a moment being in the clinic, and when I became clear I was in another ward. My mind worked very rapidly but disconnectedly. I remembered an experience that happened at the age of seven when I saw a swallow strike a telephone wire and fall to the ground. I picked it up, laid it on the backsteps of my home, where it finally revived and flew away. I recalled that on the same day there was an article in the paper about the sun being faceted like a diamond with two small facets on either side. This is something I did not see myself, and so far as I can recall I had not thought of it since that time. The recollection of these early memories was strange to me because of my memory being poor as a rule.

In some way I attributed this whole experience to some prediction from God about the ending of this earth. Voices from the other world have indicated that it meant that God willed that this world is to be vacated by mankind in one hundred fifty years. In connection with this experience, however, I came later to think how foolish it was to place any significance in the idea that the sun looked like a diamond, but I did think it strange that I remembered it in conjunction with the swallow. This clarification of my thinking came one day while I was going home in my car and upon driving into the garage there was a swallow who apparently had become confused and could not get out. This coincidence made quite an impression on me.

While I was at Johns Hopkins, after my period of amnesia, I refused to eat anything for days, not wishing to die but just waiting for some reason—not knowing why. The doctor finally told me that if I refused to eat, they would have to feed me forcibly. I told them that would be all right, and submitted without opposition to their inserting a tube in my nose which went down into my stomach. I was fed night and morning in this manner.

Two years ago when I was in Palm Beach there would be a group of Chinese that came down and stayed awhile and then left. Other groups that I cannot recall just now also came and left. At times there would seem to be small snakes that would stick out of the pupils of my eyes—all these things had a meaning—and I would have to pull them out. There would be devils that would be in my side and then would appear in the shape of bags like a blownup hog bladder—just horrible things that I would have to pull out of my side. There would be octopuses, crocodiles, horrible creatures of all kinds. I saw these things—and without being intoxicated, too! All of that has cleared up now.

I happened to be in Florida at the time of the radio broadcast of the "Invasion from Mars." This broadcast upset many people, which I believe was entirely due to coercion from the spiritual world. Even the authorization of it by Orson Welles came from the spiritual world, and I also believe that at this same time there occurred an invasion of the spiritual world by souls from Mars. They say the Martians caused the upset so that mankind would think twice before having children.

*   *   *

The Influence of Spirits

The spirits of the other world have a strange effect on me. They do this with me: they make me turn suddenly to look at a woman or a man in a place where I might be unaware of that person's presence. This happened to me once while I was in Florida. I had forgotten someone's name and had started out with the letter "A" trying to remember it. I don't remember just what reaction I was to get from the other world, but then I went to B, C, D and so on, until they let me know which was the right letter. I did this until I had spelled out the entire name.

Some people call this spiritualism, but this is incorrect, as man has thought of it. Spiritualism is an instrument of the devils. So far as this is concerned, all religions are instruments of the devils. It is my feeling that even in the use of prayer we deal with an ineffective instrument. I do not mean that there is no God, but that God does not answer our prayers because He knows nothing of them, as far as being able to grant them and they would if proper even before the request. In a perfect world one would not dare pray for anything.

In a religion such as Christian Science, any apparent benefit that a patient might receive is due to the releasing of the evil souls in the spiritual world from the patient by Scientists there. The same thing is true, just as if you pray for somebody and the person gets well. Just think how often you pray for a person and the person does not get well. We might use Rickenbacker as an illustration. What happened to him is that he was frightened, so it brought him to his senses and the realization that there was a God, and those in the other world allowed the Supreme Beings to send rain.

During my first trip to the sanitarium in Baltimore, I got the idea that I was Jesus Christ. I laid down in a tub and baptized myself several times in the water. It was John the Baptist making me do it; I had part of his soul. Also while there, I was lying on my cot writhing for days, feeling as if my body were full of static electricity. My muscles had become so drawn that I would have to put my foot over the side of the bed and touch the metal in the bed, which seemed to relieve my body of the current that seemed to be there.

I was lying in bed one night having in my mind an accounting to God of my many frailties and claiming one trait that I thought I had of honesty, when almost in a delirium I asked God if in return for my honesty He would allow me to rule the universe for a day.

On the night of December 31st at midnight I heard some cannon firing and sounds of a celebration which I thought meant that there was some warfare taking place. This caused me to have a crack-up, and I remember jumping up and down on the bed. The next morning, although I was very weak physically, I made up my mind that I would make every effort in my power to recover and carry on the best I could. I seemed to make rapid progress from then on, and regained my equilibrium.

*   *   *

Des Wasser Des Vergebens

German for the Water of Forgetfulness expresses well the meaning of Baptism in Hell in contrast to baptism in which they pull a mental block on a sinful soul to forget the many evils of the past which include for each soul all diseases, lusts, wars and premature aging of all bodies of every nature. I was just told this morning that this is the last world in the Universe, that those on earth do not know of both Gods and Goddesses.

I am told that there have been many civilizations here that were better than the one we now have. The fall of these civilizations has been due to either at their deaths in disgust, realizing their thievery in stealing to not be perfect did not pay, giving up what they had stolen or staying stubbornly on and going down in sure defeat.

The Opera La Boheme was composed really by a couple in the soul world who were French, the wife having died of tuberculosis while on earth, but it was not composed for the nobleless of the tuberculosis germ. A group of negroes gave me the thought that the expression, "The road to hell is paved with good intentions," really means in the soul world that they think often of giving up and accomplishing much and in delaying doing so they face what they call Hell which is judgment. But I understand that judgment is not as unpleasant as that which they face there. So, I believe, even delay leaving for that reason and become deranged in so doing.

In all perfect worlds they, having suffered, know of sin somewhat to understand as the Supreme Beings themselves understand and to understand one another meaning mankind and all other life and the Supreme Being.

Moles Are of Negroes Sold in the Soul World

A raised mole is part negro in the soul world and part hog and other forms of life that reflect in the body. I want negroes to understand that no negro is a perfect soul and only about 2,500 humans are perfect beings on this earth; they are all as I understand to be perfect again. No negro will ever be a Gentile or a Jew, a Jew or Chinese or any other race what they have been for sometime because you should know that they would and could not give birth but to perfect souls all of one kind. The expression "Hells Bells" that I just heard from the soul world means Christmas bells for Christ which are evil for those there and for you if you follow unreason still. The soul world suddenly grew worse about the start of the first World War when the Supreme Beings were first able to start placing real pressure on all there to vacate the most damnable place of all time. They started sinning more heavily in retaliation by war, lust, or babies, crime and insanity.

It is said in the soul world that one of the thieves who was crucified with Christ was a perfect soul, but it is strange that souls in the other world refuse to know and refuse to let this world know the truth.

It is strange, indeed, that a Supreme Being of the Universe would send a son of his here to this world and have a female dry his feet with her hair. God would not create any form of life to be degraded in such an act upon himself.

All flowers have given themselves the names they are called by as well as trees and other vegetation, although man on earth may think otherwise. I was in my bathroom a moment ago and, looking out the window, I could see faintly a dinosaur which they told me was about the last one there and was turned loose.

The Bible (which they often want me to write with a small letter) speaks of the Son of God being tempted on the Mount. Can you with any reason at all believe that the son of God could be tempted? I cannot. They tell me that just as man on earth thinks it only will have eternal life with their foolishness of religion so in your denial in thought through those in supposed Heaven the poor animals, birds, fish, microbes, and vegetation on earth do not know of immortality on earth and so much of it there. They take the position that all build character on darkness, ignorance and crime. Deranged souls in the soul world take in every form of life there, and if mankind were not demented no other soul could be. They tell me, which seems strange, that if you know their greatness, all vegetation speaks a language, even here, to one another something like a radio wave. It is strange in a way unless one understands that in a sinful soul world souls cannot keep from sinning equally; for if one permits the other to sin, saying, "I will not sin myself," you sin as much in so doing.

This may have a tendency to weaken my book with readers, but a "tumble bug" in the soul world played the best game of bridge that has ever been played, and you will know it some day and the reason for it. It was permitted by the Supreme Being to show that an obedient soul with their help can do better than the stolen wisdom of Gentiles, Jews and others. I do not know that grown people play any game as the great outdoors and thought of it as well as perfect humor and what we think of as deep thought which with them is simplicity itself.

1946 ⇥

The Snake Pit, by Mary Jane Ward

While the population of the United States in 1944 had little more than doubled that of 1880, the number of psychiatric patients in state institutions increased twelve times—to more than half a million.[1] The number of institutions increased as well: from 13 in 1830, to 190 in 1945. The trend toward centralization also continued: by 1945 there were 33 federal institutions. But the most notable change over the century was in the size of the institutions themselves. Asylums in the first half of the nineteenth century had capacities of one or two hundred. New York State's Willard Asylum broke with all tradition when it opened in 1866 with an astonishing 1,500 beds. By 1945, however, several American psychiatric institutions had become the size of small cities, with thousands of patients. Perhaps the three largest were New York Central Islip State Hospital with more than 7,000 patients, the Georgia State Hospital at Milledgeville, with 9,000, and New York's Pilgrim State Hospital, with a capacity of 10,000.

Were these mid-century institution-cities any better than their nineteenth-century predecessors? Nineteenth-century asylums were notable for the physical abuse of patients. We read again and again in patient writings of beatings, overt abuse, and tyranny over patients by attendants. Furthermore nineteenth-century institutions were almost wholly custodial, with no serious plans for treatment. Nurses were usually poorly trained, and attendants were untrained. The heads of these institutions called themselves "medical superintendents," and were invariably occupied with problems of management rather than concerns about treatment. Their management was typically narrow and authoritarian. The non-restraint system, popular in England, took hold much more gradually in America, in large part because of the continued resistance of the Association of Medical Superintendents of American Institutions for the Insane (now the American Psychiatric Association). A patients' rights association, the National Association for the Protection of the Insane and the Prevention of Insanity, founded in 1880, lasted only four years, largely because of the antagonism of this group of superintendents.[2] In the

---

[1]Deutsch, *The Mentally Ill in America,* p. 507.
[2]Ibid., p. 313.

238

1870s, however, the first courses in psychiatry were introduced in some American medical schools, and in 1882 the first permanent school of psychiatric nursing was established at the McLean Asylum in Massachusetts.

Conditions within American psychiatric institutions did improve somewhat during the first decades of the twentieth century. Most crucial in this improvement was the National Committee for Mental Hygiene, established in 1909 by Clifford Beers, a former mental patient and author of the protest *A Mind That Found Itself* (1908). The National Committee promoted research, legislation, hospital care studies, information programs, and community guidance centers. During the Depression, the committee lobbied in Washington for WPA money for state institutions, influencing the flow of more than ten million dollars.

The depression and World War II—with all the concomitant shortages of personnel and supplies—reversed much of that earlier improvement. In 1945 historian Albert Deutsch made a two-year survey of mental institutions in America and witnessed "scenes that rivaled the horrors of the Nazi concentration camps—hundreds of naked mental patients herded into huge, barn-like, filth-infested wards, in all degrees of deterioration, untended and untreated, stripped of every vestige of human decency, many in stages of semi-starvation." He discovered "hundreds of sick people shackled, strapped, strait-jacketed and bound to their beds" and "mental patients forced to eat meals with their hands because there were not enough spoons and other tableware to go around." He found "dormitories filled with twice or three times their normal capacity." He saw "in institution after institution, cold unappetizing food placed before patients at mealtime—food that patients either wolfed down to get the ordeal over quickly or else left untouched."[3]

Probably the most significant improvements over the century have been in therapy. The lack of therapeutic treatment in nineteenth-century asylums has been replaced by an abundance of therapies in our time. We can divide these therapies into two types: the psychotherapies and the somatic therapies.

The psychotherapies are the least radical and the least divergent from nineteenth-century treatment. At the beginning of the nineteenth century Pinel and others recommended the use of "moral

---

[3]Ibid., p. 449.

treatment," which was essentially a form of psychotherapy in which the unspoken assumption was that madness was an ailment of the personality that could be corrected by judicious interaction with a healthy personality. The rise of psychoanalysis led to a number of other therapies that were essentially refinements of moral treatment. Freud himself thought that mad people were not accessible to psychoanalysis and did not work with institutionalized patients. But psychoanalysis has been tried in many American clinics and institutions. Dr. John Rosen in 1947 claimed to have successfully treated thirty-seven cases of chronic schizophrenia by a method he called "direct analysis," a relationship therapy in which the therapist first establishes emotional contact with the patient by participating in the patient's fantasies and then gradually draws the patient into a more realistic model of the world.[4] Dr. Frieda Fromm-Reichmann used a similar approach with schizophrenic patients with some positive results; one of her patients, Joanna Greenberg, wrote a best-selling novel about her recovery, *I Never Promised You a Rose Garden* (1964). Unfortunately, in spite of the impressive publicity surrounding the psychotherapies based on traditional Freudian psychoanalysis, their actual impact on institutional populations has been minor. Other psychotherapies include behavior modification and various forms of group interaction. But probably the most lasting and important result of psychoanalysis and other twentieth-century versions of moral treatment has been an increased emphasis upon the need for humane and reasonable—psychologically positive—interactions between the patient and his or her keepers.

The therapies which have most distinguished twentieth-century American institutions, however, for better and for worse, have been the somatic therapies: shock, lobotomy, and chemotherapy.

It has been known since 1928 that chemically induced convulsions could cause some improvement with certain mental patients. Sometimes patients were put into a coma with large doses of insulin, and there is one patient's autobiographical account of her dramatic remission from five years' severe depression, after a short course of insulin shock treatment.[5] In Rome in the early 1930s Dr. Ugo Cerletti decided to try inducing convulsions with electricity to see if he could get similar results. With the permission of a Professor Torti, director of a

---

[4]Ibid., pp. 491, 492.
[5]McCall, *Between Us and the Dark*, 1947.

large Roman slaughterhouse, Cerletti first experimented on pigs so as to differentiate between lethal and non-lethal shocks. Cerletti then proceeded to human subjects, first working with a vagrant, a forty-year-old madman whose identity and home were unknown, who talked in "an incomprehensible gibberish made up of odd neologisms." The patient was put into bed and two electrodes were attached to his temples with an elastic band. The first jolt was given, but it was too low a voltage to produce a coma. As the doctor prepared for the second shock at a higher voltage, the patient sat up and said his first comprehensible words: "Not a *second*. Deadly!" Dr. Cerletti ignored the patient's wishes, however, and proceeded; the second shock did cause a seizure, after which, according to Cerletti, the patient improved rapidly. He stopped talking gibberish, was eventually able to give information about himself, began to be interested in his surroundings, and after eleven complete treatments, was discharged in "complete remission."[6]

In 1938 Cerletti demonstrated his invention at the Rome Medical Academy. Within the year electroshock therapy was being used on mental patients in America, quickly achieving popularity, partly because of its cheapness and ease of administration. Electroshock is sometimes effective for reversing severe depression, for unknown reasons; but at first, and for many years, electroshock was used in American institutions indiscriminately. Although it was supposedly therapeutic and painless, patients were terrified of it. Without question, during the height of its popularity as a treatment, there were many cases of foolish and abusive practices.

Lobotomy was introduced in 1936 by Egas Moniz of Portugal. Moniz believed that mad behavior could be reduced or cured by a simple cutting of certain nerve pathways in the frontal lobes of the brain. In his first operation Moniz drilled holes in a patient's skull, then inserted a hypodermic needle into the brain, injecting at several fixed points cell-destroying alcohol. Because the dispersement of the alcohol was too imprecise Moniz invented a cutting instrument which was essentially a hollow needle with a retractable wire loop at the tip. The instrument was inserted into the brain and then extended and rotated once in a circle, cutting out a small core of tissue. The loop was then retracted and the needle taken out. Four to six cores would be cut out in the same manner. On his first twenty patients, Moniz reported seven recoveries, seven cases of improvement, and six cases

---

[6]Cerletti, "Old and New Information about Electroshock," pp. 90, 91.

of non-improvement.[7] In 1939 the doctor was shot and nearly killed by one of his patients. He was awarded a Nobel Prize in 1949.

After Moniz's promising reports in 1936, lobotomy was tried in America. It quickly became popular, at first enthusiastically used as a miracle cure for chronic cases. As with electroshock, however, its initial cures led to excessive, incautious use and abuse. Between 1936 and 1949 over five thousand lobotomy operations were performed in the United States, on patients as young as sixteen. Lobotomy often had positive results—some patients experienced lowered tension and agitation after the operation, some were well enough to leave their institutions. Often enough, however, the operation produced irreversible negative surprises. From 2 to 5 percent of the patients died on the operating table, and 5 percent had convulsions from brain scarring. Many patients considered "overactive" before the operation were "underactive" afterward and vice versa. In short the results were erratic and unpredictable.[8]

Perhaps one of the worst things about both shock and lobotomy was their effect on the imagination: their simple existence and the very images they called up brought an atmosphere and mythology of terror and brutality to American institutions. In terms of actual, tangible, effects, electroshock and lobotomy, like psychotherapy, did not significantly decrease the large institutional populations of the 1940s and 1950s—especially when compared to the third major somatic therapy, chemotherapy.

Since the beginnings of medicine, there have been various chemotherapies available to mad people. But traditionally these have been, at best, simply narcotics and sedatives designed to tranquilize and induce sleep. Opium derivatives were long used in American institutions, and in the last two or three decades a number of other powerful tranquilizers have come into use. In the 1950s, however, an entirely new class of medicines was introduced. These new "antipsychotic" medicines (among them, the phenothiazines and lithium carbonate) can control and actually eliminate some of the more disturbing and disabling experiences of madness.

Sometime during the 1940s Mary Jane Ward was confined to a public institution near New York City. Her several months' res-

---

[7]Freeman and Watts, *Psychosurgery: Intelligence, Emotion and Social Behavior Following Prefrontal Lobotomy for Mental Disorders*, p. 13.

[8]See Greenblatt, *Studies in Lobotomy*.

idence there provided the basis for a highly successful autobiographical novel, *The Snake' Pit*. The book is unlike any protest we have seen so far. For one thing, it is the first fictionalized account we have examined. Though the basic elements of the story are true, and the descriptions of the institution, called Juniper Hill, seem wholly taken from real life, the entire work is constructed in the form of a novel—with scenes, extended dramatic dialogue and flashbacks. Unlike most of the protests we have seen so far, there is no attempt to establish the veracity of the narrator. There is no prefatory statement about "the unvarnished truth." There is no editorializing against asylum conditions in general. Nonetheless, *The Snake Pit* operates only partly as an experience of fiction. In large part the book works as a detailed, realistic, convincing study of a mid-twentieth-century American psychiatric institution. And the book's ultimate effect was as a protest. The expression "snake pit," now commonly used to describe the worst sort of mental hospital, was brought into the language in the 1940s, apparently by the appearance of Ward's novel. A movie based on the book, released in 1947, won fifty-two awards and was the largest-grossing A picture of the year. The coauthors of the screenplay received the award of the year for the best dramatic screenplay from the Screenwriters' Guild. And, according to Millen Brand, one of the coauthors, the film ultimately inspired greater state appropriations for mental institutions.[9]

During much of the novel the main character, Virginia Cunningham, is confused and disoriented. She cannot see well; her glasses are missing. Nor can she remember much; her memory is wholly unreliable (one common effect of electroshock). As the novel begins, she is sitting outside, enjoying the warmth of the sun. We observe her thoughts, as they wander randomly over past events and through confused present perceptions. Though she is actually sitting somewhere on the grounds of an institution, she thinks she is sitting in a park. When a woman orders Virginia and others back inside, she concludes she is visiting a school for delinquent girls, doing research for a novel. As she enters the hall the sight of wire mesh screens and the pungent smells suggest she may be at a zoo. However, the women in authority treat her and others harshly, curtly, as if they were criminals: so Virginia thinks she might be investigating a prison for a prison novel. She finally comes to the shocking realization that she is an inmate in a mental institution.

---

[9]Personal letter from Millen Brand, May 2, 1974.

The most striking thing about *The Snake Pit* is the detailed, precise picture of one institution at a particular time in history. Surprisingly, perhaps, we see almost no actual violence in the institution. But its very atmosphere is brutal. Patients are lied to. A nurse speaks to them "as if they and she were separated by a thick wall." Sometimes the nurses seem to think that "the patients were unable to hear anything that was not shouted." A request to see the doctor is evaded rather than straightforwardly answered. Patients are treated "as if they were criminals," or "like cattle." The power of the staff is often used arbitrarily. In one ward that Virginia enters the nurse forbids patients to walk on a new rug in the dayroom.

Very little attention is given to patients' personal appearance. Quick showers are permitted twice a week. There is no laundry service, so patients wear the same clothes indefinitely. Once a week is "fine-comb night," when the nurse goes through each patient's hair with a fine comb, searching for lice. On some wards, women's hair is cut short, for the convenience of the institution. Restraints such as the straitjacket and the "wet pack" are seen by the patients as humiliating rather than helpful. Treatments often look and feel more like punishment than therapy, while the very physical layout of the institution seems almost expressly designed to depress, humiliate, and abrade individuality. In at least one ward the walls, floors, and curtains are either brown or dirty. In the lavatory there are no doors to the stalls and no toilet paper. Clothes are stamped with a number. There are four wash basins for a ward of forty or fifty patients and two shower stalls. In one of the wards the furniture consists of four of five long benches. There are shortages of mattresses, linen, toilet paper, and tissue; patients use rags for tissue.

During the novel's progress we closely follow Virginia's mental processes, confusion, and forgetfulness. At the same time we can look slightly beyond her limited awareness and see the larger world of Juniper Hill. The difference in viewpoints, so skillfully handled, lends a great dramatic tension to the entire work. Virginia is an innocent, a sheep among wolves—we are sympathetic, and apprehensive. We see the dangers and the hardness. When her point of view at last converges with our greater awareness and when she more fully recognizes her position, that recognition is the beginning of her progression toward health. She sees at last that she is in a "snake pit" and the shock of that perception seems to give her the strength and clarity and will to survive: "Long ago they lowered insane persons into snake pits; they thought that an experience that might drive a sane

person out of his wits might send an insane person back into sanity.
. . . They had thrown her into a snake pit and she had been shocked
into knowing that she could get well."

That particular conceptual or psychological turning point is very
dramatic. I know of no such "snake pit" treatment in the past
(although there may have been something similar at the ancient
Greek healing temple at Epidaurus). But the idea that mad people
could be shocked out of their madness is an old one. Eighteenth- and
nineteenth-century treatments included the "bath of surprise," in
which the unsuspecting patient was dropped through a trap door
into a pool of ice-cold water. Some physicians recommended the
"well-cure" in which the patient would be chained at the bottom of a
well, with water gradually dripping in. According to Albert Deutsch,
one American physician, a Dr. Willard, became known at the beginning of the nineteenth century for his own particular variation of the
well-cure. At his private asylum in New England, Willard kept a black
coffin with holes in it. The newly admitted patient would be sealed
inside the coffin, then submerged in a water tank until all the air had
bubbled out of the holes.[10] And we recall Ebenezer Haskell's description of the harrowing "spread-eagle cure" with "douche bath."

It is not at all clear that the coersive treatments and degrading
environment at Juniper Hill were deliberately and consciously
planned to shock the patients "back into sanity." That idea is more
dramatic than accurate. Nonetheless, Mary Jane Ward's Juniper Hill is
an accurate portrait of a typical American psychiatric institution of the
mid-twentieth century.

The following excerpts from *The Snake Pit* are meant to give a composite reproduction of Juniper Hill. In the first excerpt we follow
Virginia's progress through a maze of locked doors and halls to the
lavatory. She is then given electroshock treatment. To her, the attendants are guards, the doctor and his assistant are diabolical conspir-
ators, the treatment itself is electrocution. In the third and fourth excerpts, Virginia undergoes "hydrotherapy," extended baths in "the
room"; then she is wrapped in a wet pack for the night; she manages
to escape and finds a dry bed to sleep in. In the fifth entry, she rushes
to dinner with the rest of her ward through the underground tunnels
connecting buildings. And in the final entry, Virginia comes face to

---

[10]Deutsch, *The Mentally Ill in America*, p. 82.

face, in the tunnels, with a straitjacketed patient who had been her friend several months earlier when she first entered "the snake pit."

THEY LINED UP in front of the dining-room door. When the door was unlocked they marched out. Miss Cut-the-Shoving was checking on her board. To see if any of them had died of the meal?

They marched up the brown hall and stopped at the door at the end of it. Miss Hart unlocked the door and they went into the waiting room. They crossed that room and paused at another door. Miss Hart unlocked the door. They went into another hall. They stopped at another door. When it was unlocked they went into a room that was stunningly different.

It was a large light room. There was tile on the floor, tiny octagonal pieces of tile charmingly fitted together and so white and clean. The walls had the two-color paint job but they seemed more cheerful. It was a lovely room. Virginia studied the floor as if it was an exceptional mosaic and she thought suddenly of her beautiful Kelim rug and had then to suppress a ridiculous and unexpected sob. Don't be a baby. Suppose you had to stay here.

If I had to remain in this prison I would choose this room, she thought. But presently her enthusiasm waned. There were four booths. The women stood and waited for their turn. Anyhow, that was the idea. Your turn wasn't necessarily when you thought. It depended a good deal on where Miss Hart was. The pushing was done quietly and with no hard feeling. Virginia changed from line to line but it was no use; none of the booths had a door.

When at last it was her uncontested turn she discovered that an even more vital accessory was missing. There was no wooden seat and the old joke about not falling in was in this case no joke. But she forgot how frightful this was when she saw there was no toilet paper, no toilet tissue as you would call it in Evanston. There wasn't even an empty container. Nor any holes to indicate that there had ever been a dispenser. She was about to call to her next neighbor, but then she remembered the cleansing tissues in her handbag.

When she left the booth she peered at the walls of the other three. None of them had paper. This must be reported.

As a rule she held back and let others do the reporting but now she was angry and she went to Miss Hart to say what is the idea of not providing these women with toilet paper. When she reached Miss Hart she saw that the woman was providing toilet paper. Miss Hart was the dispenser. If you required paper you asked her for it in advance and she doled it out for you.

*   *   *

"Good morning, ladies."

Who had got into the room? Stealthily she groped for Robert. I must put my hand over his mouth so he won't speak out. But the bed was narrow and she was alone. The room was dark but she saw pale shapes rising up. One of the shapes said her name and then she remembered that she was not at home. February to August.

"Yes," she said. She got out of the cot, fumbled for the bag under the bed and then put on her shoes.

"Hurry up."

"I am." Always the command to hurry and you hurried nowhere, you arrived nowhere. The shoes were cold and clammy and they squished up and down when you walked.

After she had followed Grace into the hall she remembered the letter and so she went back and took it from under the pillow. When she returned to the hall Grace had vanished but there were other ghosts that rushed in the dimness. It was far too dark to be morning and she wondered if this might be a fire drill.

She followed the shapes into the washroom. Although it was the same room it had been moved to the other end of the hall. She would not give them the satisfaction of commenting on the change. She found her hanger and began to dress.

"Virginia! You don't take breakfast this morning."

Then why not let me stay in bed, fool? She turned and there was another guard, not Miss Hart, a smaller one but with a big voice. Not that I took dinner last night, but thank you just the same for saving me the bother of the trip. "All right," she said.

Perhaps Robert is coming to take me away. She continued to dress.

Now this one that was not Miss Hart came over to her and took her by the shoulders and shook her. "You put your clothes right back on that hanger." This guard had puffy cheeks and her rouge was in purple splotches and her hair was scooped into a black-silk net and she looked as if she had been up all night. "You know you go for shock. Hurry up or you'll be late."

It was quaint of the guard to think you had to go elsewhere for a shock. But Virginia put her clothes back on the hanger and again got into the grotesque nightgown.

"You'll have to concentrate," whispered Grace. "It makes her so mad when you forget. And it counts against you."

"Where am I going?"

"For shock. You remember."

Do I? I remember it no more than I remember the house where I was born and the little window. Going for shock. An odd, foreign expression. Sensation seekers go to be shocked; I never heard anyone say go for shock, as if it was a commodity like the morning milk.

Presently she and the guard were the only ones left in the washroom. The guard handed her a gray terrycloth robe. "Put this on," she said. "Put your nightgown back on the hanger. Hurry up."

In the hall the guard turned her over to another one in blue and white, one who hadn't put on any rouge this morning. Virginia and the pale one went through the large room and they reached the outer corridor in time to trail along with the last of the breakfast ladies, but they did not go into the dining room with the breakfast ladies.

As they turned at a door just beyond the dining room door Virginia noticed a third door. It had gold letters on it. It looked familiar but she was unable to make out the letters. The pale one unlocked the door she had selected and they went into a cement stair-well and started to climb. After several flights the pale one unlocked another door and they went into another brown corridor. The pale one escorted her to a small room and left her there. All of this was done without any comment. Well, I don't feel like talking before I've had my coffee either.

There were wooden benches around the walls of the small

room and there were two windows. Virginia tried to open one of the windows and was surprised to find that she could. The window opened down the center to make two slits. They might as well have had bars. It was beginning to get light. The sky had a sick, lemon cast at the horizon.

Three robed women were ushered in. One of them sat down; the other two stood in the center of the room. No one said anything.

After a while a guard came and took one of the robed women away. There was pink in the sky now. The pink was turning to red when another woman was taken away. It was nearly light when Virginia was taken.

She was taken down the hall to a little room and the moment she saw that room she knew she had been shocked previously and that she did not care for another helping. The room smelled like her old electric egg beater and there was a dull red glass eye in the wall. "I think I'll go back downstairs," she said.

"You go right on in," said the guard.

"Good morning, Virginia." This was quite a different voice. It was so pleasant that it was silly. It dripped the sort of cheery good will that is hard to take any morning, especially a morning when you have a formaldehyde hangover.

"Good morning," said Virginia in a tone which she meant to indicate that she wished not to discuss it further.

There was a high table, like an operating table, and she knew she was supposed to get up on it. She got on it and the woman with the silly voice fussed around her. This woman was in an R.N. uniform and the room had somewhat the appearance of an operating room. I'd forgotten I was to have an operation. You don't eat before an operation, of course. I should have remembered. I wonder what I am being operated on for. What haven't I had removed? I believe I still have my gall bladder.

"Well, Jeannie. And how is Jeannie this morning?"

It was he, the Indefatigable Examiner, come out from the bushes. He was wearing a white coat. He had blue eyes and a hawkish nose and a very slender face and his hair was fair and curly, like Grace's, only shorter.

"And did you enjoy being outside in the park yesterday?" He said this with a heavy accent that you had never been able to place. It wasn't German, French, Italian or Scandinavian.

Polish, perhaps. He began to talk at great rate but you could tell he didn't care if you translated or replied. He and the silly woman were busy with their hands. Evidently it was to be a local anesthetic.

They put a wedge under her back. It was most uncomfortable. It forced her back into an unnatural position. She looked at the dull glass eye that was set into the wall and she knew that soon it would glow and that she would not see the glow. They were going to electrocute her, not operate upon her. Even now the woman was applying a sort of foul-smelling cold paste to your temples. What had she done? You wouldn't have killed anyone and what other crime is there which exacts so severe a penalty? Could they electrocute you for having voted for Norman Thomas? Many people had said the country was going to come to that sort of dictatorship but you hadn't believed it would ever reach this extreme. Dare they kill me without a trial? I demand to see a lawyer. And he—he always talking about hearing voices and never hearing mine . . . He, pretending to be so solicitous of me and not even knowing my name, calling me Jeannie. If I say I demand a lawyer they have to do something. It has to do with habeas corpus, something in the Constitution. But they and their smooth talk, they intend to make a corpus of me—they and their good mornings and how are you.

Now the woman was putting clamps on your head, on the paste-smeared temples and here came another one, another nurse-garbed woman and she leaned on your feet as if in a minute you might rise up from the table and strike the ceiling. Your hands tied down, your legs held down. Three against one and the one entangled in machinery.

She opened her mouth to call for a lawyer and the silly woman thrust a gag into it and said, "Thank you, dear," and the foreign devil with the angelic smile and the beautiful voice gave a conspiratorial nod. Soon it would be over. In a way you were glad.

*   *   *

Occasionally she was aware of being moved from a tub to a bed. From a wet hammock to a wet bed. During this long period there was no normal eating. The tube business happened again and again and eventually she understood that it was a way of feeding her. When she neared the top of the hole and found the tube in her nose she wanted to tell the Young Jailer she would gladly eat if he would give her an opportunity, but she was unable to speak. The quicksand of the hole pulled her down and stifled her attempts at speech.

Then gradually she began to come out of it; gradually the periods of being out of it lengthened and now she walked from bed to tub and from tub to bed. And the time came when she went to a small room that had a table and two long benches and there, along with several other robed creatures, she ate meals of gravy and gruel. She ate eagerly. The food was revolting looking and tasting stuff but she had learned that by eating it she avoided the tube feeding.

Sometimes the real Robert came to see her. She tried to talk to him, to tell him how cold she was, but all she could do was cry. She wept while Robert talked quietly to her. She liked to hear his voice, but she never knew what he was saying. It was terrible when he went away. He went away and the old routine of tub and bed and meals in the little room was resumed.

An icy draft blew in around the windows at the end of the tub room. In front of the windows a nurse sat at a desk and marked on papers. She wore a sweater and had a coat over the back of her chair. All of the nurses in the tub room wore sweaters but the patients went from tub to tub in sheets or in cotton robes. When the wind was blowing hard and cold the tub water, when you first got into it, felt good. It always cooled, though. The nurses said not, but by the time you had to move on to another tub the water seemed as cold as the winter wind.

*   *   *

After the meal the nurse came and took them away. Usually two nurses called for Virginia. Great strapping women with large arms, they lifted her up to a bed as if she was a baby. They bounced her on the wet sheets and expertly wrapped her into the frigid cocoon.

"That's quite a trick," she said to them one night. "A dirty trick."

The nurses looked at each other. "Well," said one of them, "it's nice to know you can talk. You are always so quiet."

They spread a dry sheet over her. Why? No bit of the dry sheet touched her. It was not to be endured. Hurry and get out, you two, so I can hurry and get out.

She watched with a purpose this night but they worked too rapidly. She was unable to memorize the motions that created the cocoon. It was not, however, to be endured. So when the nurses left she began to get out of the mummy trappings.

It took a long time.

First she wriggled under the wide binder that was tucked between the mattress and springs. This took a very long time. For a while, when her head was under the binder, she thought she would never manage it; it was like crawling out of your own skin. Free of the binder she twisted her body until she could swing the lower part of it over the side of the bed. After sliding to the floor it was comparatively easy. Using her teeth, good strong teeth and none missing, she loosened the twists that went over her shoulders and then swayed from side to side until the sheets unwound.

She stood naked and free in air that felt comfortingly warm. She took the dry sheet to the radiator and made herself a tent. To be warm in winter. One of the very finest things in life.

When she became sleepy she went back to the bed. She shoved the wet sheets way down to the foot of the bed and, wrapped in her dry sheet, curled up on the rubber mattress. She would, she promised herself, wake up early enough to rewrap herself in the wet sheets but instantly a voice was screeching.

"Virginia—how on earth! Who put you in pack last night?"

"I don't know," said Virginia.

"How did you get out?"

"I was cold." Why had morning to come so quickly?

"Well," said this morning nurse, "I'll attend to your pack myself tonight and that's for sure."

Yes, this one who thought she was so smart, this one attended to Virginia's pack that night and maybe it did take Virginia longer to get out of it. Maybe it did. But she got out and she had another comfortable sleep. And the next night they put a large canvas spread over her bed and they laced this spread under the springs in some way. The spread had one hole in it, for your head.

*   *   *

"Supper, ladies," shouted Miss Vance. She was an amazon of a woman. There was a nurse, a long time ago, that I thought was large; I hadn't seen anything.

The ladies scrambled over to Miss Vance. Virginia tried to keep a little air between herself and the others. However, such foul-smelling air was undoubtedly as thick with germs as were the ladies.

"I don't know yet," the nurse was saying. "Wait a sec." She cocked her head in the direction of the hall and then she bellowed, "Tunnel!"

She unlocked the door and the ladies sped down the stairs. Virginia had a hard time keeping up with them. They raced into a basement and then into a tunnel.

The tunnel was something for a horror story. There were lights but the pale glow they gave off was swallowed in the midnight pools between the lights. The walls were cement patterned with cracks. Water seeped slowly from some of the wider cracks and on the uneven floor were puddles of dark water.

The tunnel was divided into two lanes. The dividing wall was of some sort of heavy chicken wire and on the other side of it ladies scurried along like gray-blue rats. Now and then there was a lady in a canvas jacket laced up the back. Virginia saw her breath in the pale light as she panted to catch up with her crowd.

They came to a staircase. This also was divided into two parts but the dividing agent in this case was merely a railing made by two iron bars. A very fat old lady crawled between the bars and went up the other side. It made no difference. You all came out on the same landing.

At the door was a nurse, oh, such a large nurse. She unlocked the door, but she held an arm across the opening and the ladies shoved against her. When she dropped her arm the ladies spilled into an enormous room and rushed for a line that was forming on one side.

*   *   *

Virginia was thinking this as she went back through the tunnel. She was not able to think and to hurry at the same time and so now she fell behind the crowd that was running back to the ward. She was pretty much alone when she saw Grace.

Grace, the fair girl who had worn a hoover apron, the girl who had been almost well enough to go back to her job on the newspaper. "Oh, Grace," wailed Virginia.

The girl on the other side of the wire partition stopped when

Virginia called her name. She stood very still and looked through the fence.

"But I thought you'd gone home," said Virginia. "Months and months ago."

Grace stared at her.

"I'm Virginia. You remember me. We were good friends. We used to sit in the sun and talk. Remember? It was in Ward Three, Grace. You used to tell me where my bed was and what number my hanger was and things like that. I was always forgetting everything but you always knew."

Grace's eyes were nearly black in the dim light of the tunnel. They were fixed on Virginia but they seemed not to see.

"They have cut your pretty hair so short," said Virginia. She put her hands up to her face to brush her tears away. "I'm sorry. I'm really glad to see you. Of course I'm not. You know what I mean. I'd thought you were back home."

Grace said absolutely nothing.

And then Virginia noticed that her friend was wearing one of the canvas jackets. She had seen many of these jackets since coming to Building Five and she supposed they were what are called strait jackets. Previously she had thought a strait jacket was something that covered all of you but perhaps the kind she was seeing here was semi-formal. They looked like lumberjacks. The armlike appendages were crossed and fastened in the back. The whole contraption was laced up the back. It looked as if there might be straps or something for the patient to rest her arms in, at any rate the arms did not dangle. The ladies who wore these jackets went directly to seats in the dining room and nurses took them trays and fed them. Just yesterday Virginia had sat next to a lady who was being fed. Between bites she told the nurse about a trip she had had in Europe some years back. She was an aristocratic-looking woman with a Best Bostonian way of speaking. The nurse appeared to be listening to her with interest and respect. Both of them gave the impression of being too well bred to notice that one was being fed by the other. Virginia had seen this Boston woman many times and always the woman was wearing a canvas jacket. You were tortured by curiosity. It was impossible to imagine that so dignified a person needed to be tied up.

Grace started to move away from the barrier. "Don't go," said Virginia. "Come back, Grace. Turn around and maybe I can reach through and unfasten that thing. It is ridiculous for them to . . . I never knew a kinder person, a more gentle person. As if you would . . ."

Grace paused long enough to give Virginia a look which made her grateful for the jacket and the fence. Yes, it was as if she would. Even the thought of Robert's coming visit failed to remove the memory of Grace's parting glare.

1952 ✑

Wisdom, Madness and Folly, by John Custance

Though he had suffered previous bouts of depression and one experience of unusual elation, John Custance's first severely abnormal mental experience happened in 1938 when he was thirty-eight years old. On Armistice Sunday, he attended a church service commemorating England's heroic dead. Suddenly he knew the meaning of the millions of war deaths in Europe. They were part of a Divine Plan and Custance realized he was to have a part in that plan. He began to notice unusual physical sensations: "shivers" in the spine and "tingling of the nerves," and that night he experienced his first "true" hallucination:

> How shall I describe it? It was perfectly simple. The great male and female organs of love hung there in mid-air; they seemed infinitely far away and infinitely near at the same time. . . . I was not sexually excited; from the first the experience seemed to be holy. What I saw was the Power of Love—the name came to me at once—the Power that I knew somehow to have made all universes, past, present and to come, to be utterly infinite, an infinity of infinities, to have conquered the Power of Hate, its opposite, and thus created the sun, the stars, the moon, the planets, the earth, light, life, joy and peace, never-ending.

After that vision his entire life changed. His sense of sin and guilt vanished, and his experiential world seemed transformed into a garden of extraordinary beauty and pleasure. He felt in love with the universe, and believed he had found the solution to all problems: love. Custance concluded that love was the force of attraction in the universe, the essence that causes spirit and matter to cohere, while its opposite, hate, causes repulsion, the essence that disintegrates spirit and matter. Furthermore, he concluded that the traditional Christian antithesis between sacred and profane love was false, that sexual attraction was indeed an essential element of spiritual attraction. What landed him in an asylum was not that insight, however, but the actions he justified by it. He was wandering the streets of London when a prostitute came up to him. He considered her solicitations to be a call for love which he could not refuse; he felt he loved her and wanted to express that love. Consequently he went with her to her room, read the Bible with her, gave her five pounds, and left. Within

256

a short time Custance had given away all his savings, some three hundred pounds, in similar enterprises. Since he saw himself as divinely inspired, he approached a Christian Science church for more money to help another prostitute. When they refused Custance tried to destroy everything in the church within his reach, hoping to make himself a martyr, "and thus showing up the meanness and hypocrisy of churches in general." The police came and Custance was put in a mental hospital for three weeks. During the next fifteen years—while in and out of asylums undergoing treatment for recurring "manic-depressive psychosis"—Custance wrote *Wisdom, Madness and Folly*, the story of his mad experiences and philosophy.

In large part *Wisdom, Madness and Folly* is presented as a psychiatric document. The foreword describes the book as "a first-hand document for the study of . . . psychosis." There are appendices describing Custance's reactions to specific psychiatric treatments and the results of two psychometric examinations. Much of the book lists in clear, methodical fashion the qualities of manic-depressive madness as Custance sees them. What is most striking is Custance's continuing insistence that his madness brought to him "an intense emotional religious experience." Surely Custance is not writing a "spiritual autobiography," as we understand the term. He seems neither aware of nor interested in the traditional forms of such an autobiography; and before speaking about matters of the soul and spirit, he carefully justifies his new vector by invoking the authority of Jung and William James. Yet finally Custance persists in describing his unusual experiences as akin to or identical with religious experience and discussable in those terms.

It may be relevant here to consider why, given all the advantages of scientific thought, so many mad people continue to speak of their experiences in spiritual terms. In the first place it is probably a mistake to assume that science and religion are antithetical. Science is one particular discipline for confronting reality, but it has limitations. It is biased towards the atomistic, rather than the holistic vision. It seems most effective when dealing with tangible and measurable material reality. And for all the successes of scientific method, we can still see its beginning in some unanalyzable assumptions and its end in some unanswerable questions. What is consciousness? What is the origin and destiny of "I" and "Not-I?" What is infinity?

It is part of the function of the brain to limit awareness, to filter, to systemize in some coherent fashion the raw, infinite chaos of reality. It may be that all ways of knowing serve as part of that complex filter. And the mind, confronted with infinity, gropes for the dark glass of system—both the mythic and metaphorical system of religion, and the logical system of science—in a response not much different from the flower seeking light. What some mad people and some mystics at times may have in common is a temporary or permanent, whole or skewed, loss of the ordinary biological and cultural filters, and a naked encounter with reality in its infinite form. Having passed through the gates of perception, having encountered reality in some unusual and perhaps overwhelming form, they return and begin speaking of old truths in new or reconstructed systems—logical, or mythic and metaphorical. We may find their mythic expressions both strangely different from and strangely like traditional religious systems; but I believe we will find them meaningless only if we try to comprehend the mythic by logic, or the logical by myth.

Following are three excerpts from *Wisdom, Madness and Folly*. First, Custance describes, in summary form, what "manic-depressive psychosis" is like for him. In the next entry, his first serious attack of mania is portrayed. In the final excerpt he describes an experience of mad depression in great detail. His feeling of despair becomes so overwhelming that he concludes his soul has been taken by Satan. The reader may want to compare this account, and the mythical thinking that leads him to ideas of demonic possession, with George Trosse's eighteenth-century description of his mad depression.

WE ALL KNOW the type of individual who is "up in the air" at one time and "down in the dumps" at another. Psychologists call this kind of temperament "cyclothymic"; it is quite common, and only when there is serious nervous disturbance does it lead to true manic-depressive psychosis. When elated, either for genuine reasons to be found in external circumstances, or sometimes for no apparent reason at all, the subject sees the world through rose-coloured spectacles. He feels particularly fit; his reactions to his environment are rapid and well-defined; he has an inner certainty that he will succeed in any plans he may have formed in embryo in his mind; the world, in fact, is his oyster. When depressed, on the other hand, he feels more or less ill; he looks on the black side of everything; he is convinced he will fail in anything he undertakes; he is uncertain and doubtful, particularly about himself; he cannot concentrate properly; his reactions are slow, though often his mind is revolving very rapidly about his own troubles and fears.

When the nervous system is thoroughly deranged, the two contrasting states of mind can be almost infinitely intensified. It sometimes seems to me as though my condition had been specially devised by Providence to illustrate the Christian concepts of Heaven and Hell. Certainly it has shown me that within my own soul there are possibilities of an inner peace and happiness beyond description, as well as of inconceivable depths of terror and despair. Normal life and consciousness of "reality" appear to me rather like motion along a narrow strip of table-land at the top of a Great Divide separating two distinct universes from each other. On the one hand the slope is green and fertile, leading to a lovely landscape where love, joy and the infinite beauties of nature and of dreams await the traveller; on the other a barren, rocky declivity, where lurk endless horrors of distorted imagination, descends to the bottomless pit.

In the condition of manic-depression, this table-land is so narrow that it is exceedingly difficult to keep on it. One begins to slip; the world about one changes imperceptibly. For a time it is possible to keep some sort of grip on reality. But once one is really over the edge, once the grip of reality is lost, the forces of the Unconscious take charge, and then begins what appears to be an unending voyage into the universe of bliss or the universe of horror as the case may be, a voyage over which one has oneself no control whatever.

*   *   *

It began in the autumn of 1938, when I was just 38 years of age. For some years I had suffered from bouts of nervous depression, and I had had one attack of elation. None of these had been really serious, however; at any rate I had not had to be confined in a Mental Hospital or Asylum. I had been free of trouble for rather more than a year and had settled down in a congenial job.

The first symptoms appeared on Armistice Sunday. I had attended the service which commemorates the gallant dead of the "War to end Wars". It always has an emotional effect upon me, partly because my work has had a good deal to do with the tragic aftermath of that war in Europe. Suddenly I seemed to see like a flash that the sacrifice of those millions of lives had not been in vain, that it was part of a great pattern, the pattern of Divine Purpose. I felt, too, an inner conviction that I had something to do with that purpose; it seemed that some sort of revelation was being made to me, though at the time I had no clear ideas about what it was. The whole aspect of the world about me began to change, and I had the excited shivers in the spinal column and tingling of the nerves that always herald my manic phases.

That night I had a vision. It was the only pure hallucination I have ever experienced; though I have had many other visions, they have always taken the form of what are technically known as "illusions". I woke up about five o'clock to find a strange, rather unearthly light in the room. As my natural drowsiness wore off, the excited feelings of the day before returned and grew more intense. The light grew brighter; I began, I remember, to inhale deep gulps of air, which eased the tension in some way. Then suddenly the vision burst upon me.

How shall I describe it? It was perfectly simple. The great male and female organs of love hung there in mid-air; they seemed infinitely far away from me and infinitely near at the same time. I can see them now, pulsing rhythmically in a circular clockwise motion, each revolution taking approximately the time of a human pulse or heartbeat, as though the vision was associated in some way with the circulation of the blood. I was not sexually excited; from the first the experience seemed to me to be holy. What I saw was the Power of Love—the name came to me at once—the Power that I knew somehow to have made all universes, past, present and to come, to be utterly infinite, an infinity of infinities, to have conquered the Power of Hate, its opposite, and thus created the sun, the stars, the moon, the planets, the earth, light, life, joy and peace, never-ending.

*   *   *

In my previous states of depression I had never really lost my grip of reality. I had begun to slip off the table-land down the slope to the left, but there was still as it were a ridge in front of me which might hold me up. I was utterly miserable and wanted to die, but my fears, troubles and worries were of normal human mischances which might happen to anybody. I feared poverty, failure in life, inability to educate my children, making my wife miserable, losing her, ending up in the gutter as the most revolting type of beggar and so on. My fears had in fact become so overpowering as to appear to me like certainties, but they were only earthly, human fears. Beyond the ridge bordering this ordinary universe of common human experience unending horrors awaited me. But I did not know; I had not crossed it, at any rate in that direction.

Had I had anything like the insight into my own mind that I have now attained, I should have known what to expect, for during the foregoing manic period I had crossed the ridge down the slope to the right of the plateau. I had experienced unearthly joys; I had imagined myself in Heaven; in the padded cell at Brixton I saw vision after vision, and though I rather doubt whether orthodox Roman Catholics would allow those visions the predicate "beatific", they were undoubtedly my particular form of the Vision Beautiful.

If you are a saint, you may, I suppose, aspire to see the Beatific Vision without experiencing its opposite, which I will call the Horrific Vision. You struggle and sacrifice and mortify your flesh; you pass through the "Cloud of Unknowing" and the Dark Night of the Soul when you feel, like St Theresa, that God has deserted you, but you need not necessarily go through the terrors of Hell. None the less, many famous religious leaders—Martin Luther and John Bunyan are notable cases in point—have experienced something of the kind, and for the ordinary sinner it is sound Catholic doctrine that Heaven without Purgatory is inconceivable.

Thus, since I had had experience of Heaven, it was only reasonable to expect that I should be shown Hell in due course. Let me try to summon up all my descriptive powers to give some idea of the pass to which conscience can bring a human soul, once it has slipped over the ridge to the left of the narrow plateau and lost its foothold on reality.

I lay in my bed in the ward of the Hospital dominated above all by an overpowering sense of fear. At first I did not know exactly what it was that I feared, except of course that my mind, which I strove as hard as I could to keep blank, would insist on working about the ordinary, human fears I have outlined above. Wisely, no attempt was made to get me up, and I lay as motionless as I could, covering my head as a rule with the bedclothes, partly to shut out the sights and sounds of the ward, and partly as a sort of instinctive reaction.

Dr W. H. R. Rivers in his suggestive work *Instinct and the Unconscious* has given one of the probable reasons for this attitude. It was the reaction of the animal who under the compulsion of the fear-emotion remains absolutely immobile, "paralysed by fear" as the popular locution has it. It does so, of course, because in the course of evolution immobility, "lying doggo", has proved a sound means of defence. The reaction is what Rivers calls an "all or nothing" reaction, because for gregarious animals it is absolutely essential that all the members of the group should remain equally immobile; if one moves, the whole purpose of the reaction is defeated.

About the second reason I am not so clear. I believe, however, that to cover oneself up with the bedclothes suggests, at any rate to some extent, the safety of the mother's womb, the ultimate refuge, according to good Freudian doctrine, towards which so much psychological striving is directed.

Anyway, there I lay for some days, only putting my head outside the clothes to eat my food, take my drugs, and for absolutely necessary purposes. Gradually, however, the sounds if not the sights of the ward forced themselves in on my consciousness.

In the bed opposite me there lay, also in a state of extreme misery and dejection, a patient named Bar——. He moaned unceasingly; I could not help hearing what he said. He only said two words, at least I never remembering hearing him say anything else. Those words were, "no hope, no hope, no hope," ceaselessly repeated in a hollow moan. I soon learnt his name; it began with the fatal syllable Bar.

I was barred, my mind began to repeat to me, barred from hope, there was no hope for me. The obvious association soon followed. I do not know much Italian, but I had once made an attempt to read parts of Dante's *Inferno* in the original.

Lasciate ogni speranza voi ch'entrate.

So that was where I was going was it? No, I tried to argue with myself, it was impossible. There must be some hope, some escape from Hell. A Creator who condemned his creatures to eternal punishment, whatever their sins, would be a monster, and the God of Jesus was a God of love. This reasoning, I may say, represents a considered view that I have always held. It comforted me for a time.

There was a very charming Anglican parson in the ward, whom I will call G.G., as he may prefer me not to mention his name. On various occasions he had done me little kindnesses, and though I hardly talked to anybody, I did now and then talk to him. As the subject of Hell was getting on my mind, I broached it to him in an endeavour to get some reassurance.

G.G., however, was not impressed by my reasoning. He brought his little Bible along and produced texts to prove his thesis that an eternal Hell was a part of God's purpose and Word, and that Jesus Christ explicitly endorsed this view. "Everlasting fire prepared for the Devil and all his Angels", "and these shall go away into eternal punishment, but the righteous into eternal life", and so on. How could I argue away the plain meaning of the words concluding the great parable of the sheep and the goats?

I tried hard; G.G. did not defeat me in argument. But unfortunately the inner voice of conscience told me that he was right.

Forgiveness of sins, G.G.—a most human person—went on to explain, could be attained by those who truly repented. I need not, indeed I should not worry about my sins; all I had to do was to repent of them. This did not comfort me in the least. My reasoning went roughly like this.

First of all, I had by now become quite convinced that I was finished for good and all. There was no possible chance of my coming out of the Hospital alive. In fact though not actually dead, I was as good as dead. For some inscrutable reason, perhaps because I had committed "the unforgivable sin" or just because I was such an appalling sinner, the worst man who had ever existed, I had been chosen to go alive through the portals of Hell, in an ordinary English lunatic asylum. Therefore it was obviously too late for repentance. It was, I knew, quite unsound theology to imagine that people got another chance after they were dead. Obviously when they saw what they were in for they would repent; anybody would. But they would be cast into outer darkness and the Lord would not bother about them any more, however much they wept and gnashed their teeth. I knew what I was in for; I had been before the Bar (Bar——); I had been told there was no hope of a reprieve; and that was the end of it.

All this I kept to myself, of course; I did not argue with G.G. about it. Nor did I tell the doctors. They were not particularly sympathetic and did not invite confidences; moreover I was quite astute enough to realise that to talk on these lines would be regarded as further proof of insanity; I might even be certified. As long as I was voluntary, there was perhaps just the faintest chance that I might get out and succeed in making away with myself.

My wife, who visited me nobly at least twice a week for the whole eleven months of my confinement, never could understand the logic of this attitude. She was the only person to whom I dared confide my horrors, and I tried hard to show my train of reasoning. Roughly it was that I was a sort of opposite of Jesus Christ. Satan's job had been to catch a man, get him to sell his soul to him completely and utterly, like Faust, and then take him down alive into the pit. That was a sort of necessary counterweight to the resurrection of Jesus and the elect. I was the man. But if I could only kill myself, it might blow up the whole Universe, but at least I would get out of eternal torture and achieve the oblivion and nothingness for which my soul craved. I did in fact make three attempts at suicide, the most serious of which was when I tore myself from my attendant and threw myself in front of a car, with my poor wife, who was visiting me, looking on.

Although my attempts at suicide failed, they had one satisfactory effect; the doctors increased my drugs. As long as I was able to attain unconsciousness at night (with the aid of three or four doses of paraldehyde), and to maintain a fairly soporific state during the day (with anything up to four tablets of allonal), I could just keep the horrors at bay. My whole conscious effort was now directed towards the aim of putting off the moment when I would disappear finally into Hell. I visualised this process as happening quite naturally. Some day, at some moment, the iron control I kept on my terrors would break. I should start shrieking in agony. Naturally the attendants would then shut me up in a side-room, probably in one of the worse wards. After that the process of torturing a human soul in the living flesh would just go on. I should shriek, but so do many lunatics; nobody would do anything for me; they would naturally think my pains were imaginary. But they would be real pains; anyway I knew that the philosophical distinction between real and imaginary was very difficult to make. It did not matter much when I "died" in the body. I might spend days, months, or years shrieking in my side-room before they buried me. For me, it would all be the same process of eternal, progressively increasing torture.

Progressively increasing, that was the appalling part of the picture. It seemed to me as I brooded on the problem, that the ancient prophets, thinkers and poets, including of course Dante, must be wrong in regarding Hell, eternal punishment, as something static. Nothing in the Universe seemed to be static; why should Hell be so? Nor, in fact, could Heaven be static either. It was borne in upon me that the creative process was all one, really. The vast evolutionary process, from the whirling spiral nebulae to man, superman, God, was a progressive movement forwards, or upwards, if you prefer it. But there must always be balance, otherwise nothing would work. So the progressive movement forwards or upwards must be compensated by a regressive movement backwards or downwards.

The progressive revolutionary movement upwards had its counterpart in the world or worlds outside space and time. This was "Heaven". The regressive movement backwards (I was not quite clear what it actually was in the physical world, but I knew it must exist somewhere) had its counterpart in Hell. In Heaven, the souls of the just, of the "elect", progressed towards increasing enjoyment, knowledge, power, love, life. In Hell, the souls of the unjust, Satan's elect—probably an approximately equal number to those of the just, in order to maintain balance—regressed down an equally infinite scale first of mental, then of physical torture. It was a remarkably logical picture, given the premises; I am sure it would have delighted Calvin to see his views so scientifically worked out.

About the time I had reached this point in my compulsive

train of reasoning, possibly three months or so after my arrival in the Hospital, I was lying one afternoon—I can't remember when; it was after I had begun to get up after breakfast—in the company of an old patient. As if specially sent by the Powers of the Universe to confirm my train of thought, he began to recite, in a monotonous but rhythmic voice:—Opposites, opposites; down, up; backwards, forwards; clockwise, anti-clockwise; push, pull; hot, cold; black, white; earth, air; fire, water. I don't remember exactly how many opposites he mentioned, but that gives the general idea. Jung, incidentally, regards the 'opposites' as an important part of the Unconscious, and I have often heard mental patients refer to them in their delusionary or compulsive trains of thought.

Perhaps I might just remark here in parenthesis that gradually all the associations of my environment came to confirm the ideas which were being forced upon me. When the wireless happened to be on, it often seemed to be speaking to me; something would be said to confirm or increase my fears. This is of course a common delusion. The fact is that the whole mechanism of 'association', to which reference has been made in the previous chapter, automatically came to work in the same direction as my thoughts. Every word, almost every letter, of a newspaper I might chance to look at, would contain some dire message of evil.

To illustrate this, I will try to put myself back in the condition of mind I was in at that time, and then take the first suggestive association that comes to hand. In front of me is a pad of Basildon Bond writing-paper, blue. Looking at it with my eyes of eight years ago I see St Basil damning me (D) ON a blue bond. Blue stands for Heaven, which is BLasting me (i.e. yoU) Eternally. I hope this makes the associations clear. They are, of course, typical of certain types of mental disease.

In such a state of mind any normal behaviour becomes virtually impossible. Yet at about this time I began to lead a rather more normal life, getting up, as I said, after breakfast, playing croquet, billiards, badminton, and so on. This was partly due to my wife's persuasive efforts, partly to the efforts of the attendants, and most of all, I think, to the fact that even with the drugs I was taking I was no longer able to keep myself in a state of drowsiness. Bed, alone with my horrors, thus became intolerable, and occupation did keep my mind off them for the moment. Even though my incorrigible mind related everything, even billiards and croquet, to my terrible predicament, as long as I could get through the time somehow without losing control and thus starting my eternal punishment, that was something gained.

I used to concentrate on getting through the intervals between my wife's visits and seeing her again. As she left me, each time, I would tell her that she would not find me there when she came next time, and as the door shut behind her, something clanged in my soul and I felt sick to death. But I used to pull round and concentrate on being there for the next visit.

By this time, say four or five months after my arrival, I had evolved a definite technique to help me in this effort of getting through the days and nights. I had frankly admitted my position. God had turned His back on me and left me to Satan, but perhaps I could persuade Satan to put off the evil day a bit. That was all I asked for, and it seemed to me I stood a chance of getting some postponement if I could worship Satan really properly. So I evolved my own little rituals—they incidentally have little to do with genuine Satanism, which is obviously much more closely associated with my manic periods.

Every night I said the Lord's Prayer backwards, letter by letter, smoking three ritual cigarettes as I did so. By that time the drug I had taken used to begin to work, and I always got to sleep before I had finished the prayer. Letter by letter, beginning with NEMA (AMEN), and continuing REVE DNA REVE ROF (for ever and ever), and so on, the Lord's Prayer is very complicated indeed. It probably takes about twenty minutes, and I cannot recall that I ever finished. I am sure Mr C. S. Lewis's Screwtape enjoyed the performance; it must have gratified him immensely; anyway neither he nor his master seemed to bear me any ill-will for not finishing.

This superstition was a great help. My mother is very superstitious; she has a horror of magpies, thirteen at a table, and so on. I evolved little superstitions which helped to build up my self-confidence. One was that if, as I left any room, I fixed my eyes on something red (Satan's colour), he would manage to get me back to that particular room or place again. I was thus certain to be preserved from eternal punishment until I went back to that room. This was the most reassuring of my superstitions, and I did not abandon it, nor for that matter did I dare to pray the right way round, till long after I had got back home again. There were many others; some depending on pure suggestion, like an idea I had that as long as I had a box of *dates*, I could be sure of having a *date* with my wife. Many were connected with my games. For example in billards God was represented by the plain ball and the devil by spot. In no game in which I was concerned, therefore, could I allow plain to win. As long as spot won the devil would save me. If spot looked like losing I would make some excuse and leave the game.

Further details would only be wearisome. I come now to the central feature of my whole experience. Somehow I want to find adequate words to describe the dawn of what I may call the Horrific Vision.

I am not quite sure when it began to break in upon me, but it was certainly within the first month or so, when I was still in bed. Thereafter it progressed *pari passu* with my ideas; it never left me for an instant.

A crumpled pillow is quite an ordinary everyday object, is it not? One looks at it and thinks no more about it? So is a washing-rag, or a towel tumbled on the floor, or the creases on the side of a bed. Yet they can suggest shapes of the utmost horror to the mind obsessed by fear. Gradually my eyes began to distinguish such shapes, until eventually, whichever way I turned, I could see nothing, but devils waiting to torment me, devils which seemed infinitely more real than the material objects in which I saw them.

They had names, too. There was the god Baal, with a cruel mouth like a slit (a wrinkle in the side of a bed), waiting to devour me as a living sacrifice. There was Hecate, who used generally to appear in pillows, her shape was, I think, the most horrible of all. When I went out I saw devils by the hundred in trees and bushes, and especially in cut wood, generally in serpent form. Even now, I can still see them on occasion; the trick of illusion by which they appeared remains with me to some extent; and now that I am depressed again I cannot help wondering if they will reawaken the sense of utter terror that they did when they first appeared. I thought I had exorcised them, but now I am not so sure.

With these visions surrounding me it is not strange that the material world should seem less and less real. I felt myself to be gradually descending alive into the pit by a sort of metamorphosis of my surroundings. At times the whole universe seemed to be dissolving about me; moving cracks and fissures would appear in the walls and floors. This, incidentally, is a phenomenon which I have often noticed in the opposite state of acute mania, though it has then, of course, a totally different underlying feeling-tone. The climax of this sense of unreality was an extraordinary vision which is difficult to classify under the normal head of "illusion", though it was not a hallucination or apparition either. It seems to me to have interesting philosophical and psychological implications.

There was a series of sporting prints round the walls of the ward day-room. They were so placed that, if you sat in an arm-chair with your back to the large windows, and facing the prints, you could see, reflected in the picture-glass, the buildings of No. 9 ward, on the opposite side of the small lawn on to which the windows looked out.

I used generally to sit concentrating on a novel—that was another good way of keeping the horrors at bay—with my back to the windows; there seemed to be fewer devils in the ward than there were outside, somehow. Little by little, over a period of about a month or six weeks probably, the reflection of No. 9 ward was distorted. The chimneys left the vertical plane and moved round to the horizontal, eventually to forty or fifty degrees below the horizontal, while the reflection of the building itself became correspondingly curved, until the whole vertical structure formed a sort of inverted U. This puzzled me greatly; I don't think I was horrified at first. What could it mean? My vision was otherwise quite normal; I could play badminton, billiards, and so on. But whenever I sat in one of those chairs and looked at the prints, I could see this strange phenomenon.

Certainly I was bewitched. But that was no new discovery; it did not frighten me more than I was frightened in any case.

Then, suddenly, the answer came. Bishop Berkeley was right;

the whole universe of space and time, of my own senses, was really an illusion. Or it was so for me, at any rate. There I was, shut in my own private universe, as it were, with no contact with real people at all, only with phantasmagoria who could at any moment turn into devils. I and all around me were utterly unreal. There in the reflection lay proof positive. My soul was finally turned into nothingness—except unending pain.

1955 ⊷

Voices Calling, by Lisa Wiley

Superficially Lisa Wiley's *Voices Calling* seems an unremarkable work. It has no medical or psychiatric introduction. The book caused no particular controversy, nor was it particularly successful or even re-printed. The experience of madness described there is not half so dramatic as that in Schreber's account or many others. It is an obscure psychiatric autobiography, yet *Voices Calling* is an unusually truthful and unembellished account—a good antidote to the romanticization of madness. It is also one of the most detailed self-studies of schizo-phrenia covering an extended period of time (two decades). It also renders an unusually clear picture of a slow, insidious onset of schizophrenia. Finally, the schizophrenic experience detailed here fits unusually well traditional models of schizophrenia and one recent biochemical model.[1]

Lisa Wiley expected early to be an asylum inmate. When she was three her father became a mental patient. She was raised from that age to the age of fifteen by an emotionally cold, old-fashioned grand-mother who often compared Wiley to her mad father. At six she became, as she described it, "acutely aware of the terrifying forces in life," and instituted rituals to keep those forces under control. She did things in groups or multiples of four. She would rub or knock on doors or furniture four, eight, or twelve times. She would look behind herself or step on a corner of a rug four times.

She often visited her mother who, unfortunately, pressed upon her an excessively rigid moral code. The young woman developed great feelings of guilt. Her mother permitted no swearing or slang, and though Lisa tried to uphold her mother's demands, slang and obscen-ities intruded upon her mind. When she was approximately eleven, she began to have absurd, blasphemous thoughts: "inwardly I began calling God a devil and Jesus a prize fighter." She tried to keep such thoughts under control, but the harder she tried, the more she be-came aware of them.

---

[1]Interestingly enough, some of Wiley's overt behavior, the uncontrollable mutterings and blasphemies, must have resembled medieval ideas of a typical case of possession; superficially at least, it also may have resembled a disease known today as Tourette's Syndrome (see chapter 2).

In the seventh grade Lisa sensed her own isolation and her difference from her peers. As if to aggravate that isolation her mother made her dress in outmoded styles. She did unusually well in school but in the ninth grade began to have trouble with homework, having to reread sentences and parts of sentences because she was disturbed by compulsive, threatening, and blasphemous thoughts. One morning upon waking she called God "a damn fool." Thereafter such thoughts seemed to come upon her with increased intensity. She felt she hated God and the words of the Bible; at the same time, she maintained a mask of docility and conformity to her mother's harsh standards of piety. In high school her thoughts and fantasies began to take on sexual significance: "I ascribed to God all the organs of a man and handled them." Eventually, these feelings were transformed into external voices and visions that were almost possible to control. She heard voices instructing her to do certain things and avoid others, and saw threatening visions of God's face. Even music, previously a source of comfort, now became a part of her torment: "The words and hymns more and more became twisted and turned around and gradually I could not sing anything without wanting to concoct some swearing or obscene expression."

She went away to college, hoping to start a new life and overcome her problems. Instead, the stresses of college merely intensified them. At last, on a June day of her junior year, she had a crisis, what she describes as "the final crash." The voices seemed to take over, telling her to "turn against God." For five weeks she went through "just one big mass of hellish, sexual thoughts and inward mutterings without a break night or day." She felt her "will and self-control snap" and an "emotional poison took entire possession." She felt her brain crack and sputter and hiss; intense pain wracked her body; she had a feeling of an emotional death spreading through her. She felt she had committed a profound "spiritual suicide."

> The sensation of an active mind faded away, and I discovered I was dead and had no God-consciousness. Although I could still think and knew what I was doing, my thoughts were lifeless. These thoughts compared to real thoughts were as a whisper is to a loud voice. I noticed that I was losing my faculties one by one. When I tried to play the piano no longer could I look ahead mentally as before. Strange to say, my fingers just didn't want to move ahead nor could I anticipate actively what was coming. All feeling seemed to have gone out of my fingers. Materials all felt the same. The sensitivity of immediate distinction was not there. Each day I mentioned that I had lost one more faculty. I told Mother that my soul had gone, and she said one's soul didn't leave the body until physical death. Therefore, I declared I must

have a dead soul. It dawned upon me that I had committed a spiritual suicide, for I had no sense of personality or character.

At twenty-two Lisa Wiley entered a mental hospital. For several months, during the most acute phase of her madness, she was tormented by voices, visions, confusion; but her continual and most profound complaint was of an emotional or spiritual death: "I wasn't sick, I was dead." Despite the severity of her experience, and the prolonged encroachment of madness, Wiley did get better. In the hospital she underwent psychotherapy and a program of resocialization. Gradually, she reentered the outside world, took a job, lived with her psychiatrist's family for two years, and returned to school. She finally cut all ties with the hospital and struck out on her own, apparently cured.

Wiley herself suggests that certain events and insights taking place during psychotherapy had an importance in her recovery: she came to realize that a recurring, threatening vision of God's face was really a visual memory of her grandmother's face. She also suggests that guilt over masturbation was "the very core of my trouble," and that the kind reassurances of her psychiatrist were of great importance. At another point, Wiley describes her psychiatrist's theory about the self-healing course of her madness: "He said that it was impossible to help me until I had broken completely and the emotional area was deadened and they could get hold of my reason and intelligence." But the most striking thing about Wiley's therapeutic treatment is the consistent, long-term, stable, supportive, and mutually responsible relationship with her psychiatrist.

Wiley's description of her early family life recalls some theoretical descriptions of the schizophrenogenic family.[2] But perhaps most remarkable is the young woman's descriptions of her madness in ways greatly reminiscent of the early Bleuler and Kraepelin models of schizophrenia. Though Wiley describes hallucinations, strange behavior, unusual thoughts and perceptions, she most particularly emphasizes that horribly disturbing "emotional death"—which echoes both Kraepelin's description of the "dementia" in "dementia praecox" and Bleuler's description of the "disturbance of affectivity" in his concept of schizophrenia.

Other elements in Bleuler's model—"autism" and "ambivalence"—are quite vividly presented in *Voices Calling*. There is also a "disturbance of association" in the description of Wiley's dif-

---

[2]See, for instance, Laing, *Self and Others*.

ficulties with homework and piano playing: "When I tried to play the piano no longer could I look ahead mentally as before. Strange to say, my fingers just didn't want to move ahead nor could I anticipate actively what was coming." It may be that with her emotional death, the loss of emotional connection to her life in the present, Wiley also lost any sense of anticipation—the desire for and emotional connection to the future. This loss of goal-directed activity can account at least partly for the disturbance of association described by Bleuler: perhaps in the same way that Wiley lost her ability to play the piano because she could not plan ahead, other schizophrenics lose their ability to plan out logical, sequential sentences and thoughts.[3]

One recent biochemical theory of schizophrenia, developed by Larry Stein of Wyeth Laboratories in Philadelphia, particularly emphasizes the abnormal absence of emotional connection or pleasure and the loss of pleasure anticipation or goal-directed activity.[4] Stein believes that the loss of emotionality and the resulting loss of goal-direction can be related to an hereditary enzyme deficiency. Through a complex biochemical chain the ordinary person continually produces certain crucial chemicals in the pleasure center of the brain which enable the normal transmission of nerve impulses. In the schizophrenic, however, low levels of an essential enzyme cause inadequate production of crucial neurotransmitters and the subsequent production of a toxin. The lack of crucial nerve impulse transmitters combined with the production of a toxin cause a temporary or permanent demise of a part of the brain associated with pleasure and, consequently, an "emotional death" and loss of goal-directed activity. Stein also believes that one by-product of the abnormal chemical reaction is an hallucinogen, thus accounting for some of the perceptual changes associated with schizophrenia.

In the following excerpt from *Voices Calling*, Wiley describes the final crisis which brought about her emotional "death" and subsequent hospitalization.

MONDAY MORNING was a beautiful day—roses, peonies, sunshine and the chirping of birds—a lovely day for Commencement. Young men and women one year ahead of me in college

---

[3]See Appendix II.
[4]Stein, "Neurochemistry of Reward and Punishment," pp. 345–61.

were to go out into a new world—some on to further schooling and some were anticipating the joys of marriage. A day of days when all seemed exceedingly happy!

I drew in the aroma from the roses and peonies, just as if the fragrance would disappear and not be so lovely next year. Suddenly I heard a strange and uncanny voice say, "You'll never get the wonderful delight from roses and peonies again."

What was the meaning of this? What was the omen? It left me with a very depressed and empty feeling. Never before had I experienced such a wierd and strange sensation, and it haunted me as I trudged over to the college to practice with the choir before the service.

At Baccalaureate the previous day I had sung especially sincerely, "Create in me a clean heart, O God, and renew a right spirit within me." I had a desperate feeling of wanting to hang on and be helped, but didn't know why the need for help seemed so urgent.

After the Commencement exercises I registered for two summer school courses in English—two that I could not have hated worse—poetry and Shakespeare. Though I hated the very thought of these courses, I needed the credit as so much of my time during the year had been spent on music and I wanted to take still more music in the fall.

About the middle of the afternoon I lay down to rest a while, but just before touching the bed something seemed to rush through me saying, "Go ahead, it's O.K. Do it this summer," meaning it was an opportune time to turn against God. Another very tender voice seemed to answer, "Don't, you'll wish you hadn't." I obeyed the first voice and lay down on the bed, starting the worst siege of blasphemy inwardly anyone could imagine.

This time I turned against the whole Trinity with all the vehemence and hate I could bring forth and with especial emphasis on the third part. I was going to get this dreadful urge over once and for all. All my life though I had called Jesus and God strange things, I had been able to refrain from attacking the Holy Ghost. I had read how bad it would be to do that, and knowing my weakness, had felt I would certainly yield to the urge someday. My greatest fear from the age of fourteen years was that someday I might attack the Holy Ghost sexually. Though I had tried to make myself like songs about the Holy Ghost, I felt the Holy Ghost hated me and would never save me. I couldn't stand even to see the name without trembling from head to foot. If only that terrifying power didn't have to be. Not being able to develop proper appreciation for God's greatest gift to mankind and because I was afraid I might some-day attack this power, every year I planned activities that would keep my mind off the Holy Ghost. I covered up the name and gritted my teeth every time I saw it to keep from doing any-thing. But seven years of such strain had sapped my will and energy to the point I finally felt I'd have to let it come. I was bound and determined to get everything out of my system and have it over with.

There was no rhyme or reason to any of my willful concoc-tions, nor was there any established order or series as before. It was just one big mass of hellish, sexual thoughts and inward mutterings without a break night or day for five solid weeks. No longer was I making any effort to stop. Previously my thoughts were just thoughts without consciously made mental pictures. The mental pictures that had been present had always forced their way through the unconscious and I had tried to hold them back. Now I consciously made up all the screwy pictures imag-inable. Rain always made me think of urination. I made a man out of God and spit on Him, kicked Him and beat Him. It was a joy to see Him fall back helpless as I beat Him, and I laughed and hissed inwardly. I attached the name of the Spirit to every-thing imaginable, vile and otherwise, eggs, apples, even to square roots in Geometry problems. Thoughts and pictures seemed to be forming at the rate of a million a minute, mostly of excretory functions and of the nose, too. I knew I was guilty but was unable to care. I knew I was actually to blame and was doing all this very willfully. With these thoughts was a voice that seemed to say, "It's your own fault this time."

The first week of the siege was something similar to that of seven years earlier. I was not greatly concerned. The only differ-ence at first was that I actually went at it as if I were making of it sort of a project like one country starting to invade another. But by the end of the week things were beginning to happen. I had expected a depressed feeling but not the particular kind that was taking place. It seemed serious enough that I felt I had better say something to my sister about it. I had her go walking with me on Sunday afternoon and told her how I was going through what I had seven years earlier. I didn't tell her exactly what it was, but asked her to pray for me and asked her whether or not she felt I should tell Mother.

This was all very new and strange to Beth, so I didn't say much. I had just more or less wanted consent to be able to go ahead with my "project" anyhow. Two days later I felt I'd better tell Mother—sort of feel her out so she wouldn't be too shocked. I approached her in quite a childish fashion, so it wouldn't upset her, and I received a rather silent consent to continue. Mother was very nice and sweet to me for a while. I didn't tell her enough to let her know what was going on, but just enough to get some sympathy, so I cannot exactly blame her for all that followed.

I told Beth and Mother that I always felt this way when I took English courses. To myself I felt that because I was having to take the hated Shakespeare, my behavior was somewhat justified. How could I be expected to control myself at such times? When summer school would be over perhaps I could get control over myself again. Little did I know that the psychic bell was tolling for me.

The greatest difference between this siege and that of former years was that now I was suffering intense physical pain. At the age of fourteen the worry and mental agony were terrible and I felt weak and depressed, but there was no headache or pain other than that which came from crying. But during the summer of 1937 I suffered the worst physical pain, in addition to mental torment, that anyone could possibly endure. The pain at first was not severe, but by the end of the second week so great was it that I had to go to a doctor, and he gave me some medicine to calm my nerves and make me sleep. Because of the bombardment of thoughts all night, too, I could sleep only a few hours.

The visit to the local physician did no good because I wasn't intending to cooperate with anyone. The reason I went to him was that I didn't like the bad headaches. However, he tried to help me and asked about my thoughts. When I told him I was calling God names, he wondered what my attitudes toward God were and what I actually thought about heaven. He tried to straighten out my thinking, but after a few interviews he could see that it was impossible to reason with me. After all, I was as versed in theology as I cared to be, and wasn't seeking further information. What surprised me was that he didn't interpret the Bible literally, nor did Mother, to tell you the truth. Although I was pitting my very soul against God, still I stuck up for the truth of the whole Bible from cover to cover.

I was too acutely ill to cooperate, though I did not think of my behavior as illness. Just as an appendix bursts and sends poison through the whole system, so did my will and self-control snap and the emotional poison took entire possession of me. Although I knew exactly what I was doing and saying and can remember to this very day, still my ordinary personality had temporarily been side-tracked and I had no command of the situation. I was a person with a great deal of energy and when I made up my mind to do anything, I did it regardless of the consequences. As long as I could be assured that I'd come out O.K. I felt it was all right to continue with my evil thoughts and mutterings.

I kept asking Mother to pray for me and told her to ask God if it was all right to do it and asked her if He would think of me as a child or as just crazy, and she said He would. Then I told her that she was just making that up, for God didn't really say anything to her. Also I asked her if she thought I'd better describe for her the type of things I was thinking so that she would know, and she said that she didn't think I needed to for she had always had a pure undefiled mind and didn't want it to be spoiled by what I would say.

The front that I was putting up concealed the real truth even from the doctor. All that I said was true but I didn't say enough. I wasn't willing to say what I was thinking about God, but did say that I was thinking bad things. He asked about some of my sex habits, but I quickly passed that by so he didn't go into that deeper. He told Mother that possibly I would have to go to a hospital, but she would not consent to that as my father already had been taken from her, and thus he did not push the matter.

Every day brought more physical suffering and mental torment. My brain cracked and sputtered and hissed as never before, and it seemed that my mind was caving in just as a brick building would crumble and fall. Severe pain shot through my entire body. One evening while mowing the lawn, it seemed that my brain cracked right through the middle and divided into two sections. I could hardly stand it. I thought I was slowly dying. In fact one night about two or three o'clock in the morning I went into Mother's room and told her I was dying, for there was a strange jumping around my heart. Even before I went to a doctor, the physical change that I noticed decidedly was that intense darkness was setting in at the back of my head. This darkness enclosed my entire mind very slowly but completely in a period of about two and one-half weeks. The light of life had gone. When this darkness began to creep in, a feeling of deadness came over me, for I found I was losing emotion little by little. The first time I saw the doctor I told him I felt sort of dead in the upper part of my body, "dead" in a sense that I had little emotional sensation, but of course he thought I just imagined that. However, the feeling of pulsing, vibrant life had gone.

Every time I would inwardly say something bad about the Spirit, it seemed that a fierce dart would shoot through me and life gurgled out of me like water gurgles out of the narrow neck of a bottle when you hold it upside down. Sometimes it oozed out. Each of these "ka thuds" left me empty, and I was emotionally dying inch by inch until by the end of five weeks I had no feeling at all.

While my brain was cracking and sputtering I noticed that no longer did I have a strong consciousness and subconsciousness. The partition had broken down and it was all one. The sensation of an active mind faded away, and I discovered I was dead and had no God-consciousness. Although I could still think and knew what I was doing, my thoughts were lifeless. These thoughts compared to real thoughts were as a whisper is to a loud voice. I noticed that I was losing my faculties one by one. When I tried to play the piano no longer could I look ahead mentally as before. Strange to say, my fingers just didn't want to move ahead nor could I anticipate actively what was coming. All feeling seemed to have gone out of my fingers. Materials all felt the same. The sensitivity of immediate distinction was not there. Each day I mentioned that I had lost one more faculty. I told Mother that my soul had gone, and she said one's soul didn't leave the body until physical death. Therefore, I declared I must have a dead soul. It dawned upon me that I had committed a spiritual suicide, for I had absolutely no sense of personality or character.

While all this was going on I continued in school. At the end of two weeks I wanted to quit, but Mother thought I should continue for it would give me something to occupy my mind. When I told her I had always called Jesus names when I read, she thought that was very silly. My aunt helped me with the lessons this time so I wouldn't have to do the actual reading, but even this did not help for the battle was on and I had lost all ability to control my thoughts at any time.

In the English classes I paid very little attention and my mean thoughts registered all over my face. I looked like the most dejected of earthly creatures. I'll never understand how the professor put up with me and why he didn't suggest that I leave. But not a word was said. He just let me sit there and make faces when some terrible sex thought passed through my thinking. I began telling people in the classes about how awful I was and what freaky things were taking place. I told them I was doing something that couldn't be forgiven, that I was always afraid I would do it and now I really was.

Lady Macbeth's hands were lily white compared to mine. She had murdered only a man. I was beating up and attacking sexually the whole Trinity. Not even if 10,000,000 people got down on their knees and begged God to forgive and restore life for me would He do it—not even if every person in the United States— not even all the people in the whole world! God would never again have anything more to do with me. I had "murdered sleep" forever.

No one sensed what was going on and no one did anything about it. I was slipping right through humanity before their very eyes. And God was protecting everyone from the knowledge of what was happening to me.

Trees and everything went around in circles while my mind was sputtering and trying to adjust to the darkness that was closing in. No longer did I have the feeling of attachment to Nature as before, and my sense of perspective seemed to have departed. I could see everything and saw it as it was, but it was all a dead, lifeless mass. I was dead mentally, having no conscience of anything and having no emotion. I could still think and apparently reason but it was all silent thoughts.

Even in respect to time I was dead. There was no future and no past. Everything was just an endless black nothingness. Except for the physical pain that had not gone away yet, I was not suffering actually. The only quiet agony came when I thought back to the time when I was alive. I could still remember that I once did have feelings and that it once was light, but the farther away I went the harder it was to remember, until finally I lost all sensation that there ever had been light and life. After I lost all feeling (emotional drive) I quit calling God names, for there was no urge. It was over!!! Just a few days before I finished, it seemed something said "Eternal darkness" and then for days I was tantalized by the thought that I didn't have to do all that. I could have stopped if I had wanted to.

The acute siege during which time the actual battle took place and also the physical changes lasted somewhat over five weeks. This period was followed by a continuation of the intense physical pain. The last of the pain didn't go away until the middle of August.

After the summer session at college, I went to a church camp at a lake for a week in July. I didn't see any point in going for I knew it was useless, but I wanted to please Mother, so I went. She felt I'd get a new vision. Although I had told her all that was taking place, she figured that it was my imagination, as did the doctor, and although worried she wasn't greatly concerned. She was blind to all that was happening and had happened because her firm faith in God made her believe that her children would be protected from any very serious trouble, inasmuch as she had always been a faithful servant to the Lord.

What a week was ahead! The classes and lectures meant nothing, but I did take notes religiously so that my folks at least would benefit from my going. The young folks there treated me kindly, but it was very evident to them that I was not well. I had told Mother I would try to control myself and not talk, but I couldn't. I talked to every person I could about what had taken place. I was batting around in a sea of inner darkness without an ounce of emotional motivations, and the pain in my head was so great I thought I might be dead physically any day. I could not sleep well at night on account of the pain and really felt like telling my minister to tell Mother that I would be dead soon. The pain in my head was not like an ordinary headache, for normally I was not subject to headaches, and the actual sensation of mental torture was over for I had no feeling. This excruciating pain was what remained after the crackling and sputtering ceased—after all these other physical changes had taken place.

Some of the counselors in the group took an interest in me and were greatly concerned. Mrs. Clark, unlike some of the others, was not telling me to keep still, but seemed keenly interested and wanted to know more and really help me. The first day she met me she didn't think things were serious, but the more I told her the more she realized that it was not theology alone that was bothering me. My whole outlook was warped in more ways than one.

The pain was so great and nothing was being accomplished by being at camp as far as acquiring this spiritual revelation that Mother thought I was going to get was concerned, so I began to contemplate physical suicide. I didn't wish to return to Mother in the same condition as I left. But I was afraid to commit suicide, for I didn't want to see God any sooner than absolutely necessary. So I didn't know what to do. When I told Mrs. Clark I didn't want to go home, she told me maybe I could find work somewhere away from home. I hadn't thought of that. Well, time passed and we didn't say more about that. However, she did say that she knew someone who could help me and she would talk to this person when she got back home.

Just before leaving the camp I told Mrs. Clark not to worry about me or try to find help for it wouldn't do much good. But her parting words to me were that she'd find a way out. A few weeks later she came to my home and asked me to go home with her for a few days.

Mrs. Clark had made an appointment for me with a psychiatrist. During the time that had elapsed after coming home from camp I had begun asking God to perform a miracle and give my feelings back to me and the light. I had enough sense to know such a thing couldn't happen so kidded myself into thinking God could do it while I was asleep. I spent most of the day sleeping and waiting for a miracle to take place. I thought maybe this psychiatrist had a miraculous something or other that could help. Mrs. Clark said she thought he could. However, she didn't know what I was after.

The interview with the psychiatrist was very disappointing, for I knew more than he did—so I thought. It was very brief. I told him what I had done and about the voices that I thought I heard at the first of the summer and that there was no hope for me. I told him I had been dead for a good many weeks. He didn't take me very seriously for he was used to people telling him all kinds of things like that. Mrs. Clark, too, was a bit disappointed, for she thought the doctor would say something that would give me a ray of hope—but I knew no such thing could be. After all, a psychiatrist was just a human being and wasn't endowed with divine power to perform miracles. What was gone was gone and could not be brought back.

When I went home I didn't tell Mother about the interview, for she wouldn't have permitted me to go to such a place. However, a few days later a letter came from this hospital saying that the doctors felt I needed a period of hospitalization to get over my nervous conditions, and Mother would have to go through some red tape to get me in. Mother was very cross at me. She said, "See what you've done." It disgraced her terribly. I told her that it was too late now; she should have thought about that earlier. She should have made me stop being such a devil earlier in the summer.

1964 ⟨⊟⟩

I Never Promised You a Rose Garden, by Joanne Greenberg

Joanne Greenberg's immensely popular novel, *I Never Promised You A Rose Garden*, was first published in 1964 under the pseudonym, Hannah Green. It is the story of an adolescent girl, Deborah Blau, who is hospitalized for something called "schizophrenia." She is finally cured through the love and therapy of her physician, Dr. Fried. Although much of the novel's popularity has arisen from the presumption that *Rose Garden* is a first-hand account of madness based upon autobiographical experience, I believed the opposite, that *Rose Garden* was simply a well-wrought piece of fiction, based upon historical research, written by a professional novelist.

In fact the basic plot of *Rose Garden* appears in the writings of the well-known psychoanalyst, Dr. Frieda Fromm-Reichmann. In her essay, "Psychotherapy of Schizophrenia," Fromm-Reichmann tells the story of a young schizophrenic patient of hers, who had been "living for eleven years in an imaginary kingdom which she populated by people of her own making and by the spiritual representations of others whom she actually knew. They all shared a language, literature, and religion of her own creation." In a parallel fashion the main symptom of Deborah's schizophrenia in *Rose Garden* is her withdrawal into a fantasy world, the Kingdom of Yr, which is peopled with beautiful, powerful, sometimes threatening gods, who speak to her in a special language called Yri. In the essay Fromm-Reichmann says that her patient suffered from a compulsion to burn her skin with matches and lighted cigarettes. In the novel the same happens with Deborah Blau. Fromm-Reichmann warned her patient against "expecting life to become a garden of roses after her recovery." Coincidentally, Deborah's therapist, Dr. Fried, similarly insists: "I never promised you a rose garden."[1]

Further, Deborah Blau's schizophrenia closely resembles Fromm-Reichmann's theoretical concepts. Fromm-Reichmann believes that schizophrenia may be caused by unsatisfying or traumatic relationships with parents experienced as an infant. Normal infants go

---

[1] See Bullard, *Psychoanalysis and Psychotherapy*, pp. 204–07.

through alterations of euphoria and low-level anxiety according to variations in the relationships with the parent-figures around them. Normally the parents have a love relationship with the infant that gives him messages of an acceptance of his essential "self," his individual being. In the pre-schizophrenic infant, however, there is a warp in the relationship; the parents do not love or accept the infant in some essential way, and the infant experiences that lack with massive anxiety. This failure in the primary parent-infant relationship produces a weak, flawed sense of self in the growing child. The child becomes abnormally sensitive, unresilient, incapable of handling the ordinary vicissitudes and rebuffs of everyday relationships with people. The original warp of the primary infant/parent relationship repeats itself in later relationships—and to such a painful, anxiety-producing degree that at last the person retreats into a schizophrenic break. The break can be marked by such experiences as hallucinations and delusions, but it functions primarily as a withdrawal from the too painful real world.[2]

Deborah's schizophrenia fits that theoretical pattern very well. It is made clear that her relationship with her parents was in some way flawed. "How did we share in the thing? What awful things did we do?" her mother asks. But the cause of the original warp is too deeply buried and never fully brought to light. However, as Deborah grows, she remains abnormally sensitive to the problems of growing up—jealousy of a sister, lack of friends, lies by adults, an operation. Three different summers her parents send her to a camp which turns out to be anti-Semitic. Deborah is Jewish. She begins to enter a fantasy world, the seductive Kingdom of Yr: "Its gods were laughing, golden personages whom she could wander away to meet, like guardian spirits." This withdrawal into fantasy is so necessary for Deborah that she finds she cannot do without it. What originally began as something akin to a normal childhood fantasy becomes filled with such emotional energy that it becomes more real than the real world: it takes over and Deborah becomes "schizophrenic."

Eugen Bleuler felt that there were four central symptoms of schizophrenia: disturbance in association, disturbance in affectivity, autism, and ambivalence. But Fromm-Reichmann believes that autistic

---

[2]See Bullard, ibid., and Fromm-Reichmann, *Principles of Intensive Psychotherapy.* Fromm-Reichmann can be considered an "interpersonalist," following and elaborating upon the teachings of Horney and Sullivan.

withdrawal into a fantasy world is really the core symptom and that the other symptoms can be explained in terms of that withdrawal. The disturbance in association, for instance, may be the result of regression to an earlier magical level of thought which does not test reality and therefore primarily serves to reinforce the withdrawal into fantasy. The verbal productions of that disturbance in association, "schizophrenic speech," can function as verbal evasive action, designed to throw about a protective screen of confused, thwarted communication between the schizophrenic and the outside world.

This is all certainly true of the picture of Deborah's schizophrenia. Her central symptom is that self-protective withdrawal into the autistic world of Yr. Her attacks of "schizophrenic thought" are seen as sudden dissolvings of previously learned reality-testing concepts, to enable withdrawal into magical thought and fantasy: "All direction became a lie. The laws of physics and solid matter were repealed and the experience of a lifetime of tactile sensation, motion, form, gravity, and light were invalidated." Her schizophrenic speech—the use of the Yri language—is also seen as a protective withdrawal: "English is for the world—for getting disappointed by and getting hated in."

In Fromm-Reichmann's theory the function of the therapist is simply to reverse the process of the schizophrenia, to break through that protective withdrawal and to provide the schizophrenic with what he or she most longs for but is most afraid of: a relationship with another human being. Freud had assumed that psychoanalysis could not reach mad people because they were supposedly regressed to a narcissistic state and were incapable of forming relationships with other people, including the psychoanalyst. But Fromm-Reichmann insists that schizophrenics are capable of, and desperately need relationships with others and that it is a primary goal of the therapist to form—slowly, with sensitivity, consistency, honesty, and directness—a relationship with the patient, to be "a bridge over which he might possibly be led from the utter loneliness of his own world to reality and human warmth."[3] And with Deborah and Dr. Fried, exactly that form of therapy is pursued. Insight is sought—and finally achieved—but the real therapeutic battle of the book is an emotional one which ends with Dr. Fried's success at forming a secure relationship with Deborah.

Joanne Greenberg has written three novels other than *Rose Garden*

---

[3]Ibid., p. 119.

which may have in common some similar approach. One is a historical novel about love and anti-Semitic persecution in medieval England; another is a novel about two deaf people; and the third is about a social worker and his clients. What all three appear to have in common is the historical approach to creating fiction. At least in the novel of medieval England, Greenberg might have begun with a small core of historical data which she embellished and dramatized. It seems likely that the other two novels began in the same way. One certainly looks as if it had its origin in the case histories of a social worker.

Knowing something of Greenberg's habits as a novelist and knowing that a case history by Fromm-Reichmann almost exactly parallels *Rose Garden*, I originally assumed that *I Never Promised You a Rose Garden* was simply a skillfully written historical novel based upon research into the writings of Fromm-Reichmann. So many people have assumed for so long that *Rose Garden* is an authentically autobiographical account, however, that I felt compelled to pursue my suspicions further. I wrote a letter to Joanne Greenberg, in care of the publisher, asking about the origins of the book; I received a response from the author's literary agent telling me politely that it was none of my business. I wrote a similar letter directly to the publisher; they suggested I write the author. I wrote letters to two physicians who had been associated with Fromm-Reichmann while she treated her "rose garden" patient, asking if Greenberg had been that patient; both declined to answer my question. I interviewed another physician who knew Fromm-Reichmann well; he did not know the patient's identity. I composed a second letter to Greenberg, carefully worded, asking once again if the book was autobiographical. Shortly thereafter I received an unsigned note, informing me in cryptic and rather circuitous terms that the book was indeed based upon autobiographical material. This response so upset my expectations that I wrote Greenberg again asking very directly if *she* had been Fromm-Reichmann's rose garden patient, or if the book was autobiographical in a more general sense. I received a note from her with a phone number, asking me to call. I did and almost immediately it became clear that she had indeed been Fromm-Reichmann's "rose garden" patient.

Nonetheless, we should keep in mind that well over a decade passed between the original experience and the telling of it. We might notice, also, how different Deborah's schizophrenia is from many other subjective accounts of madness which might be called "schizophrenia." Her hallucinatory experience of the Kingdom of Yr is remarkably coherent and stable, radically different from the wild hallucinations of Mark Vonnegut (1975) or the ever-changing possession of E. Thelmar (1909).

I have selected the first chapter and part of the second to reproduce here because all the dramatic elements of the book are immediately introduced and juxtaposed in these first pages: the failed parents, the great and humane physician, the flawed child, and the enticing world she has made for herself. The movement of the book consists in the struggle and resolution of these four elements. In these first few pages we can get a good sense of Greenberg's portrayal of Deborah's inner experience of madness. It involves a profound fragmentation of the material world and an entry into an amazingly coherent fantasy world.

THEY RODE THROUGH the lush farm country in the middle of autumn, through quaint old towns whose streets showed the brilliant colors of turning trees. They said little. Of the three, the father was most visibly strained. Now and then he would place bits of talk into the long silences, random and inopportune things with which he himself seemed to have no patience. Once he demanded of the girl whose face he had caught in the rear-view mirror: "You know, don't you, that I was a fool when I married—a damn young fool who didn't know about bringing up children—about being a father?" His defense was half attack, but the girl responded to neither. The mother suggested that they stop for coffee. This was really like a pleasure trip, she said, in the fall of the year with their lovely young daughter and such beautiful country to see.

They found a roadside diner and turned in. The girl got out quickly and walked toward the rest rooms behind the building. As she walked the heads of the two parents turned quickly to look after her. Then the father said, "It's all right."

"Should we wait here or go in?" the mother asked aloud, but to herself. She was the more analytical of the two, planning effects in advance—how to act and what to say—and her husband let himself be guided by her because it was easy and she was usually right. Now, feeling confused and lonely, he let her talk on—planning and figuring—because it was her way of taking comfort. It was easier for him to be silent.

"If we stay in the car," she was saying, "we can be with her if she needs us. Maybe if she comes out and doesn't see us . . . But then it should look as if we trust her. She must feel that we trust her. . . ."

They decided to go into the diner, being very careful and obviously usual about their movements. When they had seated themselves in a booth by the windows, they could see her coming back around the corner of the building and moving toward them; they tried to look at her as if she were a stranger, someone else's daughter to whom they had only now been introduced, a Deborah not their own. They studied the graceless adolescent body and found it good, the face intelligent and alive, but the expression somehow too young for sixteen.

They were used to a certain bitter precocity in their child, but they could not see it now in the familiar face that they were trying to convince themselves they could estrange. The father kept thinking: How could strangers be right? She's ours . . . all her life. They don't know her. It's a mistake—a mistake!

The mother was watching herself watching her daughter. "On my surface . . . there must be no sign showing, no seam— a perfect surface." And she smiled.

In the evening they stopped at a small city and ate at its best restaurant, in a spirit of rebellion and adventure because they were not dressed for it. After dinner, they went to a movie. Deborah seemed delighted with the evening. They joked through dinner and the movie, and afterward, heading out farther into the country darkness, they talked about other trips, congratulating one another on their recollection of the little funny details of past vacations. When they stopped at a motel to sleep, Deborah was given a room to herself, another special privilege for which no one knew, not even the parents who loved her, how great was the need.

When they were sitting together in their room, Jacob and Esther Blau looked at each other from behind their faces, and wondered why the poses did not fall away, now that they were alone, so that they might breathe out, relax, and find some peace with each other. In the next room, a thin wall away, they could hear their daughter undressing for bed. They did not admit to each other, even with their eyes, that all night they would be guarding against a sound other than her breathing in sleep—a sound that might mean . . . danger. Only once, before they lay down for their dark watch, did Jacob break from behind his face and whisper hard in his wife's ear, "Why are we sending her away?"

"The doctors say she has to go," Esther whispered back, lying rigid and looking toward the silent wall.

"The doctors." Jacob had never wanted to put them all through the experience, even from the beginning.

"It's a good place," she said, a little louder because she wanted to make it so.

"They call it a mental hospital, but it's a place, Es, a place where they put people away. How can it be a good place for a girl—almost a child!"

"Oh, God, Jacob," she said, "how much did it take out of us to make the decision? If we can't trust the doctors, who can we ask or trust? Dr. Lister says that it's the only help she can get now. We have to try it!" Stubbornly she turned her head again, toward the wall.

He was silent, conceding to her once more; she was so much quicker with words than he. They said good night; each pretended to sleep, and lay, breathing deeply to delude the other, eyes aching through the darkness, watching.

On the other side of the wall Deborah stretched to sleep. The Kingdom of Yr had a kind of neutral place which was called the Fourth Level. It was achieved only by accident and could not be reached by formula or an act of will. At the Fourth Level there was no emotion to endure, no past or future to grind against. There was no memory or possession of any self, nothing except dead facts which came unbidden when she needed them and which had no feeling attached to them.

Now, in bed, achieving the Fourth Level, a future was of no concern to her. The people in the next room were supposedly her parents. Very well. But that was part of a shadowy world that was dissolving and now she was being flung unencumbered into a new one in which she had not the slightest concern. In moving from the old world, she was moving also from the intricacies of Yr's Kingdom, from the Collect of Others, the Censor, and the Yri gods. She rolled over and slept a deep, dreamless, and restful sleep.

In the morning, the family started on its trip again. It occurred to Deborah, as the car pulled away from the motel and out into the sunny day, that the trip might last forever and that the calm and marvelous freedom she felt might be a new gift from the usually too demanding gods and offices of Yr.

After a few hours of riding through more brown and golden country and sun-dappled town streets, the mother said, "Where is the turn-off, Jacob?"

In Yr a voice shrieked out of the deep Pit: *Innocent! Innocent!*

From freedom, Deborah Blau smashed headlong into the collision of the two worlds. As always before it was a weirdly silent shattering. In the world where she was most alive, the sun split in the sky, the earth erupted, her body was torn to pieces, her teeth and bones crazed and broken to fragments. In the other place, where the ghosts and shadows lived, a car turned into a side drive and down a road to where an old red-brick building stood. It was Victorian, a little run-down, and surrounded by trees. Very good façade for a madhouse. When the car stopped in front of it, she was still stunned with the collision, and it was hard to get out of the car and walk properly up the steps and into the building where the doctors would be. There were bars on all the windows. Deborah smiled slightly. It was fitting. Good.

When Jacob Blau saw the bars, he paled. In the fact of this, it was no longer possible to say to himself "rest home" or "convalescent care." The truth was as bare and cold for him as the iron. Esther tried to reach him with her mind: We should have expected them. Why should we be so surprised?

They waited, Esther Blau trying still to be gay now and then. Except for the barred windows the room was like an ordinary waiting room and she joked about the age of the magazines there. From a distance down the hall they heard the grate of a large key in a lock and again Jacob stiffened, moaning softly, "Not for her—our little Debby. . . ." He did not see the sudden, ruthless look in his daughter's face.

The doctor walked down the hall, and steeled himself a little before entering the room. He was a squared-off, blunt-bodied man and now he dived into the room where their anguish seemed to hang palpably. It was an old building, a frightening place to come to, he knew. He would try to get the girl away soon and the parents comforted enough to leave her, feeling that they had done the right thing.

Sometimes in this room, at the last minute, the parents, husbands, wives, turned with loathing from the truth of the awful, frightening sickness. Sometimes they took their strange-eyed ones away again. It was fear, or bad judgment well meant enough, or—his eyes appraised the two parents again—that straying grain of jealousy and anger that would not let the long line of misery be severed a generation beyond their own. He tried to be compassionate but not foolish, and soon he was able to send for a nurse to take the girl to the wards. She looked like a shock victim. As she left, he felt the wrench of her going in the two parents.

He promised them that they could say good-by to her before they left, and surrendered them to the secretary with her pad of information to be gotten. When he saw them again, leaving after their good-by, they, too, looked like people in shock, and he thought briefly: wound-shock—the cutting-away of a daughter.

Jacob Blau was not a man who studied himself, or who looked back over his life to weigh and measure its shape. At times, he suspected his wife of being voracious, picking over her passions again and again with endless words and words. But part of this feeling was envy. He, too, loved his daughters, though he had never told them so; he, too, had wished confidences, but was never able to open his own heart; and, because of this, they had also been kept from venturing their secrets. His oldest daughter had just parted from him, almost eagerly, in that grim place of locks and bars, turning away from his kiss, stepping back. She had not seemed to want comfort from him, almost shrinking from touch. He was a man of tempers and now he needed a rage that was cleansing, simple, and direct. But the anger here was so laced with pity, fear, and love that he did not know how he could free himself of it. It lay writhing and stinking inside him, and he began to feel the old, slow waking ache of his ulcer.

They took Deborah to a small, plain room, guarding her there until the showers were empty. She was watched there also, by a woman who sat placidly in the steam and looked her up and down as she dried herself. Deborah did what she was told dutifully, but she kept her left arm slightly turned inward, so as to hide from sight the two small, healing puncture wounds on the wrist. Serving the new routine, she went back to the room and answered some questions about herself put to her by a sardonic doctor who seemed to be displeased. It was obvious that he did not hear the roaring behind her.

Into the vacuum of the Midworld where she stood between Yr and Now, the Collect was beginning to come to life. Soon they would be shouting curses and taunts at her, deafening her for both worlds. She was fighting against their coming the way a child, expecting punishment, anticipates it by striking out wildly. She began to tell the doctor the truth about some of the questions he was asking. Let them call her lazy and a liar now. The roar mounted a little and she could hear some of the words in it. The room offered no distraction. To escape engulfment there was only the Here, with its ice-cold doctor and his notebook, or Yr with its golden meadows and gods. But Yr also held its regions of horror and lostness, and she no longer knew to which kingdom in Yr there was passage. Doctors were supposed to help in this.

She looked at the one who sat fading amid the clamor and said, "I told you the truth about these things you asked. Now are you going to help me?"

"That depends on you," he said acidly, shut his notebook, and left. *A specialist,* laughed Anterrabae, the Falling God.

Let me go with you, she begged him, down and down beside him because he was eternally falling.

So it shall be, he said. His hair, which was fire, curled a little in the wind of the fall.

That day and the next she spent on Yr's plains, simple long sweeps of land where the eye was soothed by the depth of space.

For this great mercy, Deborah was deeply grateful to the Powers. There had been too much blindness, cold, and pain in Yr these past hard months. Now, as by the laws of the world, her image walked around and answered and asked and acted; she, no longer Deborah, but a person bearing the appropriate name for a dweller on Yr's plains, sang and danced and recited the ritual songs to a caressing wind that blew on the long grasses.

For Jacob and Esther Blau the way home was no shorter than the way to the hospital had been. Although Deborah was not with them, their freedom to say what they really wanted to say was even more circumscribed than before.

Esther felt that she knew Deborah better than her husband did. To her, it had not been the childish attempt at suicide that had begun this round of doctors and decisions. She sat in the car beside her husband wanting to tell him that she was grateful for the silly and theatrical wrist-cutting. At last a dragging suspicion of something subtly and terribly wrong had had outlet in a fact. The half-cup of blood on the bathroom floor had given all their nebulous feelings and vague fears weight, and she had gone to the doctor the next day. Now she wanted to show Jacob the many things he did not know, but she knew she could not do it without hurting him. She looked over at him driving with his eyes hard on the road and his face set. "We'll be able to visit her in a month or two," she said.

Then they began to construct the story that they would tell their acquaintances and those relatives who were not close or whose prejudices did not allow for mental hospitals in the family. For them, the hospital was to be a school, and for Suzy, who had heard the word "sick" too many times in the past month and had been puzzled too often and deeply before that, there was to be something about anemia or weakness and a special convalescent school. Papa and Mama would be told that everything was fine . . . a sort of rest home. They already knew about the psychiatrist and his recommendation, but the look of the place would have to change in the telling, and the high, hard scream that they had heard from one of the barred windows as they left, and that had made them shiver and grit their teeth, would have to be expunged. The scream had made Esther wonder if they had not really been wrong after all; the scream would have to be kept locked in her heart as Deborah in That Place.

Doctor Fried got up from her chair and went to the window. It faced away from the hospital buildings and over a small garden beyond which lay the grounds where the patients walked. She looked at the report in her hand. Against the weight of three typewritten pages were balanced the lectures she would not be able to give, the writing she would have to neglect, and the counseling of doctors that she would have to refuse if she took this case. She liked working with patients. Their very illness made them examine sanity as few "sane" people could. Kept from loving, sharing, and simple communication, they often hungered for it with a purity of passion that she saw as beautiful.

1965 ✑

Beyond All Reason, by Morag Coate

Beyond All Reason provides another example of the psychiatric auto-biography used as documentation to support a particular theory of madness. The introduction was written by R. D. Laing, who stresses the need to understand the mad experience from the inside. He then proceeds to give an "existential" interpretation of Coate's madness.

Basically Laing rejects the notion that there is such a thing as "mental illness," feeling that the concept of an "illness" implies an alien disease process which attacks the body or mind from without and which must be treated by a counterattack with the techniques of modern medical science. One may see the person's behavior as symptoms of a disease, but Laing would prefer to see it as "expressive of his existence."[1] According to Laing, what we call "normal" is simply one form of alienation or estrangement from reality, and madness is simply another form of alienation which happens to be "out of step with the prevailing state of alienation."[2]

The particular form of alienation called "schizophrenia" begins in certain family situations where there is an unconscious conspiracy to deny autonomy, individual identity, and sense of self to the growing child. The child fights to develop a separate identity and eventually begins a severe split between his or her outer self—a mask of conformity and acquiescence to the family—and his or her inner self. When the child's need for identity falls victim to the family's needs for their idealized image of the child, the split in the child's personality between an inner and outer self comes to a crisis—the child at last reaches a state of behavior and experience defined as "schizophrenic." Laing believes that schizophrenia is nothing but the forceful takeover of the outer self by the inner self in a spontaneous and naturally-occurring attempt of the human personality to heal itself. Instead of trying to "treat" this takeover of the inner self, cutting short the natural process by shock or chemotherapy, the "true physician-priest," as Laing phrases it, should instead help the person go through this natural healing experience—to take a journey into madness in order to confront and integrate the inner self.[3]

---

[1] Laing, *The Divided Self*, p. 31.
[2] Laing, *The Politics of Experience*, p. 28.
[3] Ibid., p. 162.

Laing feels that there may be certain biochemical abnormalities in schizophrenia, but that they are probably the result of earlier psychological and interpersonal situations.[4] Actually Laing's differences with some biochemical theorists—Larry Stein, for instance—are extreme. Where Laing believes that chemotherapy inhibits true recovery because it blocks recognition and integration of the mad experience and thus cuts short the natural healing process of schizophrenia, Stein says that schizophrenia is *caused* by the presence of a toxic substance in the brain and that this substance can best be blocked by the ingestion of antipsychotic medications such as the phenothiazines. Failure to block that toxin with medication, Stein believes, will eventually lead to the irreversible damage of certain neuron terminals in the brain, resulting in the syndrome of chronic "burnt-out" schizophrenia.[5]

Laing maintained a therapeutic center at Kingsley Hall in a working-class neighborhood of London's East End, where people could "go down and come out," that is, experience their madness in a supportive community without medication, restraint, or interruption. Unfortunately, no conclusive results of this experiment have been presented. In 1971 one Kingsley Hall patient wrote an autobiographical account of her madness, published along with her therapist's perspective of the experience, under the title *Mary Barnes: Two Accounts of a Journey Through Madness*. But the book does not give a very clear description of her madness or the dynamics of her recovery.

Morag Coate's account in *Beyond All Reason*, however, is clear and interesting and does support the Laingian theory of schizophrenia. As a child Coate shed religious orthodoxy. Late in adolescence she devoted much energy to serious philosophical inquiry. Then she had some kind of spiritual experience, what she called an "illumination," and from that she concluded that it was possible to have a personal relationship with a personal God. Her thought and behavior quickly became irrational, however, more magical and atavistic, until she finally was hospitalized. She experienced five different breaks over a period of fourteen years, two of which were dramatically ended by electroshock therapy. But she seemed finally to be cured by a relationship with an understanding psychiatrist who encouraged her to accept and integrate the experience of her madness.

In his introduction Laing promises that Coate's description will raise questions beyond the reach of psychiatry and medicine, to a

---

[4]Laing, *Sanity, Madness and the Family*, p. 18.
[5]Stein, "Neurochemistry of Reward and Punishment," pp. 354–56.

"domain of relevance that takes us to the very horizons of human existence."[6] He suggests that priests, theologians, and philosophers will find relevance in the account and that this psychiatric autobiography might best be read as a spiritual autobiography.

> Since natural science studies only the relation between things, we are thus in a context of relevance that is outside the domain of natural scientific investigation. We have to realize the phenomenal existence of an "inner" world, that goes beyond the realm of imagination, reveries, dreams, and even of unconscious fantasy. I can think of no better word for the experiential domain that lies "beyond" the reach of perception, thinking, imagination, dreams, fantasy, than the spiritual world—or the domain of spirits, Powers, Thrones, Principalities, Seraphim, Cherubim, The Light.[7]

The following excerpts were selected to illustrate the writer's psychiatric and/or spiritual progress. She first describes the beginning of her unusual mental experiences which she enters into with tremendous intellectual curiosity. In the next entry her first acute break and subsequent hospitalization are described. Writing retrospectively, she portrays it as an experience of insanity, but it is clear that at the time she felt she was going through powerful experiences of spiritual significance. Her experiences involve a few hallucinations, some delusional interpretations, but mostly a state of awareness in which she experiences herself and others as shorn of their contemporary identities and participating in a more universal or archetypal identity. In the third excerpt Coate describes her first contact with Dr. Upton, who tells her—as Laing would recommend—that much of the content of her religious experiences may be valid. In the last excerpt, Coate writes of her resolution and cure through her therapeutic relationship with Dr. Upton. She is able to achieve an emotional release through the support of this relationship and to "resolve and integrate" her madness.

I GOT UP from where I had been sitting and moved into another room. Suddenly my whole being was filled with light and loveli-

---

[6]Laing's intro. to Coate, *Beyond All Reason*, p. viii.
[7]Ibid., p. ix.

ness and with an upsurge of deeply moving feeling from within myself to meet and reciprocate the influence that flowed into me. I was in a state of the most vivid awareness and illumination. What can I say of it? A cloudless, cerulean blue sky of the mind, shot through with shafts of exquisite, warm, dazzling sunlight. In its first and most intense stage it lasted perhaps half an hour. It seemed that some force or impulse from without were acting on me, looking into me; that I was in touch with a reality beyond my own; that I had made direct contact with the secret, ultimate source of life. What I had read of the accounts of others acquired suddenly a new meaning. It flashed across my mind, "This is what the mystics mean by the direct experience of God."

It did not necessarily follow that God was a person as we understand the term; my initial state of illumination was highly abstract and gave no clue of that. It might be a life force, an inorganic source of spiritual power transcending all our own notions of individuality; but that it was the external, transcendent source of life and beauty and of truth, I did not doubt. I had never feared people, and it did not occur to me now to be afraid of God; I was astonished and awed at the magnitude of what had happened to me, but I responded simply, warmly and intensely as my natural self. It was, from that first instant, a direct, reciprocated love relationship. It remained to be seen what was its cause and purpose and what I should make of it.

*   *   *

One Saturday, feeling that the crisis point was now at hand, I decided that the only thing to do was to call God back to earth to see and take charge of matters for himself. I finished my work in an orderly fashion and stood up in my office at midday. I clasped my hands tightly together and with my whole strength called on God. There was a sudden feeling as of a strong current running through me from above downwards. It lasted for about six seconds. It left me feeling dehydrated, as though I had been in some literal sense burnt out. I went across to the canteen to have my lunch, and drank nearly a quart of water before I ate my food. I was quite untroubled now. I had done all that was needed, and my period of lone responsibility was over. From now on I would be instructed what to do. I no longer held tentative beliefs, or was puzzled at the idea of what seemed strange or unlikely happenings. I took the situation perfectly for granted. I knew.

In the short space between one half minute and the next I had lost my reason and become insane. Not that this was apparent yet to anyone, and least of all to me. Months earlier when I was alarmed in case I might be losing my sanity, the fact that I could feel this fear showed that I was not more than partly submerged in my own inner mind. I was like a swimmer who has gone out of his depth and fears drowning; sometimes my head was above water, sometimes under the surface, and the comparison and contrast between the different views kept me clearly aware of which was which. Since that time, although getting into deeper and deeper water, I had so to speak kept my head above it, and I remained clearly conscious of the normal aspect of the outside world. Suddenly I had gone deep down under, as though it were a kind of water of Lethe I had sunk into, I forgot immediately and completely my normal, rational view of life.

I finished my lunch and walked out into the town, ready for whatever adventure should befall. I was under direction. All I needed to do was to go wherever the impulse took me, and sometime during the day I would meet the special messenger who was being sent.

If anyone suspected my state of mind and had tried to reason with me, they could have had no influence. I was no longer the same person who had gone to work in the morning. This new me had direct and certain sources of knowledge, shared only by those who, for some special purpose, might have been called to play a part in the important event at hand. The messenger I was waiting to meet would, no doubt, be one of them.

The sun shone brightly, reflecting off the chromium of parked cars and refracting tiny fans of iridescent rainbow colouring. I could have spent hours observing the subtle qualities of light, but there was not time to linger on the way. I passed by my flat and glanced in through the window. A man was kneeling beside the armchair on which I had laid my head while deep in thought the previous night. I passed on quickly. If I had stopped to look closely I would have seen no one there. I saw the man only abstractly with my inner eye; I was aware of his attitude and general build, but we were apart in time and on different planes of existence and we were not meant to meet that day.

The city was crowded. There was a big football match on, and that was significant, for part of the plan for the future was that aggressive and competitive impulses should be channelled into sports and games as a substitute for war. I pressed on purposefully towards the cathedral which was my immediate destination, and I was soon joined by an unseen companion who walked beside me on my right. Unlike the man in the flat who was, as it were, the invisible shadow of the form of a man, this person was totally unseen but vividly present in strong spirit, and my right hand curled its fingers lightly against his. I was glad to have him there, and I was surprised when he held back fifty yards from the cathedral and would not come any nearer to it. I went on alone, went in, genuflected towards the high altar, and came straight out again. My unseen visitor had not waited for me, he was gone; but within a few yards of where I had left him a man of flesh and blood fell into step with me. We walked in silence; I felt no need to talk; I knew I had at last met my special messenger.

When we reached the quiet backwater where I lived he started, still in complete silence, to make love to me. This astonished me; it was the last thing I had expected in the circumstance. I thought quickly. No doubt some special demonstration and tuition had been called for. I planned my actions accordingly, and I noted that the man's hands shook when I lit him a cigarette. Eventually he spoke.

"Do you know who I am?"

"No."

"I'm David."

"David Stronsay?"

"Yes."

This was the only conversation that we had. It was quite sufficient for me; it identified him as my grandfather's great-grandfather come back from the dead.

My contact was in fact a real and ordinary man. So much the worse for him, for he had been nervous from the start, and he got a serious fright when I told him suddenly that he was upside down. He ran away from me, after a short struggle in which I tried to stop him; and after that the solar system started to fall apart. I had certain, but purely abstract, knowledge of the danger that now threatened, and it was up to me to keep my head. The running man, as he went out of sight, could be seen now as four different men all present in one body at the same time. There was the stranger of my own time and district; there was the eighteenth-century ancestor; there was another contemporary man living at that time in a different place; and there was a semi-divine personage as well. They had all simultaneously panicked.

I retired to my flat, dismissed from mind the stranger and the ancestor, who were no longer relevant, and concentrated my attention on the other two. The superhuman personage was in blind flight and racing round the planets widdershins. The planets were arranged in a circular ring around the sun, all on the same plane, and spaced evenly enough to provide a series of stepping stones. I could not see this from my room, but I knew it; and I knew also, as the racing figure did not, that at one point one of them was missing and he would fall through and disrupt the equilibrium of the others in his fall. I could not call him back, and the only person who could help was the contemporary whose identity I knew, who had now fled to his own part of the country. He, if he could be induced to do it, could rise up like Atlas and, by strengh of personal stature, support not only this world but the whole disrupting system. I called out to him, "Stand up. Be a man." It was in vain. He could not be roused, and I had not the strength. I was tempted to run away myself, but checked the impulse and thought quickly what I could do. The main risk was that the balance of the moving planets would be lost. If I could provide some kind of counterpoise, all might be well. I stood in a passage swinging my arms like pendulums until the danger point had passed and all was well. I became elated after that.

I was found soon afterwards, dancing naked in front of a mirror. My eyes were very wide open so that the whites were visible on both sides of the iris. From this I knew that I was now a priestess of the Minoan snake goddess, or perhaps the goddess herself; it did not seem to matter which. I found it easy enough to make the transition back to modern times when my visitor, whom I knew well, helped me into a dressing gown. To keep me talking while expert help was being sought, he told me about a recent journey he had made. I understood clearly what he was saying, but I was puzzled by it. What was the special significance of this journey, and why, at this precise moment, did the knowledge of it have to be conveyed to me? To my mind then there were no such things as ordinary, everyday events. Everything was charged with an immense significance.

The visiting psychiatrist looked in and spoke to me briefly. I made what must have seemed a highly delusional reference to Eve. I had recently spent some time playing with a child who had that name, and it seemed relevant and important to refer to the fact.

After the ambulance took me away, I became so ill that there are now some gaps in memory, but I found myself before long lying on a mattress in a small and otherwise empty room. I was inside out and upside down, and the visible sign of this was that I was lying on the ceiling. How did I know it was the ceiling and not the floor? In the first place there was the absence of a bed. In hospital you are put to lie on a bed if you are nursed by ordinary gravity. But if you had to lie on the ceiling, you would want to be as close to it as possible; so that was why I only had a mattress. These things are quite simply explained if you keep calm, but at the same time it is as well to make sure. I got up and looked out through the small peephole in the observation cubicle. There were shelves alongside, and on them parcels tied up in newspaper. I looked closely. The print was upside down. That proved conclusively that in this place gravity had been reversed.

I knew I was in hospital because I was attended there by girls in nurses' uniform. I knew also that I was in prison because I was locked in. As I had done no wrong, I waited hourly for a friend in whom I trusted to release me. I was disappointed when he failed to come, but not deeply troubled. I had forgotten about him by the time I was transferred elsewhere. I have no memory of being moved.

On arrival at the distant hospital, my first memories are of struggles and of forcible sedation. Soon afterwards I adapted myself to my new environment and acquired a different personality. My experiences were now filled with religious content, but of a kind quite different from what had occupied my mind over the previous half-year. I was submissive, pious, and at the same time elated. I was not concerned with understanding anything; I had been specially chosen to be a kind of star actress in a celestial mystery play. I accepted this unquestioningly and with delight, while at the same time never completely identifying myself with the role I played. At one time I took the part of the Virgin Mary, at another I was the boy David; sometimes I was an anonymous figure representing a boy and a girl at the same time. Always my point of reference and of distant veneration was the black-robed, sandalled figure who sat motionless for hours at a time at the end of the aisle of a cathedral. The building was long enough to fit in with this interpretation, and the tall windows were suitable, and the flowers were appropriate. The presence of beds there could be conveniently dismissed from mind. The black-robed figure was a priest, the head of a religious order, who represented and at times actually became Christ. At meal times we filed into an adjacent, circular building, the chapter house, in which the ceremony of the Last Supper was recurrently enacted. The priest-figure served out the food which I helped, with due reverence, to carry round. Then, after seating myself at one of the wooden trestle tables, my duty was to see that the salt was passed up and down and especially from one side to the other. This was vitally important, for the two sides were not, as it seemed, a mere arm's length apart. The opposing rows of people seated there were really in far different places and in different centuries as well. Space and time converged here to make a meeting point.

I awoke one day, as my normal self, to the consciousness that I had recently been mad. I tried to hope that this was not true, that I had dreamed it, and that nothing had really happened. This hope quickly died. Further and seemingly insoluble problems now arose. I had certainly been mad, my recent actions proved it; how could I be sure I was now sane? I believed I was in hospital, but was I? This place bore no resemblance to the traditional hospitals with which I was familiar. I looked out of the windows at a mountain, but it was different in outline from any that I knew. The faces that surrounded me were strange.

The place and people might all be a hallucination of my own. If one's personal yardstick for reality has once proved faulty, it is hard in strange surroundings to recover confidence in it. I was allowed no visitors. The nursing and medical staff had no conversations with me. I had to work the problem out from first principles as best I could. Two points of reference eventually fixed my orientation. I received letters, undoubtedly authentic because of their characteristic handwriting, from people that I knew. I also eventually recognised by name and by appearance one member of the staff whom I had happened to meet, elsewhere and in a very different context, a year ago. I was after all among real people and in a real place.

I sought out the doctor in charge of my section of the hospital and asked what had happened to me. He said, "You have had a nervous breakdown, and you must now forget all about it." I found this singularly unhelpful at the time.

*   *   *

I moved to a larger city not long afterwards. I had some contacts there and I hoped to build up a fuller and more satisfying social life. In that I was, for various reasons, less successful than I had hoped. The general tone of my life was an even grey. My youth was past, and I had nothing to look forward to in later life.

I thought it might be wise to put myself under the supervision of a psychiatrist. I was too depressed to expect much benefit from this, but I found it unexpectedly most helpful. In the past I had only had occasion to speak to doctors about my illnesses or about my spiritual experiences at times when I was too ill to think and express myself with ease. It was a relief to be able to talk freely at last. Unlike the psychiatrists in the mental hospitals, Dr. Upton was not a persistent questioner. Once the ice was broken he just let me talk, and it was his quality as a listener that led me on. He did directly influence me, but in a quiet and non-dominating way. He suggested to me that I had cast out too much when I rejected the whole content of my spiritual experiences. There might still be much that was valid in them. I was impressed by his comments, and by the way he listened, and by his quickness to link up experiences of mine with those of other people. I no longer felt inwardly alone, and hope began to stir within me. My outside interests revived, I could listen to music with enjoyment, the world became a brighter place.

All this was of immediate value to me, and it was also dangerous. Only I knew how I induced my experiences and what effect they had and what they meant to me. I should have been wiser not to reverse too quickly the verdict of renunciation which I had earlier made. But I jumped eagerly at the excuse that I might have been wrong; I felt that I was so to speak licensed to go ahead, and that I now had a safe support behind me. I decided to seek direct contact with God again.

I started one Saturday evening. The experience I had was intense and emotionally demanding. I slept dead out afterwards until half-way through the following morning, and found myself hard pressed to get through my commitments during the rest of the day. That did for a moment give me pause to wonder about the physiological effect of what I was doing. But I chose to explain it differently; God had missed me and wanted more of me because of my long absence. I soon adjusted to a comfortable balance between spiritual and other day-to-day activities. I told Dr. Upton nothing about all this. When I saw him I was still busy talking about events in the past, and I felt no need to discuss present-day affairs that, from my point of view, presented no problem. I felt undisturbed and confident. From Dr. Upton's point of view I seemed to be progressing well. He little knew that inadvertently he had done the equivalent of sending a reformed drug addict back to addiction.

Not that, on a long-term view, his judgement was at fault. I needed to pick up where I had left off in order to resolve and integrate my whole experience. But a more watchful check on what was currently happening to me might have been advisable. Direct questioning has its values too.

Some months went by before anything unusual happened. In the past I had tended to expect too much too soon. I felt less impatient now because I was, correspondingly, more confident. Outside events would undoubtedly confirm before long the indications I received in private. It was just a matter of keeping in readiness, and of dealing with such matters as came my way meanwhile.

The first surprising thing that happened was that I met the

devil in a restaurant. I had been to an official meeting and took myself out to dinner afterwards. I had a leisurely meal and was daydreaming about certain friends whom I wanted God to meet. Suddenly something about the quality of my inner feeling told me that another person had intruded into my private, personal relationship with God. The newcomer was unrestrained and rather sentimental, and I knew that it was the devil, though he was not a person I had thought about or believed in before. But, if he existed, he was clearly a deprived person, so it was perhaps not surprising that he should be sentimental in private when his outer façade was not in evidence. I was angry at his intrusion and lost my appetite; I quickly paid my bill and left. The devil had made contact from within; I projected him now outside me where I would have more control over him. I half thought of sending him to heaven as a punishment, as I reckoned that he would be bored. But no, on second thoughts that would be dangerous; among innocent and unsuspecting people he could do too much harm. The only thing to do was to take him home with me. That was an inconvenient plan, but not specially dangerous. He could have no power over me unless I feared him, which I did not. I was still cross, and mentally I reduced him to the status of an animal, a kind of farmyard version of a dinosaur that I negotiated through the traffic on a lead. But to treat a potential human as an animal is meant and felt as an insult, and it is particularly inappropriate to behave towards a deprived person in that way. I therefore changed my tactics and accorded him human status, and I began to tease him a little, mainly to reassure myself because I was in fact rather frightened of him after all. That clearly boosted his self-importance too much. The best way was to accept him and take him for granted in the simplest way possible. When we got home, I offered him the run of the flat for as long as he wanted. But one thing I made clear. He would have no opportunity of intruding on my privacy with God. So long as he was around, I would abstain from direct contact with God. I took no further notice of him and was not sure when he actually went. At most, he did not stay more than a few days.

I wondered about him afterwards. Was it the spirit of some man who identified himself as the devil? Or was the devil really a person, and if so what had happened to develop him into a twisted, thwarted adversary of the good? There was clearly a place for adversaries in any stable spiritual ecology; healthy resistance and challenge keep up the vitality and quality of goodness; unopposed, steam-roller benevolence is a spurious substitute. But evil is a form of sickness . . .

I was thinking about this and switched on the wireless and a traveller was speaking of a Persian sect who worship the lord of darkness who fell to earth as a wounded peacock. The speaker linked the story with his journey home and the English child in the train listening to a fairy tale—could it have been Beauty and the Beast? I have forgotten now.

A week or two later I attended church on Sunday as a kind of thanksgiving, for I had a feeling that all was going well. The quality of the service disappointed me; a good deal of rather tatty ceremonial, but no sense of spiritual depth or inspiration. I was glad to get out into the fresh air. It was a very lovely day. I decided to visit a park on the outskirts of the city.

Time was becoming altered again, but I was not alarmed. It had merely been lengthened to allow more to take place per minute than would otherwise be possible. This meant that the time I had to wait for a bus appeared much longer than in fact it was. The bus itself was quite normal when it came.

I went in at the park gates and was overwhelmed by the glory of the colour of the rhododendrons. I had forgotten that they would be in full bloom. Crimson and pink and white they blazed in the sunlight, and beyond them the yellow-gold and orange of azaleas and the creamy tumbled remnants of overblown magnolias spread out under the light, spring-green trees. I drank in the colour as if it had been wine, and I returned with special delight to the rhododendrons because of their association with a very special experience which happened in the early days of my spiritual adventures.

I was enjoying these outward beauties so wholeheartedly that it was not for some time that I sensed I was in danger. A slight shift in the spectral quality of the colours warned me; they became just a shade too crude and bright. A split between the spiritual and physical components of reality was taking place, as had happened some years earlier when I found myself in Vanity Fair among fake people. A fake version of the flowers and the park and people in it would shortly be projected away from earth, taking me too, unless I could arrest the process. Forces from elsewhere had once again credited me with a power and importance that was not mine, and were attempting to kidnap me. I would be given greater status than I could hope for here, but I would never see earth and my friends again. And I would, in subtle, imperceptible ways, lose my own soul.

I lay face downwards on the grass. I had been through so much in different ways over the years, I now felt spent. I looked down as I lay and remembered lying in this position on my bed twelve years ago. I used to look in imagination through the earth and visualise the ocean where I would surface if I slipped straight through. I looked further and, looking downwards, knew I was looking up towards far distant stars. To look in that way used to delight me; it increased my sense of danger now. I closed my eyes and put my face close to the grass and whispered into the earth and asked that a friend in whom I trusted would call my spirit home. I had a sense of being shriven. I got up quietly and returned.

*   *   *

It was in the end an outside stimulus that triggered off a sudden, unforeseen emotional release. I went, a shade reluctantly, to see *David and Lisa*, a film that tells the story of a mentally sick boy and girl in a school for severely disturbed adolescents. The opening shots reminded me of my own horror of the mental hospitals I had been in, but I soon forgot that and became absorbed completely by the personal human drama— tense, beautifully acted, and at times deeply moving. The central characters were presented with a reality that struck me as perfectly authentic, and with a sympathy that implied absolute acceptance. So, by involving myself in their experience as I did, I was not only accepting my past sickness, but feeling it accepted too. This was something which I had so needed, but had lacked in hospital.

I had gone to the film by myself, and was glad afterwards to come out alone. I walked slowly along the river bank, and let the chattering groups pass me by. The black waters of a big river at night are threatening when seen in the context of insanity; I was not troubled by them now, but awed a little, certainly impressed. And a planet shone out in the clear sky above, as piercing in its light as a single sharp note of music, and the lights on the far bank were gay with a warming brightness, and I myself was feeling human and humane. I had quite lost my dread of mental hospitals. On the contrary, I felt that was where I would now like to be, that I had gifts which I could use and that, instead of trying to forget and to deny my kinship with people who were mentally ill, I wished to work directly with them.

I climbed up some steps onto the bridge, and as I did so it dawned on me what this new-found impulse meant. I had at last forgiven my sick self. It did not in fact greatly matter whether I could use my gift for making contact with deeply disturbed people, but I felt sure this was something that I had, and the important thing was that I should know and value it.

My involvement in the film brought home to me how sick I had been in my past life at times when I had outwardly seemed well. I saw with sudden insight the relevance of minor neurotic symptoms, and I remembered the terrors of infancy which had been revived for me in my last time in hospital. I began to reach down towards the roots of a forgotten fear of absolute destruction and annihilation.

I explored further into this hidden region on the same evening after I got home. But this was something that I could not have done alone. I was thinking of Dr. Upton at the time. At first I had felt inclined to write to him, and then I knew there was no immediate need to write and I would rather wait and talk to him direct. Meanwhile, in spirit I took him by the hand with the same confidence and comfort that a child holds someone's hand when retracing their steps to the place where they have had a terrifying accident. I pressed down into the darkly bright intensity of my hidden life and broke through to the perilous secret that my adult defences had guarded me from coming near. Damned up and firmly sealed off down inside myself my primal, urgent need was still intact. And somewhere, in the uncharted time of early infancy, I had given myself and taken in return; I had needed and enjoyed and later felt that I had lost a mother's love. The sudden, living sense of need and loss came upon me so strongly that I wept. And then, refreshed as by a sudden storm of rain, I fell asleep.

During the next few days a tremendous emotional upheaval took place. I was able to recover into consciousness and to assimilate the terrifying feelings that stemmed from my first relationship in infancy. The barrier against them had been so strong that, except during periods of acute psychosis, it had never lifted until now. And it could not have lifted without disaster or destruction if there had not been a new relationship to take its place. It did not matter feeling I was an infant in dire need—I could need Dr. Upton now. And need him I did, quite unrestrainedly. I just didn't mind. I didn't feel embarrassed or that my inner stature had lessened, rather the reverse. For there was something about this primal urge, stemming from the very source of life, that was bigger, brighter, deeper and stronger than any of the feelings of my remembered childhood. It was also something that could have been overwhelming if I had been alone with it. Dr. Upton was my safe anchorage. I could let my feelings free.

This direct, completely uninhibited relationship gave a profound new sense of freedom to the rest of my emotional life. My sense of urgent, overwhelming need for the doctor whom I freely loved and trusted subsided gradually as I worked through and left behind my childhood terrors. The curious experiences which I went through at that stage would take too long to recount in detail here. Once that phase was over I could return to the interests and joys of normal adult life. But the personal relationship remained, giving a deep, warm sense of security that enriched all aspects of my life. Mind, body and spirit were now at peace with one another. I had been made whole.

So, despite all that has happened, I can feel that nothing has been wasted, and my worst experiences have had constructive value for me in the end. I have lost some transitional beliefs that I based on experiences which bewildered and sometimes gravely misled me at the time. But I have regained and strengthened my faith that life has a purpose and a meaning. I can honestly say I now have every reason to believe that living is worthwhile.

Is that an irrational belief? Of course it is. Reason is a tool; a valued tool which it is our pride and privilege to use as best we may. But life and love and loveliness, whose existence reason confirms and must accept, are in themselves beyond all reason.

1975 ↩

The Eden Express, by Mark Vonnegut

Mark Vonnegut is the son of the novelist Kurt Vonnegut. Mark graduated from college just when his father was becoming famous as an
author who was especially popular with the counterculture of the late
sixties and early seventies. The son embraced the styles and values
of the counterculture wholeheartedly: he renounced the barber, experimented with psychedelic drugs, was once arrested for possession
of marijuana, and went to British Columbia to found a self-sufficient
farm commune.

The counterculture emerged as a reaction to the Vietnam war, to
apparent secrecy and distance in government, and to what it perceived as the aggressive and destructive tendencies of American
mainstream culture. Although there was a radical leftwing element
that was perhaps as coercive and institutionally oriented as its right-
wing counterpart, the important core of counterculture values was a
kind of benevolent anarchism—with a distrust of institutions, of coercion, of authority, a belief in the importance of the individual and the
power of goodness, and a fascination with the organic and the
spiritual.

The theories of R. D. Laing happened to mesh quite well with the
attitudes and values of the counterculture folk. His rebellion suited
theirs. His distrust of psychiatric institutions matched their distrust of
institutions. His distrust of traditional psychiatry paralleled their distrust of traditional authority. His insistence on the spiritual validity of
schizophrenic experience reflected their own fascination and trust in
spiritual systems of understanding. His theory that schizophrenia is a
natural, organic attempt at the self-healing of the psyche was akin to
their own fascination with the natural and the organic. His therapy of
kindness, empathy, guidance, and care embodied their own trust in
the value of benevolence.

Mark Vonnegut worked in a mental hospital for several months
and at the time firmly believed in Laing's ideas: he described himself
as a "Laing-Szasz fan" who "didn't believe there was really any such
thing as schizophrenia. I thought it was just a convenient label for
patients whom doctors were confused about." He believed that if the
patients were acting a little strangely, it was nothing but "a reasonable reaction to an unreasonable society." After living in British
Columbia, however, Vonnegut had a severe experience of madness,

later labeled "schizophrenia," which had apparently been triggered by a weekend mescaline trip. His friends took care of him as well as they could, and eventually his best friend took him into Vancouver to a commune which tried to treat him in what was essentially a Laingian therapeutic milieu. The results were disastrous. He was finally taken to a psychiatric institution called Hollywood Hospital where, after a short period of Thorazine treatment, he recovered. After his discharge he stopped taking Thorazine and soon again became disoriented and began hallucinating. Eventually he was readmitted and again, after Thorazine treatment, his madness receded. After his discharge this time Vonnegut continued to use Thorazine and also began taking megavitamins. His interest in Laing ended and his interest in biochemistry began. He went east, wrote *The Eden Express*, and entered medical school.

A review in *Newsweek* magazine downgrades the importance of the book, describing Vonnegut as "an immensely likable young man with no distinct capacity to write."[1] The reviewer appears to have reacted not so much to Vonnegut's ability to write, however, as to his use of what the reviewer calls the "hippie cant." But it seems to me that Mark chose deliberately, with skill, humor, and intelligence, to write in a particular voice—that of counterculture slang—fully appropriate for the subject. For not only is *Eden Express* a fascinating account of madness, it is also one of the clearest published accounts of the American youth culture of the late sixties and early seventies.

In the following excerpts, the author describes the Vancouver commune, where, roughly and with little preparation, a therapeutic environment is prepared to help him go through his "journey" à la Laing. In medieval times, and to a large degree until the great age of asylum construction in the nineteenth century, most mad people were treated at home, probably much in the improvised way that the writer was cared for. The reader will have to judge for himself or herself the efficacy of that approach as compared to the Thorazine treatment at Hollywood Hospital; I have included Vonnegut's opinion on that subject as the last excerpt.

What Was Really Going On. All I was catching was itty-bitty snatches. A word here, a sentence there. A funny smell, a

[1]Taylor, "Bad Trip," pp. 85A, 86.

funny face. Now and then a whole vignette. Putting it together was like trying to make a movie from a bunch of slides that had nothing to do with each other.

Why is Simon turning green? Why is Sy beating me up? What's that awful smell? Why is André winking at me? Why won't they let me go outside? What the fuck is going on?

What was going on was several people dealing as best they could with a very difficult, unfamiliar situation: a friend gone psychotic.

Apparently suffering a great deal. Incoherent most of the time. Incapable of understanding anything said to him. Moaning, screaming, smashing things. Completely unpredictable. And the cherry on the whole show—he doesn't sleep. Some six-day house guest.

What was really going on was Simon's job. I had other things to do. But when I did manage to check in, that I was very different from other people and being treated very strangely, and in a great deal of physical pain and not hearing, seeing, smelling, tasting, walking, or talking right, was hardly delusional.

What could they do? Putting someone in a nut house isn't a nice thing to do to someone. There are lots of pressures in the hip community that make that sort of decision even harder to come to than normally. Doctors don't know anything, mental hospitals are repressive, fascist, etc. Hippies are supposed to be able to take care of their own. "Schizophrenia is a sane response to an insane society." "Mental illness is a myth." The Sanskrit word for crazy means touched by the gods.

I vaguely remember Sy's threatening me. "If you don't shut up we'll have to put you in a nut house. You've been yelling all night." I laughed. "Fine hippie, fine revolutionary, fine peace-love brother you turned out to be."

It was a cosmic barroom brawl. Like most it had something to do with religion. My team was fighting for minority plank No. 234: Everyone gets saved. Fighting against notions of chosen people. Trying to convince everyone that no one really knew much. For sure no one had come even close to putting it all together. So the best we could do was present a united front of ignorance rather than our pathetic fragmented pretensions.

I was the clock. As long as I could keep breathing, there was still time. We were badly behind and needed all the time we could get. One of our key strategies was to find out what everyone knew or thought they knew and then publish-broadcast-ESP it to everyone. And all the time thinking that what I was thinking was absurd and very unlikely but a bet that had to be covered.

Suddenly Sy was shaking me by the shoulders, looking very unfriendly. He must have been frustrated to the point of tears.

Fuck shit if my crazy hunch didn't turn out to be right. Here's a Jew who wants to stop the clock. Well, if it comes down to one on one, me vs. Sy, no sweat. I'm not in the greatest shape but he couldn't do much damage. Besides, wasn't he into pacifism, peace-love, etc.?

Boomzapplewomp! Wow! Where the hell did he learn how to throw a punch? I never saw it coming, which didn't mean that much. There was lots of stuff I wasn't seeing. He was slugging my chest. It was hard to tell the heartbeats from the punches. It all just rolled together. I was having a heart attack. Sy hit me a few more times. I went down hard.

Sy was making me get up. Someone had slashed my temples with razors. There was blood. Something had something to do with Maharishi, with my old girl friend, Betsy, in Houston with Harry Reasoner and mission control and gay bars, and watching on tv something called Operation Jack-in-the-Box battling against some acid-freak mutant from the year two thousand, into time travel, trying to have things his way. I wasn't sure which side he was on, but he had a thing about black people and electroshock and Thomas Edison and heroin and being wired to the fact that my father, besides being wanted by Israeli zealots, wasn't able to give up smoking. And someone making me hold on to the refrigerator door handle and not being able to move a muscle. And André, where the hell were those French when you needed them, came in saying something about Paris burning and telling Sy to let up on me and that he'd be in pretty rough shape too if he'd had my dose of bad news. And I cried and cried and cried, begging Sy to just give me a little time. Maybe if I had paid more attention to Bucky Fuller. "I'll adjust better. Please, another chance. I'll pay better attention. Please, another chance."

After a while a reasonable routine for dealing with me was

worked out. A twenty-four-hour watch was set, sharp and dangerous objects were put away, and things calmed down a little. There was some talk about hospitals but Simon held fast to his promise to me. There was a lot of telephoning. The Barnstable house, which was the only number I could remember, still never answered. Simon somehow managed to get my sister Edie in N.Y.C. on the line.

"Mark?"

"Don't worry, Edie, I won't tell them a thing," and I slammed the receiver down.

Many hours were taken up trying to decode my ravings, in hopes that if they knew more about what was going on in my mind they could snap me out of it. Most of the time I was honestly trying to be as informative and straightforward as possible, but there was so much to tell and things kept getting more and more confusing and it was so hard to understand what they were saying or make my own voice and words act right. But things seemed to be working out all right.

Hello. I am here. I am Mark Vonnegut and all that that entails. That's Simon there and Sy there and André there and Sankara there. We all went to Swarthmore. We are in Vancouver, British Columbia, Canada. I can remember lots of things. I can think about things. I can understand what people are saying and they can understand what I am saying.

It never lasts very long. It's lasting less and less. I keep going away. It keeps getting harder and harder to come back. I stop being Mark Vonnegut. Simon stops being Simon and so on. I stop being able to remember things, think about things, or understand what people say. It stops being Vancouver, British Columbia, Canada. I get swept away. I keep making it back, but it's getting tougher and tougher.

In a funny way it's almost fun, having everything be so fucked up and managing to adjust. I guess you might say I'm proud. Proud of me, proud of my friends for managing to deal with this thing so well. For most people this would be the end of the world. They'd panic, their friends would panic. Things would get trampled in the stampede. But we've kept our heads, made the necessary allowances, and can just ride this thing out.

I'm pretty much just putting in time waiting for this cloud to blow over. Waiting for something to come along to make some sense out of all this. Killing time, waiting for some sort of cavalry to come over the hill. There's really not an awful lot I can do but wait. As long as there's no panic, we can hold out damn near forever.

And Then Along Came Warren. Actually we went to see him. Warren was a holy man of sorts who was supposed to drive the evil demons out of me or maybe just talk me down or at least come up with some explanation for what was wrong with me. The Stevens Street folk and Simon were getting desperate.

We first heard about Warren from Luke. Luke was wandering around the Kootenays feeling very untogether. One day he came across this old man who, as Luke put it, was living the most together organic, spiritual life he had ever seen. It was Warren. Vibes happened and something like a guru-disciple relationship went on for a few weeks. Luke credited Warren with having helped him a great deal. All this had taken place a year or so ago.

Then we heard from Sankara, André, and Sy that they had run into a really far-out man, long white hair, flowing white beard. He did Ching reading, numerology, and other things and had spiritual powers of some sort. They were getting more and more into him.

Sure enough, it was Warren. I had had lots of opportunities to go see Warren but always managed to pass them up. Maybe if I had met him earlier it would have helped lessen the shock of our first encounter.

Now there was lots of talk about Warren and all his spiritual gifts, wisdom, and powers, and that he probably knew all about whatever had gone wrong with me. I dreaded going to see him or having him come to see me. I'd never gotten on very well with guru types and was perfectly happy with the adjustments that had been made for my disabilities. Killing time till the cloud blew over. But maybe the cloud wasn't going to blow over until I faced Warren. Maybe Warren was in charge of the cloud.

I don't know how many of us went. I don't remember how we got there. I don't even remember whether I knew we were going to see Warren.

The door was opened by this white-haired, white-bearded

man, skinny as a rail, with sunken raving eyes and a huge hook nose, in a white-robe, holy-man outfit.

"Welcome to my temple."

Lots of white, incense, burning candles, little altars here and there, a mishmash of religious symbols and objects. We were supposed to sit on cushions on the floor. He had a chair.

I can't believe that I and these other people here are really sitting on cushions in front of this guy doing a white-robe bit in such a rinkydink put-up job of a temple.

Gurus as a group are generally a kindly lot. But there was nothing gentle or kindly about Warren in his appearance or manner. His face and the face that had engulfed me some weeks earlier had a lot in common.

I don't remember much of what was said. I blocked it out at the time: Whatever else happens here, don't let the joker trick you into saying the Lord's prayer backward. A limited objective, you might say, but it seemed the most I could handle at the time and when I left I wasn't even sure I had managed to achieve that.

"Look, sweetheart, I don't give a shit what you say."

"OK, pops, snap-fizzle-crack-pop. Sure, War."

Nothing pissed Warren off more than my calling him War, but I didn't dig his calling me sweetheart much so I figured we were even, at least on that score.

Disbelief, naked terror, frustration, towering rage. This can't be happening. I have to sit here and take this shit? I was furious at Simon. I had put him in charge of reality and he had really botched it. Judas? Was this what he had been up to all along? To deliver me into the hands of War? All that feigned fuzziness, leading me along? What was in it for him? Could I come up with a counteroffer? He wouldn't look at me. He had the look of a guilty child.

From not eating for quite a while I had developed a facial tic to go along with the general shakiness of my whole body. I was confused, upset, scared. Warren did everything he could to amplify all this. He challenged me to try to stop the tic in my face. He seemed to be trying to impress upon me the fact that he and not I was in control of my body.

"You are dust dust dust. You will die and nothing will remain." True enough, but not really what I needed to hear at the time.

Someone from the Stevens Street apartment had briefed him about me. He used the information as if he had just divined it clairvoyantly.

"You had a girl. She is not with you now."

War was hooked on notions of spiritual power, satanic or angelic didn't make much difference to him. If I had had an inclination to believe that maybe he was somehow hypnotizing me or in control of my heartbeat or an important part of some cosmic plot—candy to a baby, dope to an addict. He did everything to expand and amplify such notions.

He talked about earthquakes and other cataclysmic events. "All this will pass away. There will be nothing left. Nothing."

He kept changing subjects so often or jumbling them all together that it was hard to keep anything straight.

"Do you see the way the light comes through the curtains? Mountains will crumble into the sea. You had a girl but you didn't love her, all you wanted to do was fuck her. I have the mayor in my pocket. I know the Koran backwards and forwards. The forests are burning out of control. The Kennedys will all be dust . . ."

There was a long, long recital of my sins and transgressions. Lust was the biggie. Maybe he was going to straighten everything out by slipping me a whomping dose of acid. There was a direct link between my fuck-ups and mountains crumbling, forests burning, and all of human suffering.

Everything was dying outside. The earth was passing away. Like the tic in my face, it was something I could do nothing about. The only safe place was in Warren's rinkydink temple. It was like what happened when Atlantis sank, the end of the land of Mu. I had a feeling Warren and I had both been there and had more or less the same conversation. It would probably happen again at the next apocalypse. What a bore.

I looked around the room. No women and no blacks. A petty point, I suppose.

Warren was real. I wasn't hallucinating him. The other people were acknowledging him as real. If Warren was real, anything was possible. His antics made my hallucinations pretty pale.

The voices were the soul of rationality, salt-of-the-earth common sense, next to what he was saying. My wildest thoughts suddenly seemed much too conservative to deal with what was really happening.

If I had been difficult to deal with before Warren, it was nothing compared to what I became afterward. A nuisance turned menace. There was indeed something very heavy and of vast proportions going on. All those thoughts, the voices and the visions, weren't just ways to while away the time, things that I might some day turn into short stories. There was, in fact, a danger, and I was an important player in whatever was being played out.

A clinical psychologist's view of the situation might be that before Warren got into the act I was not actively suicidal or combative. Afterward I was. My paranoia, previously vague and intermittent, almost playful, became full-time focused and anything but playful.

Paranoia was the best way to deal with my situation, the most hopeful way to make any sense of the things that were happening to me. If there was no sense to what was happening, no intention, malignant or benign, then there was no hope. Would you rather be chased by a pack of wild dogs that were hungry or a pack of dogs that had a master who could, if he wanted to, call them off?

Warren himself was hauled off to the nut house a few weeks after I was. As I found out later, it wasn't his first such trip. An interesting footnote to the whole thing is that he was picked up by the cops from the lawn in front of the Stevens Street apartment. The diagnosis: paranoid schizophrenic. A couple of weeks after that, a freak wandered in off the street claiming that God had led him there. He wrote poetry all over the wall and claimed that there was someone after him. He was right. He had busted out of a nut house somewhere in Ontario. I don't know what it was about the Stevens Street apartment, but the odds of such a chain of events says something.

Suicide. The twenty-four-hour watch system broke down from time to time. I remember coming out of a long blank during which I had made love to every living thing, ingested gallons of every poison known to man, and called the devil's bluff in a game a lot like seven-card stud in an end-of-the-world bacchanal. I was still moving but Simon and everyone else were out cold. I had relived the history of man and it was mostly ugly, brutal, and macho. My dead grandfather was congratulating me on winning. I was the toughest bastard who had ever lived and my forefathers were very proud of me.

I got up and went into the bathroom. The mirror in there was the best way to broadcast back to planet earth.

"First I'd like to thank all the billions of people, animals, and plants who made this possible."

Looking in the mirror I could see that my body had become a composite of all bodies. Half my face was Asian, an arm and a leg were black. But it was more subtle than that. Everything that had ever lived had contributed their best cell to make what I now called me.

I tried to open the bathroom door but it wouldn't budge, and I finally understood what I had to do. My life had been spiraling toward this place and moment, pulled closer and closer to the vortex, and now I was there. I cheerfully drew myself a nice hot tub, found the razor blades they hadn't hidden very well and a gallon jug of Clorox. I wasn't unhappy or bitter, I was humming tunes from "My Fair Lady." I thought it would be lots of fun to see if I really could kill myself, but Simon interrupted my little party before I could decide whether it would be better to slash my wrists and then drink the Clorox or vice versa.

At other times suicidal longings came from desperate unhappiness, but everything was so confused I couldn't do a decent job of it. I'd become convinced that something like sitting in a certain chair, looking crosseyed at a psychedelic poster while I chanted Om and clicked my heels together, would do the trick. It became very hard for me to tell when I was committing suicide and when I wasn't.

I had thought a fair amount about suicide before I went nuts. It was often in connection with thinking about what sort of positive move I could make toward solving the problems of the world. The only way out of the mess the world was in that I could see was to have fewer people. Maybe killing myself and thereby making one less mouth to feed, one less body to clothe, one less excuse for the *New York Times* to kill trees, would do more good than anything else.

I believe now that if I placed a twelve-gauge shotgun in my mouth and pulled the trigger, I would cease to have consciousness. I find it a comforting belief. Much of the terror of then was that I had done that or the equivalent and it hadn't worked.

Before the crackup, suicidal impulses had been prodded by my mortality: Since some day, why not now? But suicide now sprang from desperate fear of immortality. I kept dying and maintaining some form of consciousness.

Down from one fifty-five to about one twenty-five pounds, deaf, dumb and blind, convulsing in my own puke, shit and piss. If something wanted me to suffer, how much more could they want? If there was a finite amount of suffering in the world, I was sparing someone somewhere something, I was a first-rate safety valve.

I don't pretend to know any more than anyone else about what happens after death, but if there is such a thing as hell and it's anything like some of the things I went through when I was nuts, and you can avoid it by doing things as petty as not coveting your neighbor's ass, by all means, DO NOT COVET YOUR NEIGHBOR'S ASS.

At some point I gave up clothing. It was just too sticky and confining, almost like drowning. No clothes would have maybe been OK if I hadn't taken it into my head to make a break for it. André and Simon tackled me before I got very far, but a neighbor saw me and told them that if he saw me anywhere near his kids, he'd shoot me. Other neighbors were going to call the cops about all the noise I was making, but the Sunshine Boys always managed to calm them down. Somewhere in there I threw a huge rock through the living-room picture window.

Gradually it became clear even to Simon that they might have to put me in a hospital, if only to save their own sanity.

*   *   *

February 14: Valentine's Day. Oh, God, it was awful. The end. So fucking hopeless, so fucking lonely. And getting more and more so and worse and worse. And harder and harder to hang on. And oh, Mother, how did your poor son end up in such a depressing hopeless meaningless mess? And oh, Father, what's gone so terribly wrong?

No more chances. No more people, trees, music, dogs. No more anything.

But then suddenly I had allies. "I thought you guys would never get here." Simon and my father, or damn convincing hallucinations, were holding me up and talking about getting me the hell out of that apartment. I hadn't been allowed outside since my nude sprint around the block.

We were in a car going somewhere. The fuckers didn't have me yet. My waiting game had paid off. I had allies.

I'd give almost anything for a tape of my ride to the hospital. My father had a lot on his mind, but still, not to have brought along a recorder verges on criminal neglect. My finest rave is lost forever unless you believe in that big cassette in the sky.

I didn't think my rave was being lost at the time. I didn't know it was just a normal day with a normal father and a normal friend of his son taking his son who had gone crazy to the sort of place you normally take someone who's gone crazy.

It was bop talk. Like a '50s DJ. I wasn't thinking, it was just all there. Words a mile a minute. No second thoughts. No need or time for them. Music.

Wazzzzzzzzzzzzz Wassa what I thought my rave-a-rap a' doin'. Passwords. Getting through to different teams and getting them to climb aboard. Start a bandwagon. For what to start a bandwagon? For to show those fuckers for to keep life going. I had something that made H-bombs look like ladyfingers. I had rhythm. And ain't no mother fucker nowhere nohow gonna take it away.

"Hey Giuseppe, how good you think that joker swim with some nice new cement booties?"

"Get the fuck out of the way. The team is coming together, coming through. Anybody I ain't talkin' to ain't gonna get talked to by nobody. Climb aboard or get run the fuck over, Jack. Get with it, Jack, or get off it."

I had some modest goals. Like letting a few people know I wasn't dead, that I was still in there somewhere. That I was salvageable. I had some immodest goals, like saving the world.

One thing a tape of my ride to the hospital would show was

how I was responding to outside events. It was a dialogue. I'd give some sort of a blues rap and then there'd be some horn or something which was a "yes" or "amen" from all blue freaks. I'd do a Mafia thing and they'd answer, a woman's thing and they'd say yes yes. A videotape would be even better. Flashing neon signs and I had some very good raps. Jackhammers had some very encouraging things to say. And big Diesel trucks and fire sirens. Who would be dumb enough to try to mess with me with Mack trucks, sirens, electricity, jackhammers, and traffic lights all on my side?

Hospital. Back at the apartment Simon had asked me if I was ready to go to the hospital. Sure I'm ready to go to the hospital. I'll go anywhere. Father seems very worried, very nervous. I guess there's no time to ask questions. Maybe everything will be explained at the hospital.

Remember Lot's wife. Full speed ahead. This train is bound for glory. Simon's driving beautifully, the car's running perfectly. Who's against us? How can we lose? We're on our way, great God, we're on our way.

The shifting is music to my ears and the lights are all turning green. Hold on tight, we're goin' to make it. We're passing everything on the road, and I hear myself rapping, cursing nonstop, hitting every password just right.

And Simon gives a "Wa hoo," double-clutches down to third, and passes another car. What a ride!

Why are they taking me to a hospital? Why is everything whizzing by faster and faster? Why am I holding my breath? Why do I feel so strange? Whatever is wrong is very strange. This will doubtless be a very strange hospital.

When the car finally came to a stop, the place looked like the Hyannisport Kennedy compound. I complimented Simon on his driving. My father and Simon turned and looked at me somberly.

When they left me, when three guys dressed in white started walking me down that long hall, half holding me up, half holding me down, I understood. I had gone too far. I was putting too much on the line. Simon and my father couldn't go the whole way with me.

In a way, it was a relief not having any allies any more. Now if

I fucked up, I fucked up on my own. I wouldn't drag a lot of people through the shit with me. But maybe it was just a holding action. They were putting me in cold storage and going out to get more allies.

Clunk, into that little room. Cuzzzunk, a huge mother bolt ran the whole width of the door. A separation chamber? No one could breathe the sort of stuff I had to breathe to keep alive.

*   *   *

Biochemistry. At first my friends and I were doubtful that there was any medical problem. It was all politics and philosophy. The hospital bit was just grasping at straws when all else failed.

It took quite a bit to convince us that anything as pedestrian as biochemistry was relevant to something as profound and poetic as what I was going through. For me to admit the possibility that I might not have gone nuts again had they given me pills when I left was a tremendous concession.

It's such a poetic affliction from inside and out, it's not hard to see how people have assumed that schizophrenia must have poetic causes and that any therapy would have to be poetic as well. A lot of my despair of ever getting well was based on the improbability of finding a poet good enough to deal with all that had happened to me. It's hard to say when I accepted the notion that the problem was biochemical, it went so hard against everything I had been taught about mental illness. At the farm we were coming more and more to seeing physical illness as psychological. A cold or slipping with a hammer and smashing a finger was psychological. Schizophrenia was biochemical?

But the idea had a lot to recommend it. The hopelessness of dealing with it on a poetic level was the start. The doctor who had apparently been able to bring me out of it was working from a biochemical model. According to most authorities who believed in this or that poetic theory, my case was hopeless. The biochemists said otherwise. The poets in the business gave little hope and huge bills. The chemists fixed me up with embarrassingly, inexpensive, simple nonprescription pills. Vitamins mostly. The biochemists said no one was to blame. The poets all had notions that required someone's having made some mistake.

The AMA had no particular affection for megavitamin therapy. That was something. Anything the AMA hated couldn't be all bad.

The more research I studied, the more impressed I was. I remain converted.

1976 ⊶

Insanity Inside Out, by Kenneth Donaldson

A central issue in the psychiatry of our time is that of the civil rights of patients. Kenneth Donaldson, carpenter, factory worker, law student by correspondence, and for fifteen years, "professional patient," has been intimately acquainted with this issue.

In 1943, at the age of thirty-four, Donaldson was working as a milling machine operator for the General Electric Company in Syracuse, New York. He began to feel that other workers in the plant were against him, that people were watching him. He heard swearing behind his back and threatening remarks that seemed to refer to him. One day, on the way to the parking lot, he became confused. Hours later he found himself wandering downtown. He was taken to Marcy State Hospital near Utica and given electroshock therapy that seemed to do little except disturb his concentration and memory. For thirteen years Donaldson moved from job to job around the country. It seemed that wherever he went, hard luck and persecution followed. In Arizona he heard people speaking behind his back. Barbers were calling him a sex deviant. Fellow workers played tricks on him. He overheard some women planning to medicate his food in order to control his sex life. In St. Louis strangers insulted him. When he went to the toilet, noises were made to insult him. People still talked about him. In Savannah, Georgia, the persecution continued so he went to South Carolina, where the same kinds of events persisted. He returned to Syracuse, but the people at work seemed to be ridiculing him because he "shunned sex." Each time he used the toilet a horn blew. In Los Angeles clerks in several stores and banks seemed to be hazing him. Someone put medicine in his food. He eventually returned to Florida to live with his parents in a trailer court.

In 1956 two police officers arrested him on the authority of his father, who had initiated commitment proceedings. After several days in jail and brief conversations with two physicians and a judge, Donaldson was sent to the White Male Department of the sixty-eight-hundred-bed Florida State Hospital at Chattahoochee, where he remained for almost fifteen years. There he witnessed incredible abuses—vicious beatings, teasing, and other manipulations by attendants—and seldom saw a physician. Introducing himself as a Christian Scientist he was usually able to avoid the two kinds of treatment

Chattahoochee had to offer: pills and electroshock therapy. During the entire fifteen years Donaldson insisted he was sane, although his commitment papers described him as a "schizophrenia paranoiac who was seeing and hearing things and was possibly dangerous to the people of the state." He behaved reasonably, even though at times his feelings of persecution recurred. A previous study of law by correspondence came in handy; he was able to have a fellow patient released by court order. Donaldson petitioned nineteen times to various courts for his own release. The first eighteen were rejected. Typically, the court asked for the opinions of Chattahoochee physicians, but the physicians would simply repeat what was written on the original admittance papers. Although they were not treating Donaldson, they held him because he had been placed there by a legal commitment. They continued to label him as a "paranoid schizophrenic" who was "possibly dangerous." For fifteen years the man insisted on his insanity, writing letters asking for help and taking notes for a book to expose the asylum system. Unfortunately, the doctors saw these activities as firm evidence of his mental incompetence. One physician described Donaldson this way: "This is to certify that I have this date, again interviewed Kenneth Donaldson . . . he does not realize he is mentally ill. . . . He states that if he is released he will obtain a civilian job and publish a book of his hospitalization for the past 20 years which illustrates he has little insight of his own condition."

In 1971 Donaldson was able to get a court hearing of his case, asking for his release and $100,000 in damages. While the case was in court, physicians at Chattahoochee decided to release him but he continued his suit. It was demonstrated in court that Donaldson had not resided in Florida long enough for a legal commitment, had never threatened anyone, had not been properly examined before commitment, had received very little attention and no psychiatric treatment during his fifteen years' incarceration, and that to all appearances he was sane and competent. As part of the evidence justifying his imprisonment, Chattahoochee physicians testified that when Donaldson drew stick figures on a psychological test he did not put pupils in their eyes. A psychologist described that as one indication of paranoid schizophrenia. Under cross-examination, however, the psychologist admitted that although Little Orphan Annie's creator never put in pupils either he had somehow managed to survive outside an institution. The jury concluded that two of Chattahoochee's physicians had acted "maliciously or wantonly or oppressively" and awarded Donaldson

$38,500 damages. The two physicians went on to appeal the case, and it was eventually brought before the bench of the United States Supreme Court. That court also ruled in Donaldson's favor, stating that his "constitutional right to liberty had been violated." The court referred the particular issue of monetary damages back to a Florida district court.

Donaldson was the first American psychiatric patient ever to win damages against his physicians, and he was the first ever to be heard by the Supreme Court. It is important to understand, however, that his is not really an isolated case. Examination of patients' periodicals such as *Madness Network News* (San Francisco, Glide Press) or *Constructive Action* (Syracuse, Shirley Burghard) reveals numerous similar cases of questionable psychiatric practice. Donaldson made it to the courts because he was tremendously persistent and because some powerful lawyers and law organizations took an interest in his case.

Among other things his lawyers hoped that Donaldson's case would establish a "Right to Treatment" precedent in the courts—that people confined in a psychiatric institution have a right to either adequate psychiatric treatment or release. Since Donaldson had received virtually no treatment for fifteen years, his seemed a good test case. Unfortunately the right to treatment issue is a red herring. It was created with the hope of releasing large numbers of untreated patients from confinement. However, as long as physicians define what they are doing as "treatment" they can justify their use of confinement.[1]

Donaldson's case was so clear-cut that the Supreme Court was able to consider it by sidestepping the broader, much more important issue of the constitutionality of commitment. In many states, simply on the word of one or two experts, people alleged to be "a danger to themselves, or to others, or severely disabled" can be deprived of many of the civil rights ordinarily guaranteed by the constitution. They can be imprisoned without having committed a crime and various treatments can be administered without their consent. If the case somehow goes to court, judges will traditionally defer to the opinions of the knowledgeable psychiatric professional.

Thomas Szasz compares the contemporary issue of commitment to the issue of slavery as it was seen in the early nineteenth century. Because slavery already existed in many parts of America, it was

---

[1] See Szasz, *Psychiatric Slavery.*

assumed to be acceptable, a necessary evil. People didn't ask how to do away with slavery but how to improve plantations. The real issue, however, was not whether slaves were happy, or whether slavery was good for them, but rather, was slavery morally right? Donaldson was held as a "possible danger," yet who has the moral right to determine what is "possibly" going to happen? Do we hold people for "possible thievery" or "possible murder"?

Donaldson has achieved some prominence since his trial. *Insanity Inside Out*, the autobiographical account of his life as a patient, appeared in 1976, supplementing his career on the lecture circuit. The book is a hodgepodge of descriptions of ward life, sketches of interesting patients, verbatim accounts of conversations with his physicians, legal documents, and notes on his case from the Chattahoochee files, all placed in a vaguely chronological sequence.

Donaldson presents a very fair, balanced self-portrait. From what he openly tells us, he did indeed hear things, imagine peculiar tastes in his food, imagine a conspiracy. Beyond these elements of suspiciousness and exaggerated self-reference, however, the man displays an impressive intelligence and rationality.

Some of the sketches of fellow patients and ward life are tremendously precise and well-observed; but most interesting are the accounts of his encounters with Chattahoochee physicians—giving a most frightening vision of authority as seen from underneath, from "inside out." Having the law and the prestige of their positions to back them up, these psychiatrists hardly strain in justifying their treatment of Donaldson. The resulting conversations seem to be right out of *Catch-22*, and the overall narrative is reminiscent of Kafka's *The Trial*. A number of doctor-patient conversations are excerpted here.

MY MAIN INTERRUPTION in a plodding summer was a call by Gumanis. "What ward are you on . . . ?" he asked.

Then I interrupted, "How is my transfer coming to New Jersey? I wrote you about it nine months ago?"

"Doctor Rogers wrote them that you were a resident of Florida."

"But that's not so."

"Your commitment papers—and I read them myself—say

you lived in Florida for four years. Rogers says there is nothing he can do and New Jersey has dropped the matter."

"But—"

* * *

"Doctor O'Connor," Davis began, "asked me to have a chat with you."

"Before we start anything," I said, "I would like to get one thing straight. It was nine months after I saw you, that I saw Gumanis again, and when I asked how I did on the tests he said you said I had hallucinations. Just what hallucinations did I have?"

"I don't remember. Let me go check." He left me alone for five minutes, then reported, "There is nothing in your record about hallucinations."

Here was proof Gumanis had lied, so I thought.

"Shall we proceed to take some tests, Mr. Donaldson?"

"I'd rather not. I don't need any tests. There was nothing wrong with me when I came to Florida and there is nothing wrong with me today. You can't tell anyone that I'm out of my head—you just said there were no hallucinations. Then why are you holding me? Why didn't Chattahoochee let my home state of New Jersey take me?"

"I'm sure no one in Chattahoochee would want to keep you if you were eligible for transfer."

"But that's just what they are doing."

"I know better because that was my first job and if you are entitled to one you'll get it."

"But somebody lied and—"

"Nobody at Chattahoochee lied about you—least of all a doctor!"

* * *

"You have been 'seek' all your life," were Char's first words to me. "You have spent half your life in state hospitals."

I let that pass, figuring the reasonableness of my story would discount whatever Gumanis had told him. I took some notes from my shirt pocket, which I had jotted down during a restless night. I brought up the first point: "Why should Florida hold me when my home state offered to take me back?"

"What have you got there?" Char asked excitedly, grabbing

the small piece of paper. "I can read. I can read. You think you have to read them to me?" His bushy black brows pushed over the top of his glasses.

"No, no. They are only notes so I wouldn't forget something."

Char read aloud: "last letter, 1957" and "have place to go." His face was triumphant. He gloated, "See, you don't make sense. You can't even write a complete sentence."

I gave up. Another morning wasted. But Char was too excited to restrain himself. Opening my chart to my letter, he said, "See—here—you say you saw me seventeen times. You're seek when you say something like that."

"I have a copy of the letter. Show me where I said that." Pointing it out, he read aloud: "'. . . when you saw me on seventeenth instant.' That means you thought you saw me seventeen times. So you see for yourself."

"Oh, my God!" I thought. "What have I drawn this hand?" But I kept from laughing, feeling that such a jerk I should be able to find some way to lead.

"In English," I said politely, "that means the current month. That meant the seventeenth of February, the month I wrote it."

"I know what it means," he snapped. "You don't have to tell me. You are seek. Besides, why do you save your letters? What good are they to you?"

Still hoping to salvage something, I said, "Tell me one way in which I am mentally ill."

"I cannot do that. It would take too long. I have tried to explain it to some of the others. I have spent hours—it is a waste of time."

But there was kindness in his voice too. I felt it worth another try: "Look at it this way then. I sleep and eat regularly. I have no crazy ideas. I don't bother people. I'm not nervous. Name just one way in which I am sick."

"I can't."

"Just one way."

"You are seek."

*   *   *

Rich said, "You're schizophrenic. I'll tell you what, Donaldson. I promise to let you go one year from now if you'll take a course of medication for six months."

"No," I said. That would give them the proof they needed and leave me no recourse. "I don't need any medication."

"What do you say, Gumanis?"

"I agree with you, Doctor Rich. Why don't you try it, Kenny? You've tried everything else."

"But I don't need any pills."

"Then you'll stay here forever!" Rich said. "Either you take pills for six months or I'll never let you go."

"That's coercion," I said.

"We could give you the needle. That would be coercion, wouldn't it?"

Any further remarks by me, I feared, would only cause him to double whatever the pill man was bound to have for me at supper.

"Don't you know we have the right to treat you when they send you here?"

I answered with a craven "Yes."

*   *   *

The day of staff, March 21, Hanenson called me to say: "You must not show any hostility. Hostility is the one thing that bothers Rich. Don't argue. If some doctor says something you don't like, don't answer. Do I make myself clear? You don't belong in here, I've got the votes to get you out. Don't argue with the doctors."

I was the first one called. O'Connor was not present. My chart, top one of five, lay open in front of Rich, who leafed a few pages. The two letters from John Lemboke were on the very top.

Rich: "The next time you come to staff, I hope you have a plan to present."

Me: "There—"

Rich: "The only reason the hospital has not released Mr. Donaldson to his friend in New York is because his friend has not shown interest enough to so much as notify the hospital he is willing to take him out."

Hanenson (with his hand on my arm): "I will work something out for Kenneth."

(There were a number of questions by younger doctors on the details of the case.)

Dunin (sitting at far end of table this time, which was half filled, about fifteen present): "You remember me. . . . You say your parents put you in here. Didn't they?"

Me: "They requested I be examined."

Dunin: "That's the same thing."

Me: "But they're not doctors."

Dunin: "But members of families know best. The only thing wrong with you is that you don't know you're sick. Look at me—I have diabetes. So I take medicine for it. You have mental illness and don't know it. You can't see it—that's why you are mentally ill. But instead of being sensible like me and taking some medication for it—no, you'd rather stay here the rest of your life. That's your illness, Donaldson—you are so sick you won't admit it."

An unidentified doctor: "Florida law says you must be examined by two doctors before commitment."

Me: "I know that. That's why I object. It's fraud—absolute fraud in my case."

Doctor: "If the law says you must be examined by two doctors, then you were examined by two doctors."

* * *

R: "I'd like to put you to staff. But I couldn't get you a competency discharge. You are schizophrenic. You've been schizophrenic all your life. But you're not dangerous. There are lots of schizophrenic people outside—they don't hurt anyone. But you'd have to have somebody be responsible for you."

Me: "I had someone."

R: "No you didn't. Nobody wants you. Your family doesn't want you. Why is your family against you?"

Me: "That's not so."

R: "But your mother won't take you out. Why not?"

Me: "She's dead. And my father died last year."

R: "It says in here your children don't want you."

Me: "My children tried to get me out."

R: "All these doctors here have said the same thing. Why do you think everybody is against you?"

Me: "I never said that. The whole case consists of presumptions and assumptions. And lies."

R: "And how about all your psychological tests here? Did you know that you didn't pass them?"

Me: "Doctor Chacon told me that I had passed the last four times."

R: "I'll let you go out of state whenever you can get anyone responsible to take you." [Then, after reading in my chart.] "Here—Doctor Hanenson wrote your friend Mr. Lemboke not to ever write you again or ever to take you out, because you would never be well."

Me: "That explains that."

*   *   *

W: "What I would like to know is why the staff did not pass you two years ago."

Me: "They did."

D: "That's right, he did pass."

W: "Why are they holding you then?"

Me: "That's the question I'd like to have an answer to."

W: "There's something wrong here."

D: "There is."

Epilogue

THE INTRODUCTION of effective antipsychotic medications in the 1950s, combined with a massive federal program in the following decade and the overdue liberalization of many state commitment laws, produced a complete reversal of the century-long trend toward centralized institutional care in America. Between 1955 and 1975 the number of patients in state psychiatric institutions decreased by two-thirds, from 559,000 to 193,000. That new policy of what was called "deinstitutionalization" has, to a large degree, eliminated many of the visible vices of the institution-cities of mid-century: overcrowding, shortages, and under-staffing. But we still must ask whether it has actually improved the lives of mad people in America, or whether it is simply a retrogression toward the earlier fragmented and irresponsible systems of local care.[1]

The seeds for this profound shift in American institutional patterns were sown in 1955 when Congress established the Joint Commission on Mental Illness and Health to survey psychiatric care in America and to suggest a comprehensive national policy. In 1960 the commission recommended to Congress the establishment of a community-based care system which would emphasize outpatient care and coordinate a massive transfer of patients from the old state and federal asylums into smaller, more personal psychiatric care units, such as halfway houses, foster care homes, therapeutic boarding houses, and private residences. In 1963 Congress began to implement the commis-

---

[1] Information in this section is taken from Bassuk and Gerson, "Deinstitutionalization and Mental Health Services," pp. 46–53.

sion's recommendations by providing federal funds to build community psychiatric centers. These new centers would be run by the communities they served and would eventually become self-supporting. By 1975 over five hundred centers were built, with ninety-six more ready for construction.

The goal of "deinstitutionalization" was eventually achieved —state institutions have reduced their populations by 65 percent. The benefits of that reduction, however, are open to question. Just as nineteenth-century reformers hoped that the very institutional edifices themselves held curative power, so the reformers of the 1950s and 1960s assumed that these institutions were, in themselves, anti-curative. They may have been right. But have they provided adequate alternatives?

The hope was that these masses of deinstitutionalized patients would continue to receive psychiatric treatment within, or coordinated by, the community centers. The fact is that less than half the necessary centers have been built or even planned, and the ones that do exist are chronically short of money and staff. The hope was that those who did receive genuine treatment would improve. The fact is that we hardly know where to begin, in treating most psychiatric problems; the new antipsychotic medications have enabled some patients to control their most severe experiences, but these medications have hardly produced mass cures. The hope was that the many patients released from the large institutions would eventually be reintegrated into their communities, but the fact is that although some ex-patients have adjusted on the outside, and others are living well within smaller psychiatric care units, still others are left to bleak lives in residential hotels and substandard inner-city rooms and apartments. Sometimes marked as peculiar in behavior and appearance, isolated, often without occupation or interest, these wandering "mad people" of today may be no better off than they would have been two and three decades ago.

California commitment laws were vastly liberalized in 1969 with the passage of the Landis Petris Short Act, which provided a number of strict safeguards for people taken in as mental patients. Among the safeguards are the requirements for very short "holds," along with a number of rights for legal review. One result is that it is much more difficult to deprive a person of his or her civil rights through psychiatric measures in my state. Another result is that some people wander the streets and sleep in the alleys.

There is, in the town where I live and work, a woman who wanders about talking to herself. At the time of this writing she appears to be in the final stages of pregnancy, and I am told she sometimes sleeps in a creek bed. When I saw her a month ago, running down the middle of a busy street, shouting at herself, striking herself, I called the police. I asked them what could be done, and whether there was any way to help this young woman, or at least see to it that her pregnancy was somehow cared for. The police told me that they knew her well, she was a local transient, and that they used to pick her up in the past and take her to a hospital, but they had given up. They told me she preferred to be out on the streets, and no physician was willing to attempt to hold her—after all, she wasn't a danger to herself or others. "What about her unborn child?" I asked the police. "Isn't she a danger to it?" They refused to admit that possibility.

I think it is of immense importance that all adults are assumed to possess certain basic civil rights and that communities tolerate some measure of deviance. The postwar American vision of itself as a clean society composed of clean individuals all connected to separate nuclear families, all living in separate houses, allowed little room for deviance. Misfits were better unseen in institutions than seen on the streets. Fortunately, we have grown beyond that narrow ideal. We are more tolerant. But are we more caring? The danger is that the emptying of the old large institutions may lead not to some improved system of care for the helpless but to the old eighteenth- and nineteenth-century habits of abandonment.

Appendices

Bibliography

Appendix I

*Ancient and Medieval
Visions of Madness*

⸮ While the word was in the king's mouth, there fell a voice
from heaven, saying, O king Nebuchadnezzar, to thee it is
spoken; The kingdom is departed from thee. And they shall
drive thee from men, and thy dwelling shall be with the beasts
of the field; they shall make thee to eat grass as oxen, and seven
times shall pass over thee, until thou know that the most High
ruleth in the kingdom of men, and giveth it to whomsoever he
will. The same hour was the thing fulfilled upon Nebuchadnezzar: and he was driven from men, and did eat grass as oxen, and
his body was wet with the dew of heaven, till his hairs were
grown like eagles' feathers, and his nails like birds' claws.
[Daniel 4:31–33]

⸮ Men ought to know that from the brain, and from the brain
only, arise our pleasures, joys, laughter and jests, as well as our
sorrows, pains, griefs and tears. Through it, in particular, we
think, see, hear, and distinguish the ugly from the beautiful, the
bad from the good, the pleasant from the unpleasant. . . . It is
the same thing which makes us mad or delirious, inspires us
with dread and fear, whether by night or by day, brings sleep-
lessness, inopportune mistakes, aimless anxieties, absent-
mindedness, and acts that are contrary to habit. These things
that we suffer all come from the brain, when it is not healthy,
but becomes abnormally hot, cold, moist, or dry, or suffers any
other natural affection to which it was not accustomed. Madness comes from its moistness. [Hippocrates (c. 460–377 B.C.):
The Sacred Disease]

§ If a man is mad he shall not be at large in the city, but his family shall keep him at home in any way which they can; or if not, let them pay a penalty. . . . Now there are many sorts of madness, some arising out of disease, which we have already mentioned; and there are other kinds, which originate in an evil and passionate temperament, and are increased by bad education; out of a slight quarrel this class of madmen will often raise a storm of abuse against one another, and nothing of that sort ought to be allowed to occur in a well-ordered state. [Plato (c. 428–348 B.C.): *Laws*]

§ But in dealing with the spirits of all patients suffering from insanity, it is necessary to proceed according to the nature of each case. Some need to have empty fears relieved, as was done for a wealthy man in dread of starvation, to whom pretended legacies were from time to time announced. Others need to have their violence restrained as is done in the case of those who are controlled even by flogging. In some also untimely laughter has to be put a stop to by reproof and threats; in others, melancholy thoughts are to be dissipated, for which purpose music, cymbals, and noises are of use. More often, however, the patient is to be agreed with rather than opposed, and his mind slowly and imperceptibly is to be turned from the irrational talk to something better. At times also his interest should be awakened; as may be done in the case of men who are fond of literature, to whom a book may be read, correctly when they are pleased by it, or incorrectly if that very thing annoys them; for by making corrections they begin to divert their mind. . . . If, however, it is the mind that deceives the madman, he is best treated by certain tortures. When he says or does anything wrong, he is to be coerced by starvation, fetters and flogging. He is to be forced both to fix his attention and to learn something and to memorize it; for thus it will be brought about that little by little he will be forced by fear to consider what he is doing. To be terrified suddenly and to be thoroughly frightened is beneficial in this illness and so, in general, is anything which strongly agitates the spirit. [Celsus (First century A.D.): *De re medica*]

§ And when he was come out of the ship, immediately there met him out of the tombs a man with an unclean spirit, Who had his dwelling among the tombs; and no man could bind him, no, not with chains: Because that he had been often bound with fetters and chains, and the chains had been plucked asunder by him, and the fetters broken in pieces; neither could any man tame him. And always, night and day, he was in the mountains, and in the tombs, crying, and cutting himself with stones. But when he saw Jesus afar off, he ran and worshipped him. And cried with a loud voice, and said, What have I to do with thee, Jesus, thou Son of the most high God. I adjure thee by God, that thou torment me not. For he said unto him, Come out of the man, thou unclean spirit. And he asked him, What is thy name? And he answered, saying, My name is Legion: for we are many. And he besought him much that he would not send them away out of the country. Now there was there nigh unto the mountains a great herd of swine feeding. And all the devils besought him, saying, Send us into the swine, that we may enter into them. And forthwith Jesus gave them leave. And the unclean spirits went out, and entered into the swine: and the herd ran violently down a steep place into the sea, (they were about two thousand;) and were choked in the sea. And they that fed the swine fled, and told it in the city, and in the country. And they went out to see what it was that was done. And they came to Jesus, and see him that was possessed with the devil, and had the legion, sitting, and clothed, and in his right mind: and they were afraid. [Mark 5:2–15]

§ How wretchedly do false appearances distract men in certain diseases! With what astonishing variety of appearances are even healthy men sometimes deceived by evil spirits, who produce these delusions for the sake of perplexing the senses of their victims, if they cannot succeed in seducing them to their side! [St. Augustine (354–430 A.D.): *The City of God*]

§   *Expulsion of a Demon by Saint Martin*
The Saint, it chanced, had stopped before a house;
he went to enter, at the threshold paused,

scenting a dreadful demon's shadow there.
A cook, possessed, had grown a ravening beast,
biting his comrades and himself for food.
The others ran and feared to cross his path,
scarcely escaping safe for all their speed
and pleased enough to win unbitten out.
Our iron-heart, God's soldier, Martin, stood
and would not budge nor let the maniac pass.
He bade the Thing of gnashing plague to halt,
thrusting his holy fingers in its mouth.
"Here, wolf of evil, here is offered food.
Elsewhere you hunt, here's meat between your teeth."
The jaws of fury slowly opened out,
they dared not bite. Gaping, the beast was held
and feared the touch of flesh it longed to tear.
The cornered spirit was convulsed with pain
yet might not pass the mouth those fingers closed.
Then, leaving trails of foulness on the air,
the filthy presence backed through filth away,
blasting an outlet fit for driven fiends.

> [St. Columban (sixth century, A.D.)]

§ Of Madnes—And the Causes and Signes Therof. Amentia and maddness is all one, as Plato sayeth. . . . And as the causes be divers, the tokens & signes ben diverse. For some cryen, & lepe, & hurt & wounde them selfe & other men, & derken & hide them self in privy & secret places: of whose disposicion & difference it is reherced tofore in the fifthe boke, where it is treated of the passion of the brayne. The medicines of them is, that they be bounde—that they hurt not them selfe & other men. And namely suche shall be refreshed & comfortid—& withdrawen from cause and mater of drede and besy thoughtes. And they muste be gladded with instrumentes of Musike—and some deale be occupied. And at the laste if purgations and electuaries suffisen not—they shall be holpe with crafte of Surgery. [Bartholomaeus Anglicus (thirteenth century): *De proprietatibus renum*]

§ That demons harass men according to certain phases of the moon happens in two ways. . . . it is manifest that "the brain is the most moist of all the parts of the body," as Aristotle says. Therefore it is the most subject to the action of the moon, the property of which is to move what is moist. And it is precisely in the brain that animal forces culminate. Therefore the demons, according to certain phases of the moon, disturb man's imagination, when they observe that the brain is so disposed. [St. Thomas Aquinas (c. 1225–1274 A.D.): *Summa theologica*]

§ There are four kinds of insane people: Lunatici, Insani, Vesani and Melancholici. Lunatici are those who get the disease from the moon and react according to it. Insani are those who have been suffering from it since birth and have brought it from the womb as a family heritage. Vesani are those who have been poisoned and contaminated by food and drink, from which they lose reason and sense. Melancholici are those who by their nature lose their reason and turn insane. We must, however, note that apart from these four kinds there is another kind: these are the Obsessi who are obsessed by the devil; the various ways in which this happens are treated by us in *De spiritibus*. But here we deal with those who are insane by nature, and sufferers of these four kinds cannot become obsessed by the devil and his company, as many people say. [Paracelsus (1493–1541): *On the Origin of Truly Insane People*]

§ Another was one, whyche after that he had fallen in to ye frantike heresyes, fell soone after in to playne open fransye bysyde. And all be it that he had therfore ben put uppe in bedelem, and afterwarde by betynge and correccyon gathered hys remembraunce to hym, and beganne to come agayne to hym selfe beynge theruppon set at lyberty and walkynge about abrode, hys olde fansyes beganne to fall agayne in his hed. And I was fro dyvers good holy places advertised, that he used in his wanderynge aboute, to come into the chyrche, & there make many madde toyes & tryfles, to the trouble of good people in the dyvyne servyce and specially wold he be most besy in the tyme of most sylence, whyle the preste was at the secretes of the masse aboute ye levacyon. And yf he spyed any woman knel- ynge at a forme yf her hed hynge any thynge low in her medyta- cyons, than wolde he stele behynde her, & yf he were not letted wolde laboure to lyfte up all her clothes & caste them quyte over her hed, wheruppon I beyng advertysed of these pageauntes, and beynge sent unto and requyred by very devout relygyouse folke, to take some other order wyth hym caused him as he came wanderyng by my dore, to be taken by the constables and bounden to a tre in the strete byfore the whole towne, and there they stryped hym with roddys therfore tyl he waxed wery and somwhat lenger. And it appered well that hys remembraunce was good inough, save yt it wente about in grasynge tyll it was beten home. For he could than very well reherse hys fawtes hym selfe, and speke and trete very well, and promyse to do afterwarde as well. [More, *The Apologye of Syr T. More, Knyght* (1533)]

§ Poor Tom, that eats the swimming frog, the toad, the tadpole, the wal-newt and the water; that in the fury of his heart, when the old foul fiend rages, eats cow-dung for sallets, swallows the old rat and the ditch-dog, drinks the green mantle of the standing pool; who is whipped from tithing to tithing, and stocked, punished, and imprisoned; who hath had three suits to his back, six shirts to his body,

> Horse to ride, and weapon to wear,
> But mice and rats, and such small deer,
> Have been Tom's food for seven long year.
>   [Shakespeare, *King Lear* (1605)]

§ Arculanus will have these symptoms to be infinite, as indeed they are, varying according to the parties, for scarce is there one of a thousand that dotes alike. . . . Fear and Sorrow are no common symptoms to all melancholy; upon more serious consideration, I find some that are not so at all. Some indeed are sad, and not fearful; some fearful, and not sad; some neither fearful nor sad; some both. . . . Many fear death, and yet, in a contrary humour, make away themselves. Some are afraid that heaven will fall on their heads; some afraid they are damned, or shall be. . . . Fear of Devils, death, that shall be sick of some such or such disease, ready to tremble at every object, they shall die themselves forthwith, or that some of their dear friends or near allies are certainly dead; imminent danger, loss, disgrace, still torment others, &c. that they are all glass, and therefore they will suffer no man to come near them; that they are all cork, as light as feathers; others as heavy as lead; some are afraid their heads will fall off their shoulders, that they have frogs in their bellies, &c. [Robert Burton, *The Anatomy of Melancholy* (1621)]

₰ Casting out Devils is meer Juggling, they never cast out any but what they first cast in. They do it where for Reverence no Man shall dare to Examine it, they do it in a Corner, in a Mortice-hole, not in the Market-place. They do nothing but what may be done by Art, they make the Devil fly out of the Window in the likeness of a Bat, or a Rat, why do they not hold him? Why, in the likeness of a Bat, or a Rat, or some Creature? That is why not in some shape we Paint him in, with Claws and Horns? By this trick they gain much, gain upon Mens fancies, and so are reverenced and certainly if the Priest deliver me from him, that is most deadly Enemy, I have all the Reason in the World to Reverence him. [John Selden, *Table-Talk* (1689)]

Appendix II

Contemporary Models of Madness

Psychiatric terms such as "psychosis" and "neurosis" are used loosely, and it is not easy to establish perfect definitions. In general one can make a distinction between neurosis and psychosis on the basis of severity. A psychosis is a very severe experience likely to be so debilitating as to require intensive care and hospitalization, while a neurosis is not. In this history I intend "madness" to be equivalent to "psychosis."

According to one authority, a psychosis is an illness, or an experience, marked by the persistent misevaluation of perception, which is not produced by sensory defect.[1] The color-blind person, for example, is not "psychotic" by this definition, but the person who hallucinates is. Similarly, the person who expresses sadness at the death of a loved one is not "psychotic," but the person who expresses a deep, long-lasting despair because he or she believes his or her sins caused World War II is.

Psychoses are of two basic types: the organic and the functional. Organic psychoses have a known organic or physiological origin, such as a brain tumor. Functional psychoses have no known organic origin—and many physicians assume the origin to be psychological. Definitions are in flux, but generally we may speak of three types of functional psychoses: (1) the affective psychoses (related to extremities of emotion, such as manic-depressive psychosis and involutional melancholia), (2) paranoid psychoses, and (3) schizophrenia.[2]

Since much of my discussion of writings by mad people has to do with schizophrenia and its theories, I believe it appropriate to give here a short description of the contemporary model of this particular type of psychosis. The theory of what is today called schizophrenia

---

[1]Klein, *Diagnosis and Drug Treatment of Psychiatric Disorders*, p. 33.
[2]Coleman, *Abnormal Psychology and Modern Life*, p. 267.

was developed around the turn of the century by two psychiatrists, Emil Kraepelin (1856–1926) and Eugen Bleuler (1857–1930).

Kraepelin began by observing a great many mental patients. He attributed some of their symptoms to models of madness that were already established, such as "melancholia," and "epileptic insanity." He ascribed others to a new model. The symptoms included in this new model were very diverse, and Kraepelin accounted for that diversity by postulating some sub-types of the model, such as hebephrenia, catatonia, and paranoia.[3] One overriding symptom as described in the model was called "dementia," a kind of emotional stupor. In the following passage, taken from one of his letters at the University of Munich, Kraepelin describes a patient who appears to exhibit that symptom:

GENTLEMEN,—You have before you to-day a strongly-built and well-nourished man, aged twenty-one, who entered the hospital a few weeks ago. He sits quietly looking in front of him, and does not raise his eyes when he is spoken to, but evidently understands all our questions very well, for he answers quite relevantly, though slowly and often only after repeated questioning. From his brief remarks, made in a low tone, we gather that he thinks he is ill, without getting any more precise information about the nature of the illness and its symptoms. The patient attributes his malady to the onanism he has practised since he was ten years old. He thinks that he has thus incurred the guilt of a sin against the sixth commandment, has very much reduced his power of working, has made himself feel languid and miserable, and has become a hypochondriac. Thus, as a result of reading certain books, he imagined that he had a rupture and suffered from wasting of the spinal cord, neither of which was the case. He would not associate with his comrades any longer, because he thought they saw the results of his vice and made fun of him. The patient makes all these statements in an indifferent tone, without looking up or troubling about his surroundings. His expression betrays no emotion; he only laughs for a moment now and then. There is occasional wrinkling of the forehead or facial spasm. Round the mouth and nose a fine, changing twitching is constantly observed.

The patient gives us a correct account of his past experiences. . . . In answer to our questions, he declares that he is ready to remain in the hospital for the present. He would certainly prefer it if he could enter a profession, but he cannot say what he would like to take up. No physi-

---

[3]Arieti, *Interpretation of Schizophrenia*, p. 11.

cal disturbances can be definitely made out, except exaggerated knee-jerks.

At first sight, perhaps, the patient reminds you of the states of depression which we have learned to recognize in former lectures. But on closer examination you will easily understand that, in spite of certain isolated points of resemblance, we have to deal here with a disease having features of quite another kind. The patient makes his statements slowly and in monosyllables, not because his wish to answer meets with overpowering hindrances, but because he feels no desire to speak at all. He pays no heed, and answers whatever occurs to him without thinking. No visible effort of the will is to be noticed. All his movements are languid and expressionless, but are made without hindrance or trouble. There is no sign of emotional dejection, such as one would expect from the nature of his talk, and the patient remains quite dull throughout, experiencing neither fear nor hope nor desires. He is not at all deeply affected by what goes on before him, although he understands it without actual difficulty. It is all the same to him who appears or disappears where he is, or who talks to him and takes care of him, and he does not even once ask their names.

This peculiar and fundamental want of any *strong feeling of the impressions of life*, with unimpaired ability to understand and to remember, is really the diagnostic symptom of the disease we have before us. It becomes still plainer if we observe the patient for a time, and see that, in spite of his good education, he lies in bed for weeks and months, or sits about without feeling the slightest need of occupation. He broods, staring in front of him with expressionless features, over which a vacant smile occasionally plays, or at the best turns over the leaves of a book for a moment, apparently speechless, and not troubling about anything.[4]

Kraepelin was most impressed by the rapid progression of the patient's illness toward a final state of dementia, and labeled his hypothetical disease model "dementia praecox." "Dementia" stood for the core symptom and the prognosis, while "praecox" described both the usual time of onset (early adulthood or late adolescence) and the speed of the progression toward dementia.[5]

Kraepelin's model was altered by the work of Eugen Bleuler, who published a monograph in 1911 entitled *Dementia Praecox, or The Group of Schizophrenias*. Bleuler proposed that the characteristic process of the new model was not a movement toward dementia, but rather a loss of psychological organization and a splitting up of the various

---

[4]Kraepelin, *Lectures on Clinical Psychology*, pp. 21, 22.
[5]Arieti, *Interpretation of Schizophrenia*, p. 10.

functions of the mind. Bleuler wanted to discard the term "dementia praecox" and proposed instead "schizophrenia" (meaning "split mind"), which he felt would be more descriptive. He thought "dementia" was misleading because it implied that an irreversible loss of intellectual ability took place, while he felt that a loss of emotionality was the real symptom.[6] He considered this "disturbance in affectivity" to be one of the four central symptoms of "schizophrenia." Interestingly enough, however, it clearly resembles Kraepelin's descriptions of dementia:

> Many schizophrenics in the later stages cease to show any affect for years and even decades at a time. They sit about the institutions to which they are confined with expressionless faces, hunched-up, the image of indifference. They permit themselves to be dressed and undressed like automatons, to be led from their customary place of inactivity to the messhall, and back again without expressing any sign of satisfaction or dissatisfaction.[7]

Bleuler also paid considerable attention to an intellectual process which his predecessor noted only in passing.[8] Bleuler called it a "disturbance of association."

> In this malady the associations lose their continuity. Of the thousands of associative threads which guide our thinking, this disease seems to interrupt, quite haphazardly, sometimes such single threads, sometimes a whole group, and sometimes even large segments of them. In this way, thinking becomes illogical and often bizarre.[9]

A type of thought and inner experience that tends to be unusually divorced from reality, which he called "autism," became the third symptom. The fourth was a tendency "to endow the most diverse psychisms with both a positive and negative indicator at one and the same time," or "ambivalence."[10]

Autism, ambivalence, and disturbances in affectivity and association were the four symptoms that Bleuler suggested would be present in all cases of schizophrenia and which could therefore be considered

---

[6]Bleuler, *Dementia Praecox*, p. 71.

[7]Ibid., p. 40.

[8]Kraepelin, *Lectures on Clinical Psychology*, p. 23.

[9]Bleuler, *Dementia Praecox*, p. 14.

[10]Ibid. The place of "ambivalence" in Bleuler's system is not absolutely clear. At first Bleuler does not mention it as a fundamental symptom (p. 14), but later he does (p. 53).

the distinguishing symptoms. Bleuler considered some of the more dramatic symptoms of schizophrenia to be "accessory" because he felt they were *not necessarily* present and could not therefore be considered the distinguishing symptoms. These include: hallucinations, delusions, some disturbance of memory, various changes in personality, and changes in speech, writing, and physical functions.[11]

---

[11]Ibid., p. 95.

Bibliography

In this bibliography, I have tried to include only works which possess *all* the following six criteria. They are (1) separately published, (2) nonfiction, (3) prose works, (4) written in, or translated into, English, (5) about the experience of being mad or being a mental patient, and (6) written by a mad person or a mental patient.

I have not included unpublished accounts or accounts published in journals or anthologies but never separately published. Works by mad people or mental patients written about their experiences in well or non-patient roles have been excluded; thus, the Marquis de Sade, though a patient, cannot be found here. I have tried not to include works of which the author was merely neurotic, or deviant, or alcoholic, or undergoing psychoanalysis—unless that person was a patient in a psychiatric institution. Thus, books such as the well-known account of a "multiple personality neurosis" treated in a psychiatrist's office, *Sybil*, have not been included. But autobiographical accounts of asylum life by supposed or apparent sane persons who were mental patients have been included. "Fictionalized" accounts based upon autobiographical material are present. A few autobiographical accounts of alcoholics who seem to have gone through mad experiences have also been included.

I have tried to examine the book behind each reference to be certain it belongs in this bibliography. There are some I have not been able to examine; in those instances, I have relied on secondary material, such as index notes and other works by the same author, to make my judgment. In general I have been eager to make my mistakes on the side of inclusion, rather than exclusion.

I began my bibliographical work by examining the two important earlier bibliographies on the subject in Walter Alvarez's *Minds That Came Back* (1961) and Carney Landis's *Varieties of Psychopathological Experience* (1964). Alvarez's bibliography is annotated and Landis's bibliography has a diagnostic index: therefore, if my reference is also to be found in Alvarez or Landis, I have marked it with an "A" or "L" for the reader who wants comment or diagnosis. Alvarez's opinions on diagnosis have not always been reliable; thus I have felt compelled to drop certain of his entries—books by Albert Abrams, for example, whom Alvarez considers to be a manic-depressive. Both the Alvarez and Landis bibliographies list autobiographies of neurotics, deviants, drug addicts, and so forth, which I have not included; and Landis's bibliography includes references to several accounts not noted here because they were published in medical or psychiatric journals.

I have also gone through indexes in the British Library, the Library of Congress, the New York Public Library, the libraries of the Wellcome Institute in London, the Royal College of Physicians in London, the Institute of Psychiatry in London, the Cornell Medical School in New York, the New York State Psychiatric Institute in New York, and Stanford University and the University of California at Berkeley. Further bibliographical discoveries have come from Louis Kaplan's *A Bibliography of American Autobiographies* (1961) and William Matthews's *An Annotated Bibliography of British Autobiographies Published or Written before 1951* (1955). In rare instances, browsing in used book stores and talking with friends and acquaintances, have brought to light relevant works not found in any of the above sources. For a long time I thought I was the only person working on such a bibliography, and then I met Charles Steir, compiler of the anthology, *Blue Jolts*. Independently, Mr. Steir developed his own extensive bibliography on the same subject, and he has very generously allowed me to make use of it here. We both hope the resulting combined list—with fully half again as many entries as my original list—will prove to be a unique resource for scholars: the only comprehensive bibliography in this area. Thank you, Mr. Steir.

I have tried to use the most sensible and readable form for my entries. In cases where it is known that the book was published under a pseudonym, the book is listed under the pseudonym, followed by the annotation "[pseud.]"; if the real name of the author is known it is listed, with the pseudonym following in brackets. Use of capitalization and punctuation in titles is arbitrarily standardized. In cases of multiple publication, dates included are the last and first dates of publication, but the most recent publisher is mentioned. For translations, the date of the original foreign edition is mentioned along with the date and publisher of the last English edition. Where the author's name is not known, the reference is listed under the name of an editor or commentator, or it is cited under "anonymous." If an editor or commentator has significantly revised an author's original material in some subsequent edition, both versions are listed. Otherwise, editors or commentators are not mentioned.

Writings by Mad People and Mental Patients

Adler, George J. *Letters of a Lunatic: A Brief Exposition of My University Life During the Years 1853–1854*. New York: The Author, 1854. A.

Agnew, Anna. *From Under the Cloud; or, Personal Reminiscences of Insanity*. Cincinnati: Robert Clarke, 1886. A.

Aldrin, Edwin E. "Buzz," Jr., with Wayne Warga. *Back to Earth*. New York: Random House, 1973.

Alexson, Jacob. *The Triumph of Personal Thought and How I Became a Mason*. Washington: Ransdell, 1941.

Anderson, Dwight, with Page Cooper. *The Other Side of the Bottle*. New York: A. A. Wyn, 1950. A.

Anonymous. *Autobiography of a Schizophrenic*. Bristol: J. Baker & Son, 1951.

———. *Autobiography of a Suicide*. Lawrence, L. I.: Golden Galleon, 1934.

———. *Bedlamiana: or, Selections from the "Asylum Journal."* Lowell: For the Compiler, 1846.

———. *Crook Frightfulness—By a Victim*. London: Moody Bros. Ltd., 1935.

———. *Five Months in a Mad-house; an Actual Experience, by an Inmate*. New York: Press Exchange, 1901.

———. *Five Months in the New-York State Lunatic Asylum by an Inmate*. Buffalo: L. Danforth, 1849.

———. *I Lost My Memory—The Case as the Patient Saw It*. London: Faber, 1932.

———. *I Question*. Nashville, Tenn.: 1945. A.

———. *Life in a Lunatic Asylum: An Autobiographical Sketch*. London: Houlston and Wright, 1867.

———. *A Madman's Musings: Being a Collection of Essays Written by a Patient During His Detention in a Private Madhouse*. London: A. E. Harvey, 1898.

———. *A Palace-Prison; or, The Past and the Present*. New York: Fords, Howard & Hulbert, 1884.

———. *The Petition of the Poor Distracted People in the House of Bedlam*. London: 1620. No known copies remain.

———. *Scenes from the Life of a Sufferer: Being the Narrative of a Residence in Morningside Asylum*. Edinburgh: Royal Asylum Press, 1855.

Ansite, Pat. *No Longer Lonely*. Van Nuys, Ca.: Bible Voice. 1977.

Artaud, Antonin. *Antonin Artaud Anthology*. San Francisco: City Lights Books, 1965.

Balt, John. *By Reason of Insanity*. New York: New American Library, 1967.

Barnes, Mary, and Joseph Berke. *Mary Barnes: Two Accounts of a Journey Through Madness*. New York: Harcourt, Brace, Jovanovich, 1971.

Barnett, Francis. *The Hero of No Fiction or the Memories of Francis Barnett*. 2 vols. 1823.

Barry, Anne. *Bellevue Is a State of Mind*. New York: Harcourt, Brace, Jovanovich, 1971.

Barrymore, Diana. *Too Much, Too Soon*. New York: Holt, 1957.

Bauer, Hanna. *I Came to an Island: A Journey Through the Experience of Change*. Spec Child, 1973.

Beers, Clifford, *A Mind That Found Itself*. Pittsburgh: University of Pittsburgh Press, 1981; 1908. A, L.

Belcher, William. *Address to Humanity, Containing a Letter to Dr. Thomas Monro; a Receipt to*

Make a Lunatic, and Seize his Estate and a Sketch of a True Smiling Hyena. London: The Author, 1796.

Benson, Arthur Christopher. *The House of Quiet.* New York: Dutton, 1907. A.

———. *Thy Rod and Thy Staff.* London: Smith, Elder, 1912. L.

Benziger, Barbara Field. *The Prison of My Mind.* New York: Walker, 1969.

Berryman, John. *Recovery.* New York: Dell, 1973.

Boisen, Anton T. *The Exploration of the Inner World.* New York: Harper and Row, 1971; 1936. A, L.

———. *Out of the Depths.* New York: Harper and Row, 1960. A.

Brandt, Antholy. *The Reality Police: The Experience of Insanity in America.* New York: Morrow, 1975.

Brea, Alton. *Half a Lifetime.* New York: Vantage, 1968.

Brokenshire, Norman. *This is Norman Brokenshire—An Unvarnished Self-Portrait.* New York: David McKay, 1954.

Brown, Carlton. *Brainstorm.* New York: Farrar and Rinehart, 1944. A.

Brown, Henry Collins. *A Mind Mislaid.* New York: E. P. Dutton, 1937. A, L.

Bruckshaw, Samuel. *The Case, Petition, and Address of Samuel Bruckshaw, who Suffered a Most Severe Imprisonment, for Very Near the Whole Year, Loaded with Irons, without Being Heard in his Defense, Nay Even without Being Accused, and at Last Denied an Appeal to a Jury. Humbly Offered to the Perusal and Consideration of the Public.* London: The Author, 1774.

———. *One More Proof of the Iniquitous Abuse of Private Madhouses.* London: The Author, 1774.

Buck, Peggy S. *I'm Depressed—Are You Listening, Lord?* Valley Forge, Pa.: Judson, 1978.

Butler-Bowdon, W., ed. and trans. *The Book of Margery Kempe.* New York: Devin-Adair, 1944.

Camp, Joseph. *An Insight into an Insane Asylum.* Louisville, Ky.: The Author, 1882. A.

Chaloner, John Armstrong. *Four Years Behind the Bars of "Bloomingdale" or, The Bankruptcy of Law in New York.* Roanoke Rapids, N.C.: Palmetto, 1906.

———. *Who's Looney Now?* Roanoke Rapids, N.C.: Palmetto, 1914.

Chamberlain, Judi. *On Our Own.* New York: Hawthorne Books, 1978.

Chambers, Julius. *A Mad World and Its Inhabitants.* New York: D. Appleton, 1877; 1876. A.

Chaning-Pearce, Melville [Nicodemus]. *Midnight Hour.* London: Faber and Faber, 1942. L.

Cienin, Pawel. *Fragments from the Diary of a Madman.* London: Gryf, 1972.

Clemens, Louisa Perina Courtauld. *Narrative of a Pilgrim and Soujourner on Earth, from 1791 to the Present Year, 1870.* Edinburgh: 1870.

Coate, Morag. *Beyond All Reason.* London: Constable, 1964.

Coleman, E. H. *The Shutter of Snow.* New York: Viking, 1930. L.

Collins, William J. *Out of the Depths.* New York: Doubleday, 1971.

Cowper, William. *Memoir of the Early Life of William Cowper.* New York: Taylor & Gould, 1835; 1816. A, L.

Crowe, Anne Mary. *A Letter to Dr. R. D. Willis: to Which are Added, Copies of Three Other Letters: Published in the Hope of Rousing a Humane Nation to the Consideration of the Miseries Arising from Private Madhouses: with a Preliminary Address to Lord Erskine.* London: The Author, 1811.

Cruden, Alexander. *The Adventures of Alexander the Corrector, Wherein Is Given an Account of His Being Unjustly Sent to Chelsea, and of His Bad Usage during the Time of his Chelsea-Campaign . . . with, an Account of the Chelsea-Academies, or the Private Places for the*

Confinement of Such As Are Supposed to Be Deprived of the Exercise of Their Reason. London: The Author, 1754.

——. *The London-Citizen Exceedingly Injured; or, a British Inquisition Display'd, in an Account of the Unparallel'd Case of a Citizen of London, Bookseller to the Late Queen, Who Was in a Most Unjust and Arbitrary Manner Sent on the 23rd of March Last, 1738, by One Robert Wightman, a Mere Stranger, to a Private Madhouse*. London: T. Cooper, 1739.

——. *Mr. Cruden Greatly Injured: An Account of a Trial between Mr. Alexander Cruden Bookseller to the Late Queen, Plaintif, and Dr. Monro, Matthew Wright, John Oswald, and John Davis, Defendants; in the Court of the Common-Pleas in Westminster Hall July 17, 1739, on an Action of Trespass, Assault and Imprisonment: the Said Mr. Cruden, Tho' in His Right Senses, Having Been Unjustly Confined and Barbarously Used in the Said Matthew Wright's Private Madhouse at Bethnal-Green for Nine Weeks and Six Days, till He Made His Wonderful Escape May 31, 1738. To Which is Added a Surprising Account of Several Other Persons, Who Have Been Most Unjustly Confined in Private Madhouses*. London: A. Injured, 1740.

Custance, John. *Adventure into the Unconscious*. London: Christopher Johnson, 1954. A, L.

——. *Wisdom, Madness and Folly*. New York: Pelligrini and Cudahy, 1952. A, L.

Dahl, Robert G. *Breakdown*. Indianapolis: Bobbs-Merrill, 1959. A, L.

Davenport, Eloise. *I Can't Forget*. New York: Carlton, 1960.

David——. [pseud.]. *The Autobiography of David——*. Edited by Ernest Raymond. London: Victor Gollancz, 1946. A, L.

Davidson, D. *Remembrances of a Religio-Maniac*. Stratford-on-Avon: Shakespeare, 1912. A, L.

Davis, Miss Phebe E. *Two Years and Three Months in the New York Lunatic Asylum at Utica Together with the Outline of Twenty Years Peregrinations in Syracuse*. Syracuse: The Author, 1855.

Davys, S. *A Time and a Time*. London: Calder and Bozars, 1971.

Dawson, Jennifer. *The Ha-Ha*. Boston: Little, Brown, 1961.

Day, Beth. *No Hiding Place*. New York: Henry Holt, 1957.

Delilez, Francis. *The True Cause of Insanity Explained; or, The Terrible Experience of an Insane, Related by Himself*. Minneapolis: Kimball, 1888.

De Nerval, Gerard, see Gerard Labrunie.

Denzer, Peter W. *Episode—A Record of Five Hundred Lost Days*. New York: Dutton, 1954.

Derby, John Barton. *Scenes in a Mad House*. Boston: Samuel N. Dickinson, 1838. A. (Authenticity questionable.)

Doe, Jane. [pseud.]. *Crazy*. New York: Hawthorne, 1966.

Donaldson, Kenneth. *Insanity Inside Out*. New York: Crown, 1976.

Drake, John H. *Thirty-two Years of the Life of an Adventurer*. New York: The Author, 1847. A.

Drory, Irene. *Another World*. New York: Vantage, 1978.

Duffy, James. *The Capital's Siberia*. Middletown, Idaho: Boise Valley Herald, 1939.

Edmonds, Helen Woods [Anna Kavan]. *Asylum Piece*. Garden City: Doubleday, 1946; 1940. A.

Ellis, William B. *Sanity for Sale: The Story of American Life Since the Civil War*. Advance, N.C.: Advance, 1929.

——. *Sanity for Sale: The Story of the Rise and Fall of William B. Ellis, by Himself*. Advance, N.C.: Advance, 1928.

Etchell, Mabel. *Two Years in a Lunatic Asylum*. 1869.

Etten, Howard J. *Memoirs of a Mental Case*. New York: Vantage, 1972.

Farmer, Francis. *Will There Really Be a Morning?* New York: Putnam, 1972.

Farmer, John Harrison. *Road to Love: An Autobiography.* New York: Exposition, 1975.

Feldman, Harry. *In a Forest Dark.* New York: Thomas Nelson & Sons, 1960. A.

Ferguson, Sarah. *A Guard Within.* London: Chatto & Windus, 1973.

Feugilly, Mary Heustis. *Diary Written in the Provincial Lunatic Asylum.* The Author, 1885.

Fink, Harold Kenneth. *Long Journey; a Verbatim Report of a Case of Severe Psychosexual Infantilism.* New York: Julian, 1954.

Fischer, Augusta Catherine. *Searchlight, an Autobiography.* Seattle: 1937.

Fleming, E. G. *Three Years in a Mad House.* Chicago: Donohue, Henneberry, 1893.

Foucault, Michel, ed. *I, Pierre Rivière, Having Slaughtered My Mother, My Sister, and My Brother . . .: A Case of Parricide in the 19th Century.* Translated from 1973 French ed. New York: Random House, 1975.

Frame. *The Philosophy of Insanity.* New York: Greenberg, 1947. L.

Frame, Janet. *Faces in the Water.* New York: Avon, 1971; 1961.

Francis, Joseph H. *My Last Drink.* Chicago: Empire Books, 1915. A.

Fry, Jane. *Being Different: The Autobiography of Jane Fry.* New York: John Wiley & Sons, 1974.

Fuller, Robert. *An Account of the Imprisonment and Sufferings of Robert Fuller, of Cambridge.* Boston: The Author, 1833. A.

Fullerton, James. *Autobiography of Roosevelt's Adversary.* Boston: Roxbaugh, 1912.

Garner, Edward Dixon. *Sketchbook From Hell.* Durham, N.C.: Moore, 1974.

Gary, Looney Lee. [pseud.]. *The Bridge of Eternity.* New York: Fortuny's, 1940.

Gilbert, William. *The Monomaniac, or Shirley Hall Asylum.* New York: James G. Gregory, 1864. A.

Gotkin, Janet, and Paul Gotkin. *Too Much Anger, Too Many Tears: A Personal Triumph over Psychiatry.* New York: Quadrangle, 1975.

Goulet, Robert. *Madhouse.* Chicago: J. P. O'Hara, 1973.

Grant-Smith, Rachel. *The Experiences of an Asylum Patient.* London: G. Allen & Unwin, 1922.

Graves, Alonzo. *The Eclipse of a Mind.* New York: Medical Journal, 1942. A, L.

Gray, Jerry. *The Third Strike.* New York: Abingdon-Cokesbury, 1949. A.

Greally, Hanna. *Bird's Nest Soup.* Dublin: 1971.

Greenberg, Joanne [Hannah Green]. *I Never Promised You a Rose Garden.* New York: Holt, Rinehart and Winston, 1964.

Greiner, S. *Prelude to Sanity.* Fort Lauderdale: Master Publications, 1943.

Grigorenko, P. G. *The Grigorenko Papers.* Boulder, Colo.: Westview, 1976.

Grimes, Green. *The Lily of the West: On Human Nature, Education, the Mind, Insanity, with Ten Letters as a Sequel to the Alphabet; the Conquest of Man, Early Days; a Farewell to My Native Home, the Song of the Chieftain's Daughter, Tree of Liberty, and the Beauties of Nature and Art, by G. Grimes, an Inmate of the Lunatic Asylum of Tennessee.* Nashville: 1846.

———. *A Secret Worth Knowing: A Treatise on Insanity, the Only Work of the Kind in the United States; or, Perhaps in the Known World: Founded on General Observation and Truth, by G. Grimes, an Inmate of the Lunatic Asylum of Tennessee.* New York: W. H. Graham, 1847.

———. *A Secret Worth Knowing: A Treatise on the Most Important Subject in the World: Simply to say, Insanity, by G. Grimes, an Inmate of the Lunatic Asylum of Tennessee.* Nashville: Nashville Union, 1846.

Hackett, Paul. *The Cardboard Giants.* New York: Putnam, 1952. A, L.

Haizmann, Christoph. *Schizophrenia, 1677: A Psychiatric Study of an Illustrated Autobiographical Record of Demoniacal Possession.* Edited by Ida Macalpine and Richard Hunter. London: William Dawson and Sons, 1956.

Hales, Ella. [pseud.]. *Like a Lamb*. London: Christopher Johnson, 1958. A.

Hall, Roger. *Clouds of Fear*. Folkestone: 1978.

Hamilcar, Marcia. *Legally Dead: Experiences During Seventeen Weeks' Detention in a Private Asylum*. London: John Ouseley, 1910. L.

Hampton, Russell K. *The Far Side of Despair—A Personal Account of Depression*. Chicago: Nelson-Hall, 1975.

Harrison, Maude. *Spinner's Lake*. London: John Lane, The Bodley Head, 1941. L.

Harvin, Emily. [pseud.]. *The Stubborn Wood*. Chicago: Ziff-Davis, 1948. A.

Haskell, Ebenezer. *The Trial of Ebenezer Haskell, in Lunacy, and His Acquittal Before Judge Brewster, in November, 1868, together with a Brief Sketch of the Mode of Treatment of Lunatics in Different Asylums in this Country and in England, with Illustrations, Including a Copy of Hogarth's Celebrated Painting of a Scene of Old Bedlam, in London, 1635*. Phila.: E. Haskell, 1869.

Haslam, John, ed. *Illustrations of Madness: Exhibiting a Singular Case of Insanity, and a No Less Remarkable Difference in Medical Opinion: Developing the Nature of Assailment, and the Manner of Working Events; with a Description of the Torture Experienced by Bomb-Bursting, Lobster-Cracking, and Lengthening the Brain*. London: G. Haydon, 1810. L.

Heaslip, Barbara. *Saints and Strait Jackets: An Intimate View of Life in an Australian Psychiatric Hospital, By an Ex-Patient*. The Author, 1972.

Hellmuth, Charles F. *Maniac: Anatomy of a Mental Illness*. Philadelphia: Dorrance, 1977.

Helmbold, Henry T. *Am I a Lunatic? Or, Dr. Henry T. Helmbold's Exposure of his Personal Experience in the Lunatic Asylums of Europe and America*. New York: 1877.

Hennell, Thomas Barcley. *The Witnesses*. London: Davies, 1938. L.

————. *The Witnesses*. Edited by Humphrey Osmond. New York: University Books, 1967.

Hewitt, Harald. *From Harrow School to Herrison House Asylum*. London: C. W. Daniel, 1923.

Hillyer, Jane. *Reluctantly Told*. New York: Macmillan, 1927; 1926. A, L.

Howland, Bette. *W-3*. New York: Viking, 1974.

Hummel, James E. [James H. Ellis]. *To Hell and Back: The Story of an Alcoholic*. New York: Vantage, 1953. A.

Hunt, Isaac H. *Astounding Disclosures! Three Years in a Mad House, by a Victim. A True Account of the Barbarous, Inhuman and Cruel Treatment of Isaac H. Hunt, in the Maine Insane Hospital, in the Years 1844, '45, '46 and '47, by Drs. Isaac Ray, James Bates, and Their Assistants and Attendants*. Skowhegan: The Author, 1851.

————. *Astounding Disclosures! Three Years in a Mad House, by a Victim. Contains Also: A Short Account of Miss Elizabeth T. Stone in the M'Lean Asylum at Somerville, Mass. and a Short Account of the Burning of the Maine Asylum, Dec. 4th, 1850*. Skowhegan: The Author, 1852.

Hunt, Morton M. *Mental Hospital*. New York: Pyramid, 1962.

Jayson, Lawrence M. *Mania*. New York: Funk & Wagnalls, 1937. A, L.

Jefferson, Lara. [pseud.]. *These Are My Sisters: An "Insandectomy."* Garden City: Doubleday, 1974; 1947. A, L.

Johnson, Donald McIntosh. *Bars and Barricades, Being the Second Part of "A Publisher Presents Himself."* London: C. Johnson, 1952.

————. *A Doctor Regrets, Being the First Part of "A Publisher Presents Himself."* London: C. Johnson, 1949. A.

————. *A Doctor Returns, Being the Third Part of "A Publisher Presents Himself."* London: C. Johnson, 1956. A.

Joyce, John A. *A Checkered Life*. Chicago: S. P. Rounds, 1883. A.

Kempe, Margery. *The Book of Margery Kempe.* Rendered into modern English by W. Butler-Bowdon. New York: Devin-Adair, 1944.
———. *The Book of Margery Kempe.* Edited and introduced by Sanford Brown Meech and Hope Emily Allen. London: Oxford University Press, 1940.
Kerkoff, Jack. *How Thin the Veil: A Newspaperman's Story of His Own Mental Crackup and Recovery.* New York: Greenberg, 1952. A.
King, Alexander. *Mine Enemy Grows Older.* New York: Simon & Schuster, 1958.
King, L. Percy. [pseud.]. *Criminal Complaints with Probable Causes (A True Account).* Bound, circular letter. Ca. 1940.
King, Marian. *The Recovery of Myself.* New Haven: Yale University Press, 1931. A.
Kirk, Anne. *Chronicles of Interdict No. 7807.* Boston: Meador, 1937.
Knauth, Percy. *A Season in Hell.* New York: Harper, 1956.
Knight, Paul Slade. *Observations on the Causes, Symptoms, and Treatment of Derangement. Founded on an Extensive Moral and Medical Practice in the Treatment of Lunatics. Together with the Particulars of the Sensations and Ideas of a Gentleman During Mental Alternation, Written by Himself During His Confinement.* London: Longman, 1827.
Krauch, Elsa. *A Mind Restored: The Story of Jim Curran.* New York: G. P. Putnam's Sons, 1937. A.
Krim, Seymour. *Views of a Nearsighted Cannoneer.* New York: E. P. Dutton, 1948; 1968.
Kruger, Judith. *My Fight for Sanity.* London: Hammond, Hammond, 1961; 1959. A.
Labrunie, Gerard [Gerard De Nerval]. *Daughters of Fire: Sylvia—Emilie—Octavie.* Translated from 1862 French ed. London: Heineman, 1923.
———. *Dreams and Life.* Translated from 1855 French ed. London: The First Edition Club and The Boar's Head Press of Manaton, Devon, 1933. A.
La Marr, Dressler [Jinxy R. Howell]. *All the Hairs on My Head Hurt.* New York: Exposition, 1965.
Lane, Edward X. *I Was a Mental Statistic.* New York: Carlton, 1963.
Larkin, Joy. *Strangers No More—Diary of a Schizo.* New York: Vantage, 1979.
Lathrop, Clarissa Caldwell. *A Secret Institution.* New York: Bryant, 1890.
Lazell, David. *I Couldn't Catch the Bus Today: The True Story of a Nervous Breakdown That Became a Pilgrimage.* Guildford: Lutterworth Press, 1973.
Leach, John E. *Fear No Evil.* New York: Vantage, 1969.
Lee, Judy. *Save Me! A Young Woman's Journey Through Schizophrenia to Health.* New York: Doubleday, 1980.
Lee, Kate. [pseud.]. *A Year at Elgin Insane Asylum.* New York: Erving, 1902.
Lelchuk, Alan. *Shrinking.* New York: Little, Brown, 1978.
Levant, Oscar. *The Unimportance of Being Oscar.* New York: Putnam's Sons, 1968.
Logan, Joshua. *Josh: My Up and Down, In and Out Life.* New York: Delacorte, 1976.
Lorenz, Sarah E. *And Always Tomorrow.* New York: Holt, Rinehart and Winston, 1963.
Lowe, Louisa. *The Bastilles of England; or The Lunacy Laws at Work.* London: Crookenden, 1883.
———. Pamphlets in a series entitled *Quis Custodiet Ipsos Custodes?*
  (1) *A Nineteenth Century Adaptation of Old Inventions to the Repression of New Thoughts and Personal Liberty.* London: Burns, 1872.
  (2) *Gagging in Madhouses as Practised by Government Servants, in a Letter to the People, by one of the Gagged.* London: Burns, 1872.
  (3) *How an Old Woman Obtained Passive Writing and the Outcome Thereof.* London: Burns, 1872.
  (4) *My Outlawry, A Tale of Madhouse Life.* London: Burns, 1872.

(5) *The Lunacy Laws and Trade in Lunacy in a Correspondence with the Earl of Shaftesbury.* London: Burns, 1872.

———. *Report of a Case Heard in Queen's Bench, November 22nd, 1872, Charging the Commissioners in Lunacy with Concurring in the Improper Detention of a Falsely-Alleged Lunatic and Wrongfully Tampering with her Correspondence.* London: Burns, 1872.

Lunt, Mrs. George. *Behind the Bars.* New York: Lee, Shepard, and Dillingham, 1871.

Marchenko, Anatoly. *My Testimony.* New York: Dutton, 1969.

Marion, Woodson M. [Inmate Ward 8]. *Behind the Door of Delusion.* New York: Macmillan, 1932. A.

Marks, Jan. *Doctor Purgatory.* New York: Citadel, 1959.

Martens, David. *The Abrupt Self.* New York: Harper & Brothers, 1946. A.

Martin, Wanda. *Woman in Two Worlds; a Personal Story of Psychological Experience.* Norwalk, Conn.: Silvermine, 1966.

McCall, Leonore, *Between Us and the Dark.* New York: J. B. Lippincott, 1947. A, L.

McGarr, Margaret Atkins. *And Lo, the Star.* New York: Pageant, 1953. A.

McNeill, Elizabeth. *Nine and a Half Weeks.* New York: Dutton, 1978.

Medvedev, Zhores A. *A Question of Madness.* Translated from 1971 Russian ed. New York: Knopf, 1971.

Merivale, Herman Charles. *My Experience in a Lunatic Asylum, by a Sane Patient.* London: Chatto and Windus, 1879. L.

Metcalf, Ada. *Lunatic Asylums: and How I Became an Inmate of One. Doctors, Incidents, Humbugging.* Chicago: Ottaway and Colbert, 1876.

Metcalf, Urbane. *The Interior of Bethlehem Hospital.* London: The Author, 1818.

Middle-Aged Man. [pseud.]. *Passages from the History of a Wasted Life.* Boston: Benj. B. Mussey, 1853. A.

Mitford, John. *A Description of the Crimes and Horrors in the Interior of Warburton's Private Mad-House at Hoxton, Commonly Called Whitmore House.* London: Benbow, 1825[?]

———. *Part Second of the Crimes and Horrors of the Interior of Warburton's Private Mad-Houses at Hoxton and Bethnal Green' and of These Establishments in General with Reasons for Their Total Abolition.* London: Benbow: 1825[?]

Moeller, Helen. *Tornado; My Experience with Mental Illness.* Westwood, N.J.: F. H. Revell, 1968.

Molony, William O'Sullivan. *New Armor for Old.* New York: Holt, 1935. A.

Moore, William L. *The Mind in Chains.* New York: Exposition, 1955. A, L.

Morrison, Isabella Millar. *A Tale Told by a Lunatic.* Dumfries: Robert Dinwiddle & Co., 1956.

Mumford, Edwin. *Diary of a Paranoiac.* New York: Exposition, 1964.

Naylor, Phyllis. *Crazy Love.* New York: Morrow, 1977.

Neary, John. *Whom the Gods Destroy.* New York, Atheneum, 1975.

Nelson, Robert Quentin. *Mental.* Chichester: Quentin Nelson, 1970.

Neyer, Dix. *Wander, Wander. A Woman's Journey into Herself.* New Jersey: Prentice-Hall, 1977.

Nijinsky, Vaslav. *Diary of Vaslav Nijinsky.* Berkeley: University of California Press, 1966; 1936. A, L.

Nolan, M. J. *Exposure of the Asylum System.* 1928.

Noone, Mary. [pseud.]. *Sweetheart, I Have Been to School.* New York: Harcourt, Brace & World, 1961.

O'Brien, Barbara. [pseud.]. *Operators and Things: The Inner Life of a Schizophrenic.* London: Elek Books, 1960; 1958. L.

Ogdon, John Andrew Howard. *The Kingdom of the Lost.* London: Bodley Head, 1947. A.

Osborne, Luther. *The Insanity Racket: A Story of One of the Worst Hell Holes in This Country.* Oakland, Cal.: 1939.

Otto, John. *Twice Through the Lines—The Autobiography of Otto John.* New York: Harper, 1972.

Owens, Emerson D. [North 3–1]. *Pick Up the Pieces.* New York: Doubleday, Doran, 1929. A.

Packard, Elizabeth Parsons Ware. *Great Disclosures of Spiritual Wickedness!! In High Places: with an Appeal to the Government to Protect the Inalienable Rights of Married Women.* New York: Arno Press, 1974; 1865.

———. *Marital Power Exemplified in Mrs. Packard's Trial, and Self-Defence from the Charge of Insanity; or, Three Year's Imprisonment for Religious Belief, by the Arbitrary Will of a Husband, with an Appeal to the Government to so Change the Laws as to Afford Legal Protection to Married Women.* Hartford: Case, Lockwood, 1866.

———. *Modern Persecution; or Insane Asylums Unveiled.* New York, Arno Press, 1973; 1873.

———. *The Mystic Key; or, The Asylum Secret Unlocked.* Hartford: Case, Lockwood & Brainard, 1886.

———. *The Prisoner's Hidden Life, or, Insane Asylums Unveiled: As Demonstrated by the Report of the Investigating Committee of the Legislature of Illinois. Together with Mrs. Packard's Coadjutors' Testimony.* Chicago: The Author, 1868.

Partyka, Joseph J. *Never Come Early.* Mtn. View, Calif.: The Author, 1968.

Paternoster, Richard. *The Madhouse System.* London: The Author, 1841.

Paul, Brenda Dean. *Autobiography.* London: 1935.

Penn, Arthur. *California Justice: Is This Supposed to Be a Democracy?* San Francisco: 1941.

Perceval, John. *A Narrative of the Treatment Experienced by a Gentleman, During a State of Mental Derangement; Designed to Explain the Causes and the Nature of Insanity, and to Expose the Injudicious Conduct Pursued Towards Many Unfortunate Sufferers Under That Calamity.* 2 vols. London: Effingham Wilson, 1838 and 1840. L.

———. *Perceval's Narrative.* Edited by Gregory Bateson. New York: William Morrow, 1974; 1961.

Peters, Fritz. *The World Next Door.* New York: Farrar Strauss, 1949. A, L.

Pfau, Father Ralph. *Prodigal Shepherd.* New York: Popular Library, 1959.

Pierce, S. W. and J. T. [pseud.]. *The Layman Looks at Doctors.* New York: Harcourt, Brace, 1929. A, L.

Piersall, James and Albert Hirshberg. *Fear Strikes Out: The Jim Piersall Story.* Boston: Little, Brown, 1955. A.

Plath, Sylvia. *The Bell Jar.* New York: Bantam, 1971; 1963.

Plyushch, Leonid. *The Case of Leonid Plyushch.* Translated from Russian by Marite Sapiets. Boulder, Colo.: Westview, 1976.

Pole, J. L. *When—A Record of Transition.* London: Chapman and Hall, 1929. A.

Pollitt, Basil Hubbard. *A Lawyer's Story In and Out of the World of Insanity.* Miami: 1958. A.

———. *Justice and Justices.* Daytona Beach: College Pub., 1954. A.

Pratt, Ann. *Seven Months in the Kingston Lunatic Asylum, and What I Saw There.* Kingston: G. Henderson Savage, 1860.

Previn, Dory. *Bog-Trotter.* Garden City, N.Y.: Doubleday, 1980.

———. *Midnight Baby—An Autobiography.* New York: Macmillan, 1976.

Prouty, Olive Higgins. *Pencil Shavings—Memoirs.* Cambridge: Riverside, 1961.

Raymond, Ernest, ed. *The Autobiography of David*———. London: Victor Gollancz, 1946. A, L.

Rebeta-Burditt, Joyce. *The Cracker Factory.* New York: Macmillan, 1977.

Redfield, Mary Ellen [Ellen Field]. *The White Shirts.* Los Angeles: The Author, 1964.

Reed, David. *Anna.* London: Secker & Warburg, 1976.

Renée. [pseud.]. *Autobiography of a Schizophrenic Girl.* Edited by Marguerite Sechehaye; translated from 1950 French ed. New York: New American Library, 1970; 1951. A, L.

Riggall, Mary. *Reminiscences of a Stay in a Mental Hospital.* London: A. H. Stockwell, 1929.

Rittmaye, Jane. *Life-Time.* New York: Exposition, 1979.

Rivière, Pierre. *I Pierre Rivière, Having Slaughtered My Mother, My Sister, and My Brother . . . : A Case of Parricide in the 19th Century.* Edited by Michel Foucault; translated from 1973 French ed. New York: Random House, 1975.

Roberts, Marty. *Sojourn in a Palace for Peculiars.* New York: Carlton, 1970.

Rogers, Hope. *Time and the Human Robot.* Vinton, Iowa: Ink Spot Press, 1975.

Roman, Charles. *A Man Remade: Or, Out of Delirium's Wonderland.* Chicago: Reilly and Britton, 1909. A.

Ross, Barney. *No Man Stands Alone—The True Story of Barney Ross.* New York: Simon & Schuster, 1963.

Ross, James. *Truth Forever on the Scaffold: I Tried to Help My Country.* New York: Pageant Press, 1964.

Roth, Lillian, with Mike Connolly and Gerold Frank. *I'll Cry Tomorrow.* New York: F. Fell, 1954.

Russell, James William. *The Stranger in the Mirror.* New York: Harper, 1968.

Rutherford, Mark. *The Autobiography of Mark Rutherford.* New York: Dodd, Mead, 1885. L.

Sanger, William Cary. *1935–1935–1936.* Newark: Newark Pr., 1937.

Savage, Mary. *Addicted to Suicide—A Woman Struggling to Live.* Santa Barbara, Ca.: Capra, 1975.

Schreber, Daniel Paul. *Memoirs of My Nervous Illness.* Edited and translated by Ida Macalpine and Richard Hunter; translated from 1903 German ed. London: William Dawson and Sons, 1955. A, L.

Schumacher, John L. *Cynicism and Realism of a Psychotic.* New York: Vantage, 1959.

Scott, James. *Sane in Asylum Walls.* London: Fowler Wright, 1931.

Seabrook, William. *Asylum.* New York: Harcourt Brace, 1935. A.

———. *No Hiding Place: An Autobiography.* Philadelphia: Lippincott, 1942. A.

Sechehaye, Marguerite, ed. *Autobiography of a Schizophrenic Girl.* Translated from 1950 French ed. New York: New American Library, 1970; 1951. A, L.

Seng, Quek Lai. *A Case Between Mentally Sound and Mentally Unsound.* New York: Vantage, 1977.

Simpson, Jane. *The Lost Days of My Life.* London: Allen and Unwin, 1958. A.

Simpson, William. *Cruelties in an Edinburgh Asylum.* Edinburgh: The Author, 1925.

Sizemore, Chris Costner. *I'm Eve.* New York: Doubleday, 1977.

Skram, Bertha Amalia. *Professor Hieronymous.* Translated from 1895 Norwegian ed. London: John Lane, 1899.

Smith, Lydia Adeline Jackson Button. *Behind the Scenes; Or, Life in an Insane Asylum.* Chicago: The Author, 1879.

Smith, Nancy Covert. *Journey out of Nowhere.* Waco, Tex.: Word Books, 1973.

Snider, Benjamin S. *The Life and Travels of Benjamin S. Snider: His Persecution, Fifteen Times a Prisoner.* Washington: The Author, 1869.

Sombre, Dyce. *Mr. Dyce Sombre's Refutation of the Charge of Lunacy Brought Against in the Court of Chancer.* Paris: Sombre, 1849.

Southcott, Joanna. *The Second Book of Wonders*. London: Marchant and Galubin, 1813. A.
———. *The Strange Effects of Faith with Remarkable Prophecies*. Exeter: Brill, 1801. L.
Spencer, Walter Steward [W. S. Stewart]. *The Divided Self: The Healing of a Nervous Disorder*. London: Allen & Unwin, 1964.
Starr, Margaret. *Sane or Insane? Or, How I regained Liberty*. Baltimore: For the Author, 1904.
Stebel, S. T. *The Shoe Leather Treatment: The Inspiring Story of Bill Thomas' Triumphant Nine-Year Fight for Survival in a State Hospital for the Criminally Insane as Told to S. T. Stebel*. Los Angeles: J. P. Tarcher, 1980.
Steffan, Gregory. *In Search of Sanity: The Journal of a Schizophrenic*. New York: University Books, 1965.
Stein, Judith Beck. *The Journal of Judith Beck Stein*. Washington, D.C.: Columbia Journal, 1973.
Stern, Bill, and Oscar Fraley. *The Taste of Ashes—An Autobiography*. New York: Holt, 1959.
Stone, Elizabeth. *A Sketch of the Life of Elizabeth T. Stone, and of Her Persecution, with an Appendix of Her Treatment and Sufferings While in the Charleston McLean Asylum Where She was Confined Under the Pretence of Insanity*. The Author, 1842.
Sugar, Frank Emery. *Mindrape: A Diary of Endogenous Depression*. New York: Exposition, 1978.
Sutherland, Steward [N. S. Sutherland]. *Breakdown*. New York: New American Library, 1977; 1976.
Swan, Moses. *Ten Years and Ten Months in Lunatic Asylums in Different States*. Hoosick Falls: The Author, 1874.
Symons, Arthur. *Confessions: A Study in Pathology*. New York: Fountain Press, 1930. A, L.
———. *Spiritual Adventures*. London: Constable, 1905. A.
Tarsis, Valeriy. *Ward Seven: An Autobiographical Novel*. Translated from 1965 Russian ed. New York: Dutton, 1966; 1965.
Tempest, John. *Narrative of the Treatment Experienced by John Tempest, Esq., of Lincoln's Inn, Barrister at Law during Fourteen Months Solitary Confinement under a False Imputation of Lunacy*. London: The Author, 1830.
Telso, A. *Experience of a Criminal*. New York: 1899.
Tew, Raya Eksola. *How Not to Kill a Cockroach*. New York: Vantage, 1978.
Thaw, Harry K. *The Traitor—Being the Untampered with, Unrevised Account of the Trial and all that Led to it*. Phila.: Dorrance, 1926.
Thelmar, E. *The Maniac: A Realistic Study of Madness from the Maniac's Point of View*. New York: Books for the Few, 1941; 1909. A, L.
Thompson, Peter. *Bound for Broadmoor*. London: Hodder and Stoughton, 1972.
Titus, Mrs. Ann H. *Lunatic Asylums: Their Use and Abuse*. New York: 1870.
Trosse, George. *The Life of the Reverend Mr. George Trosse, Late Minister of the Gospel in the City of Exon, Who Died January 11th, 1712/13. In the Eighty Second Year of His Age, Written by Himself and Publish'd According to His Order*. Exon: Richard White, 1714. L.
———. *The Life of the Reverend Mr. George Trosse: Written by Himself, and Published Posthumously According to His Order in 1714*. Edited by A. W. Brink. Montreal: McGill-Queen's University Press, 1974.
Turner, Cyrus S. *Eight and One-Half Years in Hell*. Des Moines: 1912.
Valentine, Christina M. *The God Within*. Pasadena: Avante Book Co., 1957.
Van Gogh, Vincent. *Dear Theo: The Autobiography of Vincent Van Gogh*. Edited by Irving Stone. Cambridge, Mass.: Riverside Press, 1937. A.
Victor, Sarah M. *The Life Story of Sarah Victor*. Cleveland: Williams, 1887. A.

Vidal, Lois. *Magpie: The Autobiography of a Nymph Errant.* Boston: Little, Brown, 1934. A.

Vincent, John. *Inside the Asylum.* London: Allen & Unwin, 1948. A, L.

Vonnegut, Mark. *The Eden Express.* New York: Praeger, 1975.

Walford, William. *Autobiography of the Rev. William Walford.* London: Jackson & Walford, 1851. L.

Wallace, Clare Marc. *Nothing to Lose.* London: Hurst & Blackett, 1962.

———. *Portrait of a Schizophrenic Nurse.* London: Hammond, Hammond & Co., 1965.

Ward, Mary Jane. *Counter-clockwise.* New York: Avon, 1971; 1969.

———. *The Other Caroline.* New York: Avon, 1973; 1970.

———. *The Snake Pit.* New York: New American Library, 1973; 1946. A, L.

Warde, James Cook. *Jimmy Warde's Experiences as a Lunatic. A True Story. A Full Account of What I Thought, Saw, Heard, Did and Experienced Just Before and During My Confinement of One Hundred and Eighty-One Days as a Lunatic in the Arkansas Lunatic Asylum.* Little Rock: Tunnah Pittard, 1902.

Warmack. [pseud.]. *Guilty but Insane: A Broadmoor Autobiography.* London: Chapman & Hall, 1931.

Wegefarth, G. C. *A Patient's Memoirs.* Baltimore: "The Rocket Buster," 1937.

Weldon, Georgina. *The History of My Orphanage or the Out-Pourings of an Alleged Lunatic.* London: The Author, 1878.

Wellon, Arthur. *Five Years in Mental Hospitals: An Autobiographical Essay.* New York: Exposition, 1967.

West, Robert Frederick. *Light Beyond Shadows: A Minister and Mental Health.* New York: Macmillan, 1959.

White, John. *Ward N-1.* New York: A. A. Wyn, 1955. A.

Wilcox, Gerald Erasmus [Thomas G. E. Wilkes]. *Hell's Cauldron.* Atlanta: Stratton-Wilcox, 1953. A.

Wiley, Lisa. *Voices Calling.* Cedar Rapids: Torch Press, 1955.

Anthologies

Alvarez, Walter C. *Minds That Came Back.* New York: J. B. Lippincott, 1961.

Aswell, Mary Louise. *The World Within.* New York: McGraw-Hill, 1947. A.

Fadiman, James, and Donald Kewman. *Exploring Madness: Experience, Theory, and Research.* Monterey, Calif.: Brooks/Cole, 1973.

Glenn, Michael. *Voices from the Asylum.* New York: Harper & Row, 1974.

Hirsch, Sherry, et al. *Madness Network News Reader.* San Francisco: Glide, 1974.

Johnson, Donald McIntosh, and Norman Dodds. *The Plea for the Silent.* London: C. Johnson, 1957. A.

Kaplan, Bert. *The Inner World of Mental Illness.* New York: Harper & Row, 1964.

Landis, Carney, and Fred Mettler. *Varieties of Psychopathological Experience.* New York: Holt, Rinehart and Winston, 1964.

McCaghy, Charles, and James K. Skipper. *In Their Own Behalf: Voices from the Margin.* New York: Appleton, 1968.

Mental Patients Association. *Madness Unmasked: Mental Patients Association Creative Writing Book.* Vancouver, B.C.: Mental Patients Publishing Project, 1973.

Mental Patients Liberation Front. *Our Journal.* W. Somerville, Ma.: 1977.

Russell, Alice Margaret Bingham. *A Plea for the Insane, by Friends of the Living Dead.* Minneapolis: Roberts, 1898.

Stanford, Gene. *Strangers to Themselves—Readings on Mental Illness.* New York: Bantam, 1973.

Steir, Charles. *Blue Jolts: True Stories from the Cuckoo's Nest.* Washington: New Republic Books, 1978.
Ten Ex-Patients. *Breakthru—Dear Society, Open Your Mind: Ten Ex-Patients of Hillcrest Psychiatric Hospital Tell Their Stories.* Australia: Liberation, n.d.
Winslow, L. Forbes. *Mad Humanity.* New York: Mansfield, 1898. A.

Works Consulted

Alvarez, Walter C. *Minds That Came Back.* New York: J. P. Lippincott, 1961.
Arieti, Sylvano. *Interpretation of Schizophrenia.* 2nd. ed. New York: Basic Books, 1974.
Bassuk, Ellen L., and Samuel Gerson. "Deinstitutionalization and Mental Health Services." *Scientific American,* February 1978, pp. 46–53.
Bateson, Gregory, ed. Introduction to *Perceval's Narrative: A Patient's Account of His Psychosis.* Stanford: Stanford University Press, 1961.
Bleuler, Eugen. *Dementia Praecox or the Group of Schizophrenias.* Translated by Joseph Zinkin. New York: International Universities Press, 1950.
Bottrall, Margaret. *Everyman a Phoenix: Studies in Seventeenth-Century Autobiography.* London: John Murray, 1958.
Brink, A. W., ed. Introduction to *The Life of the Reverend Mr. George Trosse: Written by Himself and Published Posthumously According to His Order in 1714.* Montreal: McGill-Queen's University Press, 1974.
Bullard, Dexter M., ed. *Psychoanalysis and Psychotherapy: Selected Papers of Frieda Fromm-Reichmann.* Chicago: University of Chicago Press, 1959.
Burton, Robert. *The Anatomy of Melancholy.* Edited by Lawrence Babb. East Lansing: Michigan State University Press, 1965.
Cerletti, Ugo. "Old and New Information About Electroshock." *American Journal of Psychiatry* 107 (1950): 87–94.
Chambers, R. W., ed. Introduction to *The Book of Margery Kempe.* Translated by W. Butler-Bowdon. New York: Devin-Adair, 1945.
Cockayne, Thomas Oswald, ed. *Leechdoms, Wortcunning and Starcraft of Early England, Being a Collection of Documents, for the Most Part Never before Printed, Illustrating the History of Science in This Country before the Norman Conquest.* 3 vols. London: The Holland Press, 1961.
Coleman, James C., and William J. Broen, Jr. *Abnormal Psychology and Modern Life.* 3rd ed. Glenview, Ill.: Scott, Foresman and Co., 1972.
Conolly, John. *The Treatment of the Insane without Mechanical Restraints.* London: Smith, Elder, 1856.
Davies, John. *The Poems of Sir John Davies.* Edited by Clare Howard. New York: Columbia University Press, 1941.
Deutsch, Albert. *The Mentally Ill in America, A History of Their Care and Treatment from Colonial Times.* 2nd ed. New York: Columbia University Press, 1949.
Dudek, Louis. *Literature and the Press.* Toronto: The Ryerson and Contact Press, 1960.
Ellenberger, Henri F. *The Discovery of the Unconscious: The History and Evolution of Dynamic Psychiatry.* New York: Basic Books, 1971.
Foucault, Michel. *Madness and Civilization, A History of Insanity in the Age of Reason.* Translated by Richard Howard. New York: Random House, 1965.
Freeman, Walter, and James W. Watts. *Psychosurgery: Intelligence, Emotion and Social Behavior Following Prefrontal Lobotomy for Mental Disorders.* Springfield, Illinois: Charles C. Thomas, 1942.

Freud, Sigmund. *An Autobiographical Study.* Translated by James Strachey. New York: W. W. Norton, 1963.

Fromm-Reichmann, Freida. *Principles of Intensive Psychotherapy.* Chicago: University of Chicago Press, 1950.

Hall, Walter Phelps; Robert Greenbaugh Albion; Jeannie Barnes Pope. *A History of England and the Empire-Commonwealth.* New York: Ginn and Co., 1961.

Haller, William. *The Rise of Puritanism: or, The Way to the New Jerusalem as Set Forth in Pulpit and Press from Thomas Cartwright to John Lilburne and John Milton, 1570–1643.* New York: Columbia University Press, 1938.

Howard, John. *The State of the Prisons.* Edited by Ernest Rhys; introduction by Kenneth Ruck. New York: E. P. Dutton, 1929; 1777.

Hunt, F. Knight. *The Fourth Estate: Contributions Towards a History of Newspapers, and of the Liberty of the Press.* London: David Bogue, 1850.

James, William. *The Varieties of Religious Experience.* New York: New American Library, 1958.

Kaplan, Bert, ed. *The Inner World of Mental Illness.* New York: Harper and Row, 1964.

Klein, Donald F., and John M. Davis. *Diagnosis and Drug Treatment of Psychiatric Disorders.* Baltimore: Williams and Wilkins, 1969.

Kraepelin, Emil. *Lectures on Clinical Psychiatry.* Edited by Thomas Johnstone. London: Bailliere, Tindall and Cox, 1913.

Kunitz, Stanley J., ed. *British Authors of the Nineteenth Century.* New York: Wilson, 1936.

Laing, R. D. *The Divided Self.* New York: Random House, 1969.

———. *The Politics of Experience.* New York: Ballantine, 1967.

Laing, R. D., and A. Esterson. *Sanity, Madness and the Family.* Baltimore: Penguin, 1970.

Landis, Carney, and Fred A. Mettler, eds. *Varieties of Psychopathological Experience.* New York: Holt, Rinehart and Winston, 1964.

Ludwig, Arnold W. "Altered States of Consciousness." *Altered States of Consciousness.* Edited by Charles Tart. New York: John Wiley & Sons, 1969.

Macalpine, Ida, and Richard Hunter. "John Thomas Perceval (1803–1876) Patient and Reformer." *Medical History* 6 (1962): 391–95.

———. Introduction to *Memoirs of My Nervous Illness,* by Daniel Paul Schreber. London: William Dawson & Sons, 1955.

———. "The Schreber Case: A Contribution to Schizophrenia, Hypochondria and Psychosomatic Symptom Formation." *The Psychoanalytic Quarterly* 22 (1953): 328–71.

Malleus Maleficarum. Translated from 1489 Latin ed., with an introduction, bibliography and notes by Montague Summers. London: John Rodken, 1928.

Meech, Sanford Brown, and Hope Emily Allen, eds. Introduction to *The Book of Margery Kempe: The Text from the Unique Ms. Owned by Colonel W. Butler-Bowdon.* London: Oxford University Press, 1940.

"Memoirs of Alexander Cruden," introducing *A Complete Concordance to The Holy Scriptures of the Old and New Testament; or, a Dictionary and Alphabetical Index to the Bible,* by Alexander Cruden. New York: Dodd, Mead, 1823.

More, Sir Thomas. *The Apologye of Syr Thomas More, Knyght.* Edited by Arthur Irving Taft. London: Humphrey Milford, 1930.

Neaman, Judith S. *Suggestion of the Devil: The Origins of Madness.* Garden City: Doubleday, 1975.

Nijinsky, Romola. *Nijinsky.* New York: Simon and Schuster, 1936.

Orwell, George, ed. Introduction to *British Pamphleteers.* 2 vols. Edited by George Orwell and Reginald Reynolds. London: Allan Wingate, 1948.

Osmond, Humphrey, ed. Introduction to *The Witnesses,* by Thomas Hennell. New Hyde Park: University Books, 1965.

Parry-Jones, William Llewellyn. *The Trade in Lunacy, A Study of Private Madhouses in England in the Eighteenth and Nineteenth Centuries.* London: Routledge & Kegan Paul, 1971.

Pinel, Philippe. *A Treatise on Insanity.* Translated by D. D. Davis. New York: Hafner, 1962; 1806.

Reed, Robert Rentoul, Jr. *Bedlam on the Jacobean Stage.* Cambridge: Harvard University Press, 1952.

Schatzman, Morton. *Soul Murder, Persecution in the Family.* New York: Random House, 1973.

Sechehaye, Marguerite. *A New Psychotherapy in Schizophrenia: Relief of Frustrations by Symbolic Realization.* Translated from French by Grace Rubin-Rabson. New York: Grune & Stratton, 1956.

———. *Symbolic Realization: A New Method of Psychotherapy Applied to a Case of Schizophrenia.* Translated from French by Barbrö Würsten and Helmut Würsten. New York: International Universities Press, 1951.

Shea, Daniel B., Jr. *Spiritual Autobiography in Early America.* Princeton: Princeton University Press, 1968.

Stein, Larry. "Neurochemistry of Reward and Punishment: Some Implications for the Etiology of Schizophrenia." *Journal of Psychiatric Research* 8 (1971): 345–61.

Stow, John. *A Survey of London.* 2 vols. Edited by Charles Lethbridge Kingsford. Oxford: Henry Frowde, 1908.

Szasz, Thomas. *Psychiatric Slavery.* New York: The Free Press, 1977.

Tart, Charles, ed. Introduction to *Altered States of Consciousness.* New York: John Wiley & Sons, 1969.

Taylor, Frank E. "Bad Trip." *Newsweek,* October 6, 1975, pp. 85A, 86.

Thilly, Frank. *A History of Philosophy.* Revised by Ledger Wood. New York: Henry Holt, 1951.

Tuke, Daniel Hack. *Chapters in the History of the Insane in the British Isles.* London: Kegan Paul, Trench & Co., 1882.

Whyte, Lancelot Law. *The Unconscious Before Freud.* New York: Basic Books, 1960.

Wright, Luella M. *The Literary Life of the Early Friends, 1650–1725.* Introduction by Rufus M. Jones. New York: Columbia University Press, 1932.

Zilboorg, Gregory. *A History of Medical Psychology.* New York: W. W. Norton, 1941.

CONTEMPORARY COMMUNITY HEALTH SERIES